Homosexuality and the Law

A Dictionary

CONTEMPORARY LEGAL ISSUES

Homosexuality and the Law

A Dictionary

Chuck Stewart

ABC CLIO

Santa Barbara, California • Denver, Colorado • Oxford, England

Special recognition and thanks are given to the National Gay and Lesbian Task Force for their permission to use content from their publication *Legislating Equality*, by Wayne Van de Meide (1999) in Appendix A: State and Local Laws.

Library of Congress Cataloging-in-Publication Data

Stewart, Chuck, 1951–
Homosexuality and the law : a dictionary / Chuck Stewart.
p. cm.
Includes bibliographical references and index.
ISBN 1-57607-267-3 (hbk. : alk. paper) — ISBN 1-57607-590-7 (e-book)
1. Gays—Legal status, laws, etc.—United States—Dictionaries. 2. Homosexuality—Law and legislation—United States—Dictionaries. I. Title.
KF4754.5.A68 S74 2001
346.7301'3—dc21 2001001344

07 06 05 04 03 02 01 10 9 8 7 6 5 4 3 2 1

ABC-CLIO, Inc.
130 Cremona Drive, P.O. Box 1911
Santa Barbara, California 93116-1911

This book is printed on acid-free paper ♾.

Manufactured in the United States of America

To those people who have worked to make society safe
for all people. From them, we can learn the courage
and fortitude to stand up for our rights.

Contents

Preface

The inclusion of lesbians, gay men, bisexuals, and of transgendered, transsexual, and intersexed people into the everyday life of American culture has created legal, social, and religious conflicts at every level. Until the 1950s, homosexuality was, as Lord Alfred Douglas, Oscar Wilde's lover, called it, the "love that dare not speak its name." Homosexuality was hidden and ignored, yet at the same time viciously persecuted. Those few homosexuals who became known to communities and police were often arrested, imprisoned, and sometimes killed.

The homophile movement of the 1950s and 1960s paralleled the civil rights movement and set the stage for outright rebellion against New York City police by drag queens, queer street kids, and avant-garde homosexuals at the Stonewall Inn in 1969. This was the spark needed to bring diverse groups of otherwise hidden homosexuals together to fight for their rights in what has become known as the modern gay rights movement.

Legal challenges are continually being mounted to remove discriminatory laws that keep homosexuals in second-class status. Antigay forces continue to erect new hurdles against same-sex marriages, lesbian or gay parent adoptions and child custody, and other privileges enjoyed by heterosexuals. The law concerning sexual orientation is in constant flux, making any book on the topic a snapshot of one representative time.

A false impression exists in the minds of many average Americans that the "gay community" comprises only one identifiable group, which is male and white. In truth, the gay community is as diverse as the United States, and other groups within the community need to be named. Thus, most homosexual groups that included the term *gay* in their names changed their names to *gay and lesbian.* Then it became clear that the plight of women required extra effort and attention and most groups renamed themselves *lesbian and gay.* Bisexuals, transgendered, transsexual, and intersexed people also make up the gay community. Most homosexual groups now use the term *lesbian, gay, bisexual, and transgender* or LGBT in their names. An effort was made in this book to alternate between these terms in addition to using the terms *queer* and *homosexual.*

This book is written for high school, college, and postgraduate students, as well as researchers and people interested in gay issues. No prior knowledge of the subject is assumed and everyone can immediately benefit from the book. Lesbians, gay men, bisexuals, and transsexual people are found in every occupation, every religion, every organization, every school, and most families. This book is aimed at educating everyone about gay issues because these issues affect more than just a few gay activists.

Entries are comprehensive to reduce the number of cross-references needed to understand the topic. This law book is different from other law books in its extensive reference to sociological, psychological, and medical information on homosexuality. For example, understanding why courts are beginning to recognize gay families requires an understanding of the evidence presented in court to show that there really are no differences in parenting styles and their affects on children in heterosexual and homosexual families. So much of the controversy concerning lesbians and gay men stems from misinformation and antigay stereotypes.

Terms that have their own entries in the book are in boldfaced type the first time they appear in another entry. Cases are generally woven into the text and lists of cases and statutes referred to in the text are provided at the end of the book. A comprehensive appendix of state and local laws affecting sexual orientation, along with an appendix listing federal and state agencies and state human rights commissions for filing discrimination complaints, are provided. A bibliography and index complete the book.

This book will not make a legal expert out of the reader. However, it will give him or her a solid and well-researched explanation of gay issues and the law.

Acknowledgments

I want to thank my parents, John and Margaret Stewart, for their emotional and financial support. Without them, this book could not have happened. I want to thank Arline Keithe for her generous offer to edit the manuscript. It was important to me that this book be as accurate as possible. I need to thank Sage Publications for their permission to use some materials and graphs from my book, *Sexually Stigmatized Communities—Reducing Heterosexism and Homophobia: An Awareness Training Manual.* ABC-CLIO should be congratulated for their foresight to bring this controversial topic in dictionary form to high school and college readers. Finally, I want to thank the Institute for the Study of Human Resources, D/B/A One Inc., for their generous financial support toward the completion of this book.

Chuck Stewart

Homosexuality and the Law

A Dictionary

Introduction

It is impossible to discuss the legal changes with respect to homosexuality without also examining the social, philosophical, medical, psychological, and anthropological beliefs that were so often used to support the legal oppression of lesbians and gay men. The "scientific" evidence used to support the belief that homosexuality is a deviance from the norm worked in synergy with laws that punished deviant behavior. Together, homosexuals faced a world that taught them that homosexuality was morally and biologically wrong and that they deserved punishment by police and the legal system. The following history weaves these strands.

History of the Gay Rights Movement

Although there have always been and always will be people who engage in homosexual behaviors and relationships, the concept of gay identity is the outgrowth of modern gay political history. The modern gay rights movement began in Germany during the mid-nineteenth century, but was soundly crushed by the rise of Nazism in the twentieth. The idea of equal rights for homosexuals did not die with World War II, but rose again in the United States and paralleled much of the general civil rights movement that began in the 1950s.

The German Homosexual Emancipation Movement

Karl Heinrich Ulrich is recognized as the "Grandfather of Gay Liberation." He published in Germany many social and juridical studies concerning same-sex love between men. His twelve books represented the largest body of work on homosexuality in the 1860s, and were collectively known as *Researches on the Riddle of Love Between Men.* Ulrich used the term *Uranian* in reference to male homosexuality. This was taken from Plato's *Symposium* in which love between two men was referred to as a beautiful love that belonged to the "Heavenly Muse Urania."

The Hungarian doctor Karoly Maria Benkert (who went by the pseudonym K. M. Kertbeny) coined the word *homosexual* in 1869. The term *heterosexual* was not used publicly until ten years later in 1880 and then in a written defense of homosexuality. In 1871 the newly united Germany enacted the New Prussian Penal Code, which included Paragraph 175 outlawing "unnatural sexual acts between men, and men and beast" and specified imprisonment for up to four years (Plant 1988, 33).

The medicalization of homosexuality influenced British doctor Havelock Ellis to coin the phrase "sexual inversion" to characterize homosexual behavior and further influenced Freud in the early 1900s to characterize homosexuality as an "immature" stage of development.

Heterosexuality was being medicalized as the norm and homosexuality as the "deviant" condition. However, not everyone accepted this. Magnus Hirschfeld organized his Scientific Humanitarian Committee in Germany in 1897 with three goals: (1) to influence legislative bodies to abolish the antihomosexual Paragraph 175 of the German Penal Code; (2) to educate and enlighten the public concerning homosexuality; and (3) to interest homosexuals in participating in the struggle for rights.

For three decades Hirschfeld was a tireless champion for homosexual emancipation. He had the support of the women's emancipation movement and the Social Democratic Party. However, he had little success in organizing the many homosexual groups in Germany. By the time World War I occurred, there were forty gay bars in Berlin and the Committee had distributed over 50,000 copies of the pamphlet *What People Should Know about the Third Sex.*

In 1919 Hirschfeld opened the Institute for Sexual Research. This was a library of more than 20,000 volumes of rare anthropological, medical, legal, and social documents, including over 35,000 photographs—an incomparable collection. The Institute employed four physicians and several assistants. It eventually led to the creation of the World League for Sexual Reform with over 130,000 members.

The effort to reform Paragraph 175 ended in 1929 when the Nazis gained control of the Reichstag. Hirschfeld was often physically beaten by the followers of German nationalism and the German police. Hitler was named chancellor on January 30, 1933. One month later all pornography and all homosexual rights organizations were banned. Four months later, on May 6, 1933, a band of 100 young fanatics surrounded and entered the Institute for Sexual Research. They smashed everything and carried out all books and photographs. Four days later these materials, along with a bust of Hirschfeld, were burned in a public ceremony.

The Nazis staged a campaign against homosexuals for the next two years. Bars were closed, groups and meetings were banned, and homosexuals were arrested by the thousands. On July 3, 1934, Ernst Roehm, leader of the Brown Shirts (SA) and a known homosexual, along with hundreds of other SA members were executed by Hitler for being homosexual (known as the "night of the long knives"). By 1935 the entire homosexual reform movement was extinguished. Heinrich Himmler, chief of the Gestapo (SS), was the architect of the antihomosexual campaign that threw homosexuals into concentration camps, where they were identified with a lavender triangle sewn to their clothes. It is estimated that a minimum of 50,000 homosexuals died in the concentration camps. Tragically, when the war ended some legally minded Allied commanders forced the homosexuals who survived the concentration camps to return to prison to serve out their sentences for violating Paragraph 175.

The American Homosexual Emancipation Movement

Very little evidence exists of efforts toward homosexual emancipation in the United States in the nineteenth and early twentieth centuries. Some members of the German Scientific Humanitarian Committee came to the United States to share their information and perspective. A few lectures were given, but homosexuals continued to stay hidden. In 1924 the first homosexual emancipation group formed in the United States. The Chicago Society for Human Rights structured itself after the German groups and was granted a nonprofit corporation status from the state of Illinois. It was founded by Henry Gerber, a German American immigrant, along with a number of working-class homosexuals.

The Society for Human Rights created a newsletter and distributed two issues. Law enforcement obtained a copy of the newsletters and all board members were arrested (without warrant). The men were jailed, brought to trial, and ultimately set free. The group disbanded and Gerber lost his job with the Post Office.

In the 1920s the number of novels with lesbian and gay themes published in the United States increased, although not without great controversy. A growing gay and lesbian underground developed in Harlem in New York and in other major cities such as San Francisco and New Orleans. However, the Great Depression and World War II crushed the homosexual emancipation movement and outward forms of discrimination increased against lesbians and gays.

World War II and the Exodus of Lesbians and Gays to the Cities

World War II caused major disruptions in family patterns, social networks, and cultural systems. Millions of men left their homes to enter the military. Millions of women entered the workplace to help produce materials and equipment for the war. Both men and women left their provincial towns to travel to unfamiliar settings, where segregation by race and sex was common.

The crush of personnel in the military exposed many men and women to same-sex living and working conditions in which personal space was limited. Soldiers often had to share bunks. While waiting to be shipped out to war, men could be found sleeping in each other's arms at the train depot, in the YMCA, and on public benches. Men were sometimes seen dancing together at army canteens. Although these were activities that could have resulted in arrests during peace times (homosexuality was treated as a criminal act in the military during the 1920s and 1930s, and many thousands of gay soldiers and sailors were imprisoned), the war provided an excuse to ignore these behaviors. Gay men and lesbians benefited from the tolerance and were able to find one another without attracting undue attention (Blumenfeld and Raymond 1993, 291; D'Emilio and Freedman 1988, 25–26). Approximately 10,000 men and women were expelled from the military for homosexuality during the war and immediately afterward (known as "blue discharges" because the document was printed on blue paper). Although this may seen like a large number, it was a very small percentage of the total number of people in uniform.

After the war an effort was made to reduce the number of personnel in the military. One way was to enforce the 1943 regulations banning homosexuals from all branches of the military. Many more men and women were then dishonorably discharged. Thousands of gay men and lesbians did not return to their hometowns. Instead they flocked to New York, Los Angeles, and San Francisco to form gay enclaves. It is within these enclaves that the gay community found relative safety and, eventually, its identity.

Like most people, lesbians and gay men wanted peaceful, productive lives with few altercations. The cold war period immediately following World War II was characterized by a number of factors that led to the development of the modern gay movement. The 1948 release by Alfred Kinsey of his study of American male sexual habits, *Sexual Behavior in the Human Male,* and the subsequent study of American female sexual habits in 1953, *Sexual Behavior in the Human Female,* sent shock waves through American culture. These reports forever shattered the stereotypes and myths concerning American puritanical codes of sexual conduct. The reports showed that many Americans had sex out of wedlock, had sex in their teens, and had engaged in a variety of sexual behaviors including bisexuality and homosexuality.

Another factor was the attempt by Joseph McCarthy to purge communists and homosexuals from the federal government. The hearings resulted in thousands of homosexuals losing their government employment. (Interestingly, many more homosexuals lost their jobs in these purges than did alleged communists.) Yet the hearings provided unprecedented exposure for homosexuals and homosexual oppression. Together with the Kinsey reports (for which Kinsey was accused of aiding the cause of world communism), homosexuality was discussed and written about in the press in ways never before seen. Although much of the media coverage was negative, it allowed closeted and isolated homosexuals to know that there were many others like them.

The Homophile Movement

One of the key founders of the homophile movement was Harry Hay (previously known as Henry Hay) who wrote under the pseudonym Eann MacDonald. Hay was a communist organizer in Los Angeles and a sought-after teacher of communist theory. In 1948 he conceived of organizing a gay group. In 1950 he assembled enough friends to launch the International Bachelors Fraternal Orders for Peace and Social Dignity (sometimes referred to as Bachelors Anonymous). Initially, the group was set up as underground guilds that were separated so that no one would know anyone else—a secret society structure used by the old political left.

The group refocused itself in 1951 and incorporated in California as the Mattachine Society. It wanted to unify homosexuals and educate homosexuals and heterosexuals about how the homosexual rights movement would parallel other minority rights movements. A separate entity, the Mattachine Foundation, provided a legal front for the Society.

Late in 1951 *The Homosexual in America* by Donald Webster Cory was published. In the book Cory related his own coming out and—to his surprise—how psychoanalysis did not help him overcome his homosexual drives, but rather only his feelings of guilt and remorse (Marotta 1981, 6). Cory was much influenced by the NAACP in New York and Gunnar Myrdal's landmark study of race relations presented in *An American Dilemma: The Negro Problem and Modern Democracy* (1944). Cory incorporated the Swedish sociologist's thesis that the root of the "Negro problem" was discrimination by whites. Cory argued that the problems experienced by homosexuals stemmed from societal disapproval rather than from homosexuality itself. *The Homosexual in America* was an important book. However, American society was not ready for it. The publisher was charged with publishing an obscene book and ordered to cease publishing books with homosexual themes.

The Mattachine Society set up another organization—ONE, Incorporated—to publish a newsletter, which began publication in January 1953 and served as the voice of the homophile movement during the early years. The U.S. postmaster refused to allow the newsletter to be sent by U.S. mail. ONE, Inc. sued and eventually won in a U.S. Supreme Court decision (*One, Inc. v. Olesen*). The Court ruled that homosexual materials were not automatically deemed "obscene" and could be sent via the mail.

Liberal factions took control of the Mattachine Society and made it more open and democratic. While all this work and organizing was occurring on the West Coast, homosexuals in New York were meeting informally in a group called The League, the residuum of a gay social group formed after World War II known as the Veteran's Benevolent Association. Rumors of a police investigation ended The League. Sam Morford and Tony Segura decided that New York needed a branch of the

Mattachine Society. Both men were frustrated by the flimsy nature of The League and wanted to participate in writing and editing a newsletter for the Mattachine Society. In December 1955 a group of friends met at Sam Morford's Greenwich Village apartment to launch the *Mattachine Review* and discuss launching the Mattachine Society New York (MSNY). One month later the first public meeting of MSNY was held at the Diplomat Hotel. Approximately thirty persons showed up. These initial steps had to be taken with extreme caution because homosexuality was a felony in New York state and was punishable by up to twenty years in prison.

Within a year after MSNY formed, a group formed in Washington, D.C., that was specific about wanting to work for the repeal of laws inimical to homosexuals. Immediately, the Mattachine leadership in New York, San Francisco, and Los Angeles wrote: "[The] Mattachine cannot pursue any path but the educational and research. . . . Our charter is placed in jeopardy whenever we try to influence legislation through any other means publicly. . . . We can endorse the action of other agencies working in this field, and 'ride on their shirttails,' so to speak, with relative safety. But we cannot lobby on our own, and must be careful how we recommend changes of law so that our charter and the right to solicit funds through the mail is not in danger" (Call 1956).

The Mattachine Society was very concerned about protecting its legitimacy; rightfully so, because at this time in U.S. history police regularly entrapped men for lewd conduct, raided bars and baths, and suspended the business licenses of gay establishments with no provocation or legitimacy. Most members of the Mattachine Society were secretive, and even the leaders often used pseudonyms.

Women were always involved with the Mattachine Society, although they constituted a very small percentage of the membership. Del Martin and Phyllis Lyon in 1956 transformed their lesbian social club into a lesbian activist organization named the Daughters of Bilitis.

The early 1960s marked a turning point for the homophile movement. The fears and inhibitions of the Mattachine Society attracted few members and they remained unassertive. The Mattachine Society tried to bolster membership by reasserting its educational and professional role. When involved in official business, the Society required members to dress conservatively—suits and ties for men, dresses and heels for women. The members avoided overly effeminate or ultramasculine mannerisms. They wrote polite letters, planned scholarly publications, and invited experts to lecture on "sexual variation" before serious audiences in respectable halls.

The conservatism of the Mattachine Society and Daughters of Bilitis did not fulfill the needs of many homosexuals. Many felt resentment from professionals who continued to tell them that they were deviants and immoral. Many homosexuals wanted to take direct political action to reduce police harassment and to change laws.

The civil rights movement of the 1950s and 1960s influenced many homosexuals to focus on direct political action. Frank Kameny, a Harvard astronomer, was one such activist. He had been dismissed from his army post in 1957 and contested the dismissal all the way to the U.S. Supreme Court. The Court would not review the case. He formed the Mattachine Society of Washington (MSW). He cited research that showed that simply communicating the facts about prejudice and discrimination did little to eliminate bigotry. He wanted the group to take direct political action.

In arguing that discrimination was squarely to blame for the homosexual's problems and that boldly challenging discriminatory policies was the most effective way to make progress, Kameny advocated a militant homophile approach to gay political activity (Marotta 1981, 25).

Taking the lead of African American militants whose motto was "Black Is Beautiful," Kameny coined the phrase "Gay Is Good." Together the more militant members of the Mattachine Society became involved in political struggles over police searches, police raids of bars, bar licensing, government employment, and entrapment. In 1964 ten participants from the Homosexual League of New York and the League for Sexual Freedom picketed the Army Induction Center on Whitehall Street in New York City, protesting the army's dishonorable discharges of gay soldiers. Later, in 1965, the Mattachine Society held its first public demonstration in front of the White House. Seven men and three women dressed in conservative attire participated. Although only a few members ever participated in political activism in the early years, it began to make an impact and planted the seeds for future activism.

Efforts made in the 1960s to form coalitions of the many diverse homophile groups were relatively unsuccessful. The conservative Daughters of Bilitis held beliefs similar to the beliefs of the Mattachine Society. Both were reluctant to engage in activities that could threaten their legal status. However, gender became a decisive issue. The militants were unable to engage the mainstream homophile groups, and men's and women's organizations were often separate. However, the militants were successful at getting a few laws changed in a number of situations, including rescinding city ordinances that prohibited people of the same gender from dancing together, or prohibited bars from serving alcohol to homosexuals.

At the same time that gay activism was increasing, research by UCLA psychologist Evelyn Hooker and other psychiatrists in the 1950s and 1960s demonstrated that homosexuality was as adaptive and psychologically sound as heterosexuality. This led the National Institute of Mental Health (NIMH) Task Force on Homosexuality to recommend in 1969 the repeal of sodomy laws and better public education about homosexuality.

Later, from 1973 to 1974, the American Psychiatric Association (APA) reviewed its position on homosexuality and found that the classification of homosexuality as a mental disorder was groundless. They removed homosexuality from the *Diagnostic and Statistical Manual of Mental Disorders* (*DSM*). This was important progress at normalizing homosexuality and became the primary argument used in courts to decriminalize homosexual behaviors.

The Stonewall Riots and Activism

At some junctures in history many forces come together to mark the creation of a major shift in the social paradigm. The riot at the Stonewall Inn in New York's Greenwich Village was such an event. Late on the night of June 27, 1969, officers from the Public Morals Section of the New York City Police Department attempted to shut down this small local bar. After many of the drag queens had been arrested, a crowd of the Inn's patrons exploded by throwing bottles and stones at the police. A battle cry was heard throughout the Village. For the next couple of nights, street demonstrations raged that were more political in nature and aimed at police abuses.

Michael Brown was a new-left homosexual who was thrilled to see homosexuals fight against the police. Days after the riots he met with Dick Leitsch of the MSNY to discuss sponsoring more demonstrations against police and others. When Leitsch adamantly insisted that the MSNY could not engage in such activity without jeopardizing its legal status, Michael Brown set up an independent action committee that became the Gay Liberation Front (GLF).

Although the GLF never became a formalized organization and was composed of a series of small groups in the United States and other Western countries, it represented an important transitional phase for the homophile movement. Its goals were to build coalitions with other disenfranchised groups as a means of dismantling oppressive economic, political, and social structures. Many of the participants had been members of the new left, such as the Students for a Democratic Society (SDS). Because many leftist organizations accepted the antihomosexual discrimination found in communist countries, they often excluded members who declared themselves homosexual. Also, the GLF attracted those who rejected strict social norms, such as pacifists and people who later would be classified as "hippies." Bound by the belief that a total transformation of society was needed to obtain equality and freedom for all marginalized people, they engaged in consciousness-raising sessions in people's living rooms, church basements, and storefronts. These groups typically did not have a leader and strove to achieve a nonhierarchical structure. Building upon the belief that the "personal is the political," these groups introduced new ways of thinking. A number of small newsletters were launched.

The GLF engaged in a number of demonstrations, but it was primarily social and was responsible for the beginning of many college lesbian and gay student groups. The GLF soon broke apart. The ideological differences between the revolutionaries, social radicals, and reformers were too great to maintain the loosely held organization. A handful of revolutionaries formed the Red Butterfly cell in New York based upon Marxist principles. Another set of third-world members formed its own group. Likewise, many of the younger members formed youth organizations throughout the nation. Importantly, these people took with them many of the principles that distinguished them from their conservative colleagues in the Mattachine Society, Daughters of Bilitis, and others.

Many, if not most, of the gay reformers felt alienated by the radical politics of the GLF. They did not hold a deficit view of homosexuality as did the conservative homophile groups, and they did not want to overthrow the entire political and social system as advocated by the GLF. Instead they wanted a more activist organization that sought political change to eliminate discrimination against homosexuals. These reformers created the Gay Activists Alliance (GAA) in December 1969.

The GAA held social functions, but it primarily engaged in petition drives, political "zaps" (in which politicians were directly confronted in public by homosexuals and asked pointed questions or chastised for antigay statements), and street theater (holding a "gay-in" or "kiss-in" in which members of the same sex would hold hands or kiss in public). The actions of the GAA garnered media attention and brought gay issues to the forefront of public discussion.

The early 1970s was a time when many different groups formed that reflected the identity of their gay members. Gay separatists advocated separatism as the solution to heterosexual oppression. The lesbian feminist movement challenged the status quo and urged the National Organization for Women (NOW) and other feminist groups to explore their internalized fear of homosexuality. Radical lesbians argued that the overthrow of sexism required all women to collaborate and challenge male privilege and heterosexist institutions. In 1969 the Eastern Regional Conference of Homophile Organizations (ERCHO) proposed that each June 28, celebrations be held nationwide to celebrate the Stonewall Riots; these later became known as the Christopher Street Liberation Day celebrations, attended by tens of thousands in most major cities. Bisexuals made their needs known and became a voice within the lesbian and gay liberation movement.

Equal Rights and Community Building

After Stonewall, there was a decline in radical activism in the gay community. Instead, the 1970s saw significant community building and political activism. By 1973 there were over 1,100 organizations nationwide devoted to lesbian and gay concerns. This number would more than double by the 1980s and again more than double by the 1990s. These organizations provided support for lesbian, gay, bisexual, and transgendered (LGBT) business owners, LGBT students concerned with school harassment, LGBT scientists fighting against federal government refusal to issue security clearances, LGBT artists who had their funding withdrawn because of political controversy over the content of their art, LGBT people who sought acceptance from organized religions, LGBT people who found their own racial and ethnic communties denying their existence, LGBT athletes who were routinely excluded from participating in organized sports, and more. A flood of publications and media attention devoted to lesbian and gay concerns also poured forth.

As cities became aware that their social services were being underutilized by homosexuals and that they had failed to provide for the unique needs of the lesbian and gay community, a number of them developed entire centers to provide services for lesbians and gays. These centers developed mental and physical health clinics, vocational services, counseling, lesbian advocacy, telephone hotlines, roommate referral, rap groups, other medical services, legal help, and more. These centers often consulted with city administrators concerning lesbian and gay legal and political issues, without actually being political activists.

One of the most influential political groups formed in the United States was the National Gay and Lesbian Task Force (NGLTF). It blended the old homophile movement with the newer reformist, liberationist strategies. Since its beginnings in 1973, it was influential in the 1974 American Psychiatric Association's removal of homosexuality from its list of mental disorders, countered the 1977 antigay "Save Our Children" campaign spearheaded by singer Anita Bryant that tried to exclude homosexuals from teaching children in Florida, worked tirelessly to eliminate state sodomy laws, and was involved in many other projects.

The NGLTF often worked in conjunction with the Lambda Legal Defense and Education Fund, the American Civil Liberties Union, the National Conference of Black Lawyers, and the National Organization for Women's Legal Defense and Education Fund, among others. It is from these coalitions that many of the antidiscrimination policies enacted by businesses, cities, and states have originated. Political parties had to take notice of the "gay" vote. A gay rights plank was included in the Democratic Party platform for the first time in 1980 and remains part of the platform as of the year 2000.

Over the past thirty years, a steady march toward equal rights for homosexuals has taken place. Here are some highlights: In 1975 the federal government eliminated its ban on homosexual employment within the civil service. Over 200,000 people participated in the first gay march on Washington in 1979. In 1981 a court decision in Dallas forbade the police from further discrimination against lesbians and gays in employment as police officers (*Childers v. Dallas Police Department*). In 1982 Wisconsin became the first state to pass a wide-reaching law prohibiting discrimination against lesbians and gay men. A high school support program for lesbian and gay children was established in 1984 (Project 10 in Los Angeles). In 1987 the second gay march on Washington took place with over 600,000 people attending. The National Education Association in 1988 adopted a resolution calling for every school district to provide counseling for students struggling with their sexual orientation. The U.S. military dropped homosexuality as a trait identifying spies in 1991. The third gay march on Washington in 1993 attracted an estimated 1.2 million participants. In 1996 the U.S. Supreme Court ruled Colorado's Amendment 2 unconstitutional (this was an attempt by Colorado's voters to block antidiscrimination protection based upon sexual orientation; see ***Romer v. Evans***). In 1998 President Clinton signed an executive order banning discrimination based on sexual orientation in the federal civilian workforce, which greatly expanded the 1975 civil service act.

Lesbians and gays have made significant legal strides in the United States in the past half century. Censorship of books, plays, and films with explicit homosexual content was common until the late 1960s and into the 1970s. Through the heroic efforts of many lesbians, gay men, and homosexual organizations, many freedoms were won. Lesbian and gay organizations have the right to incorporate (*Gay Activists Alliance v. Lomenzo*), even in states with sodomy laws. Gays and lesbians may peacefully demonstrate and picket under the same terms and conditions applied equally to all demonstrators (*Olivieri v. Ward*). Changes in the obscenity laws, as interpreted by the U.S. Supreme Court, have made it such that homoerotic materials are not automatically judged obscene (*Miller v. California*). First Amendment protections are probably the most powerful tools gays and lesbians have against heterosexism.

MAJOR TOPICS

The civil rights process described above is one in which lesbians and gay men take a few steps forward toward equality with heterosexuals, only to experience a backlash from conservatives and members of the religious right. For example, a number of states have enacted antidiscrimination statutes based on biological sex and socially constructed gender. Same-sex couples in Hawaii and Vermont sued their respective states in the 1990s claiming sex discrimination when they were not allowed to marry. These lawsuits brought the issue of same-sex marriage to the forefront of national debate. Many state legislatures and the federal government responded by passing preemptive laws that barred same-sex marriage and allowed states to ignore same-sex marriages performed elsewhere.

Gay marriages, gays in the military, and other gay-related topics are plastered across newspaper banners and TV news shows. Radio and TV talk shows sensationalize gay topics. Many religious groups see gay rights as an attack on their values and on traditional family structures. To better understand these topics, it is important to get past the sensational headlines and look at the evidence and how it is being reflected in the law.

Military

Homosexuality is still considered to be incompatible with military service. As early as 1957 the Crittenden Report concluded that homosexuals posed no security risk to the United States. The Pentagon denied the existence of the report for twenty years. Two more research projects were commissioned by the military analyzing the participation of lesbians and gay men in military service. Again, both the 1988 and 1989 Personnel Security Research and Education Center (PERSEREC) reports found no reason to deny lesbians and gay men the right to serve in the military. Again, the reports were buried, but leaks to Congress and the press brought them and the Crittenden Report to the surface in October 1989.

In 1993 President Clinton reneged on his campaign promise to lift the ban on gays serving in the military. Instead, he implemented the "Don't Ask, Don't Tell" policy. The persecution of lesbian and gay military personnel soared instead of declining as expected. It was revealed in 2000 that the Naval Criminal Investigative Service (NCIS) conducted undercover surveillance operations in District of Columbia gay-friendly bars and nightclubs. While there, NCIS agents solicited military personnel to engage in conduct that carries administrative or criminal penalties. These actions were attempts to skirt the provisions of "Don't Ask, Don't Tell," which allow servicemembers to engage in associational activities such as going to gay bars (Servicemembers Legal Defense Network 2000c). A number of lawsuits were filed against the military in the 1980s and 1990s by lesbian and gay personnel who were discharged for homosexuality. With few exceptions, the suits were not successful and the Supreme Court refused to review any of the cases that directly challenged the "Don't Ask, Don't Tell" policy.

Courts often made illogical and irrational decisions in this area. For example, the Ninth U.S. Circuit Court of Appeals ruled in 1997 in *Holmes/Watson v. California Army National Guard* that the "Don't Ask, Don't Tell" policy was not discriminatory because it treated homosexuals and heterosexuals equally since neither are allowed to say they are gay and are required to prove that they have not, or will not, engaged in homosexual conduct. This ruling was utterly confusing and shows to what extent courts are willing to go to avoid resolving conflicts over military policy.

Until some president or Congress takes action to make the military safe for lesbians and gay men by following the lead set by President Harry Truman in racially desegregating the military, more witch hunts, prosecutions, lawsuits, and conflicting court rulings involving gays can be expected.

Family

Lesbian and gay family issues continually make the news and engage the courts. The prospect of same-sex marriage has conservatives and members of the religious right petitioning their state legislatures and Congress to enact laws to "defend" heterosexual marriage. The federal Defense of Marriage Act (DOMA), passed in 1996, and similar state measures attempt to define marriage as a union between one woman and one man, and allow states to deny recognition for same-sex marriages that may originate in other states.

The controversy surrounding this issue stemmed from the possibility that Hawaii, Vermont, or both were soon to allow same-sex marriage. The constitutions of both states provide antidiscrimination protections based on sex or gender. The courts interpreted this to mean that disallowing same-sex marriage was a form of sex discrimination. Before the Hawaii Supreme Court could render a decision, the voters of Hawaii enacted a DOMA amendment to their state constitution that rendered moot the lawsuit that began the whole controversy. Vermont took a different approach. Again, the Vermont Supreme Court determined that barring same-sex marriage was a form of sex discrimination and that the state was not able to provide compelling reasons for the ban. Instead of the court approving same-sex marriages, it referred the issue back to the state legislators to find a solution that would place same-sex relationships on the same legal footing as opposite-sex relationships. The legislators created a civil union designation in 2000 for same-sex couples that conferred all the rights associated with marriage. In a way, they created a super domestic partnership status for same-sex couples.

The controversy over same-sex marriage is expected to last a decade or longer. Because there are no residency requirements for Vermont's civil unions, it is expected that many lesbian and gay couples will fly to Vermont for these legal unions, return to their states, and demand to be recognized. This will set the stage for court tests of DOMA and related issues. It takes about ten years for local cases to be heard by the U.S. Supreme Court. If these cases are successful, same-sex marriage will probably not receive national legal recognition until the second decade of the twenty-first century.

An equally volatile issue is the right of lesbians and gay men to retain legal rights to their children or to gain custody of children through second-parent adoptions or foster care. The controversy over this issue originates with stereotyping that homosexuals are unfit parents, that they molest children, and that they will influence children to be homosexual. The more academic researchers examine parenting skills and styles with regard to child development, the more evidence suggests that in these areas there are no differences between opposite-sex or same-sex parents. Also, there is no evidence that child molestation is related to sexual orientation, or that parental sexual orientation has an influence on the sexual orientation of children. These important findings are making their way into court decisions. In state after state, courts are slowly placing homosexual parents on the same footing as heterosexual parents.

Education

Gay rights issues in schools are also a volatile mix. There always have been and always will be homosexual students. Schools have been dangerous places for lesbian and gay students. It is estimated that a child hears twenty-five antigay remarks each day in the public schools, and when these are said in front of a teacher, 97 percent of these teachers make no effort to stop the comments (Carter 1997). Some homosexual students have experienced criminal assaults, such as Jamie Nabozny, who was mock raped by two boys in front of twenty other students, urinated upon in the bathroom, and beaten so badly that he required surgery to stop the internal bleeding. Nabozny and his parents complained to the school, but a school official said he should get used to it because he was a homosexual. Nabozny sued and, for the first time, the court found the school liable for his mistreatment (*Nabozny v. Podlesny*). The school was fined almost $1 million and it was established that harassment of lesbian and gay students that was sexual in nature constituted sexual harassment. In 1997, the U.S. Department of Education clarified Title IX of the Civil Rights Act of 1964 to emphasize that schools are responsible for providing a safe environment, free from sexual harassment—including harassment toward lesbian and gay students. Only at the turn of the century is this ruling and its implications filtering down to the local schools.

Another volatile issue is the right of lesbian and gay students to form support organizations. The Equal Access Act of 1984 required that schools that receive federal funding provide access to all extracurricular clubs on an equal footing. This act was the result of religious groups influencing Congress to ensure students the right to conduct Bible study programs during lunch and after school. The Act requires that if a school allows even one extracurricular club access to school property, all clubs must be given equal access. With the formation of lesbian and gay clubs, some schools rebelled against the law. The Salt Lake City School District, for example, canceled all extracurricular clubs and activities rather than allow lesbian and gay students the same access. Unfortunately, many parents and students blamed the lesbian and gay students instead of the actions by the school board for the cancellation of the clubs.

Particularly after the *Nabozny v. Podlesny* case and the expansion of Title IX, courts now are issuing injunctions against school districts that try to block lesbian and gay students from organizing. These conflicts are likely to continue in the future, particularly in conservative communities.

Lesbian and gay teachers face somewhat different challenges. Historically, being lesbian or gay automatically disqualified persons from obtaining state teaching credentials. If closeted and found out after obtaining employment, these teachers could be terminated and have their credentials revoked. Not until 1969 in *Morrison v. State Board of Education* did a court rule that homosexuality itself was not cause for termination, but rather shifted the burden of proof to the schools to demonstrate that the actions of an openly lesbian or gay teacher affected teaching efficiency and school functioning. However, other courts have found differently, and lesbian and gay teachers run great risk of losing their jobs if they are open about their sexual orientation.

Politically, there have been attacks on the right of lesbians and gay men to teach. In 1978 California state senator John Briggs drafted Proposition 6, which specifically declared that homosexuals could not teach in public schools. This was modeled after the efforts in Florida by Anita Bryant and her "Save Our Children" campaign. The proposition was not passed. Other cities and states have faced the same ordeal.

Some lesbian and gay educators' organizations have a national presence. In general, it is believed that no school district today could fire a teacher for simply being homosexual. The legal gray area is how "open" they can be. Many open gay teachers have shared knowledge of their sexual orientation with a few colleagues, but no students. A few open teachers have shared knowledge of being gay with students. It is the act of sharing knowledge with students that results in community backlash. Here the rulings of the courts and the actions of enforcement agencies in states that have antidiscrimination statutes providing employment protections based on sexual orientation have been mixed. Sometimes teachers who are open with their students are fired, whereas other times they experience no problems. Legally, the demarcation line of what constitutes "too open" is not clear, and crossing that line can result in teachers being accused of promoting homosexuality and acting unprofessionally. Interestingly, no city, state, or union contract has ever specified what constitutes "professional" conduct by teachers. Teachers are advised to be careful about being open to their students.

A recent change in tactics by parents who are members of conservative religions is to sue school districts, claiming that their First Amendment rights to freedom of religion and association are violated when teachers bring up topics concerning homosexuality or when teachers make it a classroom policy that antigay remarks will not be tolerated. Courts so far have rejected these parental claims.

Criminal Law

Criminal law regarding homosexuals has changed significantly since the 1950s. At one time police routinely entered gay and lesbian bars and arrested anyone they wanted. For example, in some cities and states, there were laws that required bar patrons to wear clothing appropriate for their gender. Often police would enter a lesbian bar and seek out the manliest looking patron. They would take her outside to the sidewalk and make her strip off her clothing. They were making sure that she wore at least three items of clothing that were "feminine." If she wore boxer shorts she could be arrested (Snyder 1984).

Slowly, statutes that criminalize sexual behaviors (sometimes known as sodomy laws) have been rescinded in most states. They were inherently discriminatory and used primarily to harass lesbians and gay men. It has been important to the gay community to see sodomy laws overturned because their existence often affected other areas of their lives. For example, children were routinely removed from the custody of lesbian mothers in states that had sodomy laws because the law made the mere existence of the lesbian mother criminal. Because the lesbian mothers were criminals, the courts concluded that they were unfit to keep their children. Likewise, the criminalization of homosexuality often resulted in people being fired from their jobs, losing their housing, losing their children, and more.

Hate crimes against lesbians and gay men have exploded nationally. The brutal murder of gay student Matthew Shepard in Wyoming in 1998 and of Billy Jack Gaither in Alabama in 1999 received national attention. The movie dramatization (*Boys Don't Cry,* 2000) of the murder of transgender Brandon Teena netted the Best Actress award for Hilary Swank at the Oscars. The rise in antigay hate crimes is probably due to the greater exposure gay issues receive from the media and politicians, the increased number of lesbians and gay men who are open, the greater economic disenfranchisement of minorities, and the increase in reporting procedures by police. Regardless of the reason, more and more police agencies are making the effort to include hate crime information on crime reports. In 1990 the federal government passed the Hate Crime Statistics Act. The

Act provides for the collection of statistics on hate crimes, including crimes based on sexual orientation, but does not carry any authority to make policy. Because of conservative forces in Congress, the Act specifically excludes taking action on sexual orientation hate crimes. In the future, every state will probably enact hate crime statutes and participate in federal efforts to track the problem.

Too often, teenagers who come out to their parents are brutalized and thrown out of the home. With nowhere to go, these "throwaways" and "runaways" are forced to live in the streets, often resorting to prostitution for survival. The street is a dangerous place, and the longer an adolescent remains there, the greater the chances that he or she will become infected with HIV and other sexually transmitted diseases. Police and courts of major cities are showing greater sensitivity to the needs of these teenagers. Instead of incarceration, they are often referred to shelters and government agencies that can better address their needs.

Employment

Employers are able to hire and fire without cause in most cases. The "employment at will" doctrine was established in 1884 in *Payne v. Western Atlantic Railroad.* The doctrine has been restricted by the Civil Rights Act of 1964 and by recent enactment of antidiscrimination statutes in cities and states. In general, lesbians and gay men are not protected from termination by private employers. Many states and the federal government have enacted employment antidiscrimination statutes and policies that provide some protections based on sexual orientation. But still, the military and other related agencies specifically discriminate against lesbians and gay men. It is expected that more cities, states, and businesses will enact protective laws and policies for gay employees.

Many businesses have instituted domestic partnership benefit programs for partners of same-sex couples that parallel the benefits provided married couples. Benefit programs are a tool to attract and retain employees. By providing employment benefits only to married couples, companies were ignoring the desires and needs of same-sex couples, who consider it an issue of fairness. Employment benefits have monetary value, and granting them only to traditional married employees gives these couples a raise that is unavailable to same-sex couples. It is expected that more companies will provide benefits to their gay and lesbian employees.

Sexual harassment in the workplace has become a major liability for both business and government employers. Once sexual harassment has become sufficiently severe or pervasive, it is said to create a hostile environment. A number of court cases in the 1990s help clarify the rights and responsibilities of employers and employees concerning sexual harassment. Employees must report problems of sexual harassment to employers so as to give them the opportunity to rectify the situation. Employers have the responsibility to document and resolve sexual harassment complaints and exercise reasonable care to prevent potential sexual harassment.

In *Oncale v. Sundowner Offshore Services, Inc.*, the U.S. Supreme Court determined that sexual harassment can occur between people of the same sex. In this particular case, it was heterosexual male workers harassing another heterosexual male through the use of sexual language and threats. The Court determined that sexual harassment does not need to be sexually motivated, but rather that harassment is the goal and sexual threats are the tool used for the harassment.

Speech and Association

The First Amendment to the U.S. Constitution provides protected status for the right of free speech and association. As it has been for African Americans, Jews, women, and other oppressed groups, the First Amendment is the most powerful tool available to lesbians and gay men to secure equality.

A U.S. Supreme Court decision in 1958 removed the automatic classification of homosexual materials as "obscene, lewd, lascivious and filthy," which thereby allowed the U.S. Postal Service to deliver homosexual materials (*One, Inc. v. Olesen*). This led to a boom in the publishing and distribution of lesbian and gay magazines, books, newspapers, videos, and films. The dissemination of knowledge concerning lesbian and gay issues within the lesbian and gay community helped reduce internalized homophobia and helped in political organizing. Similarly, the dissemination of knowledge about lesbians and gay men helped heterosexuals to overcome their homophobia and recognize that homosexuals should be treated fairly and equally. If the U.S. Supreme Court had not made this decision, the gay rights movement might never have been born.

The Internet is a new technology that our social and legal systems are not yet ready to handle. Attempts by Congress to regulate the Internet have been struck down by the Supreme Court in *ACLU v. Reno I* and *ACLU v. Reno II* as being unconstitutional infringements on the First Amendment. Legislatures seem unable to construct laws that clearly define "harmful," "offensive," "community standards," or regulatory schemes that can be upheld by the courts. Lesbians and gay men are concerned about protecting children from harmful information that may be on the Internet, but they are also concerned that legislation and filter software not interfere with the free transmission of ideas or knowledge concerning homosexuality. It remains to be seen how this problem will be resolved.

An area of politics and law that is also underdeveloped concerns the right of lesbian and gay men to come out and be open about their homosexuality. For example, the California Supreme Court ruled in 1979 in *Gay Law Students' Association v. Pacific Telegraph and Telephone Company* that a person's affirmation of homosexuality was analogous to expressing a political view, and, as such, is protected under the state labor code. But what constitutes "affirming" ones homosexuality? Does this mean a person has the right to declare that he or she is gay? What about answering questions about one's beliefs or personal life? Is that protected? With homosexuals, these rights are underdeveloped.

Antidiscrimination Statutes

Many cities and states have enacted antidiscrimination statutes based on sexual orientation. The protections are often limited to public employment, but some are more comprehensive and extend to private employment and public accommodations. As lesbians and gay men have gained more legal protections, conservatives and members of the religious right have fought back. The most chilling example was the passage of Amendment 2 in the state of Colorado in 1992. This amendment rescinded all existing antidiscrimination laws based on sexual orientation in the state of Colorado and precluded the adoption of future laws that would provide protections against discrimination based on sexual orientation. The U.S. Supreme Court reviewed the case in 1996 and ruled that Amendment 2 violated the fundamental right of lesbians, gay men, and bisexuals to participate in the political process on an equal basis with other Coloradans.

This was an important ruling because similar attacks were being mounted in other states against antidiscrimination laws designed to protect lesbians and gay men. What was most revealing from the entire process was the deeper understanding gained about the motivation and strategies used by the religious right in mounting the campaigns. Correspondence between the lawyers and leaders of the religious right showed that they understood that antidiscrimination laws are meant to help stigmatized groups attain equal status with the dominant group. Yet they purposely chose the motto "no special rights" because of its impact on the minds of voters and its ability to raise money. The religious right's mantra, "no special rights," is a deception of which they are fully aware. Because of its effectiveness, it is expected that "no special rights" will be used in future attempts to keep lesbians and gay men from gaining equality with heterosexuals.

Reparative Therapy

In July 1998 full-page paid advertisements were placed in major national newspapers promoting the "ex-gay" movement. The ads were purchased by a coalition of fifteen Christian right organizations and represented a reframing of its longstanding condemnation of homosexuality. The emphasis on condemning homosexuality as a sin then shifted toward curing homosexuality as an act of redemption.

Evidence suggests that sexual orientation cannot be changed. The American Psychiatric Association (APA) declassified homosexuality as a mental disorder in 1973. Thus, it can be argued that there is no reason to attempt to convert someone from homosexuality to heterosexuality, because all sexual orientations are equally healthy. In their "Fact Sheet on Reparative Therapy," the APA states that there is no scientific evidence to support the effectiveness of any of the conversion therapies that try to change sexual orientation. The APA concluded that all conversion therapies only exacerbate feelings of inadequacy and guilt and violate ethical standards.

The alignment of the Christian right with the reparative therapy movement has legal implications. They are attempting to stop the tide of scientific evidence that is deconstructing antigay stereotypes. Their objective is to convince people that sexual orientation is a choice and is a choice they believe is morally wrong. As such, they conclude that lesbians and gay men should not be granted antidiscrimination protection, and, in fact, should not be granted any rights. That is the agenda of the religious right: to keep lesbians and gay men from attaining equal rights. Some leaders of the religious right advocate the death penalty for homosexuals with the state carrying out the sentence (see Religious Right Agenda entry).

Transgendered, Transsexual, and Intersexed

Another area of law that is severely underdeveloped is the rights of transgendered, transsexual, and intersexed people. Courts have repeatedly rejected claims of sex discrimination against transsexuals because they are "transitioning" from one gender to another, or against intersexed people because they are neither one gender nor the other. Gender confuses our social and legal system. Gender is thought to be comprised of two polar opposites—male and female. In actuality, it is much more complex, with at least eight different characteristics involved to which many humans do not precisely conform. In many ways, transgendered, transsexual, and intersexed people do not legally exist; they can legally be terminated from their jobs, denied housing, and experience other legal discriminations.

The legal issues of transgendered, transsexual, and intersexed people should be a concern for all. Many would claim that there are so few of them that it is not necessary to address their concerns. That position of not protecting the rights of minorities is adamantly rejected by legal theorists and would have been rejected by the founders of the Constitution. There are tens of thousands of transsexual surgeries performed each year in the United States. It is estimated that at least 400,000 Americans are intersexed. Some religions have fewer adherents, yet they are still guaranteed the highest legal protection through the First Amendment.

Transgendered, transsexual, and intersexed people challenge our legal system and reveal a deep confusion in the courts and legislatures about the construction of gender. Some states have passed antidiscrimination statutes that include gender as one of the protected classes. But it is clear that they mean men and women, not those who are between or shifting between gender. The confusion shown by the courts about this issue demonstrates that the trend for the past fifty years to specify which groups are to be afforded protection is coming to an end. The U.S. Supreme Court has been reticent to increase the number of characteristics that are afforded suspect class status. Perhaps it is time to consider a new approach to guaranteeing equality for all Americans.

Separate but "Equal"

The gay rights movement parallels the civil rights movement. The process of overcoming prejudice is the process of deconstructing a social bias. For example, we have seen African Americans move from being nonpersons and property when slavery was legal to gaining citizenship through the adoption of the Fourteenth Amendment to the U.S. Constitution. But there was a backlash by Southern conservatives who influenced state and local authorities to enact Jim Crow laws that kept the races separate. For almost 100 years, "separate but equal" was the law of the land and terror perpetrated by white supremacists was used to keep blacks "in their place." Then in 1954 the U.S. Supreme Court ruled that "separate but equal" was inherently unequal. Only then was the United States faced with fully integrating African Americans into the society. Still, the Civil Rights Act of 1964 and other legislative acts were required to ensure the equal participation of people of different races. This process deconstructed the concept of race and the allocation of rights and privileges associated with that attribute.

Lesbians and gay men are entering the second phase of overcoming the stigmatization associated with their sexual orientation. Until the beginning of the civil rights movement, homosexual behavior was illegal and lesbians and gays were often arrested, prosecuted, and imprisoned, and were constantly at risk of losing their jobs, homes, and children. Slowly, cities and states have removed antigay laws and replaced them with antidiscrimination laws aimed at providing some protection in the areas of employment and housing. With the possibility of same-sex marriages being recognized, there has been a backlash by Christian conservatives who have influenced federal and state governments to define and defend marriage as an exclusively heterosexual institution. Some states are attempting to ameliorate the situation by providing domestic partnership status for same-sex couples while retaining marriage for heterosexuals. Vermont implemented a "civil union" program that confers all the same legal rights and responsibilities associated with marriage without having to call such unions "marriage." Thus, lesbians and gay men are entering the "separate but equal" phase of civil rights. But civil unions, which may not be recognized in other states, are still not the full equivalent of marriage. This is similar to the recognition by courts that separate schools for blacks do not confer all the same benefits that whites enjoy in segregated schools, even when the schools appear similar in terms of facilities, teachers, and funding. It is expected that the courts will eventually rule that any scheme that attempts to give lesbians and gays the same rights enjoyed by heterosexuals without giving them exactly the same rights is inherently unequal. Ultimately, gay liberation will render sexual orientation irrelevant to the legal enjoyment of civil rights, much as African American and women's liberation movements have helped to make race and gender irrelevant to an individual's status before the law.

The same process will occur for intersexed and transgendered people. They are currently legal nonentities. Perhaps some laws and some courts will attempt to define a third sex. But with existing laws specifying, for example, that a marriage can be legal only if it involves one man and one woman, intersexed people will only achieve a status somewhere between the earlier stage of being nonpeople with no rights, and the later stage of being separate but supposedly equal. Ultimately, intersex liberation will make sex per se irrelevant to one's status before the law. This will be achieved when we no longer have to list the sex of a person on a birth certificate, driver's license, and other documents, and no law favors one sex over another.

As legislatures and courts overcame their history of bias, they recognized the need to provide protection for disenfranchised groups. The antidiscrimination laws enacted did not provide special rights, but helped minorities attain the *same* rights held by those in power. But as the number of disenfranchised groups has grown, the courts have been less willing to expand the list of persons qualifying for additional protection because of their status as a suspect class. The city of San Francisco exemplifies the problem. Groups that are protected under city antidiscrimination ordinances have grown to include the transgendered, the transsexual, "looks," and many more—a virtual laundry list of attributes. Some legal theorists believe that this process of specifying groups for heightened legal protection is nonproductive. Instead, they claim the law should emphasize equal rights for all, that is, enforcement of the First and Fourteenth Amendment for all people. They believe this will better counter the moral wars being waged by bigots. It will be interesting to see how laws in this area develop over the next generation.

Before closing, I want to focus attention on the personal side of the law. Each of the cases listed in this book represents someone who somehow came in conflict with the law over their sexual orientation. Many of the cases shattered lives. Most lesbians and gay men who fought against the system lost their suits. For example, think of Mr. Gaylord, a teacher of many years who was fired for engaging in noncriminal same-sex conduct. His case was dragged through the press, yet he still decided to sue. After years in court, he lost. He was barred from working in his chosen field. Today, it is more difficult to fire a teacher for being gay, but Mr. Gaylord was one of the first and he paid a high price to fight for his rights. Even those who withstand years of court battles and eventually prevail pay a high personal cost, such as disruption of their lives due to media attention, loss of income, and often even loss of their families. It is not easy being a vanguard for civil rights. Please remember the sacrifices these people made to help make the United States safe for lesbians, gay men, and bisexuals, and for transgendered, transsexual, and intersexed people.

References

Blumenfeld, W. J., and D. Raymond, eds. 1993. *Looking at Gay and Lesbian Life.* Rev. ed. Boston: Beacon Press.

Call, Hall. 1956. Letter to Dwight Huggins, Sam Morfora, Tony Segura, et al., 30 August. Reported in T. Marotta, *The Politics of Homosexuality.* Boston: Houghton Mifflin.

Carter, K., 1997. "Group Monitors Pervasiveness of Comments: Gay Slurs Abound, Students Say." *Des Moines Register* (7 March 1997): B3.

D'Emilio, J., and E. B. Freedman. 1988. *Intimate Matters: A History of Sexuality in America.* New York: Harper & Row.

Kinsey, A. C., W. B. Pomeroy, and C. E. Martin. 1948. *Sexual Behavior in the Human Male.* Philadelphia: W. B. Saunders Co.

Kinsey, A. C., W. B. Pomeroy, C. E. Martin, and R. H. Gebhard. 1953. *Sexual Behavior in the Human Female.* Philadelphia: W. B. Saunders Co.

Marotta, T. 1981. *The Politics of Homosexuality.* Boston: Houghton Mifflin.

Plant, R. 1988. *The Pink Triangle.* New York: New Republic Books/Henry Holt.

Servicemembers Legal Defense Network. 2000c. "Military Surveillance of Gay Bars and Nightclubs." Press release on Servicemembers Legal Defense Network website: www.sldn.org/templates/press/index.html?section= 2&record=146.

Snyder, Patricia Ginger, producer. 1984. *Silent Pioneers: Elderly Gays and Lesbians Tell Their Struggles.* (30 min.) New York: Filmmakers' Library.

ABSURD SEX LAWS Laws intended to control sexual behavior have been used throughout the world. Many seem absurd by today's Western standards.

Sex is promoted everywhere in the Western world. We see it on our television soap operas and prime-time sitcoms. It is discussed from religious pulpits to afternoon talk shows. And it is argued on the floor of the U.S. Congress. Sex is discussed, shown, and sensationalized. Sex seems to be free of legal constraints, yet there are statutes on the books in many states intended to control certain sexual activities. (See also **Criminal Law**.)

Robert Pelton reviewed some of these laws in his book *Loony Sex Laws That You Never Knew You Were Breaking* (1992). Some of these are listed below. While reading the list, remember groups of people became involved in creating and enforcing these laws. Much time was spent on these issues. Ask yourself, for example, why anyone would care about a man shooting off his gun when his wife has an orgasm or about a person masturbating in his or her own home? Who benefits from such laws and who is controlled? Women usually fare far worse than men in cases concerning adultery. Why the inequality? And why such drastic measures (death penalty) to control homosexuality?

SEX LAWS IN THE UNITED STATES

Courting and sexual activity:

- It is illegal for a man in Hogansville, Georgia, to use his lariat to lasso and seduce his girlfriend.
- It is illegal for male skating instructors to have sexual relations with their female students in Indiana and Ohio.
- Because of Michigan's sodomy statutes, single men and women caught having sex could be sentenced to five years in prison or $5,000, or both.
- Female toll collectors in Harrisburg, Pennsylvania, are prohib-

ited from engaging in sex with truck drivers while working in their booths.

- It is illegal for a husband to swear or curse during sex in Willowdale, Oregon.
- In Connorsville, Wisconsin, it is illegal for a man to shoot a gun off when his female partner has an orgasm.
- Skullbone, Tennessee, has made it illegal for a woman to "pleasure a man" while he is sitting behind the wheel of a moving vehicle.
- It is illegal in Oblong, Illinois, to make love on your wedding day if you are also hunting or fishing.
- In Carlsbad, New Mexico, you must have tightly drawn curtains on your parked vehicle if you engage in sex in it during a lunch break.
- It is illegal for a husband and wife in Cattle Creek, Colorado, to make love while bathing "in any lake, river or stream."
- Couples are specifically banned from having "sex while standing inside a store's walk-in meat freezer" by a bizarre ordinance in Newcastle, Wyoming.
- In Alexandria, Minnesota, a wife may legally force her husband to brush his teeth or stop having sex if she objects to his bad breath due to "garlic, onions, or sardines."

Masturbation and adultery:

- Michigan's sodomy laws require prison time and a fine for any man who masturbates.
- Adultery can be punished by a small fine of $20 to $100 in Arkansas, to $1000 or one year in prison, or both, in California.

Youths:

- In Hawaii the parents of a girl under the age of eighteen may be arrested and sentenced to three years of hard labor if they know their daughter engages in coitus. Interestingly, the law does not apply to young men under eighteen years of age, nor does it apply if the daughter engages in sex other than coitus.
- In Indiana and Wyoming it is illegal to entice or help a person under the age of twenty-one to masturbate.

Condoms and sex toys:

- Hawaii, Kentucky, Massachusetts, Pennsylvania, and Wisconsin prohibit the sale of condoms by vending machine.
- Vending machines in Maryland may sell condoms, but only "in places where alcoholic beverages are sold for consumption on the premises."

- Only physicians can sell condoms in Nebraska and Arkansas.
- Condoms must be used in Nevada brothels.
- Alabama passed an antiobscenity statute in 2000 that made it unlawful to produce, distribute, or otherwise sell sexual devices that are marketed primarily for the stimulation of human genital organs. What makes this statute interesting is how its constitutionality was upheld by the 11th Circuit Court of Appeals (*Williams v. Pryor*). Several sellers of such items, along with two married women who used them as marital sex aids, filed suit with assistance from the American Civil Liberties Union to challenge the statute's constitutionality. The court agreed with the state of Alabama's contention that it had the right to promote "morality" by discouraging "autonomous" sexual expression, that is, masturbation. The court found support for this argument in *Bowers v. Hardwick,* noting that the U.S. Supreme Court ruled that the Constitution does not automatically extend the right to privacy to protect all private, consensual sex between adults, and specifically does not protect same-sex (homosexual) conduct. From this, the circuit court concluded that Alabama had the right to bar "homosexuals" from buying such items. As such, the statute had some clearly constitutional uses and could not be stricken as a whole. This is an example of a law that affects heterosexuals but is based on the persecution of homosexuals. (Alabama Obscenity Code)

Unique laws:

- The state of Washington has an archaic sex statute that makes having intercourse with a virgin female punishable with substantial prison time or a monetary fine, or both. Surprisingly, this law also applies to newlyweds.
- In Sioux Falls, South Dakota, the hotel room a couple rents for only one night must have twin beds placed a minimum of two feet apart.
- A cleaned and pressed nightshirt must be provided to every hotel guest in Hastings, Nebraska. Guests are also prohibited from sleeping together in the nude (married or not).
- In Kansas City, Kansas, women can be arrested for going out alone at night in the streets.

SEX LAWS OUTSIDE THE UNITED STATES

Sexual activity:

- In Georgetown, Guyana, if two people are caught engaging in sex while skinny-dipping, both people are first covered with paint, then "attached to an ass and taken on a tour of the village," whereupon they are banished.

- Newlyweds in Cali, Colombia, are watched by the bride's mother while they engage in sex.
- Male specialists are paid to have sex with virgin girls in rural Guam because the law does not allow virginal females to marry.
- Couples in the People's Republic of China must obtain governmental permission to marry. After the wedding, they must obtain government permission to have sex.
- Women in Johannesburg, South Africa, can legally charge their husbands every time they engage in sex.
- A husband in Equatorial Guinea may force his wife's boyfriend to become his slave for life. However, if his wife's lover is not a man but another woman, the husband may force this woman to be his mistress for the rest of her life.
- It is illegal for couples in the community of Bristol, England, to engage in sex while under their automobiles. Interestingly, in this same community, a dog has the legal right to observe sexual activities, whereas a cat does not.

Adultery, rape, and illicit lovemaking:

- In most of Central and South America, adultery by women is severely punished. For men, adultery is perfectly legal and expected.
- A man must divorce his unfaithful wife in Matagalpa, Nicaragua. If a woman catches her husband with another women, the wife is not permitted to divorce him.
- In Colombia, South America, a husband may legally murder his wife if she is caught in bed with her lover.
- A husband in Uruguay who catches his wife in bed with her lover may legally either kill both of them or castrate her lover and slice off his wife's nose.
- In Paramaribo, Surinam, a rapist will not be punished if the woman he raped agrees to marry him.
- A woman accused of illicit lovemaking in Guatemala may be stopped on the street, spat upon, and beaten by the citizenry.

Bestiality:

- According to Islamic Law it is forbidden to eat a sheep after having sex with it.
- In Oman, a camel, a cow, or a ewe is to be slaughtered and the carcass burned if a man has sex with it. The man is also required to pay its owner the dead animal's full market value.

- In Lebanon men can legally have sex with female animals. However, if a man has sex with a male animal, the man is put to death.

Genital observations:

- While conducting a gynecological exam, it is forbidden in Bahrain for a physician to look directly at a woman's genitals. He must use a mirror.
- Muslim morticians are not allowed to look at the genitals of the corpse they are preparing. While preparing the corpse, a brick or piece of wood must be placed over its genitals.

Homosexuality:

- Men who are arrested for homosexual behavior in Panama are castrated. Friends of the arrested homosexual have their heads shaven and receive 100 lashes and banishment.
- In many countries homosexuals are arrested and executed. For example, Saudi Arabia and other Islamic countries classify homosexuality as "deviant sexual behavior" and publicly execute homosexuals.

Reference

Pelton, R. W. 1992. *Loony Sex Laws That You Never Knew You Were Breaking.* New York: Walker Publishing Co.

ADOLESCENCE

ADOLESCENCE Homosexuality in adolescence until recently was viewed by classic pediatric specialists as either a short-term phase of sexual experimentation or as an arrested form of development. Psychologists and psychiatrists held negative beliefs concerning adolescent homosexuality. These views have changed, and the **American Psychiatric Association (APA)** eliminated homosexuality as a mental illness in 1973. It now considers both homosexuality and heterosexuality normal. For certain youths, a gay or lesbian identity is a natural developmental outcome (Martin 1982; Remafedi 1987a; Remafedi and Blum 1986; Rig 1982). Nevertheless, old prejudices remain, even within the professional communities working with youth.

Many adolescents engage in sex, including homosexual and heterosexual expressions. If approximately 10 percent of the population is (primarily) homosexual, then perhaps 2.9 million of the 29 million American adolescents are lesbian or gay (Bidwell 1992).

DEVELOPMENTAL TASKS

Adolescence is a time of exploration and discovery. Ideally, adulthood is reached upon the accomplishment of certain developmental tasks (Hammer 1982). These include establishing a stable identity along with enhanced self-esteem, adapting to an adult sexual role, achieving emancipation from the **family**, and developing a career or vocational goals.

In a heterosexist society, only those who are not heterosexual can fully understand the unique experience of those teenagers who must slowly come to terms with their homosexuality. Lesbian, gay, bisexual, transgendered, transsexual, and intersexed children experience confusion and pain when they realize they do not fit the heterosexual norm. With luck they will gain strength from being survivors in a largely hostile environment.

Many of the male-female rites of passage that other teenagers encounter are not available to the gay or lesbian adolescent. The simple things society takes for granted—glances and shy smiles exchanged across a classroom, sending a valentine at school, the awkwardness of the first telephone call asking for a date, sharing a bag of popcorn in a movie theater, walking home with arms about one another, the first kiss—are not possible for most gay and lesbian teens. Sometimes lesbian or gay teenagers have these experiences with members of the opposite sex, but with a sense of falseness and confusion. The greatest stress gay or lesbian youths have is daily living with a terrible secret that cannot be shared. The greatest fear they have is being found out or exposed. Gay adolescents are always on guard to make sure they do not give themselves away by a glance or quiver in their voice should a conversation turn suddenly to the homosexuality of a friend or should a "queer joke" be told. (See also **Heterosexism**; **Homophobia**.)

Gay youths experience an overwhelming sense of loneliness and isolation. To whom can they tell their terrible secret? Their parents? Their friends? All these people expect the adolescent to be heterosexual, and if he or she is not, they often reject the youth. Thus, lesbian, gay, and bisexual youth often feel victimized.

All people affirm their normality through the use of role models. However, there are few role models for lesbian and gay adolescents. The sexual orientation of those who are not heterosexual is often ignored, passed off as a phase, or viewed as a terrible character flaw. Often, these negative views come from the very people the lesbian or gay youth most loves and trusts. These negative views become internalized in gay youth and lead to a sense of self-contempt and guilt. They begin to feel powerless and isolated. Without healthy ways to explore their sexuality, gay youths often have their first sexual experiences in "the baths, bars, or bushes" (Bidwell 1992, 27). Here anonymity provides a false sense of safety. However, such a setting does not promote genuine intimacy, commitment, and self-esteem. Studies have documented the physical and emotional turmoil experienced by many gay male adolescents (Roesler and Deisher

1972; Remafedi 1987b). The experience of lesbians is less well documented but is presumed to be similar. (See also **Coming Out**.)

ADAPTATIONS

The more we learn about human sexuality, the more we realize that sexual identity is not a matter of choice. However, people can choose how to respond to their feelings. Many lesbian and gay teenagers repress or suppress their sexual selves and put all their attention and energy into scholastics, athletics, or the arts. Others may engage in self-destructive behaviors, including risk taking and drug and alcohol abuse. Many go on to marry and raise families. Over time some come to accept their lesbian or gay identities, whereas others carry their "awful secret" for a lifetime. A small number of lesbian or gay youths come out and admit their homosexuality or are exposed involuntarily. These teenagers face real risks of rejection by family and friends along with possible physical and mental abuse (Remafedi 1987a). Many gay teens are thrown out of their homes or become runaways. There are few safety nets for these homeless youths. Because those under sixteen cannot legally work, they are often forced into theft, drug dealing, or prostitution to survive on the streets. Many youths in Hollywood, California, became HIV-positive within weeks of living on the streets (*Youth Runaways* 1999). For some teens, the stress is too great and they commit suicide. Roesler and Deisher (1972), and Remafedi (1987c) found that more than one-third of the gay and bisexual adolescents in their studies had attempted suicide, a rate three times higher than for heterosexual youths.

Not only are lesbian and gay teens denied their sexuality, but their adolescence as well. Being unable to openly admit or express one of the most important parts of human identity—their sexuality—they are prevented from accomplishing the expected developmental tasks of adolescence (Malyon 1981).

SEPARATION FROM FAMILY

Children are subject to the direct control of their parents or guardians. Some parents react poorly to learning their child is lesbian, gay, bisexual, transgendered, transsexual, or intersexed. Because parents have the right to direct the education of their children, some have attempted to "educate" their children into traditional heterosexuality. This education has included parents separating their child from the home and placing him or her into mental hospitals. Approximately 48,000 adolescents are involuntarily placed in psychiatric institutions each year (Robson 1997, 65). A disproportionate number of these youth are lesbian or gay. The diagnoses used by health care professionals to justify hospitalization include "borderline personality disorder," "gender identity disorder," or "confusion over sexual identity." Although the American Psychiatric Association declassified homosexuality as a mental illness in 1973, many mental health providers still consider homosexuality as a problem.

Once committed to these institutions, either by their parents or by the state, gay youths are often subjected to therapy that attempts to change their sexual orientation. Treatments that attempt to "repair" or "reorient" sexual orientation are not successful and lead only to anger and resentment. There are reported cases of adolescents being subjected to forced heterosexual sex as part of their therapy (Robson 1997, 66). This is most likely illegal since it was decided in 1976 that "fornication therapy" was illegal when applied to adults (*Roy v. Hartogs*), and, thus, should apply to adolescents. The legal framework concerning reorientation therapy is confused, and the nonadult status of adolescents compounds the problem. (See also **Reparative Therapy**.)

Some lesbian and gay youth are simply thrown out of their homes. Others flee for their safety. Adolescents can seek to separate themselves from their parents by filing a lawsuit accusing them of abuse or neglect and obtaining a *guardian ad litem* from the courts. If the court agrees to a separation from the parents, the adolescent may prove to the court that he or she is mature enough to live on his or her own away from all adult supervision and obtain "emancipation"; or the child may be adopted by another adult or adults and all rights of the biological parents severed in what is known as "divorce"; or, the child may convince the court that he or she should be removed from the parents' supervision and placed in the care of another adult, adults, or institution in a foster status (here, the biological parents' rights are not severed unless abuse is proven). (See also **Child Adoption and Foster Care**.)

Parents can also separate themselves from their children. If parents kick their child out of the home, child protective agencies may become involved. This requires a hearing with strict standards of evidence and representation to determine what is in the best interest of the child. Sometimes the child is returned to the home under strict supervision by the state. Other times, the child may become a ward of the state and placed in foster care or an institution. Parents who kick their minor children out of their home can be prosecuted for neglect and their parental rights terminated. Even then, they may still be liable for financial support of the minor child.

In other cases, parents voluntarily request that a child welfare agency seek foster care or institutionalization for their child. Parents may claim severe financial or health reasons. Some parents claim the child is "uncontrollable" or "incorrigible." Unfortunately, this claim is too often used against lesbian and gay youths. Most states have passed protective legislation regarding how children are institutionalized and what due process they must have. However, in general, the level of protection and review is less than found in juvenile courts dealing with the crime of delinquency.

References

Bidwell, R. J. 1992. "Adolescent Issues." In *Project 10 Handbook.* Los Angeles: Friends of Project 10.

Hammer, S. L. 1982. "Adolescence." In *Practice of Pediatrics,* edited by V. C. Kelley. Philadelphia: Harper & Row.

Malyon, A. K. 1981. "The Homosexual Adolescent: Developmental Issues and Social Bias." *Child Welfare* 60: 321–330.

Martin, A. D. 1982. "Learning to Hide: The Socialization of the Gay Adolescent." In *Adolescent Psychiatry,* vol. 10, edited by S. C. Feinstein. Chicago: University of Chicago Press.

Remafedi, G. J. 1987a. "Adolescent Homosexuality: Psychosocial and Medical Implications." *Pediatrics* 79: 331–337.

———. 1987b. "Homosexual Youth: A Challenge to Contemporary Society." *Journal of the American Medical Association* 258: 222–225.

———. 1987c. "Male Homosexuality: The Adolescent's Perspective." *Pediatrics* 79: 326–330.

Remafedi, G. J., and R. Blum. 1986. "Working with Gay and Lesbian Adolescents." *Pediatric Annals* 15: 773–783.

Rig, C. A. 1982. "Homosexuality in Adolescence." *Pediatric Annals* 11: 826–831.

Robson, R. 1997. *Gay Men, Lesbians, and the Law.* New York: Chelsea House Publishers.

Roesler, T., and R. W. Deisher. 1972. "Youthful Male Homosexuality." *Journal of the American Medical Association* 219: 1018–1023.

Youth Runaways. 1999. Los Angeles: Jeff Griffith Gay and Lesbian Youth Center.

ADULT ADOPTIONS An adult adoption is one strategy used by same-sex couples to obtain some of the same rights married couples enjoy. Here, each adult in a same-sex couple legally adopts the other. Overall, this strategy has not been very successful. All states developed their adoption regulations in response to the welfare of children. Adoption places the control of one individual (the child) under another (the parent). As such, most states refuse to approve adult-adult adoptions unless one of the adults is mentally or physically incapacitated and requires a conservator, mimicking the parent-child relationship. Even then, the courts prefer a conservator relationship over adoption.

Wills and trusts offer some control for same-sex couples over parts of their relationship, but these devices have limitations. They typically cover only property assignment and have been successfully challenged in court by blood relatives who may claim the lesbian or gay partner used undue pressure or influence in the creation of the will or trust. Adoption rights are implemented immediately and cover daily life, not just property after the death of one partner. Adoption provides a closeness and obligation reserved only for married couples.

In states that do not have adult adoption regulations, courts have disagreed about the validity of adult adoptions when designed for inheritance purposes only (*Doby v. Carroll*). In general, if the adoption seems simply to address inheritance, there are few problems. However, if the adoption seems to be much more and verges upon marital rights, then courts typically reject the adoption, declaring that such extensions of law must originate from the legislature. In states that disallow children to be adopted by homosexuals, same-sex couples attempting to adopt their partners' children will not be successful (for example, Florida does not allow such arrangements).

In adult adoptions that involve a sexual relationship, some courts have approved such arrangements, noting that the adoption laws are silent concerning sexuality (*East 53rd Street Associates v. Mann*). Other courts, though, have denied such adoptions because adoption statutes have moral and policy purposes that the court must uphold (*In re Adoption of Robert Paul P.*). (See also **Family**.)

AFFIRMATIVE ACTION Affirmative action programs are designed to overcome the effects of past discrimination in the United States by allocating jobs and other resources to members of historically stigmatized groups. The term *affirmative action* was first used by President John F. Kennedy when issuing Executive Order 10925, which created the Committee on Equal Employment Opportunity. Later, President Lyndon Johnson signed into law the Civil Rights Act of 1964, which included provisions for affirmative action programs that were enforced through Executive Order 11246 in 1965. The next thirty years of affirmative action were tumultuous, with courts first approving, then disapproving the use of quotas, set-asides, and other techniques.

A backlash against affirmative action occurred from what some characterized as "angry white men." Some people claimed reverse discrimination, and, in *Regents of the University of California v. Bakke,* the U.S. Supreme Court declared strict racial quotas unconstitutional, while at the same time supporting the concept of affirmative action. Eventually, conservative political forces were able to influence voters in the states of California and Washington to pass laws to abolish affirmative action in 1996.

These same conservative groups often attempt to block antidiscrimination statutes that protect lesbians and gay men. They claim that such legal protections are the first step toward affirmative action based upon sexual orientation. They further claim that affirmative action is the ultimate goal of gay activists. However, the claim is false because not one of the major national lesbian and gay organizations, college LGBT resource centers, local lesbian and gay community services centers, or professionally recognized academics on lesbian and gay culture advocates for affirmative action based upon sexual orientation. Conservatives who make such claims are engaging in scare tactics.

AIDS Acquired immune deficiency syndrome (AIDS), which is caused by a retrovirus known as the human immunodeficiency virus (HIV), has become one of the world's major epidemics. The first cases were reported in 1981 in the United States, primarily among gay men. Initially, doctors were unsure what caused this "gay plague" that was sweeping the nation and called it gay-related immune deficiency (GRID).

We have since learned that HIV infects and kills white blood cells called CD4 or T4 cells. These cells help the immune system fight infections. Without these cells, the immune system is weakened and opportunistic infections take hold, causing illness and death. It is the immune deficiency that is characteristic of AIDS.

The HIV virus is primarily transmitted through blood and semen. It is a fragile virus and cannot live long outside the human body. Its transmission occurs in three principal ways: (1) sexual contact that includes vaginal and anal intercourse; (2) direct exposure to infected blood through contaminated needles (either in medical use or illicit drug activity), through any kind of piercing in which blood may be transferred from one individual to another on unsterile tools (for example, piercing ears, "blood brother" rites, etc.), or via a tainted blood transfusion; or (3) perinatally from mother to child during pregnancy or delivery, or through breast-feeding (HIV can be transmitted to the fetus through the placenta, during the bloody process of delivery, or through mothers' milk).

The development of AIDS follows three stages. The acute infection stage occurs two to four weeks after exposure to the HIV virus. The exposed individual may experience flu-like symptoms. The second stage, asymptomatic infection, can last many years. This is a latent period in which the infected person experiences no clinical symptoms of the disease. However, the virus is replicating and causing slow damage to his or her white blood cells. Finally, the CD4 cell count drops to less than 200 and the final stage—advanced, symptomatic infection—progresses to "full-blown" AIDS with the development of opportunistic infections that cause illness and possible death. It is estimated that once the CD4 cell count drops below fifty, the patient has a life expectancy of twelve to eighteen months.

Since the Center for Disease Control began keeping records on AIDS in 1981, there have been between 650,000 to 900,000 persons infected in the

United States, of which 401,028 have died (as of 1998). That is approximately a 60 percent mortality rate. (It is estimated that approximately 2 percent of people exposed to the virus never go on to develop the disease. The reasons for this are unclear.) With such a devastating epidemic, a host of legal, social, and public health issues have developed related to HIV infection and AIDS.

Much hysteria arose during the 1980s about the causes and transmission methods of the disease. People who developed AIDS were often fired from their jobs, were forced out of their apartments and housing, lost their health insurance, and worse. Children infected with HIV who were asymptomatic were expelled from schools. Public swimming pools were emptied, scrubbed, disinfected, and refilled after a person with AIDS used them. Mortuaries refused to handle the bodies of people who died from AIDS. Airlines refused to allow people with AIDS to fly, and even heath care professionals sometime refused to care for those with AIDS. (See also **Employment**.)

People on the political and religious right used AIDS to reignite their antigay crusades. They claimed AIDS was "God's punishment" for the "immoral gay lifestyle." As such, there were calls to quarantine people with AIDS, to fire lesbian and gay teachers, and to impose other legal restrictions on homosexual behaviors. AIDS is still tied to antigay sentiments, even though it is well documented that AIDS existed in Africa long before it arrived in the United States and that in Africa heterosexual behavior is the primary method of transmission of HIV infection. AIDS was never a gay disease. Now that we understand that one of its modes of transmission is sexual activity, it makes sense that AIDS would primarily affect the gay community in the United States because this relatively closed subpopulation is where the virus first took hold. This is similar to the closed demographic circles in Africa where AIDS caused the death of virtually entire villages. (See also **Religious Right Agenda**.)

Linking AIDS with the gay community and drug users further oppressed already stigmatized groups. Massive discrimination resulted and the government initially ignored the severity of the problem. Even mainstream media refused to cover the AIDS epidemic until the first heterosexuals were reported to be infected (Shilts 1987). President Ronald Reagan did not mention AIDS until seven years into the epidemic. Yet his chief of communications, Patrick Buchanan, was very outspoken, claiming that AIDS was "God's awful retribution" for homosexual behavior and that AIDS patients did not deserve a thorough or compassionate response ("Buchanan Calls AIDS 'Retribution'" 1992).

President Reagan appointed a thirteen-member AIDS panel in July 1987. There was much infighting between members of the group and it reformed in 1988 to develop a plan of attack. The recommendations of the group were remarkably progressive, calling for massive governmental funding of research and care. The panel also recommended legislation to prevent discrimination against people with AIDS (PWA) and people infected with the virus. This was necessary because of the terrible discrimination AIDS patients with life-threatening illness were facing, including the calls by governmental units, such as states, for "mandatory contact tracing" (patients reveal with whom they had sex) and other infringements of rights.

Americans with Disabilities Act (ADA)

In 1987 a Florida court decided that tuberculosis infection was a disability protected by law (*School Board of Nassau County v. Arline*). This was an important decision because AIDS, like tuberculosis, is an infectious disease that often causes people to lose their jobs and face other discrimination. This concept of protecting those with disabilities was further developed by Congress with the enactment of the **Americans with Disabilities Act (ADA)** of 1990. Although it was not enacted primarily to cover HIV-infected individuals, AIDS was clearly on the minds of congressional representatives during the debate over this measure. For example, Senator Ted Kennedy stated, "With this measure [the ADA], we call for an end to finger pointing and fearmongering about AIDS. We know with great certainty how this disease is and is not transmitted. There is no scientific or medical reason to shun people with AIDS o[r] HIV disease" (Kennedy 1989).

In enacting the ADA, Congress intended to "provide clear, strong, consistent, enforceable standards addressing discrimination against individuals with disabilities" (ADA, § 12101[b][2]). However, court interpretation of HIV as being a disability has been anything but consistent. The unique characteristics of HIV, particularly its long asymptomatic latency, have created legal conflict over whether the disease is a disability.

Bragdon v. Abbott

The U.S. Supreme Court cleared up some of the issues in 1998 in *Bragdon v. Abbott*. Sidney Abbott went to the dental office of Randon Bragdon for an examination. She revealed that she was HIV positive on the patient registration form. Dr. Bragdon performed a routine examination, determined that she had a cavity, and told her that he would not fill the tooth in his office because of his HIV policy, but rather it would need to be done in a hospital setting and at her expense. She declined his offer and filed a complaint under the ADA and the Maine Human Rights Act (MHRA).

Both lower courts determined that Ms. Abbott's asymptomatic HIV was a physical impairment and that she was disabled as a matter of law under the ADA. On appeal, the Supreme Court used the case-by-case method of analysis. This method was first used by the Fourth Circuit Court of Appeals in *Ennis v. National Association of Business & Education Radio, Inc.* (1995), in which the court held that the plain language of the ADA required each case to be analyzed by itself. The court made three findings. First, HIV infection is an "impairment from the moment of infection" (*Bragdon v. Abbott,* 1998, 580). The court supported this position by citing several agency guidelines and judicial decisions. Second, the court agreed that HIV infection "substantially limits . . . [a] major life activit[y]" (*Bragdon v. Abbott,* 1998, 581). The court decided the major life activity impacted by HIV is reproduction. This position was further supported by the **Equal Employment Opportunity Commission (EEOC)** regulation for Title I that states that a physical or mental impairment is "[a]ny physiological disorder, or condition . . . affecting any one or more of [a number of listed body systems including reproduction]" (EEOC Guidance § 1630.2 [h][1] [1999]).

Because a case-by-case methodology was used, Sidney Abbott needed to demonstrate how her HIV status substantially limited her reproduction. First, the Court reviewed medical literature and found that HIV-positive persons impose a significant risk of infection on their partners when they engage in sexual behaviors while trying to conceive. Second, the Court determined that there was a significant risk to the fetus and newborn children from mothers who were HIV positive. Thus, the Court upheld Abbott's claim of discrimination under the ADA.

The *Bragdon* decision is exemplary for finding asymptomatic HIV a disability under the ADA. However, the Court failed to explicitly state that HIV infection is a disability per se. Because the case-by-case methodology is used in these situations, each claimant must show that the infection substantially limits his or her major life activities, and, in particular, the major life activity of reproduction. This could be problematic for lesbians and gay men on a number of levels.

Reproduction is generally viewed as a heterosexual activity. The case-by-case method places the burden on the plaintiff to demonstrate how HIV infection substantially limits his or her ability to reproduce and his or her *intention* to reproduce. Even if lesbians and gay men say that they intend to reproduce, some courts have challenged the truthfulness of such claims (Parmet and Jackson 1997). This is particularly distressing for gay men, the group that still comprises the majority of AIDS cases. Unless lesbians and gay men can convince a court that they intend to conceive children, the ADA may not provide protection against discrimination for those with HIV and AIDS.

Although a few lower courts have accepted the argument that HIV infection is a disability per se (*Hoepfl v. Barlow*), it is left to the future to see if the U.S. Supreme Court agrees. If this conclusion is ever reached, the case-by-case analysis will be circumvented and the major life activity argument will no longer be restricted only to reproduction.

HEALTH INSURANCE COVERAGE

When AIDS first appeared, insurance companies began redlining lesbians and gay men for denial of medical coverage. Challenges were made in each state against such discriminatory practices. With the advent of tests to detect the presence of the HIV virus, such as the enzyme-linked immunosorbent assay (ELISA) and "Western blot" test, insurance companies insisted that applicants for medical insurance take them. Quickly, these requirements and other mandatory testing were blocked by state and federal agencies.

The ADA also prohibits insurance companies from imposing disease-specific caps that limit health coverage for policy holders with HIV or other disabilities. But some insurance companies have ignored these rules and imposed caps on AIDS-related services. These were challenged in court with conflicting results. Recently, two Chicago men sued the Mutual of Omaha Insurance Company for establishing a cap on AIDS-related services (*Doe v. Mutual of Omaha Insurance Co.*). In January 2000 the U.S. Supreme Court declined to review *Doe* and let stand the appellate court decision that allowed insurance companies to impose such caps. Then, just three months later, Mutual of Omaha announced that it had voluntarily removed the cap on AIDS-related services and would provide coverage similar to other diseases. However, other insurance companies still maintain a low cap on AIDS medical insurance ("Supreme Court Refuses . . ." 2000).

References

"Buchanan Calls AIDS 'Retribution.'" 1992. *San Francisco Chronical* (28 February 1992): A1.

Equal Employment Opportunity Commission. 1999. *EEOC Enforcement Guidance: Vicarious Employer Liability for Unlawful Harassment by Supervisors.* Washington, DC: Government Printing Office.

Kennedy, Edward. 1989. "Senator Kennedy of Massachusetts speech," *Cong. Rec.*, 7 September, vol. 135, S10789 (daily ed.).

Parmet, W. E., and D. J. Jackson. 1997. "No Longer Disabled: The Legal Impact of the New Social Construction of HIV." *American Journal of Law and Medicine* 7: 35.

Shilts, R. 1987. *And the Band Played On: Politics, People, and the AIDS Epidemic.* New York: St. Martin's Press.

"Supreme Court Refuses to Review HIV Benefit Case." 2000. *Lesbian/Gay Law Notes* (May 2000).

ALCOHOLIC BEVERAGE CONTROL (ABC)

State alcoholic beverage control regulations are used to maintain the public safety in places that serve alcohol. Police are entrusted with the responsibility of maintaining public safety, including monitoring gay bars for overcrowding, underage patrons, or selling alcohol to patrons who are inebriated. Police departments have historically been one of the primary tools used to oppress lesbians and gay men through raiding or harassing patrons at gay and lesbian bars. Police often entered gay or lesbian bars and indiscriminately arrested people. In addition to enforcing ABC regulations, the police enforced antiquated sex statutes that limited touching between people of the same sex. For example, as late as the mid-1980s, it was illegal for people of the same sex to dance together, hold hands, or to wear non–gender-conforming clothing in many cities and states. It was the police raid on the Stonewall Inn in the summer of 1969 in New York City that sparked a riot that is recognized as the beginning of the modern gay rights movement. Celebrations are held nationwide in most cities to commemorate this event. (See also **Stonewall Riot**.)

Today, reports persist that police target gay bars more often for ABC enforcement than bars that serve a heterosexual clientele. In response to these and related abuses, many cities have gay and lesbian organizations that act as liaisons between the lesbian and gay community and the police department.

AMENDMENT 2 Amendment 2 was an amendment to the Colorado state constitution that invalidated antidiscrimination statutes based upon sexual orientation. The measure was passed November 3, 1992, by the state's voters, but the U.S. Supreme Court declared the amendment unconstitutional in a 1996 case, ***Romer v. Evans.***

AMERICAN PSYCHIATRIC ASSOCIATION (APA) The American Psychiatric Association is a professional organization that oversees ethical behaviors and other issues related to the profession of psychiatry. The APA also maintains the *Diagnostic and Statistical Manual of Mental Disorders* (*DSM*).

The APA initially classified homosexuality as a mental disorder in the first edition of the *Diagnostic Statistical Manual* (*DSM I*). Research by Evelyn Hooker and others in the 1950s and 1960s demonstrated that homosexuality was as adaptive and psychologically sound as heterosexuality. President Johnson appointed Dr. Hooker to head the National Institute of Mental Health (NIMH) Task Force on Homosexuality, which in 1969 recommended the repeal of sodomy laws and better public education about homosexuality (Thompson 1994, 69).

A committee was formed within the APA in the early 1970s to investigate the belief that homosexuality was a mental illness. The NIMH report, along with the efforts of Dr. Charles Silverstein (founding editor of the *Journal of Homosexuality*) and other respected physicians and researchers, was able to convince the board of trustees of the APA in 1973 that homosexuality should be removed from the list of recognized disorders. A vote by the entire membership the next year (1974) upheld the recommendation of the board and homosexuality was no longer listed as a mental disorder in the *DSM*.

Conservatives and members of the religious right have often portrayed the adoption of this change in the *DSM* as the result of scheming by a band of gay activists that pushed through their agenda. This is not true. Because the entire body of the APA voted on the change, it was the clear presentation of the research to the members that convinced them to change their position. The membership of the APA reflects society and is mostly heterosexual. Thus, it was primarily heterosexuals who reviewed the research and agreed that the change was needed.

Understanding this history helps explain one of the major tools used to maintain legal discrimination against homosexuals. Psychiatrists are often called upon by courts to give professional testimony. In the past psychiatrists provided support for the belief that homosexuals were mentally defective and thus unfit to have custody of their children, to teach or work with children, or to hold jobs that dealt with security and intelligence. They also supported the belief that heterosexuals would naturally respond with violence toward homosexuals who made passes at them. (See also **Child Custody and Visitation Rights**; **Employment**; **Homosexual Panic Defense**; **School Faculty Members' Rights**; **Security Clearance**.)

Objective scientific research revealed that homosexuality is not a disorder. It is the poor treatment of homosexuals by society that is the problem. Psychiatrists now educate courts about homosexuality and support lesbian and gay parents during child custody cases. Their testimony helps to defeat attempts to use the so-called homosexual panic defense and to counter negative stereotypes used to defeat lesbian and gay defendants. (See also **Homophobia**.)

The American Psychological Association supports the American Psychiatric Association in its position that sexual orientation—whether it be homosexual, heterosexual, or bisexual—is innate for all human beings and one form of sexual orientation is not better or more psychologically healthy than another. The American Psychological Association has issued position papers and a pamphlet contending that efforts to change sexual orientation violate ethical standards and that changing sexual orientation cannot be achieved. (See also **Reparative Therapy**.)

References

Diagnostic and Statistical Manual of Mental Disorders. 1994. 4th ed. Washington, DC: American Psychiatric Association.

Thompson, M., ed. 1994. *Long Road to Freedom:* The Advocate *History of the Gay and Lesbian Movement*. New York: St. Martin's Press.

AMERICANS WITH DISABILITIES ACT (ADA) An act passed in 1990 by the Senate and House of Representatives to establish a clear and comprehensive prohibition of discrimination on the basis of disability. It became apparent to Congress after the passage of the Civil Rights Act of 1964 that large numbers of Americans still faced discrimination in employment, housing, and public accommodations due to their physical and mental disabilities.

As **AIDS** spread throughout the land, large numbers of people were denied health benefits, were fired from their jobs, and experienced severe discrimination from health care professionals and others. Research showed that AIDS is not an easily communicable disease, thus, much of the hysteria was unfounded. Congress recognized these needs and AIDS was extensively discussed during the development of the act.

With the passage of the ADA, people with AIDS (PWA) had legal recourse against acts of discrimination. However, court challenges slowly eroded these protections. Some insurance companies established policies that put extremely low caps on AIDS-related expenditures. Initially, the courts found such actions illegal, but eventually the U.S. Supreme Court agreed that insurance companies could take such actions (e.g., *Doe v. Mutual of Omaha Insurance Co.*). Also, an amendment to the ADA specifically excluded transsexualism (along with transvestitism, pedophilia, exhibitionism, and voyeurism) from coverage.

ANTIDISCRIMINATION STATUTES Antidiscrimination statutes are laws that provide protection against discrimination. The Civil Rights Act of 1964 was the most significant step taken by the federal government to enact antidiscrimination provisions. It provided protections for a few categories of people based on race, color, religion, or national origin. These are known as **suspect classes** for the purpose of strict judicial scrutiny. (See also **Equal Employment Opportunity Commission [EEOC]**.)

Interestingly, sex was not initially included in the draft of the Civil Rights Act. It was then added to the bill by conservatives who hoped that its inclusion would ensure the act's defeat. However, the act passed and opened the door for the adoption of antidiscrimination policies and laws by local and state governments based on gender and sexual orientation. Sexual orientation has yet to receive suspect class status or formal protection at the federal level except in federal **employment**.

State and local governments have the ability to regulate discrimination more thoroughly than the federal government. The power of the federal government to regulate in this area is based on the commerce clause of the U.S. Constitution, which allows the government to regulate interstate commerce, or on the essentially negative power of withholding federal funding from state and local programs that discriminate unfairly. State and local governments are not as restricted. State constitutions can provide more (but not less) protection from discrimination than those protections specified in the federal Constitution and many federal statutes. State agencies, such as those regulating insurance and housing, can write additional policies providing protection from discrimination.

Every state has some types of laws providing protection from discrimination. Only a few explicitly include sexual orientation. Other states courts have made wide interpretations that sometimes exclude and other times include sexual orientation as a protected classification. For example, Timothy Curran sued the **Boy Scouts** of America for denying him the right to be a scoutmaster because he was openly gay. The California court ruled against the Boy Scouts, reasoning that California's antidiscrimination classification of sex and race was not restrictive to these classes, but rather illustrative of protected groups. The Boy Scouts appealed. The California appellate court reversed the decision and agreed that the Boy Scouts had the constitutional right to discriminate against homosexuals, based on their First Amendment rights of free association and speech. Thus, the constitutional protection of free speech sometimes comes into conflict with the constitutional protections against discrimination. In 2000, the Supreme Court upheld the Boy Scouts' right to exclude homosexuals from their organization (*Boy Scouts of America v. Dale,* 2000).

More than 100 towns, cities, and counties have passed antidiscrimination laws based on sexual orientation. Some of these laws apply only to government employees. Sometimes they include private employment and housing. Most laws represent a long process of consensus building to create the environment necessary for their passage. In a few cases, the laws have come under attack after they were enacted and were later revoked; a few were then reinstated.

The state of Colorado is a prime example of this process. A number of cities enacted legislation to provide protection based on sexual orientation. A state constitutional amendment was then passed to rescind protection from discrimination for lesbians and gay men and to preclude future protections for them. **Amendment 2** went to the U.S. Supreme Court, which ruled against Colorado. The Court found that the amendment violated federal equal protection guarantees because the law specifically made it more difficult for lesbians and gay men to participate in the political process. (See also ***Romer v. Evans.***)

It is often believed that antidiscrimination laws are a phenomenon limited to big cities such as San Francisco, New York, or Los Angeles. This is not true. Employment discrimination protection for transgendered people is provided by Louisville, Kentucky, and Iowa City, Iowa, but not yet by New York City. More than 100 cities and eighteen counties prohibit discrimination based on sexual orientation in private employment. Equality for lesbians, gay men, and bisexuals, and for transgendered, transsexual, and intersexed people has widespread support in the American heartland. Polls show that "70 percent of Americans in 1999 support the right of gays and lesbians to serve in the military . . . [and] 49 percent of Republicans support antidiscrimination laws for gay men and lesbians" (National Gay and Lesbian Task Force 2000). (See also **Appendix A: State and Local Laws**.)

The status of antidiscrimination laws throughout the world for lesbian and gay men is mixed. Some countries provide extensive protections, while others still arrest and kill homosexuals (for example, Iran, Saudi Arabia, and Turkey). The Netherlands provides legal domestic partnerships that mimic heterosexual **marriage**. Other countries have conflicting moral and legal systems that oppress homosexuals. For example, a Saudi Arabian court in April 2000 sentenced nine young men to up to 2,600 lashes each for "deviant sexual behavior." They were convicted of transvestitism and participating in deviant sexual acts. The sentence was to be carried out at fifteen-day intervals during which the men are supposed to recover enough to sustain the next beating. The process would take two years. In addition, they have been sentenced to four to six years in prison. Surprisingly, Saudi Arabia is a founding member and a signatory to the UN Convention Against Torture—yet they are torturing these nine men (International Gay and Lesbian Human Rights Commission 2000). The men are currently serving out their sentences under Saudi law.

References

International Gay and Lesbian Human Rights Commission. 2000. "Alleged Transvestites Sentenced to Brutal Flogging: IGLHRC Condemns Court Ruling in Saudi Arabia." Press release on International Gay and Lesbian Human Rights Commission website: www.IGLHRC.org/news/press/pr_000420.htm. Accessed 20 April 2000.

National Gay and Lesbian Task Force. 2000. "Nondiscrimination Laws Now Cover 100 Million Americans, New Report Finds." Press release on National Gay and Lesbian Task Force website: www.ngltf.org/press/010300.html. Accessed 3 January 2000.

ARTIFICIAL INSEMINATION Artificial insemination is the process by which a woman can be impregnated without having to engage in sexual intercourse with a man. Many lesbians desire to have children, but intercourse with a man is not desired or an option. In the early years of artificial insemination by donor (AID), the treatment was restricted to heterosexual married couples ("Artificial Insemination: A New Wave" 1977). In the last years of the twentieth century, AID for lesbians has become widely available from the medical establishment, and as many as one-third (Smolowe 1990) of all AID procedures are now being utilized by lesbians.

Four problems face the AID program:

1. There is a slight chance that two AID children with the same father may meet and begin an incestuous relationship.
2. Because the birth certificate of an AID child lists the father as "unknown," the child may face the emotional stigma of "illegitimacy."
3. Nearly all lesbians express a desire to rear a female child, yet approximately 93 percent of AID children born are male (Hanscombe and Forster 1982). This overrepresentation of male babies occurred even when using a sex predetermination method that times insemination by ovulation cycles (Shettles and Rorvik 1997). The reason for this phenomenon is unknown.
4. When the donor is known, a fear of future litigation has prompted some sperm banks and donors to sign contracts that allow the child access to his or her father's name upon legal adulthood (Sperm Bank of California 1997).

The accessibility of AID is expected to expand as lesbians and gay men obtain greater legal rights.

References

"Artificial Insemination: A New Wave." 1977. *British Journal of Sexual Medicine* 27(2) (February): 206.

Hanscombe, G., and J. Forster. 1982. *Rocking the Cradle—Lesbian Mothers: A Challenge in Family Living*. Boston: Alyson Publications.

Shettles, L. B., and D. M. Rorvik. 1997. *How to Choose the Sex of Your Baby: The Method Best Supported by Scientific Evidence*. New York: Doubleday.

Smolowe, J. 1990. "Last Call for Motherhood." *Time*, fall special issue, 76.

Sperm Bank of California. 1997. *Donor Identity-Release Policy*. Berkeley, CA: Reproductive Technologies, Inc.

B

BAEHR V. LEWIN *Baehr v. Lewin* was a Hawaii Supreme Court case that found the laws preventing same-sex couples from marrying were a form of sex discrimination and therefore unconstitutional. In December 1990 the Hawaii Department of Health denied marriage licenses to three gay couples. The three gay couples sued the department. In September 1991 Circuit Court Judge Robert Klein threw out the case, ruling that homosexual **marriage** was not a fundamental right. The ruling was appealed. In May 1993 the Hawaii Supreme Court reinstated the lawsuit and held that the state's denial of marriage licenses to the three couples violated their rights as a form of sex discrimination. Sex receives suspect class status in the Hawaii constitution and thus requires the highest scrutiny of legal review. The state was required to show a compelling reason to justify the ban. Circuit Court Judge Kevin Chang ruled in 1996 that prohibiting same-sex couples from marrying violated the state constitution's equal protection clause—specifically that the state Department of Health could not deny marriage licenses on the basis of gender. However, an amendment to the Hawaii constitution was passed by the voters in November 1998 that restricted the definition of marriage to opposite-sex couples only. At that, the Hawaii Supreme Court unanimously overturned Chang's 1996 decision.

BAKER V. VERMONT In December 1999 the Vermont Supreme Court found in *Baker v. Vermont* that same-sex couples in the state were entitled to the same protections and benefits provided by law as are given to opposite-sex married couples. The court did not decide that same-sex couples were entitled to civil marriage licenses. Instead, the court referred the matter back to the Vermont legislature to craft a solution for same-sex couples. The legislature could extend marriage to same-sex couples or form a new category that extended all the same rights and responsibilities to them. Within six months, Vermont created a new category called **civil union** to achieve this end. It is not known if civil unions will be transferable to other states.

BEING OUT AT WORK A number of studies have shown that the more a person is open about his or her sexuality, the greater is his or her psychological adjustment and well-being (Cain 1990; Cass 1979). (See also **Coming Out**.)

The social environment of the workplace has been shown to be related to employee job satisfaction in a number of studies (Andrisani and Shapiro 1978; Crosby 1982; Repetti and Cosmas 1991). A study conducted by Alan Ellis and Ellen Riggle (1995) found "lesbians' and gay males' satisfaction with coworkers is associated with openness in the workplace," that is, "openness about one's sexuality was associated with greater satisfaction with one's coworkers." Consistent with other research on the relationship between being open and life satisfaction, Ellis and Riggle found that openness at work and satisfaction with coworkers were positively related to lesbians' and gay males' overall satisfaction with life.

Thus, lesbians, gay males, and bisexuals, and transgendered, transsexual, and intersexed people obtain social acceptance and equality by being open about their personal lives. This openness supports feelings of self-worth. Being open at work fosters greater satisfaction about work.

These are important findings for businesses and schools. By making work and school environments safe for lesbians, gay males, and bisexuals, and transgendered, transsexual, and intersexed people, tensions will be reduced for all, workers will feel better working together, the potential for complaints about discrimination will be reduced, and workers will be more productive. It is to everyone's benefit to reduce and eliminate bias and prejudice. (See also **Employment**; **Equal Employment Opportunity Commission [EEOC]**.)

References

Andrisani, P. J., and M. B. Shapiro. 1978. "Women's Attitudes toward Their Jobs: Some Longitudinal Data on a National Sample." *Personnel Psychology* 31: 15–34.

Cain, R. 1990. "Stigma Management and Gay Identity Development." *Social Work* 36(1): 67–73.

Cass, V. 1979. "Homosexual Identity Formation: A Theoretical Model." *Journal of Homosexuality* 4(3): 219–235.

Crosby, R. 1982. *Relative Deprivation and Working Women*. New York: Oxford University Press.

Ellis, A. L., and E. D. B. Riggle. 1995. "The Relation of Job Satisfaction and Degree of Openness about One's Sexual Orientation for Lesbians and Gay Men." *Journal of Homosexuality* 30(2): 75–85.

Repetti, R. L., and K. A. Cosmas. 1991. "The Quality of the Social Environment at Work and Job Satisfaction." *Journal of Applied Social Psychology* 21: 840–854.

BISEXUAL Bisexuality is physical and emotional attraction to persons of either the same or the opposite gender. Bisexuals are virtually invisible in our society. When they form opposite-sex relationships, they are presumed to be heterosexual. When they form same-sex relationships, they are presumed to be homosexual. The ability of bisexuals to form relationships with either sex confuses many people and has led gays to stereotype bisexuals as self-absorbed, shallow, untrustworthy, narcissistic, and morally bankrupt (Udis-Kessler 1996; Weinberg, Williams, and Pryor 1994)—the same stereotypes applied to gays by heterosexuals. Bisexuals are often not accepted into either the gay or straight community.

Bisexuals report falling in love with "persons" and not with a particular gender (Leland 1995). The most common relationship pattern for bisexuals is not to be dating both men and women at the same time ("swinging"), but rather to form one exclusive relationship for a particular time until, at some future time, it ends, and then to form another exclusive relationship (serial monogamy)—the same as for heterosexuals and homosexuals. Bisexuals are not confused or in denial about their sexual and affectional relationships (Cabaj and Stein 1996, 154–156). Approximately 10 percent of bisexuals form long-term threesomes, also known as group marriages (Rust 1996). Overall, there is probably more bisexual behavior than there is exclusive homosexual behavior when sexual behaviors over a lifetime are considered (Diamond 1993; Janus and Janus 1993; Laumann, Gagnon, Michael, and Michaels 1994; Rogers and Turner 1992).

The Kinsey studies found that as many as 15 to 25 percent of women and 33 to 46 percent of men may be bisexual based on their sexual activities and attractions over a lifetime (Kinsey, Pomeroy, and Martin, 1948; Kinsey, Pomeroy, Martin, and Gebhard, 1953). Considering these studies were conducted in the 1940s and 1950s and society was not tolerant of homosexual or bisexual behaviors, many researchers believe these numbers are low.

The bisexual liberation movement has paralleled the gay rights movements. Primarily, bisexuals have worked to gain visibility for their concerns. In the 1970s, the first bisexual groups tended to emphasize sexual liberation as their political goal. They often aligned with heterosexual "swinger" communities and fledgling gay rights organizations. As gay activists began to espouse their identities, many bisexuals felt left out and unheard. Bisexuals resisted the trend by both the straight and gay communities to bifurcate sexuality into two opposite camps. In 1972, the

Quaker Committee of Friends on Bisexuality issued the "Ithaca Statement on Bisexuality" in *The Advocate,* delineating a new "bi-consciousness." The same year, the National Bisexual Liberation Group founded in New York and published the earliest bi newsletter, *The Bisexual Expression.* Bisexual support organizations formed in many major cities and throughout Europe.

In the 1980s, a shift occurred in bisexual organizations; whereas before they had been predominantly male, many were now founded and led by women. Many bi women experienced alienation from the women's movement, which often discriminated against lesbians, and "separatist" lesbians who thought women should live apart from men. For many bi women, their sexuality was an integral part of their feminist politics and they wanted support organizations that were respectful of their ideals and needs. Two of the earliest groups to respect bisexuality as a sexual orientation were the Boston Bisexual Women's Network (formed in 1983) and the Seattle Bisexual Women's Network (founded in 1986). Many similar groups formed across the United States, Europe, New Zealand, and Australia.

The AIDS epidemic had, and still has, a major impact on the bisexual community. Bi men were stigmatized as spreaders of HIV from homosexuals to the "general population," whereas bi women were accused of bringing HIV to the lesbian community. Neither stereotype is true. It is sexual behavior, rather than sexual orientation or identity, that causes the spread of HIV. These controversial accusations spurred discussion on the distinction between sexual identity and sexual behaviors, and many bisexual activists turned their attention to AIDS-related activism.

The 1987 march on Washington for gay and lesbian rights marked the first national gathering of bisexuals. There it was decided to create a national organization for bisexuals—the North American Bisexual Network (NABN). The first National Bisexual Conference was held in San Francisco in 1990, which more than 400 people attended. A year later, NABN renamed itself Bisexual Network of the USA (BiNet). In 1992, the First International Conference on Bisexuality was held in Amsterdam.

In the late 1980s and early 1990s, lesbian and gay college student groups and other organizations began to include the term "bisexual" in their names. This was in response to Queer Nation activism emphasizing the inclusion of all people who differ from the dominant power elite. Books and papers on bisexuality and transgenderism exploded in number. Including bisexuals on the talk show circuit became a "must." Universities began to include bisexuality in their gender studies courses. Finally, the Internet allowed bisexuals to communicate and organize in ways never before imagined.

Although bisexuals have gained greater recognition and acceptance, courts have had difficulty acknowledging a class of people who are not exclusively heterosexual or homosexual. Child custody and visitation are areas in which bisexuality is not acknowledged. When a bisexual parent divorces and becomes involved with a same-sex partner, the ex-spouse may claim the "homosexual" relationship of the other parent is detrimental to the well-being of the child and try to block visitation rights of the parent. The courts have viewed the bisexual parent as homosexual in these cases and decided accordingly. (See also **Child Custody and Visitation Rights**.) Another area of confusion has been in sexual harassment cases. In *Holman v. Indiana,* the court decided that "equal opportunity harassers" who sexually harass both genders on the job do not violate Title VII because the harassment did not occur "because of sex" (910). Surprising as this may seem, it does not mean bisexuals are free to sexually harass employees with impunity. In such situations, other state and local statutes may apply to prosecute harassment by bisexual employees. (See also **Sexual Harassment**.)

References

Cabaj, R. P., and T. S. Stein. 1996. *Textbook of Homosexuality and Mental Health.* Washington, DC: American Psychiatrist Press.

Diamond, M. 1993. "Homosexuality and Bisexuality in Different Populations." *Archives of Sexual Behavior* 22(4): 291–310.

Janus, S. S., and C. L. Janus. 1993. *The Janus Report on Sexual Behavior.* New York: John Wiley & Sons.

Kinsey, A. C., W. B. Pomeroy, and C. E. Martin. 1948. *Sexual Behavior in the Human Male.* Philadelphia: W. B. Saunders Co.

Kinsey, A. C., W. B. Pomeroy, C. E. Martin, and R. H. Gebhard. 1953. *Sexual Behavior in the Human Female.* Philadelphia: W. B. Saunders Co.

Laumann, E. O., J. H. Gagnon, R. T. Michael, and S. Michaels. 1994. *The Social Organization of Sexuality: Sexual Practices in the United States.* Chicago: University of Chicago Press.

Leland, J. 1995. "Bisexuality Is the Wild Card of Our Erotic Life." *Newsweek* (17 July 1995): 44–50.

Rogers, S. M., and C. R. Turner. 1992. "Male-Male Sexual Contact in the U.S.: Findings from Five Sample Surveys, 1970–1990." *Journal of Sex Research* 28(4): 491–519.

Rust, P. C. 1996. "Monogamy and Polyamory: Relationship Issues for Bisexuals." In *Bisexuality: The Psychology and Politics of an Invisible Minority,* edited by B. A. Firestein. Newbury Park, CA: Sage.

Udis-Kessler, A. 1996. "Challenging the Stereotypes." In *Bisexual Horizons; Politics, Histories, Lives,* edited by S. Rose, et al. London: Lawrence & Wishart.

Weinberg, M. S., C. J. Williams, and D. W. Pyror. 1994. *Dual Attraction: Understanding Bisexuality.* New York: Oxford University Press.

BOOKS, BROCHURES, PAMPHLETS

See SPEECH AND ASSOCIATION

BOWERS V. HARDWICK *Bowers v. Hardwick* was the U.S. Supreme Court's 1986 decision that upheld states' rights to regulate adult consensual sodomy through the application of sex statutes. Michael Hardwick was a twenty-eight-year-old gay man who worked at one of the well-known gay bars in Atlanta, Georgia. After a long night at the bar, he left at seven in the morning with a beer in hand. He decided he did not want the beer and disposed of it in a trash can outside the bar before getting into his car to drive home. Police officer Torrick pulled Hardwick over to the side of the highway. He asked Hardwick where he worked. Hardwick's answer indirectly indicated to the police officer that Hardwick was gay. Torrick suspected Hardwick of drinking and asked where he disposed of his beer. Hardwick was placed in the rear of the police car while Torrick drove to where the beer was discarded. They did not find the trash receptacle and Torrick issued a ticket to Hardwick for drinking in public.

The ticket Hardwick was given required him to appear in court. There was a discrepancy as to whether the court appearance was on a Tuesday or Wednesday. Two hours after the Tuesday court date, a warrant for the arrest of Hardwick was issued. Officer Torrick came to Hardwick's home to arrest him, but he was not there. When Hardwick returned home later that day, his roommate informed him about the officer's visit. Hardwick went to the county clerk, who doubted Hardwick's story because it usually takes at least forty-eight hours for such a warrant to be issued. Later it was discovered that Torrick personally processed the warrant—the first time this was done in over ten years. Hardwick paid the $50 fine and thought the case was closed.

About three weeks later, officer Torrick returned to Hardwick's home with the arrest warrant. The door was open and Torrick was allowed to enter the home by a houseguest who was half asleep on the couch. He did not know that Hardwick and his companion were together in Hardwick's bedroom. Torrick walked to the bedroom and discovered Hardwick engaged in oral sex with another man. Torrick proceeded to enter the bedroom and arrested Hardwick and his companion for violating Georgia's sex statute. Hardwick was entitled to bail within an hour after arriving at the jail, but instead he was held for twelve hours and was subjected to harassment by the other prisoners, who had been informed of the charges against him.

Hardwick was charged with committing sodomy. Gay activists saw this as a perfect test case and Hardwick decided to challenge the Georgia statute in federal court. Because the Georgia sex statutes do not refer to the gender or marriage status of offenders, a married heterosexual couple attempted to join Hardwick's action, but the court dismissed the married couple's claim.

Hardwick lost his claim in federal court, but won on his appeal to the

U.S. District Court of Appeals for the Eleventh Circuit. The case was appealed to the U.S. Supreme Court by Georgia Attorney General Bowers. The Court ruled against Hardwick in a five-to-four decision. The Court ruled that claims for "homosexual sodomy" as a protected right to privacy are "at best, facetious" (193). The Court therefore established that lesbians and gay men have no right to sexual expression under the federal Constitution. Within two weeks of the *Bowers* decision, the Missouri Supreme Court, citing *Bowers,* upheld Missouri's sodomy law from privacy challenges (*State v. Walsh*). Soon after his retirement, Justice Lewis Powell conceded that he "had made a mistake" and should have voted to strike down Georgia's sex statute (Marcus 1990).

Since *Hardwick* many within and without the lesbian and gay legal community have written scathing critiques of the ruling. If the Court had ruled in favor of Hardwick, all state sex statutes would have been overturned. Instead, the battle continues state by state. For example, the Kentucky Supreme Court decision in ***Commonwealth v. Wasson*** (1992) rejected many of the arguments made by the majority in *Hardwick.* Instead, the court held that the privacy protections contained within the Kentucky constitution were more comprehensive than those provided by the U.S. Constitution. Because many states have constitutions similar to Kentucky with regards to privacy, this decision has been instrumental in the overturning of other state sex statutes. (See also **Sodomy**.)

Reference

Marcus, R. 1990. "Powell Regrets Backing Sodomy Law." *Washington Post* (26 October 1990): A3.

Boy Scouts The Boy Scouts of America has sustained many legal challenges for its policy of excluding homosexual members. Many school districts, cities, counties, nonprofit organizations, and religious groups have severed their relationships with the Boy Scouts over this issue. The Boy Scouts claim that they have a First Amendment legal right to promote their belief that homosexuality is immoral and inappropriate. Some school districts, cities, and counties have decided that they cannot allow their facilities to be used by, and they cannot provide other government support to, an organization that excludes particular groups of people because this violates antidiscrimination policies and equal access laws. The Boy Scout organization thus has become the legal focal point over the debate between freedom of association and equal access. (See also **Antidiscrimination Statutes**.)

The Boy Scouts was founded by Robert S. S. Baden-Powell in England in 1907. He was a decorated war hero and was gay (Greif 1989; Halsall 1994). He promoted the Boy Scouts as a "character factory" to help young men find honor and learn to be helpful to society. The Boy Scouts has become an institution in American life. The policies of the Boy Scouts, embodied in over a hundred years of actions, teachings, positions, and documents, neither provide directives on nor condemn homosexuality. It is only the recent leadership that has become steadfast against homosexuality. In the United States, there are more than 5 million Boy Scouts, of whom 55 percent are in troops sponsored by churches. The Boy Scouts contends that it has an overarching objective to reach "all eligible youth."

Over the past decade courts have often ruled against the Scouts for removing openly gay troop leaders, only to see these decisions overruled by higher courts. The crucial issue of whether the Boy Scouts could discriminate against homosexual members and leaders was finally reviewed by the U.S. Supreme Court in *Boy Scouts of America v. Dale* (2000). James Dale was involved with the Boy Scouts for twelve years. He obtained the rank of Eagle Scout, was elected to the Order of the Arrow, and became assistant troop leader in 1990 at age twenty. He never made his homosexuality known to the Scouts, nor did he mention or discuss the topic of homosexuality. That same year he was interviewed in a college newspaper and was identified as the copresident of a lesbian and gay student group at Rutgers University. The paper ran a photo of him marching in the local gay pride parade. When the Scouts' Monmouth, New Jersey, council discovered this fact, they sent him a letter stating that the Boy Scouts "specifically forbid membership to homosexuals" and expelled him from the organization (*Boy Scouts of America v. Dale,* 137). Dale was not expelled for inappropriate conduct "on" or "off duty," but rather for simply being identified as a homosexual.

Dale sued the Monmouth council and the national organization in 1992. He contended that their actions violated New Jersey's antidiscrimination law. The state court threw the case out, stating that the Boy Scouts was not a **public accommodation** and therefore was not bound by state antidiscrimination laws. The case was appealed and the New Jersey Supreme Court ruled in Dale's favor. The court rejected the Scouts' position that allowing homosexuals to participate would violate the Scouts' Oath's promise to remain "morally straight" and "clean." The court decided that the Boy Scouts was a public accommodation and was subject to state regulation. (See also **Antidiscrimination Statutes**.)

The New Jersey Supreme Court made the following points:

- The Boy Scouts is a public accommodation because of its enormity and entanglement with governments and public entities.
- The Boy Scouts' policy of expelling openly gay members violated the state's law prohibiting places of public accommodation from discriminating on the basis of sexual orientation.

- To recognize the Boy Scouts' First Amendment claim would be tantamount to tolerating the expulsion of an individual solely because of his status as a homosexual—an act of discrimination unprotected by the First Amendment freedom of speech.
- The state's interest in prohibiting invidious discrimination outweighs the rights of nonsectarian organizations to exclude individuals simply because of who they are.

The issue polarized America. Together, seventy-one organizations filed briefs in this case. Every major civil rights organization including the NAACP and the American Bar Association joined with states, cities, deans of divinity schools, youth organizations, mental health and social services organizations, and rabbinical institutions in lobbying the Supreme Court in Dale's favor. The religious right, including Orthodox Jewish groups, supported the Boy Scouts.

The Boy Scouts argued the following in Court:

- No one has the "right" to be a Boy Scout leader. The Boy Scouts has the right to determine the qualifications of its leaders. Because it believes homosexuality is immoral, it has the right to disallow homosexuals from being troop leaders. It contends that Boy Scout policy is promoted through its leadership and attempts to control its leadership is, in fact, control of its speech.
- Homosexuals cannot teach "true manliness" and a boy's ultimate responsibility to women, children, and religious belief.
- Boy Scouting espouses family values, which emphasize marriage and fatherhood—neither of which homosexuals stand for.
- Requiring the Boy Scouts to accept homosexual leaders would, by word and deed, put leaders in place who disagreed with the organization's moral code.
- Applying the New Jersey law to the Boy Scouts violates the members' constitutional right to intimate and expressive association. The Boy Scouts is a private, voluntary organization and should have the freedom to "create and interpret its own moral code."
- The Boy Scouts is being forced to condone homosexuality against its will.

Dale's lawyers made the following arguments to the U.S. Supreme Court:

- The Boy Scouts does not have a history of actions or policy that excludes homosexuals. If anything, the Boy Scouts teaches tolerance and encourages an end to bigotry and hate.

- The U.S. Supreme Court has repeatedly rejected the notion that the First Amendment gives groups the right to discriminate. The First Amendment right to freedom of association and its corollary, the freedom not to associate, has never been regarded as an absolute free-floating right.
- Dale was expelled from the Scouts solely because he was gay and not for misconduct. In New Jersey, discrimination based upon sexual orientation is illegal. The Boy Scouts illegally discriminated against Dale.

There are two basic arguments to this issue.

For the Boy Scouts: The Boy Scouts have a First Amendment right to determine and promote the moral goals of a private organization. This includes the right to choose leaders who reflect the organization's goals. A few court cases back this position. For example, in *Hurley v. Irish-American Gay, Lesbian, and Bisexual Group of Boston,* the court upheld the First Amendment right of the organizers of the Boston **St. Patrick's Day Parade** to exclude gays from their event. The gay marching contingent was not barred from participating because of its gay identity, but rather because it intended to express a message in the parade contrary to that of the parade organizers.

For James Dale: Because of the size and institutional nature of the Boy Scouts, it is a public organization subject to state laws. As such, if state laws prohibit discrimination based upon sexual orientation, then the Boy Scouts should not be allowed to exclude lesbian or gay members or leaders. This position is supported by three recent cases, all dealing with all-male organizations. In *Roberts v. United States Jaycees,* the Supreme Court allowed the state of Minnesota to require that females be accepted as members into the once all-male Jaycees. In general, the courts found the clubs existed for commercial purposes and that the exclusion of women was not part of their self-described mission.

The Boy Scouts asserted that by donning the Scout uniform, James Dale would celebrate his identity as an openly gay scout leader precisely as did the gay Irish marchers who attempted to conscript the Boston St. Patrick's Day Parade for their own purposes. However, Dale argued that "learning that someone is gay tells you nothing about his or her political party, religious beliefs, lifestyle, or moral code." Thus, his exclusion from the Boy Scouts is the same discrimination based on status that the court rejected in the all-male club cases.

The balance between First Amendment rights to free speech and association and government regulation of discrimination is distinguished between identity-based and speech-based discrimination. The Boy Scouts is free to express its point of view in pamphlets, speeches, and other ways.

However, it has chosen not to do so. Heterosexual troop leaders have publicly stated that discrimination against homosexuals is wrong and that homosexuality is moral; yet the Boy Scouts has not acted against these leaders (*Boy Scouts of America v. Dale* 2000, 2455). Only those who are openly gay have been expelled. This is conduct discrimination that the courts have held to be unconstitutional for private nonsecular organizations that are deemed public accommodations.

On June 28, 2000, the U.S. Supreme Court reversed the New Jersey Supreme Court decision. The Court held that requiring the Boy Scouts to include Mr. Dale in their ranks would violate the organization's First Amendment right of "expressive association." The Court said, "We are not, as we must not be, guided by our views of whether the Boy Scouts' teachings with respect to homosexual conduct are right or wrong. Public or judicial disapproval of a tenet of an organization's expression does not justify the state's effort to compel the organization to accept members where such acceptance would derogate from the organization's expressive message" (*Boy Scouts of America v. Dale* 2000, 2458). Because Boy Scout leaders are drawn from the ranks of young scouts, it is inferred that gay people are forbidden in the Scouts at any level. The dissenting justices, John Paul Stevens, David Souter, Stephen Breyer, and Ruth Bader Ginsburg, said that the scouting precept of being "morally straight and clean" was not related to homosexuality. However, the Boy Scouts' lawyer George Davidson stated that being openly homosexual communicates the concept that this is acceptable and is against the Scouts' policy.

Because the U.S. Supreme Court failed to force an overall change in the Boy Scouts' policy, it is expected that more cities, local governments, school districts, and others will withdraw their support of the Boy Scouts because of the Boy Scouts' intransigent ban on allowing gay members to participate. For example, the day after the announcement by the Supreme Court, the mayor of Philadelphia was asked to withdraw all city support for the Boy Scouts of America (Center for Lesbian and Gay Civil Rights 2000).

Some tax scholars have queried whether the Boy Scouts should have their tax-exempt status revoked by the IRS ("Does Boy Scouts' Policy," 2000). This is based on the law that charitable institutions must demonstrably serve and be in harmony with the public interest to qualify for tax-exempt status. In *Bob Jones University v. United States*, the Supreme Court upheld the revocation of the university's tax-exempt status because it had a policy forbidding interracial dating. By 1983, the social, political, and legal climate of the United States was such that this policy violated community conscience. The Court respected the right of the university to have this policy, but ruled that the government could not provide financial support by granting tax-exempt status. At this time there is no clear public position concerning the acceptance of sexual orientation–based discrimination. Consequently, the Boy Scouts will probably retain its tax-exempt status. However, this will probably change in the future as lesbians, gay men, bisexuals, transgendered, and intersexed people gain greater social and legal acceptance.

References

Center for Lesbian and Gay Civil Rights. "Gay Group Demands City Withdrawal of Support for Boy Scouts." 2000. Press release, 28 June. Available at www.center4civilrights.org.

"Does Boy Scouts' Policy on Homosexuals Preclude Tax-Exempt Status?" 2000. *Tax Analysts' Tax Notes Today* (11 December 2000).

Greif, M. 1989. *The Gay Book of Days.* New York: Lyle Stuart.

Halsall, P. 1994. *Queers in History.* Available at www.dezines.com/rainbow/queers.htm.

C

Child Adoption and Foster Care

The adoption of children and the foster care for children by lesbians and gay men and same-sex couples are rapidly changing. A child may be adopted through a public agency or state-licensed private agency, or through private placement. All adoptions are approved through court action and the recommendations of an agency or social worker.

Children requiring temporary care until they are adopted or returned to their parents can be placed in foster homes. Foster parents are state licensed and are paid to take care of children. In either adoption or foster care, it is the child's welfare that courts supposedly use to guide their decisions.

Adoptions by Same-Sex Couples

Often referred to as "second-parent adoptions" or "coparent adoptions," these are a new development in the law. Here, one partner of a same-sex couple adopts the child of the other partner, who is the legal parent. Courts have had difficulty with these arrangements because the act of adopting a child has historically terminated the rights of the legal parent (Clark 1988). In these cases, the adoption adds a second parent to children of couples who are not married. Courts are now interpreting lesbian or gay second-parent adoptions in a manner similar to stepparent adoptions. Some states, for example Florida and Utah, still do not recognize these types of adoptions.

Second-parent adoptions also terminate the rights of other people who could legally be the child's parent. For example, if one woman in a lesbian couple has a child and the other woman adopts the child with the sperm donor's consent, the sperm donor would waive all legal rights toward the child. Similarly, if one of the men of a gay male couple is the legal parent of a child and the other man adopts the child with the consent of the biological mother, the biological mother or egg donor would lose her rights toward the child. Without a second-parent adoption, the biological mother or sperm donor may still be able to exert her or his parental rights.

Adoption rights are modeled after heterosexual unions of one father and one mother and typically do not recognize a third party. In a few cases a gay sperm donor has claimed visitation rights or the right to share custody of a child with two lesbian mothers. Courts and the lesbian and gay community have been split over the proper course of action in these cases, partially because it pits men against women and there is no accepted model for lesbian or gay families.

A few states allow joint adoptions. These are adoptions in which two people simultaneously adopt a child that is not legally related to either person. Courts have recognized that having two parents provides a protection for children that is absent when there is only one parent. However, there is still much controversy about allowing any child to be adopted into a lesbian or gay male **family**. For example, the Utah state legislature in March 2000 and the state of Mississippi in May 2000 both approved a ban on all adoptions by unmarried couples. This was the first time since 1988 that a state approved a bill to restrict the rights of lesbians and gay men to adopt or foster children (Freiberg 2000). In that same year, eight similar bans in other states were retracted because of the work of gay activists, and New Hampshire repealed its 1988 ban on gay adoptive and foster parents. This left only Florida and Arkansas, and now Utah and Mississippi, with legislation prohibiting adoptions and foster care by lesbians and gay men. Mississippi's ban went farther, not only banning same-sex couples from adopting, but refusing to recognize gay adoptions performed in other states. This legislation was modeled after the **Defense of Marriage Act (DOMA)** as a way of preempting gay adoptions from other states. The general trend is toward allowing lesbians and gay men to adopt, but it is a circuitous legal route. Lesbian and gay families are on the cutting edge of the law and reveal how traditional concepts of fatherhood or parenthood are no longer viable for large segments of our society.

FOSTER CARE BY SAME-SEX COUPLES

Courts have shown great hesitancy to allow same-sex couples to act as foster parents, often because it is believed that the child will be harmed by such placements. Some of the reasons given for denying same-sex couples the chance to be foster parents include the belief that: (1) the child's **sexual orientation** will be affected by the couple's sexual orientation; (2) the child will be sexually molested by the parents; (3) the child will be subjected to peer harassment or ostracism because of having lesbian or gay parents; (4) the child will not be able to "pass" as the natural child of the same-sex couple; and (5) by allowing such adoptions or foster care, it may seem that the state is condoning homosexuality. These arguments are also often used in cases of child adoption by same-sex couples.

Each of these concerns is easily addressed. First, there is no evidence that a child's sexual orientation is influenced by his or her parents' sexual orientation. Second, there is no evidence that homosexuals are more likely to molest children than are heterosexuals. Third, most children are unaware of their friends' home conditions. The likelihood of peer harassment is small. Even if the child's peers do find out that he or she has same-sex parents, the situation would be no different than if the children came from a religious minority home or a home with nonvisible minority status. Some children are subjected to considerable harassment, others are harassed a little, and others are not harassed at all. All parents need to teach children how to handle prejudice. Fourth, it is true that the child will not be able to "pass" as the natural offspring of a same-sex couple, but this is no different than children of one race placed with parents of a different race. Mixed-race adoptions and foster care are routinely approved. Courts have determined that congruency between the characteristics of parents and children is not absolutely required. Fifth, fear voiced by courts of appearing to encourage homosexuality by sanctioning adoptions or foster care by lesbian or gay male families is simply that: an irrational fear. This fear is interfering with the need of children for homes. "Whether or not the state is seen as encouraging homosexuality is irrelevant" (*Harvard Law Review* staff 1990, 135). (See also **Child Molestation Stereotype; Gay Fathers; Lesbian Mothers; Stereotypes**.)

Besides the sexual orientation of the prospective parents, courts consider other factors to determine the best interests of the child. The economic stability of the household, educational resources, and social and cultural outlets provided by the family are also taken into consideration. Judges often reason that children brought up in conventional families will make better citizens. Thus, adoptive or foster parents who conform to middle- to upper-class norms are the ones first considered acceptable. These same beliefs affect child custody disputes. (See also **Child Custody and Visitation Rights**.)

ADOPTION OR FOSTER CARE FOR CHILDREN WHO ARE HOMOSEXUAL

Although there have always been lesbian and gay male children who need adoption or foster care, courts have only recently recognized the special needs of these children. There has been a bias by courts that homosexuals, and particularly gay men, are child molesters. Although this stereotype is false, the combination of a homosexual parent and homosexual child forming a family has been explosive in the minds of the courts. Recently, courts in California and elsewhere have begun to acknowledge the special needs of lesbian and gay youth. They have encouraged same-sex couples to adopt or provide foster care for this class of stigmatized children. Many major cities now have group homes that are tailored for lesbian and gay adolescents.

References

Clark, H. 1988. *The Law of Domestic Relations in the United States.* 2d ed. St. Paul, MN: West Publishing Co.

Freiberg, P. 2000. "Utah Approves Gay Adoption Ban." *Washington Blade* 31(9): 12.

Harvard Law Review staff. 1990. *Sexual Orientation and the Law.* Cambridge, MA: Harvard University Press.

CHILD CUSTODY AND VISITATION RIGHTS

The issues of child custody and visitation come about when there are competing interests between adults in regard to their legal relationship to children. This area of law is quickly changing in recognition of the changes seen in **family** structures. Child custody and visitation rights become issues when there is a dispute between parents during a divorce, between a parent or parents and other relatives, between a parent and the state when there is evidence of neglect or abuse, between the parties responsible for the conception of a child, and between lesbian or gay male coparents who are ending their relationship.

The most common dispute regarding child custody comes about during divorce. All states use the "best interest of the child" as the rule guiding their decisions. However, such a rule is obviously vague and open to a wide range of interpretations. Courts have developed a list of factors to determine what is best for children, including the financial and psychological stability of the parents and the ability of parents to provide a supportive environment that meets the social, educational, and cultural needs of the child. Typically, courts have shown a bias toward keeping children in conventional, middle- or upper-class homes.

When one or both of the parents are lesbian, gay male, bisexual, transgendered, transsexual, or intersexed, the court considers this information. Historically, courts have taken a narrow view of sexual orientation and awarded custody to the heterosexual parent, sometimes denying the lesbian or gay male parent rights even to visit his or her child. As courts have taken a more moderate view, they have accepted placement of a child with his or her homosexual parent, but only if the parent was a "parent first," that is, the parent did not "flaunt" his or her homosexuality. Parents who were politically active in the gay community or had a live-in lover were often denied custody or visitation rights with their children. A third strategy is known as the "nexus" approach. Here courts try to determine if the sexual orientation of the parent actually harms the child, that is, is there a nexus between the parent's sexual orientation and the child's welfare. This incorrectly assumes that one sexual orientation is better than another, and in our heterosexist society, this presumes that heterosexuality is better than homosexuality. In practice, the nexus approach is indistinguishable from the narrow and moderate approach.

The harm the courts have ascribed to having a parent who is homosexual includes the beliefs that: (1) parents influence their children's sexual orientation and lesbian or gay parents make their children homosexual; (2) homosexual men, in particular, are child molesters and should not have custody or visitation rights in order to protect the child; (3) lesbian mothers or gay fathers cannot be good parents; and (4) the child will face peer harassment or be ostracized for having lesbian or gay male parents. None of these antigay **stereotypes** is true. Even for children who are lesbian, gay, bisexual, or transgendered, the courts often have believed that it is not in the best interest of the child to have lesbian, gay, bisexual, or transgendered parents. (See also **Child Molestation Stereotype**.)

DISPUTES BETWEEN PARENTS WHEN ONE IS GAY OR LESBIAN

In general, the law favors awarding custody and visitation rights to natural parents. In cases between parents, the sexual orientation of the parent becomes an issue if one or both are not heterosexual (Sheppared 1985). The courts have historically denied lesbian or gay parents the same custody or visitation rights given heterosexual parents ("Custody Denials to Parents in Same-sex Relationships" 1989; Harris 1989). In some states, courts have made the assumption that **lesbian mothers** and **gay fathers** will be harmful to the child and these assumptions cannot be challenged (*G.A. v. D.A.; N.K.M. v. L.E.M; Roe v. Roe*). Other states require lesbian mothers and gay fathers to prove that their sexual orientation will not harm the child. In contrast, still other states, such as New Jersey, have explicitly rejected the belief that sexual orientation should be a factor in child custody and visitation rights.

No court has ever denied a noncustodial parent the right to visit his or her child solely because the parent is homosexual. However, courts have sometimes prohibited children from staying overnight with a lesbian mother or gay father (*J.L.P.[H] v. D.J.P.*) or from allowing children to visit their parent's home if there is a live-in same-sex companion (*Dailey v. Dailey*). Because of these restrictions, lesbian mothers and gay fathers who do not live near their children are, in practical terms, denied access to their children. In these cases, because the child may not stay overnight in the homosexual parent's home, other arrangements may need to be made that would entail expenses that the homosexual parent cannot afford. Also, extended stays such as for the summer or school year become impossible.

Some courts have placed restrictions on these children: they may not be taken to functions within the gay community (*In re J.S. & C.; J.L.P.*

[H.] v. D.J.P.), may not be in the presence of their homosexual parent's same-sex companion (*Irish v. Irish*), and may not be in the presence of other "known homosexuals" (*In re Jane B.*) or even around members of their parent's sex (*Roberts v. Roberts* [1985]). However, other courts have refused to restrict overnight visitations solely due to the sexual orientation of the parents (*In re Marriage of Birdsall; In re J.S. & C.; Marriage of Cabalquinto*).

Custody and visitation orders, once issued, are difficult to change or amend. Courts require a "material" change in the parties' circumstances before reviewing such requests. Part of the reason for this approach is to reduce the potential for continued disruption of the child's routine through challenges to custody arrangements. In general, if the nonheterosexual orientation of a parent becomes known to the court after orders are issued, the court considers this a material change and the case can be reviewed upon the request of one or both of the parents (*In re Jane B.*).

DISPUTES BETWEEN PARENTS AND NONPARENTS

Persons who are not the parent of a child sometimes sue for custody or visitation rights. Usually, these cases involve grandparents or other relatives. Instead of using the "best interest" rule, the courts require these third parties to show that there are overwhelming circumstances that warrant denying or terminating the custody or visitation rights of a parent. One such notable case was the 1993 custody battle between Sharon Bottoms and her mother (*Bottoms v. Bottoms*). Sharon's mother sought custody of Sharon's two-year-old son, Tyler, by arguing that Bottoms's lesbian relationship made her an unfit mother. Also, Virginia's sodomy law criminalized Bottoms's sexual life. Thus, the grandmother argued that Tyler would be living with a criminal if he stayed with his mother. Bottoms argued that she was a fit mother and did not want Tyler visiting the grandmother's home because the man who sexually abused Bottoms while she was growing up also inhabited it. The trial judge agreed with the grandmother and Tyler was removed from Sharon Bottoms. This case caused tremendous outrage in the lesbian and gay community. Later, the Virginia appellate court reversed the lower court and gave custody of Tyler to the mother. The court said that Bottoms's sexual orientation as a lesbian did not make her unfit to have custody of her child. (See also **Criminal Law; Sodomy**.)

Unlike *Bottoms*, however, many cases are not resolved in favor of the lesbian mother or gay father. In general, if the homosexual parents are poor or nonconforming, they often lose custody of their children. For example, in *In re Breisch*, the state of Pennsylvania took custody of a preschool boy who had a speech impediment. The mother had a masculine appearance and wore men's clothing. She lived with another woman at the time of the hearing who also had two children living with them. The mother took notes at meetings with the social workers and refused, as a condition of custody, not to live with her lover. Her actions were construed by the courts to be "uncooperative." The state took custody of her child. When the mother appealed, the court decided that restricting her from living with her lover was not an act of discrimination and interference with her lesbian relationship, but rather an attempt to establish order in the child's life and to bring the mother and son closer.

DISPUTES WHEN BOTH PARENTS ARE LESBIAN OR GAY

Sometimes both parents of a child are homosexual. The reported rise in lesbian couples having children, the so-called lesbian baby boom, has given rise to custody disputes when the couples decide to separate. Courts usually decide that the woman who carried the child is the legal parent and has full custody rights. Unless the other woman adopted the child, she has no rights toward the child. The well-known case of *Alison D. v. Virginia M.* illustrates the problem. The nonbiological mother, Alison D., sued to have visitation rights with the child carried by her lover, Virginia M. Although she was not the legal parent and had not adopted the child, she argued that she was a de facto parent. The courts said that she may, in fact, be a de facto parent, but such a category had no legal claim, including visitation rights, to the child. Alison lost her right to visit the child.

The Rhode Island Supreme Court reached the opposite conclusion in a case between Maureen Rubano and Concetta DiCenzo. The two women had lived together for three years when they decided to raise a child together. DiCenzo became pregnant by an anonymous sperm donor and bore a son in 1992. The birth certificate listed the last name of the child as Rubano-DiCenzo. Although coparent adoptions are legal in Massachusetts, Rubano did not go to the effort to legally adopt the child. Four years later their relationship deteriorated and they separated. DiCenzo and the child moved to Rhode Island. At first the former couple arranged for visitations, but the schedule collapsed due to DiCenzo's resistance. Rubano filed an action in family court in Rhode Island seeking to establish her as a "de facto" parent. The court accepted her claim and granted her visitation rights. Soon DiCenzo again blocked Rubano's visits. Rubano went back to court. DiCenzo argued that the family court lacked jurisdiction over the dispute. The court agreed with Rubano; DiCenzo appealed. The Rhode Island Supreme Court decided on September 25, 2000 that the family court had jurisdiction to deal with a claim for child visitation by a lesbian coparent, thus recognizing the right of "de facto" coparents in same-sex relationships.

References

"Custody Denials to Parents in Same-Sex Relationships: An Equal Protection Analysis." 1989. *Harvard Law Review* 102(3): 617.

Harris, D. R. 1989. "Non-Nuclear Proliferation." *Utne Reader* 32 (March–April): 22–23.

Sheppared, A. 1985. "Lesbian Mothers II: Long Night's Journey into Day." *Women's Rights Law Reporter* 8(4): 219–246.

CHILD MOLESTATION STEREOTYPE One of the major stereotypes used to denigrate lesbians and gay men is that homosexuals molest children. This is not true. Studies have concluded that "gay men are no more likely than heterosexual men to molest children" (Newton 1978).

A number of difficulties exist with regard to any research into child molestation. One problem is population sampling. All studies have relied upon convicted child molesters. Thus, we do not have any profile of child molesters who were not caught, and those who are caught may not be descriptive of all child molesters.

Second is the problem of definition. When adult males molest a male child it is termed "homosexual molestation." This implies that the perpetrator is gay or has a homosexual orientation. This is not accurate. Researchers quickly discovered that many child molesters never develop the capacity for mature sexual relationships with other adults, whether with men or women. Instead, they become "fixated" on children. For those who develop adult sexual interests, they are said to have "regressed." "Thus, regressed molesters can be adult homosexuals, heterosexuals, or bisexuals. But it is meaningless to speak of fixated molesters in these terms—they are attracted to children, not to men or women" (Herek 1991).

In their sample of 175 adult males who were convicted of sexual assault against a child, researchers found that none of the men had an exclusively or primarily homosexual adult sexual orientation (Groth and Birnbaum 1978). Similarly, in response to the state of Colorado's attempt to deny rights to homosexuals, researchers reviewed the charts of all sexually abused children seen in one year in a Colorado children's hospital. The study revealed that only 3.1 percent, at most, of the sexually abused children were abused by homosexuals—a rate significantly lower than expected (Jenny, Roesler, and Poyer 1994). From these studies, it must be concluded that children are unlikely to be molested by homosexuals. In contrast, children are primarily (82 percent) molested by the heterosexual partners of a close relative of the child (Groth and Birnbaum 1978). Child molesters are attracted to children and sexual orientation is not a significant factor.

Most "scientific" claims that homosexuals are the primary perpetrators of child molestation can be traced to one individual. Beginning in 1985, psychologist Paul Cameron has self-published a number of pamphlets alleging that most serial killers, child molesters, and others who commit heinous crimes are homosexual. His publications misrepresented the findings of Groth and Birnbaum and contained his own research. Cameron came under investigation by the American Psychological Association for breach of ethics and poor research methodology. His membership was terminated. Still, he continues to be a one-man propaganda machine that the religious right has appropriated for their own antigay agenda. (See also **Religious Right Agenda**.) What is surprising is that the child molestation stereotype used to stigmatize gay men has been known to be false for more than twenty years, yet the myth persists and has impacted our legal system.

References

Groth, A. N., and H. J. Birnbaum. 1978. "Adult Sexual Orientation and Attraction to Underage Persons." *Archives of Sexual Behavior* 7(3): 175–181.

Herek, G. M. 1991. "Myths about Sexual Orientation: A Lawyers' Guide to Social Science Research." *Law and Sexuality* 1: 133–172.

Jenny, C., T. Roesler, and K. Poyer. 1994. "Are Children at Risk for Sexual Abuse by Homosexuals?" *Pediatrics* 94(1): 41–44.

Newton, D. E. 1978. "Homosexual Behavior and Child Molestation: A Review of the Evidence." *Adolescence* 13:29–43.

CHILDREN OF HOMOSEXUAL PARENTS Often the courts have relied on antigay stereotypes to deny custody of children to homosexual parents. The primary concerns expressed by courts about allowing children to live with homosexual parents include the beliefs that: (1) the child may be molested or harmed by the homosexual parent; (2) homosexuals cannot be good parents; (3) the child's sexual orientation may be influenced toward homosexuality; or (4) the child will experience peer harassment or ostracism. None of these is valid. (See also **Adolescence; Child Adoption and Foster Care; Child Custody and Visitation Rights**.)

The research on children raised by **lesbian mothers** or **gay fathers** reveals that there are no significant differences between these children and children raised in heterosexual households. Intellectual development (Flaks et al. 1995; Green et al. 1986; Kirkpatrick, Smith, and Roy 1981); gender identity (Golombok, Spence, and Rutter 1983); sexual orientation (Bailey et al. 1995; Golombok, Spence, and Rutter 1983; Miller 1979); peer group relations (Green et al. 1986); and self-esteem (Huggins 1989) are the same regardless of whether the child is raised in a homosexual or heterosexual family. The sexual orientation of the parent has no influence on the gender identity of the child (Green 1978) or on his or her independence

(Steckel 1987). The children studied preferred sex-typed toys consistent with their biological gender regardless of their parent's sexual orientation (Hoeffer 1981). Children of homosexual parents do not suffer disproportionate turmoil (Flaks et al. 1995; Weeks, Derdeyn, and Langman 1975) or depression (Pennington 1987; Tasker and Golombok 1995). In addition, there is ample evidence that the sexual orientation of the parent has no influence on the sexual orientation of the child (Bailey et al. 1995; Flaks et al. 1995; Miller 1979; Tasker and Golombok 1995).

Understanding that there are no negative impacts for children raised in homosexual households is important for many legal considerations—including lesbian and gay families, custody, child adoption, and child foster care. Courts should no longer treat homosexual parents or lesbian or gay families differently than heterosexual parents and families.

References

Bailey, J. M., D. Bobrow, M. Wolfe, and S. Mikach. 1995. "Sexual Orientation of Adult Sons of Gay Fathers." *Developmental Psychology* 31: 124–129.

Flaks, D. K., I. Ficher, F. Masterpasqua, and G. Joseph. 1995. "Lesbians Choosing Motherhood: A Comparative Study of Lesbian and Heterosexual Parents and Their Children." *Developmental Psychology* 31: 105–114.

Golombok, S., A. Spence, and M. Rutter. 1983. "Children in Lesbian and Single-Parent Households: Psychosexual and Psychiatric Appraisal." *Journal of Child Psychology and Psychiatry* 24: 551–572.

Green, R. 1978. "Sexual Identity of 37 Children Raised by Homosexual or Transsexual Parents." *American Journal of Psychiatry* 135(6): 692–697.

Green, R., J. B. Mandel, M. E. Hotvedt, J. Gray, and L. Smith. 1986. "Lesbian Mothers and Their Children: A Comparison with Solo Parent Heterosexual Mothers and Their Children." *Archives of Sexual Behavior* 15(2): 167–184.

Hoeffer, B. 1981. "Children's Acquisition of Sex-Role Behavior in Lesbian-Mother Families." *American Journal of Orthopsychiatry* 51: 536–544.

Huggins, S. L. 1989. "A Comparative Study of Self-Esteem of Adolescent Children of Divorced Mothers and Divorced Heterosexual Mothers." In *Homosexuality and the Family,* edited by F. W. Bozett. New York: Hawthorn.

Kirkpatrick, M., A. Smith, and R. Roy. 1981. "Lesbian Mothers and Their Children: A Comparative Study." *American Journal of Orthopsychiatry* 51: 545–551.

Miller, B. 1979. "Gay Fathers and Their Children." *The Family Coordinator* (October): 545–552.

Pennington, S. B. 1987. "Children of Lesbian Mothers." In *Gay and Lesbian Parents,* edited by F. W. Bozett. New York: Praeger.

Steckel, A. 1987. "Psychosocial Development of Children of Lesbian Mothers." In *Gay and Lesbian Parents,* edited by F. W. Bozett. New York: Praeger.

Tasker, F., and S. Golombok. 1995. "Adults Raised as Children in Lesbian Families." *American Journal of Orthopsychiatry* 65: 203–215.

Weeks, R. B., A. P. Derdeyn, and M. Langman. 1975. "Two Cases of Children of Homosexuals." *Child Psychiatry and Human Development* 6: 26–32.

CIVIL UNION Civil union is the legal recognition of same-sex couples in marriage-like relationships. In April 2000 Vermont became the first state to give full legal rights to same-sex couples. The civil union status confers upon same-sex couples the identical state law protections and responsibilities that are available to heterosexual spouses in a **marriage**. This includes preferences for guardianship of, and medical decisionmaking for, an incapacitated partner; automatic inheritance rights; the right to leave work to care for an ill spouse; hospital visitation rights; control of a partner's body upon death; the right to be treated as an economic unit for tax purposes under state law, including the ability to transfer property to each other during life without tax consequences; greater access to family health insurance policies; the ability to obtain joint policies of insurance and joint credit; parentage rights; and the right to divorce (called a "dissolution") with an ordered method for ascertaining property division as well as child custody and support. Because civil unions are not marriage, the 1,049 protections afforded married couples under federal law are not in effect.

Civil union legislation is the outcome of the decision by the Vermont Supreme Court in ***Baker v. Vermont*** that same-sex couples in Vermont are entitled to the same protections and benefits provided by law for opposite-sex married couples. The Vermont constitution contains an "equal protection" clause that guarantees all citizens the same treatment under the law. These clauses are similar to the equal protection provision of the U.S. Constitution's Fourteenth Amendment, which was used to secure civil rights for racial minorities, women, and other groups.

The court did not specify how this was to be done, rather leaving it to the Vermont legislature to devise a method to achieve this end. Marriage was considered, but ultimately the Vermont legislature created the civil union program. Immediately, the religious right and conservative representatives called for the impeachment of the judges making this decision and a reversal of the decision. However, many powerful Vermont politicians took great pride in the fact that Vermont was the first state to outlaw slavery in 1777 and believed that lesbians and gay men deserved to be treated fairly and equitably. Governor Howard Dean stated, "we will remain in the forefront of the struggle for equal justice under law" (Dean 2000).

By constructing a parallel institution to marriage for lesbians and gay men, Vermont created a super **domestic partnership** that is legally identical to marriage without invoking the "m" word. A term that comes from the civil rights movement describes this arrangement as "separate but equal." The U.S. Supreme Court found in *Brown v. Board of Education* (1954) that separate is inherently unequal. Some gay activists predict that courts will eventually require full legal marriage rights to be granted to same-sex couples.

It is not known what legal status same-sex couples will retain who go to Vermont for a civil union and then return to their own states. Because a Vermont civil union is not marriage, the defense of marriage acts many states have legislated do not apply. Civil unions may be viewed as contracts enforceable under tort and contract law. Vermont citizens who enter a civil union have concerns that when they travel out of the state, their legal relationships may not be recognized. For example, if one member of a same-sex couple is killed while traveling out of state, will the other partner have the right to obtain the body? This scenario does not involve any "government benefits" and is a real concern for same-sex couples. It is possible the Doctrine of Conflicts (the rules used by courts to determine which law applies to the case) may be used to resolve these issues. According to the doctrine, when the parties or the subject of a lawsuit come from or arise in a state other than the state where the court is located, the court must decide which state's law to apply. Some states apply the law of the state where the parties live, some the law of the state where the agreement or contract was formed, some the law of the state where the "res" or physical object under dispute is located, and some the law of the state with the most "significant" contacts to the case. Regardless, this is an important first step toward full recognition of same-sex couples. "By changing the focus away from the word 'marriage' and looking instead to the legal protections and responsibilities provided to married families, people in other states should be able to forge a fair common ground with lawmakers who seek to support all families," said Mary Bonauto, counsel for the Gay and Lesbian Advocates and Defenders in Boston (Bonauto 2000).

References

Bonauto, M. 2000. "Vermont House Gives Final Approval to Civil Union Bill." Gay and Lesbian Advocates and Defenders (GLAD) website: www.glad.org. Accessed 25 April 2000.

Dean, H. 2000. State of the State Address. 5 January, at Montpelier, Vermont. Vermont governor's website: www.state.vt.us/governor/0002.htm.

COMING OUT Coming out is the process of coming to realize and accept one's desires to seek affection and sex from persons of the same sex in ways not sanctioned by the heterosexual norm.

THE CHOICES FOR LESBIANS AND GAYS

Heterosexuality is enforced by most Western societies. Sexual orientation is thought to form by age three (Money and Ehrhardt 1972) and becomes an integral part of a person's gender identity. Those people who do not conform to the cultural norm often feel alienated and isolated.

Families rarely support these individuals and their negative feelings are exacerbated.

A number of options are open to gay males, lesbians, and bisexuals who realize that they have a gender identity different from cultural expectations. They can: (1) attempt to deceive themselves and others, which leads to devastating emotional consequences; (2) lead a double life by having same-sex relations in secret while living a heterosexual public life (maintaining such a front requires significant emotional effort to keep a constant vigil); (3) attempt to change their affectionate desires and sexual fantasies through therapeutic techniques (researchers have found that this is unattainable); or (4) live an honest and open lesbian, gay, or bisexual lifestyle by "coming out" of the closet.

"COMING OUT" MODELS

A number of coming out models have been proposed. Vivienne Cass (1979) proposed a six-stage "coming out" model:

1. Identity Confusion—general feelings of being different.
2. Identity Comparison—awareness of homosexual feelings, yet thinking that this may just be a phase or that the feelings are toward only one specific person.
3. Identity Tolerance—stronger identity of being homosexual and starting to reach out to contact other homosexuals.
4. Identity Acceptance—increased contact and affiliation with other homosexuals.
5. Identity Pride—the "These are my people" stage in which the homosexual individual comes out to more and more people and often starts to feel anger toward heterosexuals and devalues many of their institutions.
6. Identity Synthesis—the intense anger of Stage 5 diminishes and the individual comes to perceive "less of a dichotomy between the heterosexual and homosexual worlds" (Blumenfeld and Raymond 1993, 89), yet retains pride for gays and lesbians.

Eli Coleman (1981–1982) proposed a five-stage "coming out" model that focuses on romantic attachments:

1. Pre–Coming Out—general feelings of being different.
2. Coming Out—becoming aware of homosexual thoughts or fantasies, beginning to make contact with other homosexuals, but keeping one's sexual identity from friends.
3. Exploration—experimenting with new social interactions with an improvement of self-image.

4. First Relationship—after a period of sexual experimentation, the homosexual person desires a more stable and committed relationship.
5. Integration—the "public and private identities merge into one unified and integrated self-image. . . . Relationships are often characterized by less possessiveness and more honesty and mutual trust and can be more successful than first relationships" (Blumenfeld and Raymond 1993, 90).

The "coming out" process is estimated to take between ten and fourteen years (Kooden et al. 1979). The processes described in the two models are not followed by everyone. Some people either get stuck at some particular stage or even regress due to bad experiences. Gender influences the coming out process, with females and males having somewhat different experiences. On the average, males seem to become aware of same-sex attractions at about age thirteen or fourteen, whereas females become aware later—around age eighteen. Also, more lesbians have experienced heterosexual sex (79 percent) than have gay males (52 percent) (Saghir and Robins 1980).

RESPONSES TO HOMOPHOBIA

How a person responds to stigmatization depends on many factors. Gordon Allport's (1954) theory of victimization looks at how societies teach stigmatized groups about their social status. Lesbians, gays, and bisexuals grow up in a world that teaches them that they are morally repulsive and sick. These negative attitudes become internalized and manifest themselves in a number of ways. First, these individuals may deny their sexual orientation. Second, they may feel contempt for members of the community who are more open and "obvious." Third, they may learn to distrust other minority groups. Fourth, they may attempt to "pass" as straight, sometimes going as far as marrying someone of the opposite sex. And, fifth, lesbians and gays may withdraw emotionally and consider suicide.

However, many gays and lesbians convert the negative stigma into something positive. They may strengthen ties with members of their own group and other minorities. They may also appropriate the terms *gay, lesbian,* or *bisexual,* which were once used as epithets against them, thereby eroding the power society exerted over them. (See also **Employment**.)

OUTING

Sometimes people who are "closeted" (not open about their sexuality) are found to be lesbian or gay and revealed to others. This is called outing and has severe consequences. For example, Marcus Wayman, then eighteen years old, and a seventeen-year-old friend were parked in a lot adjacent to a beer distributor on the night of April 17, 1997. Police Officer F. Scott Wilinsky, suspicious of the car with its lights off, called for backup and then approached the two young men. The officer searched the car and found condoms, and the two men admitted they were gay and had parked with the intention to engage in sex. The men were arrested for underage drinking and taken to the Minersville police station. There, the two men were lectured by the police about the Bible's condemnation of homosexuality. Wilinsky threatened to tell Wayman's grandfather that Wayman was gay if he did not tell his family himself. After the threat, Wayman told his friend that he was going to kill himself.

When Wayman's mother came to the jail, the police forced Wayman to tell his mother that he was gay. Later, Wayman was released from custody and, that night, committed suicide at home. The mother, Madonna Sterling, sued the police for violation of privacy (*Sterling v. Borough of Minersville*). A divided Third U.S. Circuit Court of Appeals ruled against the police, stating that the law clearly protected a person's sexual orientation from forced disclosure. Judge Carol Los Mansmann took a broad view of the protections afforded by the constitutional right of privacy and said, "it is difficult to imagine a more private matter than one's sexuality and a less likely probability that the government would have a legitimate interest in disclosure of sexual identity." (Duffy 2000). However, Senior Judge Walter K. Stapleton, dissenting, believed the case should have been dismissed because the right to privacy was not clearly established.

References

Allport, G. 1954. *The Nature of Prejudice.* Reading, MA: Addison-Wesley.

Blumenfeld, W. J., and D. Raymond, eds. 1993. *Looking at Gay and Lesbian Life.* Rev. ed. Boston: Beacon Press.

Cass, V. 1979. "Homosexual Identity Formation: A Theoretical Model." *Journal of Homosexuality* 4(3): 219–235.

Coleman, E. 1981–1982. "Developmental Stages of the Coming Out Process." *Journal of Homosexuality* 7(2/3): 31–44.

Duffy, S. P. 2000. "Outing Gay Man." *The Legal Intelligencer.* Available at www.law.com. Accessed 7 November 2000.

Kooden, J. D., S. F. Morin, D. F. Riddle, M. Rogers, B. E. Sang, and F. Strassburger. 1979. *Removing the Stigma: Final Report, Task Force on the Status of Lesbian and Gay Male Psychologists.* Washington, DC: The American Psychological Association.

Money, J., and A. A. Ehrhardt. 1972. *Man and Woman, Boy and Girl: Differentiation and Dimorphism of Gender Identity from Conception to Maturity.* Baltimore, MD: Johns Hopkins Press.

Saghir, M., and E. Robins. 1980. "Clinical Aspects of Female Homosexuality." In *Homosexual Behavior,* edited by J. Marmor. New York: Basic Books.

COMMONWEALTH V. WASSON

In *Commonwealth v. Wasson* the Kentucky Supreme Court in 1992 ruled Kentucky's sex statutes unconstitutional under the state's constitution. This was an important ruling after the United States Supreme Court decision in ***Bowers v. Hardwick*** on the issue of adult consensual **sodomy**. The Kentucky sex statutes criminalized sexual behaviors using the natural, anatomically specific, and gender-specific strategies. (See also **Criminal Law**.)

Jeffrey Wasson engaged in conversation with a man for twenty to twenty-five minutes, during which he invited the other man to "come home" with him. The other man prodded Wasson to provide details about the sexual acts in which they would engage. What Wasson described violated Kentucky's sex statutes. Unknown to Wasson, the other man was an undercover police officer who was wired for sound and taped the conversation. At the end of the conversation, the police officer arrested Wasson for "soliciting" to engage in unlawful sexual behavior.

Wasson moved to the have the charges dropped against him on the grounds that the sex statutes violated the state constitution. The trial judge, appellate court, and finally the supreme court of Kentucky all agreed with Wasson, stating that "the guarantees of individual liberty provided in our 1891 Kentucky Constitution offer greater protection of the right of privacy than provided by the Federal Constitution" (Robson 1997, 30).

Reference

Robson, R. 1997. *Gay Men, Lesbians, and the Law.* New York: Chelsea House Publishers.

CRIMINAL LAW

The set of statutes, laws, and regulations used to stigmatize homosexual sexual practices, although commonly referred to as sodomy laws, is better termed "sex statutes" and reflects current changes in the thinking of the courts and legislatures. Sex statutes are used to criminalize sexual practices between consenting adults, whether they are heterosexual, homosexual, or bisexual.

The sex statutes have been the cornerstones of legal homosexual oppression. Although homosexuality is not illegal per se, by making homosexual sexual practices illegal, the sex statutes have been used to further stigmatize homosexuals. The sex statutes, although rarely enforced, have wider legal implications. For example, courts have used the existence of sex statutes to support the idea that homosexuality involves deviant behavior and thereby to deny discrimination claims brought by lesbians and gay men. Similarly, courts often cite sex statutes as the justification to deny lesbians and gay men the right to their children during custody cases. Thus, by making homosexual sexual practices illegal, the sex statutes are instrumental in restricting and denying equal rights for homosexuals.

Historically, sex statutes have been used to punish homosexuals most harshly. At one time, homosexuals charged with sodomy were put to death in America's thirteen colonies. Eventually, the sentences were reduced and Illinois led the way in 1961 with the abolition of its sodomy laws. At the beginning of the second millennium, approximately one-third of the states still have sex statutes that criminalize homosexual sexual practices. Punishment ranges from a simple misdemeanor and fine to a felony conviction and the possibility of life imprisonment. (See also **Sodomy** for greater historical details.)

SEX STATUTE STRATEGY

In general, three distinct strategies have been used to criminalize homosexual practices. The *natural* strategy used terms such as "crimes against nature" (Idaho), "unnatural copulation" (Louisiana), the "abominable and detestable" (Michigan, Mississippi, Oklahoma), or similar wording in early laws prohibiting sexual expression. For example, Florida's statute criminalizes "unnatural and lascivious" conduct, whereas the United States Code of Military Justice uses the terms "unnatural carnal copulation."

As would be expected, the vagueness of these terms has yielded a wide range of court interpretations. Courts taking a "narrow" view have limited their interpretation to criminalize oral or anal sex, or both, between men. Some states, when it has come to their attention that certain lesbian sexual practices were "regrettably" not criminalized, hastened to legislate prohibitions against these practices as part of their sex statutes. In general, state legislators have taken action to criminalize additional sexual practices when the courts have returned a narrow interpretation that included few specific sexual acts.

Courts taking a "broad" view of the sex statutes have usually included all nonprocreative sexual acts. These have been applied toward both homosexual and heterosexual encounters. As such, anal sex, fellatio, mutual masturbation, and cunnilingus have been routinely criminalized.

With such a range of responses by state courts, constitutional concerns have been raised. The due process clauses of the United States Constitution require laws to be understandable by the average person of ordinary intelligence. If a law does not meet this condition, it can be overturned or repealed. The natural strategy has been declared unconstitutional in some states due to its vague and confusing language, whereas other states have held the natural strategy to be constitutional. Because of the independence of individual state court systems, the judgments by one state court do not affect the judgments of another. However, if the United States Supreme Court were to rule that sex statutes based on natural strategy are unconstitutional, then all such state statutes would be voided. But this has not happened. In *Rose v. Locke,* the U.S. Supreme Court in 1975 upheld as constitutional a Tennessee "crime against nature" statute. The Court found the phrase "crime against nature" to be no more vague than many other terms used to describe common crimes.

If a state court declares its sex statutes unconstitutional because of vague language, the state legislature can either allow the statutes to fade away, or it can attempt to draft new legislation to continue regulating adult consensual sexual activity. If they opt for the latter course of action, lawmakers frequently employ a second approach—the *anatomically specific strategy*—in creating sex statutes.

The anatomically specific strategy uses concise language describing specific body parts during sexual acts as part of the sex statutes. These statutes specifically name the applicable genital organs of one person and states how they are used by the mouth or anus of another. For example, Arkansas's sex statute (1981) stated, "A person commits sodomy if the anus, mouth, or vagina of a person or animal is penetrated by the penis of a person or animal of the same sex." (See **Appendix A: State and Local Laws**.) This Arkansas statute is also representative of additional language used to limit the application of the strategy only to homosexual acts and to stereotype homosexual sex by linking it with bestiality. However, elsewhere the anatomically specific strategy has been used to criminalize both homosexual and heterosexual sexual encounters.

Some states have used the anatomically specific strategy to prohibit all sex outside of marriage (Alabama, Kansas, and Utah). Other states have used the strategy to prohibit specific sexual acts for all people. Some states have limited the prohibitions to homosexual acts only. The courts have usually excluded touching, stroking, or the use of anything other than a sex organ in their definition of prohibited activities. Similarly, touching or stroking of the genitals by the hands, kissing, petting, and mutual masturbation have generally not been criminalized by the courts. Also, one court has suggested that contact between clothing and flesh does not meet the requirements of sex statutes; only direct flesh-on-flesh contact is considered.

A third strategy used exclusively against homosexuals is the addition of *gender specificity.* Laws such as the Arkansas sex statute described above limit sodomy to persons of the same sex, and indirectly dismisses lesbian sexual practices. Montana is another example of a state that criminalizes "sexual contact or sexual intercourse between two persons of the same sex." Missouri is direct in targeting homosexual sexual acts by limiting sex statutes to "sexual misconduct between same sex." (See **Appendix A: State and Local Laws**.)

Sex statutes are rarely enforced. Because both persons engaging in the sexual acts can be convicted of the crime, they are considered accomplices and courts rarely convict based upon the testimony of an accomplice. Instead, there needs to be corroborating evidence, such as an eyewitness account or physical evidence. In ***Bowers v. Hardwick*** a police officer entered the residence of Michael Hardwick to arrest him for another matter and observed Hardwick engaging in sex with another man. This established the corroborating evidence needed to convict Hardwick of violating Georgia's sex statute.

Few lesbians and gays have fought against the sex statutes. When someone is arrested for violating sex statutes, they often plead guilty to quickly extinguish the potential for undue public exposure. Sometimes the charges of sex statute violations are raised in conjunction with other crimes such as rape and battery. Defendants facing multiple charges are not ideal candidates to challenge sex statutes directly. Finally, lesbian and gay activists who have wanted to challenge the statutes have been precluded from doing so because of the procedural requirement of *standing*. Standing is the requirement that the person challenging the law must have a significant stake in its outcome. This usually means that only the person charged with violating the law has the right to challenge the law. Thus, lesbian and gay legal scholars have had to wait for the appropriate cases to come about before they could argue their position before the courts.

Two cases have helped define the constitutionality of sex statutes. In the 1986 U.S. Supreme Court case *Bowers v. Hardwick,* the Court refused to strike down a Georgia law criminalizing adult consensual sodomy. In a five-to-four vote, the majority opinion stated that there was no constitutional right to engage in homosexual sodomy. However, one of the majority justices, Lewis Powell, conceded after his retirement that he "had made a mistake" (Marcus 1990) and should have voted to strike down Georgia's sodomy law. Nevertheless, that Court decision allowed states to continue enforcing sex statutes.

After *Hardwick,* the supreme court of Kentucky in ***Commonwealth v. Wasson*** (1992) found its state's sex statutes to be unconstitutional. The court decided that the constitution of Kentucky provided greater protection for the rights of privacy than that afforded by the federal Constitution. Interestingly, the Kentucky Supreme Court repudiated many of the arguments used to substantiate the U.S. Supreme Court's *Bowers v. Hardwick* decision.

Of those states that still have sex statutes, many are considering eliminating these laws or are in litigation that may lead to them being declared unconstitutional. When the last of the sex statutes are eliminated, lesbians and gay men will begin to achieve equality with heterosexuals. Even with the elimination of sex statutes, other statutes relating to **lewd conduct, solicitation and loitering**, vagrancy, indecent exposure, or disorderly conduct will need to be reviewed for bias against homosexual contact. (For a complete listing of the sex statutes and court challenges, see also **Sodomy**.)

Lesbians and Gay Men as Victims of the Criminal Justice System

Lesbians, gay men, and bisexuals, and transgendered, transsexual, and intersexed people are often the victims of crime, the perpetrators of crimes, or both in the case of domestic violence. The biases and prejudices society has toward those who do not conform to its sexual norms often influence the enforcement of laws and the outcome of court decisions. The sex statutes have played a significant role in legalizing these differences.

Bias Crimes

Violence against nonheterosexuals or those perceived to be lesbian or gay steadily increased in the United States during the 1990s. Otherwise known as **hate crimes** or gay bashings, these acts of violence have been linked to other forms of bias based upon race, nationality, ethnicity, gender, and other characteristics. It is believed that gay bashings are significantly underreported because of: (1) the hesitancy of victims to be identified as gay (particularly if the victim is heterosexual but is mistaken as gay); (2) the belief by victims that the police will harass them during the investigation or that the police and courts will not take the report seriously; (3) the fact that bashings often take place near bars and victims may be under the influence of alcohol; or (4) the belief by victims who have accepted society's moral condemnation of their homosexuality (known as internalized homophobia) that they deserve to be bashed.

The 1990 Hate Crime Statistics Act passed by Congress included sexual orientation in addition to race, religion, and ethnicity as targeted categories (interestingly, manifestations of hate against women were decidedly excluded). The purpose of the act was systematically to collect data on hate crimes throughout the United States. The inclusion of sexual orientation came about through intense lobbying by lesbian and gay activists amid much controversy in Congress. Additional language was added to the act by conservative politicians to reinforce commitment to the family and to ensure that the act was not an attempt to promote homosexuality. The act specifically stated that "[n]othing in this section creates a right to bring an action, including an action based on discrimination due to sexual orientation" (Robson 1997, 86). It is ironic that this statement was inserted, because it implicitly approves discrimination based on sexual orientation.

The act made local police more aware of bias-based crimes. Many states passed statutes of their own criminalizing hate crimes, but few included sexual orientation as a protected class. Because of the inconsistencies among local, state, and federal reporting agencies, the nonprofit organization New York City Gay and Lesbian Anti-Violence Project took it upon itself to compile the most comprehensive data on national hate crimes and to make yearly reports.

Some municipalities and colleges have made attempts to regulate confrontational actions against lesbians and gay men that are not violent in nature. These regulations attempt to criminalize speech that intimidates or harasses. Hate speech, for example calling someone a "faggot" or "dyke," attempts to intimidate the victim. However, regulating speech is problematic due to First Amendment protections. The government has an interest in preventing hate and violence, yet has the duty to protect freedom of speech. Often, when **hate speech** regulations are challenged in court, they have been determined to be unconstitutional.

Criminal Defense

Historically, courts have allowed perpetrators of antigay violence to claim that they acted as they did in response to fear toward homosexuals. Sometimes known as the **homosexual panic defense**, this strategy involves claims that a heterosexual defendant panicked when the victim came onto him or her, or that he or she witnessed homosexual behavior that the heterosexual defendant found offensive. The homosexual panic defense has depended on the courts interpreting the act of violence against the homosexual (or perceived homosexual) victim as the result of a mental defect or diminished capacity on the part of the perpetrator. Recently, most courts have refused to consider the validity of this defense strategy (*Commonwealth v. Carr*).

The sexual orientation of homosexual victims and defendants sometimes becomes known in court. Too often, this prejudices the decision of the court in the direction of either leniency toward perpetrators of antigay violence or increased sentences for criminals who are homosexual. For example, a nineteen-year-old Ohio lesbian was kidnapped by her father and three other men in an attempt to "deprogram" her in favor of heterosexuality. The men deprived her of sleep and food and repeatedly raped her. When she was released, she reported the kidnapping and violent rapes to the police. In court, the parents admitted to paying $8,000 for the services of the male deprogrammers and were fully aware of the techniques to be used. The judge dismissed all charges of sexual battery, assault, and kidnapping. He deleted all references to rape and instead redefined these horrific experiences as "heterosexual activity meant to sway [her] from her lesbianism" (Comstock 1991, 201)

Solicitation and Loitering

Techniques used to control contact between homosexuals involve the enactment and enforcement of solicitation and loitering statutes. These criminal laws are related to state sex statutes, yet their independence means that they often remain valid even after sodomy laws are overturned or revoked. In general, the solicitation statutes prohibit invitations, requests, or offers to perform illegal or improper acts—even if the acts are to be performed in the privacy of one's own home. Loitering statutes, otherwise known as vagrancy or disorderly conduct statutes, make it a criminal act to stay in a public place without apparent reason or for the purpose of engaging in illegal behavior. For both solicitation and loitering, some states have used language that specifically targets homosexual behaviors. Unfortunately, these statutes are commonly used by police to harass lesbians and gay men. (See also **Solicitation and Loitering**.)

Lewd Conduct

Lewd conduct criminalizes the exposure of one's genitals or other acts deemed immoral in public. What constitutes immoral behavior varies widely from state to state, particularly as to what parts of the body can be seen and the line between public and private spaces. Like solicitation and loitering, these statutes are commonly used by the police to harass lesbians and gay men.

Public Safety

The enforcement of **alcoholic beverage control (ABC)** regulations is considered a function of the police in maintaining public safety. Historically, the "public safety" rationale has been used by society to justify police harassment of lesbians and gay men in bars. Although enforcement of ABC regulations and fire codes is desirable, the presence of the police in gay bars is potentially very explosive.

LESBIANS AND GAY MEN AS CRIMINAL DEFENDANTS

Lesbians and gay men, like others in society, can be defendants in crimes. However, having their sexual orientation become known to the court has often resulted in prejudicing the outcome of the case.

Knowledge of Defendant's Sexual Orientation

In general, courts have disallowed knowledge of a defendant's sexual orientation unless it is relevant to the case. Comments made during opening or closing statements by prosecutors that identify the defendant's sexual orientation are generally considered nonprejudicial if the court instructs the jury to disregard them. However, cases have been thrown out if the prosecutor makes unsubstantiated statements during closing arguments concerning the sexual orientation of the defendant (*Commonwealth v. Clary; Bennett v. State*).

Jury Selection

All people are afforded the right to a fair and impartial jury. The antigay stereotypes and prejudices permeating society make obtaining an unbiased jury difficult. One way to ensure the quality of jurors is to question them and determine their competence through a process known as *voir dire.* Ensuring that there are lesbians and gay men on a jury helps to ensure the representativeness of the jury. However, this is a double-edged sword because voir dire provides the opportunity to disqualify persons who are, or are perceived to be, lesbian or gay from serving on the jury. Only recently have courts determined that jurors cannot be excluded through peremptory strikes (removing them before the trial starts) simply because they are lesbian or gay, and, further, they cannot be asked by lawyers about their sexual orientation.

Domestic Violence

Violence between lesbian or gay male partners is often referred to as spousal abuse or **domestic violence**. All states have domestic violence statutes that grew out of the hard work of feminists in response to women being battered by their husbands and boyfriends. As such, the statutes have been designed to help women avoid further abuse by using restraining orders and shelters. Also, the courts have shown an understanding of the battered woman syndrome as a defense for women who murder their abusers. However, few states have extended these statutes to lesbians and gay men. Even when laws exist to protect lesbians and gay men from abusive partners, authorities seem confused about the relationship. Police and judges often resort to gender stereotyping and assume that the more masculine partner is the abuser and the more feminine partner is the one being abused.

References

Comstock, G. D. 1991. *Violence Against Lesbians and Gay Men.* New York: Columbia University Press.

Marcus, R. 1990. "Powell Regrets Backing Sodomy Law." *Washington Post* (26 October 1990): A3.

Robson, R. 1997. *Gay Men, Lesbians, and the Law.* New York: Chelsea House Publishers.

CRITTENDEN REPORT

The Crittenden Report was a U.S. Navy report that concluded that there was no sound basis for the belief that homosexuals posed a security risk. In 1957 the secretary of the navy put together a board chaired by Captain S. H. Crittenden Jr., U.S.N. The findings, known as the Crittenden Report, examined the antigay stereotype that homosexuals are easy targets of blackmail by enemy agents who might threaten to expose their sexuality. The board found that "the number of cases of blackmail as a result of past investigations of homosexuals is negligible. No factual data exists to support the contention that homosexuals are a greater risk than heterosexuals" (Dyer 1990, xvi).

The 639-page report so threatened the navy that it refused to release it. It took twenty years and a court order to pry the report loose from the grips of the navy. Thirty years after the initial Crittenden research, two more studies were conducted. These too were buried, but were forced out through leaks in Congress. These reports also reinforced the Crittenden findings that homosexuals do not pose a security risk because of sexual orientation and, thus, the belief that homosexuals should not serve in the military because of the threat of potential blackmail remained unsupported. (See also **Security Clearance**.)

Reference

Dyer, K. 1990. *Gays in Uniform: The Pentagon Secret Report*. Boston: Alyson Press.

D

Daughters of Bilitis The Daughters of Bilitis was the first influential lesbian organization in the United States. After hearing about the **Mattachine Society** in San Francisco, Del Martin and Phyllis Lyon decided in 1956 to transform their lesbian social club into a "women's organization for the purposes of education of the variant" and "of the public at large" (Blumenfeld and Raymond 1993, 295). They named the organization the Daughters of Bilitis (DOB). The name came from Pierre Louÿs's narrative "Song of Bilitis," in which Bilitis is a lesbian poet who lived in ancient Greece on the isle of Lesbos with Sappho. Over the next few years, chapters of the DOB were established in major cities around the country and in Australia, and they produced a newsletter called *The Ladder.* The DOB was well connected with the Mattachine Society and other early gay rights organizations and was influential in effecting changes in law toward lesbians and gay men.

Reference

Blumenfeld, W. J., and D. Raymond, eds. 1993. *Looking at Gay and Lesbian Life.* Rev. ed. Boston: Beacon Press.

Defense of Marriage Act (DOMA) The Defense of Marriage Act (DOMA), signed into law in 1996 had two purposes: (1) it prevented states from being forced by the **full faith and credit clause** of the U.S. Constitution to recognize same-sex marriages validly celebrated in other states; and (2) it defined **marriage** for federal purposes as the union of one man and one woman.

Experts believe that the act is probably unconstitutional because: (1) it is the antithesis of the full faith and credit clause; (2) it lacks sufficient generality; (3) it was constructed without adequate justification; (4) it encroaches upon an area of law that has been within the traditional power of the states; (5) it restricts interstate travel; and (6) it is motivated by animus toward a disfavored group.

The state has a fundamental interest in protecting the predictability, security, and stability of marriage. For couples who marry in one state (state of celebration) and live in another, the home state (domicile state) recognizes marriages from other states as long as they are not polygamous, incestuous, and do not violate a strong public policy of the domicile state. There is a long history of courts accepting valid marriages from other states that otherwise would be prohibited or odious to the public policy of the domicile state.

Choice-of-law procedures are used to determine the acceptance of out-of-state marriages, not the full faith and credit clause. The validity of a marriage is determined by the laws of the state of celebration and the laws of the state of domicile at the time of the marriage. If both the state of celebration and the state of domicile recognize the marriage, it is valid everywhere except those states that have declared such marriages void or have passed some kind of evasion statute. Because the DOMA did not address the issue of choice of law, the DOMA does not affect this procedure. Thus, if a same-sex couple were married in one state and their domicile state also accepted the marriage as valid, no other state could refuse to accept their marriage as valid unless it was proved to be obnoxious to that state's law.

One reason this choice-of-law procedure has developed is to stop people from so-called forum shopping. For example, assume a couple create a marriage that is valid in their home state but is void in other states. Then, one partner moves to one of these other states in which the marriage would not have been allowed. Here, the person could claim that he or she was never in a valid marriage and therefore was not responsible for child support or other claims. "Because the interstate recognition of marriages involves choice of law and because of how each state's choice-of-law rules operate, only the exception involving obnoxiousness to the domiciliary state's law may invalidate a marriage" (Strasser 1997, 130).

> Currently, *according to each state's law,* the only state laws potentially applicable to determine the validity of a marriage are the laws of the states of celebration and domicile. A state which is not the domicile at the time of the marriage will be forced by its own law to recognize a marriage validly celebrated in another state as long as the domicile at the time of marriage would recognize it. Thus, because DOMA does not affect state law, the act has *no* effect on which marriages are recognized by the various states. (Strasser 1997, 133)

Surprisingly, DOMA may have more of an effect on divorce than on marriage. Divorce decrees are not subject to choice-of-law rules. Thus, divorce decrees are legal judgments that are subject to the DOMA. Thus, for example, if a state's own choice-of-law rules require it to recognize all nonincestuous, nonbigamous marriages that do not violate public policy of the domiciliary state at the time of marriage, it may have to recognize a same-sex marriage and yet will retain the right not to recognize a same-sex divorce.

The DOMA does not increase the number of states allowed to refuse to recognize same-sex marriages validly celebrated in other states. States already have that right through their choice-of-law procedures. However, the DOMA may act as a destabilizing effect on the full faith and credit clause. Congress is opening itself up to demands for other exceptions to be made to the clause.

The exception Congress created to the clause with the DOMA is highly specific. Court interpretations of the clause demonstrate a reluctance to allow the federal government to make a change to one category of the clause or to target a subgroup within a category. The DOMA lacks generality. It is unclear whether Congress had the power to differentiate between different types of judgments as covered by the clause.

The right to interstate travel is fundamental to the concept of a federal union and is virtually unqualified (*United States v. Guest*). The DOMA would have a chilling effect on the right to travel to a state or migrate to a state. For example, if a validly married same-sex couple traveled through a state that did not recognize same-sex marriage, a situation could occur in which a hospital would not let the partner of an injured person give consent for medical treatment for life-threatening injuries sustained in an automobile accident. Same-sex married couples would be justified in being reluctant to travel through or migrate to states that were hostile to their relationship.

This scenario also points out the problem that the state through which the couple was passing would essentially invalidate their valid marriage. Currently, domestic relations law does not allow a state to invalidate a previously valid marriage without the consent of one or both partners. The DOMA would overrule this. Enforcing the DOMA would result in federal intrusion into state law. The Supreme Court has made it clear that state law can be overridden when the law causes "major damage" to "clear and substantial" federal interests (*Rose v. Rose*). The discussion in Congress shows a concern over extending federal benefits to same-sex couples. It is left to future courts to decide if this concern constitutes major damage to federal interests.

Congress overreached its power without adequate justification. Congress is displacing state law with the DOMA. Marriage, divorce, child adoption, and **family** law have historically been left to the states to regulate. The DOMA will interfere with that long history. It is difficult to believe that Congress had any legitimate justification for offering this act. It is very clear from the debate in Congress that animus was the motivation behind its adoption. Courts have consistently viewed the disfavoring of a disadvantaged minority as an illegitimate role of government.

As of the year 2000, twenty-nine states have passed preemptive laws similar to the DOMA that exempt them from having to recognize same-sex marriages from other states. It is believed that these kinds of legislation will be found unconstitutional once they are tested in court.

Reference

Strasser, M. 1997. *Legally Wed: Same-Sex Marriage and the Constitution.* Ithaca, NY: Cornell University Press.

DISCRIMINATION

DISCRIMINATION Discrimination is any act of exclusion or violence based upon some characteristic. Discrimination against lesbians and gay men goes seriously underreported. According to studies conducted by the National Gay and Lesbian Task Force (NGLTF), over 90 percent of gays and lesbians have been victimized in some way on the basis of their sexual orientation (National Gay and Lesbian Task Force 1989; U.S. House 1986).

PHYSICAL ATTACK

Gay bashing is the most extreme form of antigay violence. Primarily, groups of young men target another man (81 percent of victims are male) whom they suppose is gay. Usually, they beat and kick the gay man unconscious, sometimes to death, while using a torrent of taunts and slurs. Similar to the lynching of blacks, this violence has the same social origin and function designed to keep an entire stigmatized group in line. The violence does not stop there. Police and courts have often ignored the seriousness of the violence, thereby giving implicit approval to the practice. **Hate crimes** against lesbians and gays have increased almost 400 percent between the years 1988 and 1996 (New York City Gay and Lesbian Anti-Violence Project 1996).

JUDICIAL DISCRIMINATION

Few perpetrators of antigay violence are brought to court. Even when they are, these cases are marked with inequitable procedures and results. A number of causes may be blamed for the dismissal of these cases. First, judges and juries have viewed the young gay bashers as "just all-American boys" (Valente 1984a) and their actions are deemed normal. Second, the perpetrators were tried as juveniles ("Suspects Get Youth Status" 1984; "Three Teenagers" 1984) and received reduced sentencing. Third, the testimony from the gay victims was discounted (D'Emilio 1983). For example, in the trial of seven police officers caught in a gay bar shake-down racket, John D'Emilio writes; "The defense lawyer cast aspersions on the credibility of the prosecution witness . . . and deplored a legal system in which 'the most notorious homosexual may testify against a policeman.' Persuaded by this line of argument, the jury acquitted all of the defendants" (D'Emilio 1983, 183). Fourth, the perpetrators were "justified" in their actions as a self-defense or panic against the sexual overtures made by the lesbian or gay victim (Bagnall 1984; Califia 1983). Sometimes the **homosexual panic defense** has successfully been tied with the highly improbable insanity or other "diminished capacity" defenses (Shilts 1982, 308–325; Shipp 1981a, 1981b). However, these diminished capacity defenses are rarely accepted by courts at this time. These inequitable procedures and results show that the life and liberty of lesbians and gays, like those of blacks, simply count for less than those of members of the dominant society.

EMPLOYMENT DISCRIMINATION

Many lesbians and gays have been discriminated against in **employment**. It is important to remember that discrimination affects not only the ability of gay people to support themselves financially, but also their self-esteem. Governments have been the leading offenders. Through the establishment of precedents and procedures, as well as requirements made of government contractors, lesbians and gays have had much to fear from the government. For example, the U.S. government explicitly discriminates against gays in the armed forces and other intelligence agencies such as the Department of Energy (which continues to deny security clearances to gays). Although an executive order was signed by President Clinton in 1995 barring discrimination in the processing of security clearances, many politicians vowed to fight the order. State and local governments still regularly fire gay teachers (*Gaylord v. Tacoma School District No. 10; Rowland v. Mad River Local School District*), police and fire personnel, social workers, and anyone else who has contact with the public. Furthermore, states use licensing laws to bar gays from a vast array of occupations and professions, for example, doctors, lawyers, accountants, nurses, hairdressers, morticians, schoolteachers, used car dealers, and others (Hunter, Michaelson, and Stoddard 1992).

LIFESTYLE DISCRIMINATION

Lesbians and gay men are constantly discriminated against in other sectors of society through the use of laws and regulations, for example, in private-sector employment, public accommodations, housing, immigration and naturalization, insurance of all types, custody and adoption, and zoning policies that bar "singles" or "nonrelated" couples. Lesbians and gay men are frequently barred from hospitals when they try to visit their partners. Similarly, they have no rights to the property of their partners upon their partners' death or incapacitation. Only a few municipalities have enacted nondiscrimination provisions designed to protect gays. No state in the union allows gay **marriage** as of 2000.

RESPONSE TO DISCRIMINATION

Lesbians and gay men work in all professional fields and in every sector of society. They are ministers, teachers, bank tellers, doctors, mail carriers, secretaries, congressional representatives, and so on. The widespread discrimination experienced by lesbians and gay men often leads to self-destructive, self-deluding, and self-oppressing patterns of behavior. These dysfunctional responses are exhibited by other historically oppressed minorities (for gay self-oppression, see Adam 1978; Hodges and Hutter 1979). Job discrimination (whether actual or threatened) prevents many gays from totally participating in the business culture. Some gays respond by becoming workaholics. This helps prevent others from examining them too closely and distracts them from self-examination. Becoming a workaholic is often driven by a half-conscious belief that if the homosexual person is productive enough he or she will become "a good person" and overcome his or her invisible stigma. However, this hyperactivity typically results in further alienation from themselves and others. Another response is for gays to underidentify with their jobs. As a result, they engage in a spiral of self-defeating poor work performance, insecurity, and further alienation. This becomes a self-fulfilling prophecy of society's estimates of them. These gays seek dead-end jobs, ones that do not subject them to peer review. Another response is for lesbians and gays to be self-employed or to make frequent job changes. Both strategies effectively reduce the chances that discrimination will occur, but they lead to unstable finances. Regardless of the strategy, society's discrimination impacts many lesbians and gays by not allowing them to attain self-worth through gainful employment (Eriskopp and Silverstein 1998).

References

Adam, B. 1978. *The Survival of Domination: Inferiorization in Everyday Life.* New York: Elsevier.

Bagnall, R. G. 1984. "Burdens on Gay Litigants and Bias in the Court System: Homosexual Panic, Child Custody, and Anonymous Parties." *Harvard Civil Rights-Civil Liberties Law Review* 19: 498–515.

Califia, P. 1983. "Justifiable Homicide?" *The Advocate,* 12 May, 12.

D'Emilio, J. 1983. *Sexual Politics, Sexual Communities: The Making of a Homosexual Minority in the United States, 1940–1970.* Chicago: University of Chicago Press.

Eriskopp, A., and S. Silverstein. 1998. *Straight Jobs, Gay Lives: Gay and Lesbian Professionals, the Harvard Business School, and the American Workplace.* New York: Simon & Schuster.

Hodges, A., and D. Hutter. 1979. *With Downcast Gays: Aspects of Homosexual Self-Oppression.* Rev. ed. Toronto: Pink Triangle Press.

Hunter, N. D., S. E. Michaelson, and T. B. Stoddard. 1992. *The Rights of*

Lesbians and Gay Men: The Basic ACLU Guide to a Gay Person's Rights. 3d ed. Carbondale and Edwardsville, IL: Southern Illinois University Press.

National Gay and Lesbian Task Force. 1989. *Antigay and Lesbian Victimization.* Washington, DC: National Gay and Lesbian Task Force.

New York City Gay and Lesbian Anti-Violence Project. 1996. *Anti-Lesbian, Gay, Bisexual, and Transgendered Violence in 1996.* New York: New York City Gay and Lesbian Anti-Violence Project.

Shilts, R. 1982. *The Mayor of Castro Street: The Life and Times of Harvey Milk.* New York: St. Martin's Press.

Shipp, E. 1981a. "Murder Suspect in Village Found Not Responsible: Defendant in 2 Slayings Held for Mental Tests." *New York Times* (25 July 1981): 27.

———. 1981b. "Defendant Facing Psychiatric Tests: Man Is Ruled Not Responsible in Two Murders in 'Village,' But Future Is Unclear." *New York Times* (26 July 1981): 25.

"Suspects Get Youth Status." 1984. *New York Times* (17 September 1984): D17.

"Three Teenagers Sentenced in Killing of Homosexual." 1984. *New York Times* (6 October 1984): 6.

U.S. House. 1986. Committee on the Judiciary. Subcommittee on Criminal Justice. *Antigay Violence.* 99th Cong., 2d sess. 9 October.

Valente, J. 1984a. "Two St. John's Students Given Probation in Assault on Gay." *Washington Post* (15 May 1984): A1.

DISCRIMINATION AGAINST CUSTOMERS

Discrimination against lesbians, gay men, and bisexuals, and transsexuals, transgendered, and intersexed people is sometimes overt, but more often is subtle and unrecognized. Although some businesses directly discriminate against homosexual employees and customers, most would claim they treat "them" like "everyone else."

An experimental field study conducted by A. S. Walters and M. Curran (1996) in the San Francisco Bay area explored the treatment of same-sex versus opposite-sex couples by retail employees. Over a four-month period, three couples (one female-female, one male-female, and one male-male) entered each of twenty retail stores located in the same mall. Each site was carefully selected to normalize for time of day, ratio of customers to sales clerks, approval of management participation to be interviewed (not knowing the details of the study), and other characteristics. The research couples were trained confederates in the use of a scripted presentation, appearance (plain clothing), and reporting methodology. The confederates, assumed to be heterosexual, were randomly assigned into couples immediately before entering the store. Whether the confederates were in same- or opposite-sex couples, they behaved the same and held hands while entering the store and milling about. No additional behaviors (such as kissing) were engaged in. The couples entered each store and measured the amount of time it took for a salesperson to approach them to offer assistance (greeters were not counted). An undercover cohort acting as a customer was placed in the store prior to and during the arrival of the couple. The cohort milled around inconspicuously, but in a position to watch the experiment. The cohort also measured the time with a stopwatch, recorded the interactions, and lingered after the couple left to overhear comments made by employees.

FINDINGS

It took approximately four minutes before the lesbian couple or the gay male couple was approached by sales clerks. In contrast, heterosexual couples were offered assistance, on the average, within one minute and eighteen seconds.

Besides the time differential, same-sex couples were treated differently than opposite-sex couples. The lesbian and gay male couples reported sales clerks staring, laughing, pointing, talking, and being rude toward them in every store. In some situations, sales employees refused to serve the gay male couples. The undercover observer confirmed these interactions. A difference in treatment was seen between homosexual couples—the gay male couples experienced significantly more staring, talking, and rude treatment. Sales clerks made public comments on the floor (not in the back room and sometimes to nearby customers) such as "Did you see those two fruits? They were holding hands! I wasn't going to wait on them even if [manager's name] saw me blow them off," or "Those two guys who were just in here were together—like, I mean, a couple. That is just so gross. I didn't even know it until I saw they were holding hands. I just kept not looking at them." At one store, several male employees formed a barricade and asked the gay male couple to leave. In contrast, the heterosexual couples reported no negative treatment.

Interviews of the store managers revealed that employees were trained to greet customers within an average of twenty-five seconds and to offer assistance within two minutes. Managers were aware of the composition of their customers with regards to race and gender, but most were unaware of any homosexual customers. Managers were aware and had observed employees negatively discussing customers, but they claimed that it occurred in the back and never "on the floor" or to the customers' faces. Most managers reported that they disliked having to discipline employees and only one said she would terminate an employee for rude behavior.

It was found that it made no difference whether employees were paid on a commission or hourly basis as to their conduct toward same-sex couples. This surprised the researcher because it was thought that commission-based employees would be more tolerant because their livelihood is dependent upon making sales regardless of the class of their clients.

The findings of this study are revealing. First, it must be recognized that customers who are in same-sex couples are treated differently by employees than customers who are in opposite-sex couples. Although this study was conducted in a retail environment, it most assuredly could be expanded to involve all employee-customer environments.

Management needs honestly to address this problem. There should be no more whitewashing the problem and claiming that everyone is "treated the same." The retail industry, and, in fact, all businesses, are fiercely competitive in the global economy and dismissing any segment of customers could be detrimental to the success of the business. Also, with the progress being made in gay civil rights, it is anticipated that such discriminatory practices by employees will subject the business to potential law suits.

Reference

Walters, A. S., and M. Curran. 1996. "'Excuse Me, Sir? May I Help You and Your Boyfriend?': Salespersons' Differential Treatment of Homosexual and Straight Customers." *The Journal of Homosexuality* 31(1/2): 135–152.

DISORDERLY CONDUCT

See **Lewd Conduct**

DIVERSITY TRAINING Businesses have significantly increased the amount of training they conduct for employees on social issues. Often referred to as "sensitivity training," "diversity training," or "cultural awareness training," these training programs seek to impart information to employees to help reduce bias and prejudice and to bring greater conformance between the company's antidiscrimination policies and employee understanding of them. Some employees resist attending these training programs. They may claim that forcing them to hear about lesbians and gays is against their religious beliefs and creates a "hostile" work environment (interestingly, the term *hostile* has only recently been claimed as a defense in these situations as a result in the rise in hostile environment **sexual harassment** litigation).

Can employees be forced to attend training programs on social issues? The answer is "yes." If the training has a legitimate purpose for the business, is conducted on paid time or required for continual service or promotion, and is required for all employees, then an employee cannot refuse to attend. (The EEOC has determined that "new age" training that includes biofeedback, meditation, and other unusual procedures must be voluntary.) If the training threatens or intimidates attendees to behave in ways contrary to their civil rights, then they could refuse (for example, a political party puts on a workshop at the business and administrators make it clear that attendees are expected to vote a particular way under threat of discharge). Although workers have the right to refuse to attend training programs that intimidate or harass, the reality is that unless the job is protected under civil service or specific state legislation, the employee could face employment termination without recourse.

A recent example shows the confusion over this issue. Three Minnesota prison employees protested having to attend workplace training on sexual orientation. They believed that the mandatory program was "state-sponsored propaganda" promoting homosexuality. The three men said that homosexuality went against their religious beliefs and that same-sex intimacy was sinful. The men took their Bibles to the training program and read silently during class. Afterward, the employees received written reprimands for violating prison policies prohibiting improper conduct and prejudicial behavior. Supervisors further charged that the protest was an attempt to impede efforts to prevent sexual orientation harassment. The men sued. In August 1999, U.S. District Judge Ann D. Montgomery of Minnesota ordered the state to withdraw the disciplinary notices. Judge Montgomery decided that the employees' First Amendment right to free expression of religion and the Minnesota constitution's freedom-of-conscience clause were violated by the prison's actions (*Altman v. Minnesota Department of Corrections*). Thus, requiring employees to attend diversity training can sometimes violate their rights.

DOMESTIC PARTNERSHIP Couples who have formed relationships but are unmarried sometimes gain legal recognition for their relationships, which are termed *domestic partnerships*. Increasingly, governmental entities and private businesses are formally recognizing domestic partnerships.

The acceptance of domestic partnerships arises from two cultural forces. First, the social construction of the **family** is changing. The traditional nuclear family consisting of a married heterosexual couple with children under the age of eighteen represents a minority of families in the United States. According to the 1990 Census, approximately 75 percent of all families do not conform to the traditional nuclear family model. There are almost 4.5 million families comprised of unmarried couples, of which approximately one-third are unmarried same-sex couples (Kohn 1999). Domestic partnership programs recognize and address the issue of fairness to nontraditional families. Second, the gay civil rights movement has brought to the attention of Americans the need for equity between same-sex couples and the rights and responsibilities opposite-sex couples are given through marriage. For example, it is estimated that benefits comprise approximately 40 percent of a worker's employment compensation. Opposite-sex couples who marry are able to obtain benefits for their spouses. This, in effect, gives heterosexual married employees a significantly higher rate of pay as compared with lesbian and gay employees. Domestic partnership benefits help equalize the workplace, thereby helping to attract and retain qualified employees in a competitive market.

Definition and Verification

Just as there are many definitions of what constitutes a family, there are wide variations in how domestic partnerships are defined and implemented by states, cities, and private businesses. Domestic partnership programs sometimes use other words, such as "life partner," "spousal equivalent," "functional marriage equivalent," "alternative family," and "family-type unit." In general, domestic partnership is defined as an ongoing relationship between two adults of the same or opposite sex who are over the age of eighteen, are sharing a residence, are emotionally interdependent, and intend to reside together indefinitely.

Some domestic partnership programs specify same-sex couples only. The rationale for doing so is that opposite-sex couples have the ability to marry, whereas same-sex couples do not. Some civil libertarians argue that this is appropriate because domestic partnership policies are an attempt to right an injustice toward lesbian and gay couples. Also, heterosexuals who choose not to marry by obtaining domestic partnership status are undermining legal and social marriage norms. Most lesbian and gay legal organizations, including the National Gay and Lesbian Task Force, recommend including both same- and opposite-sex couples in domestic partnership policies. Some courts have struck down same-sex only domestic partnership policies as being discriminatory based on sexual orientation or on marital status. More and more employers are designing domestic partnership programs that allow both same- and opposite-sex couples to register.

Some domestic partnership programs are all-inclusive. For example, Bank America allows employees to designate any member of their household to be a recipient of their health benefits. This may include a married spouse, unmarried domestic partner, or relative (such as a sibling or parent). Few employers have adopted such programs, but they are ideal to fit the wide range of family arrangements. Surprisingly, unmarried opposite-sex couples are the primary people who sign up for domestic partnership benefits (Donovan 1998). Also, some, but not all, domestic partnership programs extend benefits to the children of domestic partners.

Verifying domestic partnerships involves a number of strategies. In some cities and one state (California), couples may register their relationship. Sometimes they only need to swear to the accuracy of their statement: other times they must show proof, such as living together (rental agreements or home mortgages), having joint bank accounts, and other examples of joint ownership and financial interdependence. Requiring such documents may be discriminatory because married couples often either do not need to show any proof of marriage or simply need to show their marriage certificate. To be fair, businesses should require similar documentation for married couples and for domestic partners enrolling in employee benefit programs.

BENEFITS PROVIDED

Workplace benefits are often divided into two categories. "Soft" benefits usually include bereavement and sick leave, adoption assistance, relocation benefits, child resource and referral services, access to employer recreational facilities, participation in employee assistance programs, and inclusion in employee discount policies. "Hard" benefits usually include medical benefits, dental and vision care, dependent life insurance, accidental death and dismemberment benefits, tuition assistance, long-term care, day care, and flexible spending accounts. It is important to note that more than 400 benefits in the public and private sector extended to married couples are denied domestic partners (U.S. General Accounting Office 1997).

GOVERNMENTAL PROGRAMS

Domestic partnerships are recognized by governmental bodies in one of two forms. First, some cities and one state allow couples who live together to "register" their status as domestic partners. Usually, this opens the door to soft benefits for government employees who register. California's registry, the only state to offer domestic partnership, is symbolic and does not confer any rights. In the second form, some cities extend to domestic partners of city employees the same health care and other benefits as are extended to spouses of married employees. In some cases, both a registry and extension of benefits are available, in other cases, one or the other form exists.

Vermont has become the first state to provide a same-sex equivalent to marriage. This "civil union" is designed to provide all the same rights and responsibilities as opposite-sex marriage without using the word "marriage." In many ways, civil unions represent a domestic partnership policy. (See also **Marriage**.)

PRIVATE EMPLOYMENT

Over 1,000 companies include sexual orientation as a protected category in their nondiscrimination policies. Only a few hundred of these companies provide domestic partnership benefits. In June 2000, General Motors, Ford, and DaimlerChrysler announced that health care benefits would be extended to same-sex domestic partners. This action affected more than

465,000 employees around the country. Program definitions vary as to what constitutes a domestic partnership, who qualifies, and what benefits are conferred.

Many reasons can be cited as to why businesses have a vested interest in providing domestic partnership benefits. First, it is a matter of equality for all employees. By participating in benefit programs, married employees are, in fact, receiving significantly higher salaries. Lesbian and gay employees feel less valued and second rate if they do not receive the same benefits. Second, comprehensive benefit packages are one way to attract and retain talented employees. In our competitive world, employers cannot ignore the power antidiscrimination policies and domestic partnership programs have in influencing lesbian and gay employees to maintain company loyalty. Third, many of the leading companies in technology, entertainment, financial, legal, medical, academic, and computer companies provide domestic partnership programs. They find that doing so boosts employee moral and attracts customers.

In many ways, the extension of benefits to same-sex couples by businesses is more important than governmental recognition. Registries provide few real benefits, whereas company benefits affect the everyday life of employees and their families.

Concerns

When domestic partnerships are considered for businesses and cities, a number of common issues are voiced as concerns.

First, there is the fear that the program will cost too much to implement. The experiences of other cities and businesses have found this to be untrue. Part of the fear is the antigay stereotype that gay people are mostly infected with HIV and, thus, will impose significant health care costs. As of the year 2000, the lifetime costs for HIV care are approximately $109,000—which is equal to or less than the cost for cancer care or organ transplants. The cost for premature birth can exceed $1,000,000. For example, Home Box Office has found that its health care program for gay partners cost 17 percent less than for heterosexual partners because there were no pregnancy costs. The city of Seattle found that domestic partners had lower overall claim costs and fewer medical visits than married employees. The city of West Hollywood found that claims ran lower than for married couples and there were negligible increased costs. Likewise, Berkeley and Santa Cruz found domestic partner costs to be equivalent to adding an equal number of married spouses (Becker 1995). Although insurance companies initially added surcharges to their premiums to companies providing domestic partnership programs, most have reduced or eliminated these charges once they learned that costs were no higher than they were for spouses of married employees (*Report of the CUNY Study Group on Domestic Partnerships* 1993).

Typically, enrollment in domestic partnership programs is low because: (1) many lesbian and gay employees are reluctant to come out of the closet at work for fear of experiencing discrimination; (2) domestic partnership benefits are considered taxable income by the IRS; and (3) most adults work, therefore the partner of a same-sex couple is often covered under his or her own employer's benefit program.

To claim costs as a reason to deny domestic partnership benefits is not fair. Employers do not bar employees from getting married or having children—both of which raise health care costs. Companies that care for their employees should treat all employees equitably.

Besides cost, a second major concern is that domestic partnership programs are open to abuse and fraud. Some believe that employees may attempt to exploit the system by enrolling sick friends or relatives. There are no reported cases of this happening. The process of registration helps preclude such a scenario. Employees also run the risk of reprisal or dismissal from employment for engaging in such practices. More importantly, the limits insurance companies place on preexisting conditions inhibit fraudulent enrollment. Finally, the act of registering for domestic partnership creates legal documents that can be used in tort actions for damages caused by fraud. Thus, fraud is not a real problem.

A third concern involves the fear of a potential backlash from other employees and customers, which is sometimes thought to be sufficient reason to deny domestic partnership programs. Experience has shown that there are usually positive reactions to the implementation of domestic partnership programs that far outweigh the negatives. One of the most visible examples of this was when the Walt Disney Company adopted domestic partnership benefits in 1996. The Southern Baptist Convention announced a boycott of Disney's products and services. Ultimately the boycott failed, as 70 percent of Americans rejected the idea of the boycott and fewer still actually participated (Morganthaus 1997).

A fourth obstacle to domestic partnerships is that many employers do not believe they have lesbian or gay employees and, therefore, do not believe they need to provide domestic partnership benefits. This is not true. Lesbians, gay men, and bisexuals, and transgendered, transsexual, and intersexed people are everywhere. (See also **Incidence of Homosexuality**.)

TAX CONSEQUENCES

There are negative tax consequences to domestic partnership programs. Federal tax law does not recognize such relationships. Domestic partners who do not receive more than 50 percent of their support from their partners do not qualify as "dependents." Therefore, the benefits they receive become taxable income to the employee because the benefits are not excludable from the employee's gross income. Furthermore, the nonexempt benefits may be taxed at "fair market value." Health care costs are often very high and this could result in a significant amount of calculable income for which the employee would have a tax liability.

LEGAL CONSEQUENCES

Domestic partnership registration creates an enforceable contract for partners to be jointly responsible for basic living expenses. The precise nature of this obligation is dependent upon the wording of state and city ordinances. It is unknown how this will be enforced. Creditors may be able to enforce agreements between domestic partners. For example, the city of San Francisco specifically requires domestic partners to be jointly responsible for basic living expenses that can be enforced by anyone to whom the expenses are owed.

Termination of the domestic partnership needs to be made with formal notice to the state or city if it has a registry, with the employee's company, and with any third party who may have relied upon the existence of the partnership. San Francisco requires couples to give written notice to a third party under penalty of perjury. In the event of failure to give notice, anyone who suffers a loss from the dissolution of the partnership may sue to recover actual damages.

The adoption of domestic partnership registries and programs helps validate lesbian and gay relationships and families. This is having an impact on many legal issues from child custody to wills and health benefits. Ultimately, this may lead the way to full same-sex marriage.

References

Becker, L. 1995. "Recognition of Domestic Partnerships by Governmental Entities and Private Employers." *National Journal of Sexual Orientation Law* 1(1): 91–104.

Donovan, J. M. 1998. "An Ethical Argument to Restrict Domestic Partnerships to Same-Sex Couples." *Law and Sexuality* 8: 649–670.

Kohn, S. 1999. *NGLTF Domestic Partnership Organizing Manual for Employee Benefits.* Washington, DC: National Gay and Lesbian Task Force.

Morganthaus, T. 1997. "Baptists vs. Mickey: Why the Boycott against Disney Faces Steep Odds." *Newsweek* (30 June 1997): 51.

Report of the CUNY Study Group on Domestic Partnerships, The. 1993. New York: City University of New York.

U.S. General Accounting Office. 1997. *Defense of Marriage Act Report.* OGC 97–16: 58. Washington, DC: Government Printing Office.

DOMESTIC VIOLENCE Commonly referred to as spousal abuse, domestic violence is violence between intimate partners. All states have domestic violence statutes that were implemented after feminist movements raised concerns for women battered by their husbands and boyfriends. Consequently, the statutes have focused on the needs of married women or women with live-in boyfriends. The statutes provide means for restraining men from being around their intimate partners and for providing shelters for battered women. The courts have also learned to take into consideration the battered woman syndrome to help explain instances in which women have resorted to murdering their abusive spouses. (See also **Criminal Law**.)

Because of this history, few courts have understood the needs of lesbians and gay men who find themselves in abusive relationships. Only a few states have extended domestic violence statutes to lesbian and gay male relationships. Even then, there is confusion. Some states limit the applicability of protection to those who live together. For lesbians or gay men who are in relationships in which they do not reside together, protections are rarely available. Furthermore, protective agencies often have difficulty determining who is at fault. Some judges have determined that battered couples engaged in "mutual combat" (simply fighting), not battering or abuse. Police and judges often fall back on gender stereotyping and assume the more masculine partner is the abuser and the more feminine partner is the abused. Furthermore, the stereotype that women engage in "cat fights" and men should be able to "fight like a man" has influenced the decisions to extend spousal abuse protections and other consequences.

It is important to extend spousal abuse protections to lesbian and gay male relationships. Intervening between abusive couples helps to break the cycle of violence. For example, in 1989 Annette Green was abused by her lover in Florida and sought help from protective agencies. The court would not issue her a protective order because the state recognized only "persons related by blood or marriage." She attempted to flee to a shelter for battered women, but she was turned away. The shelter was partially funded by the state and was subject to its regulations. The state allowed only women who were abused by their "spouses" to use the shelter. Because the state did not recognize gay marriages, Green was not defined as a spouse and, thus, was denied shelter. Ultimately, Green murdered her lover, Ivonne Julio. At the trial, prosecutors sought first-degree murder charges. The defense claimed that Green suffered from battered woman syndrome. Green had been shot at by her lover, sustained a broken nose and broken ribs, and had a long history of abuse from Julio. Despite the objection of the prosecution to the use of the strategy, the judge allowed the defense. This became the first trial to extend the battered woman defense to situations involving lesbian or gay male partners (Robson 1997, 91).

However, the jury did not accept the defense and rendered a guilty verdict in only two and one-half hours. One juror reported hearing two other jurors in the restroom saying that they wanted to "hang that lesbian bitch." Thus, this case shows the difficulty in extending domestic violence concepts to lesbian and gay male relationships, and shows that prejudice can affect decisions reached by juries.

Reference
Robson, R. 1997. *Gay Men, Lesbians, and the Law.* New York: Chelsea House Publishers.

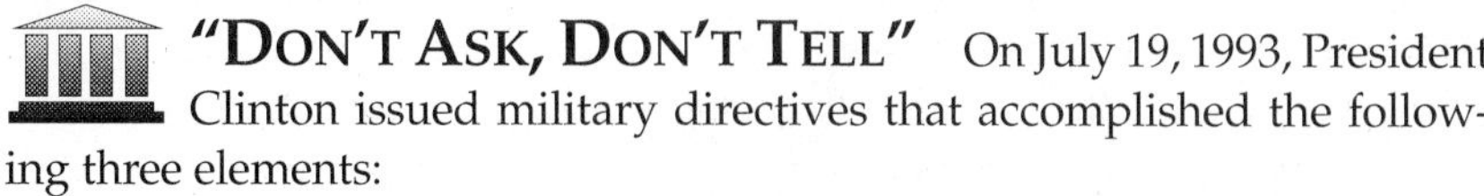

"DON'T ASK, DON'T TELL" On July 19, 1993, President Clinton issued military directives that accomplished the following three elements:

1. "Servicemen and women will be judged based on their conduct, not their sexual orientation."
2. "The practice . . . of not asking about sexual orientation in the enlistment procedure will continue."
3. An "open statement by a service member that he or she is a homosexual will create a rebuttable presumption that he or she intends to engage [in] prohibited conduct, but the service member will be given an opportunity to refute that presumption; in other words, to demonstrate that he or she intends to live by the rules of conduct that apply in the military service." (Don't Ask, Don't Tell Policy)

Behaviors that would no longer initiate an investigation or serve as the basis for separation included association with known homosexuals, presence at a gay bar, possessing or reading homosexual publications, marching in a gay rights rally, or the listing of someone of the same gender as the person to be contacted in case of emergency or the beneficiary of an insurance policy.

Has the policy been effective in reducing lesbians and gay harassment in the military? The answer is "no." "Since the regulations took effect in early 1994, the number of gays dismissed from military service has climbed 42 percent" (Graham 1997).

COURT CHALLENGES TO "DON'T ASK, DON'T TELL"

In the 1980s and 1990s, courts consistently decided that homosexual status alone could not be used to justify discharging military personnel (see, e.g., *Cammermeyer v. Aspin, Meinhold v. U.S. Dept. of Defense*). However, it was claimed the act of declaring one's homosexual sexual orientation created a presumption to engage in homosexual acts (see, e.g., *Ben-Shalom v. Marsh, Steffan v. Perry*). This conflict over status versus conduct was codified in the "Don't Ask, Don't Tell" executive order. The new policy required service members who declared their homosexuality to rebut the presumption of homosexual conduct, that is, demonstrate that they were not engaging in, attempting to engage in, did not have a propensity to engage in, or intend to engage in homosexual acts.

Two cases were combined and heard by the Ninth Circuit Court (*Holmes/Watson v. California Army National Guard*). Both Watson and Holmes challenged the constitutionality of the "don't ask, don't tell" policy's presumption of homosexual conduct (§654) that is created solely by a statement of homosexual sexual orientation. The court concluded that §654 and its implementing regulations were constitutional on their face as applied to Watson and Holmes (see, *Richenberg v. Perry, Able v. United States, Thomasson v. Perry*).

The Equal Protection Clause of the Fourteenth Amendment was applied to Holmes/Watson. Because homosexuals do not constitute a suspect or quasi-suspect class, the courts reviewed the military's "don't ask, don't tell" policy using a rational test. As such, Holmes and Watson needed to show the statute and accompanying regulations were not rationally related to any legitimate governmental purpose. The court was careful to avoid substituting its own judgement over the "wisdom, fairness, or logic of legislative choices" (*Watson/Holmes,* 9). As such, it deferred to the military's contention that "don't ask, don't tell" was needed and constitutional. Surprisingly, this ignored the exact opposite findings by the same court in *Meinhold v. United States Dep't of Defense* a few years earlier.

Watson and Holmes next contended that it was not rational for the government to presume from statements regarding homosexual sexual orientation that they will likely engage in homosexual conduct. The court was expressly aware that, unlike in *Meinhold* where the decision was narrowly construed, this issue had to be directly addressed. The court looked to other cases and agreed with the Second, Fourth, and Eighth Circuits that a declaration of homosexual sexual orientation is rationally related to the presumption of sexual conduct.

Last, Watson and Holmes argued that the policy, as applied, treated homosexual and heterosexual persons differently. The court did not agree and stated "the policy itself does not distinguish between persons of homosexual and heterosexual orientation, providing that any person who makes a statement of homosexual orientation is subject to the same rebuttable presumption that arose against Watson and Holmes" (*Watson/Holmes* 14). Thus, with an Orwellian twist of logic, the court ruled the policy is not discriminatory because it treated homosexuals and heterosexuals equally—neither are allowed to say they are gay without proving that they will not engage in homosexual conduct.

TRAINING ON THE "DON'T ASK, DON'T TELL" POLICY

The Pentagon issued a press release on February 1, 2000, announcing that the rate of discharge from the military for homosexuality was 73 percent higher than the rate in 1993—the year prior to implementation of "Don't Ask, Don't Tell." In response to this increase of persecution and reports of increased harassment of lesbian and gay service personnel at all levels, the Pentagon also announced new training programs to prevent antigay harassment and improper investigations. The training program is the first to provide servicewide guidelines on antigay harassment and the first clarification of training under "Don't Ask, Don't' Tell." The training will instruct service personnel how to report and commanders how to respond to antigay harassment. Training will instruct service members that they may seek confidential help from military defense attorneys and chaplains. The training also provides commanders with guidelines on when and when not to investigate gay service members under current law (Servicemembers Legal Defense Network 2000a). (See also **Hate Crimes; Military; Military Expulsion**.)

Reference

Graham, B. 1997. "Military Reviews Allegations of Harassment against Gays." *Washington Post* (14 May 1997): A01.

Servicemembers Legal Defense Network (SLDN). 2000a. "New Gay Discharge Figures Up 73 Percent since 'Don't Ask, Don't Tell, Don't Pursue' First Implemented." Press release on Servicemembers Legal Defense Network website: www.sldn.org/templates/press/index.html?section=2&record=98. Accessed 1 February 2000.

DRESS AND GROOMING CODES Employers can impose dress and grooming codes in the workplace. However, the rules should bear a relation to the requirements of the job. Even then, the rules are not hard and fast. For example, a pizza restaurant worker who was black was fired for refusing to be clean shaven. The employer felt there was a sanitation reason for the policy. The black worker filed suit claiming that shaving irritated his skin so much that it was impossible to shave and that it posed an undue hardship. The courts sided with the fired employee, noting that 50 percent of all black males have this common skin disorder (pseudofolliculitis barbae), of which 25 percent find they can't shave at all. Thus, a grooming code such as shaving inherently discriminated against a protected class. The employer lost the case (*Bradley v. Pizzaco of Nebraska*).

"Looks" discrimination is probably the most widespread form of discrimination. Without the right "look," employees may not fit into the "culture" of their companies and are subject to being overlooked for promotion or face outright termination. This is probably the most important issue in the debate over discrimination, yet it is not covered by any particular law.

In one particular case, *Carroll v. Talman Federal Savings & Loan Association,* a woman employee sued on behalf of herself and other female employees over disparate dress codes. From 1958 to 1969, Talman required both male and female employees to wear uniforms. Then Talman revised its policy to allow men to wear "customary business attire" although women were still required to wear uniforms consisting of a skirt or slacks paired with a color-coordinated vest, jacket, or tunic. Mary Carroll argued that these disparate requirements were a violation of **Title VII** because the employees wearing the uniforms, the women, would be considered of lesser professional status. Although the court did not find different dress norms for males and females to be offensive or illegal stereotyping, in this case, the uniforms would have indicated that the women were of lower status and this was thus a violation of Title VII.

There are many reasons employees may not want to conform to dress and grooming codes. Many religious groups require members to wear particular clothing. Political beliefs also affect the choice of clothing. For example, many feminists (including men with this belief system) refuse to wear clothing that reinforces the dominant culture and, in particular, the subjugation of women. Ties are phallic symbols and suits are symbols of wealth and power. Feminists often refuse to wear ties and suits. Yet many businesses require employees, particularly managers, to wear "professional attire." What constitutes professional attire is not stated, but is informally understood to mean suits and ties for men and dress suits for women. Feminists are often at odds with traditional corporate standards. (See also **Neckties as Phallic Symbols**.)

Another group of workers that faces severe challenges with most dress and grooming codes are **transsexuals**, **transvestites**, **transgendered**, and **intersexed** people. By not conforming to expected gender roles in their clothing choice, they often face overt discrimination. The courts have held that Title VII was never intended to address issues of length of hair or people who changed their sex (transsexuals). Thus, transgendered people are at particular risk from discrimination.

Employees are allowed to wear insignias to show their religious beliefs and union associations. This is protected under the law and dress codes or uniform requirements do not supersede the right to wear insignias. However, under certain situations, employers may be able to justify a regulation banning or limiting insignias if it is based upon a legitimate business interest. For example, an employer may be able to limit the wearing of insignias to prevent the alienation of customers (for workers who interact with the public), or if they may adversely affect patients in a health care facility. Although a total ban may not be possible, an employer could ban all but "tasteful and inconspicuous" insignias. (See also **Employment**.)

E

Effectiveness of Antidiscrimination Statutes Just how effective are antidiscrimination statutes at protecting the rights of lesbian and gay people? Chuck Stewart (1993, 1996) obtained data from the California Department of Labor Standards Enforcement (DLSE) concerning the outcome of complaints filed with the agency claiming sexual orientation discrimination in employment.

A total of 464 sexual orientation discrimination complaints were filed during the first three years of the law's existence. Of the total complaints filed, 102 were still open and pending. This was contrary to the goals of the California Employment Discrimination Sexual Orientation Act (AB2601) for expeditious investigations and settlements to protect the livelihood of lesbians and gays. When the agency was asked the average length of time required to finish a complaint or the average length of time for the still pending cases, agency representatives did not know.

Of the 372 cases disposed of within the first three years, 143 (38 percent) were dismissed, 98 (26 percent) were abandoned, 97 (26 percent) were withdrawn, and 34 (9 percent) were settled in favor of the complainant.

When the DLSE was contacted and was asked to explain why 91 percent of the complaints were not successful, the department had no answers, nor did it plan to review the cases or to conduct a follow-up to determine if there was a pattern to the unsuccessful complaints. The DLSE revealed that there was no quality assurance program in place. The agency displayed pride in having full-time investigators on its staff who were responsible for covering *all* labor law disputes in California, not just sexual orientation discrimination complaints.

When asked about the thirty-four complainants who prevailed, the DLSE did not know if the complainants kept their jobs, obtained back pay, or won damages. In general, the DLSE did not know the outcome of its own efforts. Further, the DLSE did not plan on issuing an opinion statement to summarize what it had learned.

As with any legislation, litigation helps to define what the law actually means. Both the successful and unsuccessful complaints help clarify

AB2601. For example, the attorney general's opinion that led to the implementation of AB2601 stated that being "openly gay" was a political act, and, as such, was protected under the First Amendment. But what behaviors constitute being openly gay? Without review of previous decisions, no measure can be developed.

Antidiscrimination statutes often turn out to be what many gay legal analysts predicted: a bone to placate the gay community's call for equal protection, yet toothless when faced with actually protecting lesbian and gay rights. (See also **Equal Employment Opportunity Commission [EEOC]; Prejudice**.)

References

Stewart, C. 1993. "How Effective Is AB2601?" *Edge* (8 September 1993): 12.

———. 1996. "How Effective Is the Department of Labor Standards Enforcement at Protecting Our Rights Under AB2601?" *Edge* (7 August 1996): 30.

EMPLOYMENT

EMPLOYMENT The 1884 "employment at will" doctrine established that employers could discharge employees "for good cause, for no cause, or even for cause morally wrong" (*Payne v. Western Atlantic Railroad*). Slowly, this doctrine has been eroded through litigation and the enactment of the federal Civil Rights Act of 1964. By outlawing discrimination based on race, color, religion, sex, and national origin, these measures have forced businesses to take greater care in their employment decisions. Today, employees can be fired for good or bad cause, but not for reasons prohibited by law.

Sexual orientation has not achieved **suspect class** status under the law. Nevertheless, many corporations and businesses have implemented employment policies that prohibit discrimination based on sexual orientation. Even so, lesbians and gay men are outside the arm of civil rights law in most of the country and are subject to arbitrary or malicious employment discrimination.

PRIVATE EMPLOYMENT

Unless expressly forbidden by state or local law, employers may discriminate against lesbian and gay employees and applicants. There are no federal laws that prevent discrimination against employees in private businesses based on the employees' sexual orientation. A few states and many cities have enacted antidiscrimination statutes and ordinances that provide employment protection for lesbians and gay men. (See **Appendix A: State and Local Laws**.)

PUBLIC EMPLOYMENT

Government employers are subject to constitutional requirements to act fairly toward all individuals and not act capriciously or irrationally. The issue of homosexuality and federal employment came before a federal court of appeals in 1969. Clifford Norton was employed by the National Aeronautics and Space Administration. He was arrested by officers of the District of Columbia Police Department's morals squad in Lafayette Square (directly across from the White House) for a traffic violation after they saw him attempt to make the acquaintance of another man. He was fired from his job. He sued and the court agreed that the government failed to show a specific connection between the employee's potentially embarrassing conduct and any reduction in the efficiency of the department for which he worked (*Norton v. Macy*). On the basis of this and related decisions, the Civil Service Commission issued a directive to federal supervisors in December 1973 that stated that "you many not find a person unsuitable for Federal employment merely because the person is a homosexual or has engaged in homosexual acts" (*Civil Service Bulletin* 1973). Later this concept was expanded by the enactment of the Civil Service Reform Act of 1978. Supervisors were directed not to discriminate against employees on the basis of conduct that does not adversely affect the performance of others. Finally, in 1998 President Clinton signed Executive Order 13087, specifically banning discrimination based on sexual orientation in the federal civilian workforce.

Even with these rulings and executive orders, there are departments of the federal government that still discriminate against lesbians and gay men. All branches of the military exclude homosexuals. The concern over security is given as the reason for disallowing homosexuals in the military. These concerns have been shown to be false. Also, the military has incurred great expense by excluding lesbians and gay men. Even so, the courts have been reluctant to overturn the military policy of **"Don't Ask, Don't Tell,"** claiming that security concerns are determined by Congress. Although the FBI, CIA, and other agencies officially no longer discriminate against homosexuals, openly lesbian and gay applicants are invariably turned down. (See also **Military Expulsion; Security Clearance**.)

The federal Constitution establishes a baseline of freedoms and rights. State constitutions often reflect the federal Constitution and specify additional (but never fewer) freedoms and rights. Considering the *Norton* case and federal guidelines on employment of homosexuals it would seem that state governments would also be enjoined not to discriminate against homosexuals in state employment. But this is not always the case. For example, in 1981 a Texas federal district court upheld the right of the Dallas Police Department to refuse to hire an openly gay man to work in its property room (*Childers v. Dallas Police Department*). The court believed there were legitimate doubts that a homosexual could develop the trust and respect of the other personnel with whom he needed to work.

Lesbians and gay men who work in public schools have faced an uphill battle to maintain their jobs and be open about their sexuality. Until recently, homosexuality was automatically deemed immoral, particularly in states with sex statutes. Teachers, in general, were held to a higher moral standard than people in other occupations. Thus, lesbian or gay teachers were automatically considered to be immoral and denied employment or terminated when found out. Even in states that have antidiscrimination statutes based on sexual orientation, the myth that gay people molest and recruit children make lesbian and gay teachers susceptible to dismissal and discrimination. (See also **Child Molestation Stereotype; Criminal Law; Sodomy; Stereotypes**.)

EMPLOYMENT BENEFITS

Employment benefits include "soft" benefits such as bereavement and sick leave, relocation benefits, and parental leave, and "hard" benefits such as general health and dental insurance coverage, life insurance, long-term care, and day care. Many companies have implemented domestic partnership programs to extend employment benefits that have traditionally been reserved for married couples to same-sex couples. This is done in recognition of fairness toward employees and as a tool to attract and retain employees. In the private sector, employment benefits for lesbian and gay employees are completely discretionary. In general, health benefits, as part of employment benefits, may be denied to partners of unmarried, or gay or lesbian employees (*Hinman v. Department of Personnel Administration*). (See also **Domestic Partnership**.)

ANTIGAY BEHAVIORS WITHIN THE WORKPLACE

There is wide variance in the level of heterosexism and homophobia that is legally allowed in businesses throughout the United States. In some states, it is perfectly legal to terminate gay or lesbian employees. Other states and some businesses strive to make the workplace safe for all people. Probably the strongest weapons against such discriminatory behaviors are **sexual harassment** laws. Supervisors who make antigay remarks, employees who bash gay or lesbian coworkers or customers, and customers who are abusive toward lesbian and gay employees engage in behaviors that create a hostile environment and that may constitute sexual harassment. Thus, complaints could be filed with the **Equal Employment Opportunity Commission (EEOC)**, and with the appropriate agency in those states with protective laws. (See also **Discrimination against Customers**.)

Some court decisions have held that **Title VII** of the Civil Rights Act of 1964 also protects job applicants and employees from discrimination based upon sexual orientation, whereas the courts have not. Thus, persons who feel they have been discriminated against because of their sexual orientation should focus on this act as part of their EEOC complaint.

JOB APPLICANT SELECTION

Sexual orientation has not yet received a protected suspect class status with the federal government. However, through presidential order and various state ordinances, most lesbian and gay employees are now covered by some kind of antidiscrimination policy. Employers are encouraged to treat sexual orientation as they would any other protected class during the job applicant selection. Employers should not ask any question that may elicit an applicant's sexual orientation, including questions about marital status. If such information is revealed during the application process, hiring decisions should not be made based upon this information.

TRAINING

Businesses have professional reasons for conducting diversity training for employees. Sometimes employees object to training related to homosexuality on religious grounds. They may refuse to attend training programs on lesbian and gay issues and claim that their First Amendment right of freedom of religion is violated. Courts have upheld the right of businesses to require all employees to attend such training programs, even training that is controversial, such as sexual orientation training, as long as there are legitimate business reasons for the training. (See also **Diversity Training**.)

DRESS CODES

Employers can impose dress and grooming codes in the workplace. However, the rules should bear some relationship to the requirements of the job. The imposition of dress codes can disadvantage people who do not or cannot conform to gender roles—such as transsexual or intersexed people. (See also **Dress and Grooming Codes**.)

AIDS/DISABILITY IN THE WORKPLACE

A 1987 U.S. Supreme Court decision listed three factors that could be used to determine whether an employee can be refused a job or terminated because of any contagious disease (including **AIDS**):

1. The nature, duration, and severity of the risk.
2. The potential harm to others.
3. The probability of transmission.

Although AIDS scores high on the first two of these factors, the probability of transmission in the workplace is extremely small. As such, the **Americans with Disabilities Act (ADA)** specifically included persons with AIDS as "qualified disabled individuals" and afforded them all the law's protections against discrimination in employment.

However, the ADA has different requirements concerning food-handling jobs (meat packer, cook, waiter, waitress, etc.). Here, an employer may refuse to hire someone with a communicable disease whose job involves handling food. The employer does not determine which diseases are communicable. The federal secretary of health and human services issues a list that is updated yearly. Current employees who contract a communicable disease should be offered the accommodation of reassignment to an alternative position that does not involve the handling of food. Most states prohibit involuntary AIDS testing or the use of such tests to affect employment decisions.

CONDUCT

There are no broadly applicable laws that specify generally acceptable workplace conduct. Instead, there are a patchwork of laws and court decisions that limit specific conduct. For example, the U.S. Supreme Court went out of its way in the same-sex sexual harassment case *Oncale v. Sundowner Offshore Services, Inc.* to say that these laws were never intended to be used to construct "general civility" codes in the workplace, yet at the same time, expanded the logic used in opposite-sex sexual harassment laws to include same-sex situations.

But there are some cracks in the wall of gender conduct conformity. In 1989 the U.S. Supreme Court dealt with a woman who did not conform to traditional feminine norms (*Price Waterhouse v. Hopkins*). Ann Hopkins was a successful senior manager and a candidate for partnership at Price Waterhouse. When her nomination came up, many partners at Price Waterhouse reacted negatively and accused her of being "macho," saying that she "overcompensated for being a woman," and added that she needed to take a "course in charm school." To improve her chances of becoming a partner, she was told to "walk more femininely, talk more femininely, dress more femininely, wear make-up, have her hair styled, and wear jewelry." Hopkins sued and prevailed. The Court stated:

> An employer who objects to aggressiveness in women but whose positions require this trait places women in an intolerable and impermissible Catch 22: out of a job if they behave aggressively and out of a job if they do not. Title VII lifts women out of this bind. . . . She had proved discriminatory input into the decisional process, and had proved that participants in the process considered her failure to conform to the stereotypes credited by a number of the decisionmakers had been a substantial factor in the decision. (18–34)

The First Amendment guarantees freedoms of speech, but employers have consistently terminated employees who answer coworkers' questions about homosexuality. Businesses seem to be in a tug-of-war with employees concerning dress codes, language usage, and personal interactions. The terms "appropriate" or "professional" are often tied to conduct, yet are never specified in employee handbooks or in the law. Perhaps what is considered appropriate or professional will be defined through years of litigation and through default by what is not specified.

COMING OUT AT WORK

A number of studies have shown that the more a person is open about his or her sexuality, the greater is his or her psychological adjustment and well-being (Cain 1990; Cass 1979).

The social environment of the workplace has been shown to be related to employee job satisfaction in a number of studies (Andrisani and Shapiro 1978; Crosby 1982; Repetti and Cosmas 1991). Furthermore, researchers have found that lesbians' and gay males' reported levels of satisfaction with coworkers is directly related to their own openness in the workplace (Ellis and Riggle 1995). Consistent with other research on being open and life satisfaction, Ellis and Riggle found that openness at work and satisfaction with coworkers were positively related to lesbians' and gay males' overall satisfaction with life.

Thus, we see that lesbians, gay males, and bisexuals, and transgendered, transsexual, and intersexed people obtain social acceptance and equality by being open about their personal lives. This supports feelings of self-worth. Being open at work fosters greater satisfaction about work.

These are important findings for businesses. By making the work environment safe for lesbians, gay males, and bisexuals, and transgendered, transsexual, and intersexed people, employers can ensure that tensions are reduced for all, that workers feel better working together, that the potential for discrimination complaints is reduced, and that workers are more productive. It is to everyone's benefit to reduce and eliminate bias and prejudice.

References

Andrisani, P. J., and M. B. Shapiro. 1978. "Women's Attitudes toward Their Jobs: Some Longitudinal Data on a National Sample." *Personnel Psychology* 31: 15–34.

Cain, R. 1990. "Stigma Management and Gay Identity Development." *Social Work* 36(1): 67–73.

Cass, V. 1979. "Homosexual Identity Formation: A Theoretical Model." *Journal of Homosexuality* 4(3): 219–235.

Civil Service Bulletin. 1973. (21 December). Quoted in *Aston v. Civiletti*, 613 F.2d 923, 927 (D.C. Cir. 1979).

Crosby, R. 1982. *Relative Deprivation and Working Women*. New York: Oxford University Press.

Ellis, A. L., and E. D. B. Riggle. 1995. "The Relation of Job Satisfaction and

Degree of Openness about One's Sexual Orientation for Lesbians and Gay Men." *Journal of Homosexuality* 30(2): 75–85.

Repetti, R. L., and K. A. Cosmas. 1991. "The Quality of the Social Environment at Work and Job Satisfaction." *Journal of Applied Social Psychology* 21: 840–854.

EQUAL ACCESS ACT (EAA) The Equal Access Act (EAA), passed by Congress in 1984, clearly specified that all student groups must be allowed access to federally funded public secondary schools. The debate in Congress demonstrated that lesbian and gay student groups were considered a possibility and that they were to be given access to public schools equally with other groups. The bill, in its original form, addressed only the problem of schools barring religious groups. The bill was amended to include all extracurricular groups without preference. Debate in Congress showed an understanding that: (1) high school students are sophisticated enough to understand that having equal access does not imply governmental support or encouragement for a particular religion or thought; (2) an open policy does not turn schools into "battlegrounds for souls"; (3) schools may try to thwart the limited open forum aspect, but evaluation of their attempt to bypass the EAA will be conducted upon a review of their actions; and (4) claims by schools that "hecklers" would give schools the right to veto a particular group would be unacceptable. As Senator Denton stated:

> Can students be prohibited from expressing their views if those who hold opposing views become angry and boisterous? No. . . . Can school officials keep students from forming an after-school club having a dissident point of view? No. . . . Can the school prevent students from inviting a speaker to their club meeting because he or she is too controversial? No. (130 Cong. Rec. 19211–52)

Schools cannot deny equal access to students who wish to conduct a meeting if the reason for the denial is objection to the speech of the meeting. The EAA is triggered when secondary public schools that receive federal financial assistance offer a "limited open forum." A "limited open forum" is created when a school provides access to any (even just one) "noncurriculum-related student group to meet on school premises during non-instructional time" (Equal Access Act § b). The EAA does not define "noncurriculum-related student group," but the U.S. Supreme Court found in *Board of Education of Westside Community School v. Mergens* that Congress intended the act to have a reading and a low threshold for triggering its requirements. The justices concluded that the EAA is triggered if any student group is allowed access that is not directly related to the body of courses offered by the school.

The *Mergens* Court found four factors that defined "directly related":

1. The subject matter of the group is actually taught, or will soon be taught, in a regularly offered course;
2. The subject matter of the group concerns the body of courses as a whole;
3. Participation in the group is required for a particular course; or
4. Participation in the group results in academic credit.

Thus, the connection to the curriculum must be strong.

A number of clubs have not triggered the EAA. These include the French club, student government, school band, vocational clubs, and computer clubs (with some limits). Clubs that courts have determined to be noncurriculum related and, therefore, trigger the EAA have included a scuba diving club, chess clubs, the Peer Advocates (a service group with special education classes), the Key Club (a civic service club), the Pep Club, the Girls' Club, ski clubs, bowling clubs, the Special Kiwanis Youth Club, international clubs, varsity clubs, minority student unions, dance squads, and the Future Business Leaders of America.

A number of strategies have been attempted to circumvent the EAA:

- A school claimed that all clubs were school sponsored, not "student initiated," and, therefore, that the EAA did not apply. In *Pope v. East Brunswick Board of Education* the Third Circuit Court of Appeals found that the requirement of "student initiation" is not in that part of the statute that sets forth what causes the act to apply to a school. Thus, such a ploy does not circumvent the EAA.
- A school attempted to restrict student groups meeting during lunchtime. The Ninth Circuit Court of Appeals in *Ceniceros v. Board of Trustees of the San Diego Unified School District* determined that lunch time was "noninstructional time" and if one group was allowed to meet at lunchtime, then all groups must be allowed the same access.
- Students at one school attempted to distribute religious materials to other students on one occasion. One court found that the EAA does not apply to this situation because a one-time effort does not constitute a "meeting."

(See also **School Programs for Lesbian and Gay Students.**)

EQUAL EMPLOYMENT OPPORTUNITY COMMISSION (EEOC) The mission of the U.S. Equal Employment Opportunity Commission (EEOC) is to promote equal opportunity in employment through administrative and judicial enforcement of the federal civil rights laws and through education and technical assistance.

STATUTORY AUTHORITY

The EEOC was established by Title VII of the Civil Rights Act of 1964. It began operating on July 2, 1965. The EEOC enforces the principal federal statutes prohibiting discrimination in employment, including the following:

1. Title VII of the Civil Rights Act of 1964. This law prohibits discrimination in employment based on race, color, religion, sex, or national origin.
2. Age Discrimination in Employment Act (ADEA) of 1967. This law prohibits discrimination in employment against individuals who are forty years of age and older.
3. Equal Pay Act (EPA) of 1963. This law prohibits discrimination on the basis of gender in compensation for substantially similar work under similar conditions.
4. Title I of the **Americans with Disabilities Act (ADA)** of 1990. This law prohibits discrimination in employment on the basis of disability in both the public and private sector, excluding the federal government.
5. Civil Rights Act of 1991. This law includes provisions for monetary damages in cases of intentional discrimination and clarifies provisions regarding disparate impact actions.
6. Section 501 of the Rehabilitation Act of 1973. This law prohibits discrimination in employment against federal employees with disabilities.

EEOC ENFORCEMENT ACTIVITIES

Individuals who believe they have been discriminated against in employment begin by filing administrative charges at either EEOC headquarters or at one of the agency's fifty field offices found throughout the United States. In addition to members of the general public, the agency's commissioners may also initiate charges that the law has been violated. The EEOC conducts an investigation. If it is determined that there is "reasonable cause" to believe that discrimination occurred, the agency must then seek to conciliate the charge to reach a voluntary resolution between the charging party and the respondent. If conciliation fails, a "notice of right to sue" is issued by the EEOC that enables the charging party to bring an individual action in court. Also, the EEOC may sue in federal court if conciliation is not reached.

Sexual orientation, transsexualism, transgenderism, and intersex are categories not covered by the EEOC. However, particular instances of antigay discrimination can sometimes be recast as gender or disability discrimination and complaints can be successful. (See also **Appendix B**: **Resources**.)

F

FAMILY Throughout the world the concept of the family has changed considerably since World War II. In the United States a majority of households are comprised of married couples. However, fewer than half these families take the form of the nuclear family—that is, the working father, home-based mother, and children. Approximately one-fourth of all family households consist of children being raised by a single parent. In addition, the average American marriage lasts 9.6 years, not a lifetime, and 24 percent of all American households consist of people living alone (Hunter 1991; U.S. Bureau of the Census 1990). Overall, "the majority of Americans will spend more of their lifetimes outside, rather than as part of, married-couple households" (Hunter, Michaelson, and Stoddard 1992, 74). The traditional family model has created a body of law and business practices that favors married couples and thus discriminates against unmarried couples.

There is no general consensus as to what constitutes a family. Likewise, family law (also called domestic relations) is equally vague in its definitions of family. Mostly state laws, not federal statutes, govern family law. For example, all states have laws governing marriage. The federal government was not involved with marriage until the recent passage of the **Defense of Marriage Act (DOMA).** Even so, there are over 2,000 references to family in federal law—in everything from immigration, income tax, social welfare, education, agriculture, national security, student loan, and highway safety laws (Robson 1997, 64).

Family law varies from state to state and within states. For example, how family is defined at the state level for purposes of adoption, marriage, and other matters can be very different than how family is defined by local zoning ordinances or welfare fraud statutes. The thousands of federal and state laws, ordinances, and regulations that make reference to family make it evident how important family is to our society.

The term *family* is not in the U.S. Constitution. However, courts have declared that there is a "zone of privacy protecting the family from government intrusion" (Robson 1997, 64). This has developed from court interpretations of the due process clauses of the Fifth and Fourteenth Amendments that recognize family autonomy. It is this same principle of autonomy used by lesbians and gay men to challenge judicial discrimination. At the same time that courts provide protection to the family from undue government interference, the family is of such importance to society that it is subjected to immense regulation.

Lesbians, gay men, and bisexuals, and transgendered, transsexual, and intersexed people have always formed and continue to form families. Because of heterosexist norms, there are great challenges in forming and maintaining relationships that are considered nontraditional.

SAME-SEX COUPLES

The legal definition of what constitutes families has broadened as society has accepted familial structures that are not forms of patriarchy. In 1977 the U.S. Supreme Court recognized constitutional protections to extended families—making *Moore v. City of East Cleveland* an important first step toward recognizing nonnuclear family structures. However, legislatures and courts seem unwilling to grant family status to lesbian or gay male couples.

Not extending legal status to lesbian or gay male couples, regardless of how long couples have been together, has some of the following consequences:

- Denial of workers' compensation or inability to assume the housing lease upon the death of a life partner;
- Having wills and trusts between partners challenged in court;
- Custody disputes concerning children of the relationship;
- Not receiving paid leave from employers when grieving the death of a spouse;
- Not being recognized by property laws;
- Not being able to file joint tax returns and not inheriting from one's spouse automatically under probate laws;
- Not sharing health, auto, and homeowners' insurance policies at reduced rates;
- Not having immediate access to one's loved ones in case of accident or emergency.

Although the laws regulating marriage may seem evenhanded in their treatment of homosexual and heterosexual relationships, the fact that homosexuals cannot marry makes the laws inherently discriminatory. At least 1,049 federal laws and regulations touch upon marital status, and thus give special rights to heterosexuals (Bedrick 1997). In a review of marriage laws in the state of Vermont conducted when the Vermont state supreme court ordered that gay relationships be given all rights afforded heterosexual marriage, it was discovered that 870 rights and responsibilities were triggered by legal marriage (Partners Task Force for Gay and Lesbian Couples 2000).

MARRIAGE AND DOMESTIC PARTNERSHIPS

Lesbian, gay male, and transgendered couples have used a number of legal strategies to try to obtain the same rights and responsibilities afforded partners in heterosexual marriage. Same-sex marriages are consistently refused legal recognition by every state in the union. In 1996 a Hawaii trial court ruled that the ban on same-sex marriage violated the equal protection clause of its constitution and that the state had failed to offer a "compelling" reason for maintaining the discriminatory practice. This was the first such ruling in the United States. The court reasoned that Hawaii's constitutional ban on sex discrimination was similar to antidiscrimination laws based on race. Just as laws banning marriages between people of different races violated antidiscrimination laws based on race, laws banning same-sex marriages violated antidiscrimination laws based on sex. (For greater details and legal arguments, see also **Marriage**.)

The furor originating from Hawaii's decision over the prospect of same-sex marriage resulted in the federal government passing the Defense of Marriage Act (DOMA), and many states passed similar legislation to outlaw same-sex marriages. Hawaii ultimately passed a constitutional amendment that banned same-sex marriage and that stopped its supreme court from making a final determination.

In December 1999 the Vermont Supreme Court unanimously ruled in ***Baker v. Vermont*** that same-sex couples are entitled to the same protections and benefits provided through state law for opposite-sex couples. Immediately, calls were made to impeach the judges who made the ruling. The state legislature began the process to implement the court decision. Some options they considered were to allow same-sex marriages, or to create a new category known as "civil unions." The Vermont legislature chose to create civil unions, but it is unsure how "equal" will be their status with traditional marriage.

Some gays and lesbians have turned to "Holy Unions" to sanctify their association, but these are not legal marriages recognized by the state (*Reynolds v. United States*).

Domestic partnerships are another way lesbians and gay men have tried to obtain some of the same rights afforded heterosexual marriages. Domestic partnerships are ordinances passed by some cities, municipalities, and states to help give legal recognition to nonmarried committed couples. These ordinances provide some, but not all, of the rights and responsibilities found in marriage. Although lesbians and gays applaud the effort to create domestic partnerships, ultimately it is demeaning to accept partial, instead of full, marriage status.

PRIVATE LAW BENEFITS

There are many ways in which same-sex couples and their families are treated differently by the law from opposite-sex married couples. These include policies regarding housing, workers' compensation, and tort claims.

Housing

Many cities have enacted zoning ordinances that restrict public housing to "families." Whether it is the sale of a home or rental units, typical ordinances define families only along blood or legal lines (Partners Task Force for Lesbian and Gay Couples 2000). The courts have generally accepted these restrictions and have been unwilling to extend the concept of family to unmarried couples—of either opposite-sex (*City of Ladue v. Horn*) or same-sex partners.

Rent control and stabilization are other areas in which same-sex couples are treated differently from married couples. Landlords have typically held a narrow view about who qualifies as a successor to a tenant who has died. Courts usually agree and have held that successorship rules do not apply to lesbian or gay life partners (*Braschi v. Stahl Associates Co.*). In general, antidiscrimination statutes are the only means available for lesbians and gay men to ensure access and fairness in obtaining housing. (See also **Public Accommodations**.)

Workers' Compensation

Most workers' compensation programs provide benefits for the "dependents" of covered employees. These programs are designed to compensate employees and their dependents when employees are severely injured or killed. They also act as a deterrent to employers engaging in harmful work practices ("*Donovan v. County of Los Angeles . . .*" 2000). The persons entitled to these programs are referred to in different statutes as "dependents," "family or household," "next of kin," or "legal beneficiaries." However, courts have rarely extended these benefits to cohabitants who are not related by law or by blood. As such, virtually all same-sex survivors of life partners who have been severely injured or killed on the job do not receive benefits from workers' compensation plans.

Tort Claims

Torts are claims of injury caused by the wrongful actions of another. Although courts have been reluctant to allow compensation for emotional injury, some courts have recognized that cases of extreme violence and emotional shock warrant tort recovery. A number of opposite-sex partners, but no same-sex partners, have succeeded in such actions (see, e.g., *Bulloch v. United States*). In *Elden v. Sheldon,* an unmarried heterosexual partner was denied damages for negligent infliction of emotional stress or loss. The court gave three reasons for the denial: (1) such cases needed to be addressed case by case to determine which relationships qualify; (2) clear lines of recovery needed to be established so as not to be unreasonably burdensome; and (3) the state had an interest in promoting traditional marriage.

It has been argued that these three reasons are insufficient cause for not extending tort laws to same-sex couples. First, tort laws already require courts to define and interpret standards to determine who qualifies for compensation and who does not. Also, standards already exist to help courts differentiate family-like relationships from tangential ones. Second, including lesbians and gay men in tort recovery does not expose defendants to unlimited liability. Tort laws already require plaintiffs to show why a duty for due care exists and to show that the relationship was sufficiently close to warrant recovery. Third, granting tort claims to lesbian and gay couples would not adversely affect the promotion of traditional marriage (*Dillon v. Legg*).

OTHER STRATEGIES FOR SAME-SEX COUPLES

A number of other strategies have been used by same-sex couples to try to define the legal status of their relationships:

- Property ownership. Even though it would seem that nonmarried couples should be able to buy property together when it is their primary residence, there have been court cases in which lesbian or gay male couples have not had the same degree of control over their property as have heterosexual couples (*Harvard Law Review* staff 1990, 113, n. 134). Joint tenancy is a legal arrangement some states allow that automatically transfers property ownership to the surviving tenant. Joint tenancy is not restricted to married couples or opposite-sex couples.
- Beneficiary designations. Sometimes lesbian and gay couples designate their life partners as the beneficiaries of life insurance and related policies. These have occasionally not held up in court when contested by surviving blood relatives.
- Powers of attorney and "durable" powers of attorney. Some lesbians and gay males have designated their life partners as their agents, granting them powers of attorney that enable them to engage in specific acts (such as maintaining finances and making medical decisions). If this device is to be used in the event that

one of the partners becomes incapacitated, it is known as a "durable" power of attorney. Only a few states and jurisdictions recognize powers of attorney between nonmarried members of a couple. In particular, when life and death decisions concerning medical services are involved, courts often ignore these legal instruments and defer to decisions by legal or blood relatives.

- Reciprocal wills. Using reciprocal **wills** to assign property to each other has been a fairly successful technique for the partners in a same-sex couple. However, relatives of the deceased have sometimes been successful in contesting these wills. They may claim that the will was written by the deceased while under undue influence. As a result, some same-sex couples have added a "no-contest" provision to their wills. This provision attempts to preclude others from contesting the will by completely cutting them out of the will if they attempt to contest its provisions. Courts have sometimes ignored the "no-contest" provision and ruled in favor of relatives of the deceased. Without a will between homosexual partners, the estate is distributed to the parents of the deceased, or if they are not living, to brothers, sisters, nieces, and nephews. If none of the deceased's relatives are alive, the property is forfeited to the state (*Max v. McLynn*).

Another technique is to create a revocable trust. These are virtually impossible to overturn, yet convey much of the same protection as wills.

- Trusts. When one person (the trustor) has a fiduciary relationship with another (the trustee) in which the trustor holds the property of the trustee, a trust has been formed. The trustor has the responsibility to keep or use the property to benefit the trustee. Courts have upheld these trusts between two adults only when there is evidence of mental or physical incapacitation on the part of the trustee. Also, it is demeaning to the trustee to place this kind of power in the hands of someone else when there is no need to do so.
- Contracts. Courts have approved the use of contracts for unmarried heterosexual couples as a way to define how property is owned and the mutual obligations between them (see, e.g., *Marvin v. Marvin*). However, these contracts must not include requirements for engaging in sex, otherwise they could be construed to be contracts for prostitution. Rarely have similar contracts been enforced between same-sex couples. However, in *Whorton v. Dillingham*, the court recognized that agreements

between same-sex couples are indistinguishable from opposite-sex couples and should, therefore, be similarly enforced.

- Adoptions. Some lesbian and gay male couples have attempted to adopt each other as a means of establishing a legal family. Because adoptions become final the moment they are approved, they provide a more secure mechanism for the delineation of property. Courts, in general, view adoption as a process for providing for the welfare of a child, which establishes a parent-child relationship. Therefore, adult-**adult adoptions** are usually frowned upon by the courts and are not recognized unless one of the adults is a ward of the state or in need of extensive support due to medical or mental disability. Few jurisdictions have allowed same-sex adult-adult adoptions.

CHILD CUSTODY AND VISITATION RIGHTS

Until recently, few lesbian and gay parents—even those already separated or divorced—were willing to reveal their homosexuality for fear they would jeopardize their rights as parents. The American courts and child welfare agencies have been totally unsympathetic to gays and lesbians. In the central and southern sections of the United States, homosexuality is a major impediment in child custody cases; on the east and west coasts there is greater acceptance of lesbian and gay parents. Some states have created irrefutable presumptions against granting custody to lesbian or gay parents (see, e.g., *Roe v. Roe; N.K.M. v. L.E.M.*). Other states require lesbian or gay parents to prove that their sexual orientation will not harm the child (see, e.g., *Constant A. v. Paul C.A.*). Many other states have reversed this burden of proof, requiring instead that the party opposing custody prove that the lesbian or gay parent's sexual orientation would harm the child.

In a handful of cases, grandparents, aunts, uncles, other relatives, and even the state, have successfully challenged a lesbian or gay parent's right to custody (see, e.g., *Chaffin v. Frye; Roberts v. Roberts; In re Holt*). Generally speaking, the law awards custody to the natural parent (see, e.g., *Gerald & Margaret D. v. Peggy R.; Bezio v. Patenaude; Albright v. Commonwealth ex rel. Fetters; People v. Brown*). A lesbian or a gay man who is not the natural parent and is no longer in a same-sex relationship with the natural parent usually cannot obtain custody or visitation rights. (See also **Child Custody and Visitation Rights**.)

CHILD ADOPTION AND FOSTER CARE

A few states have allowed gays and lesbians to adopt children, but only if the court finds that the best interests of the child will be served by the adoption. Other states, such as Utah, have explicit statutes against same-sex couples adopting children. A lesbian or gay man can qualify as a foster parent in some states. In general, state agencies have been more reluctant to place children with gay males than with lesbians. For example, in *Big Brothers, Inc. v. Minneapolis Commission on Civil Rights,* a nonprofit corporation providing services to boys without fathers may require adult volunteers to disclose sexual orientation and may communicate that information to the boy's family, even though the city has an antidiscrimination ordinance covering gay people (Waldron 1979). (See also **Child Adoption and Foster Care**.)

Procreation and Parenting

Homosexuals are just as capable of conceiving children as are heterosexuals and bisexuals. Some gay men and many lesbian couples are choosing to have children within their families. However, there are a number of legal barriers that may block their efforts. **Artificial insemination** (semen introduced into a woman's uterus by means other than sexual intercourse), in vitro fertilizations (eggs fertilized outside the woman's body, then introduced into her uterus), and surrogate motherhood (one woman used to carry the fertilized egg of another couple) are sometimes legally restricted from use by single people or same-sex couples. For example, fornication statutes may inhibit physicians from performing artificial insemination in unmarried women (Perkoff 1985; Strong and Schinfeld 1984). The U.S. Supreme Court in *Eisenstadt v. Baird* concluded that the "decision whether to bear or beget a child" is a constitutionally protected right of women. Thus, the fornication statutes rarely inhibit physicians from performing artificial inseminations.

For gay men there are different challenges. Establishing parental rights overshadows access to reproductive techniques. A man can always donate sperm. The problem is finding a woman with whom he can establish legal rights and responsibilities related to their child. If the child is conceived through intercourse, the father usually has equal rights and responsibilities regardless of whether they are married.

If the child is conceived through artificial insemination, state law determines the father's rights. Of the states that have artificial insemination regulations, few have detailed the rights of the sperm donor in the case of unmarried couples. Some states eliminate donor paternity rights regardless of whether the insemination takes place at home or in a physician's office. For those states that do not regulate artificial insemination, there are few cases to determine paternity rights—and these are conflicting and confounded by the method used. The best way to proceed, although not foolproof, is for the gay man and woman to form a contract detailing their rights and responsibilities with regards to the child.

Surrogacy arrangements allow lesbian or gay male couples to arrange for a woman outside their relationship to carry their baby and then relinquish all rights after the baby is born. Some states have enacted statutes that make any arrangements for paid surrogacy illegal (Gostin 1988). Likewise other states have linked paid surrogacy with baby selling and have deemed such contracts illegal. Couples contemplating a paid surrogacy service should contact a local lawyer for guidance.

Parents can relinquish their claims to a child. This can be achieved by allowing the child to be adopted by others, or, in some states, relinquishing all parental rights to a child independent of an adoption. Paid surrogacy usually includes a contract in which the birth mother agrees to give up all rights to the child. However, such agreements may be revoked by the surrogate mother up until the birth of the child.

Similarly, men can give up their parental rights in favor of lesbians with whom they have fathered a child. As long as the woman is willing to accept full financial and other responsibilities, courts have recognized contracts in which the donor man has terminated all parental rights. However, there are a few states in which preconception contracts with single women or lesbian couples are unenforceable. In these states, men may be unwilling to participate in fathering children because of possible future parental obligations.

Only the biological parent is automatically the legal parent of a child. Within same-sex couples, the nonbiological parent has no legal rights with respect to the child. If this partner wants to be a coparent, he or she must use one of a number of strategies. The coparent may be able to adopt the child. Care must be taken that by adoption, the coparent does not extinguish the birth parent's rights. This is similar to a stepparent adoption and has been recognized in a number of states for same-sex couples. However, in some states the procedures for stepparent adoption are applicable for married couples only.

Another strategy is for the coparent to claim custody of the child under the "psychological parent" theory if the birth parent dies or the couple separates. Here it is claimed that the person who provides for the child on a continuing day-to-day basis fulfills the child's psychological need for a parent. As such, the coparent assumes the role of the parent regardless of the biological relationship with the child (Goldstein, Freud, and Solnit 1973, 98). A better approach is for the birth parent to designate the coparent as testamentary guardian of the child. If the birth parent should die, the coparent then becomes the child's guardian.

In the past, courts have been reluctant to allow same-sex couples to make these coparent arrangements. It was sometimes argued that being brought up in a lesbian or gay male household would make a child homosexual. This myth has been shown to be false many times (Bozett 1993; Goodman 1977). Some courts have come to realize that the child is best served if there are two parents to see to his or her safety and needs. (See also **Child Adoption and Foster Care**.)

References

Bedrick, B. R. 1997. "Report on The Defense of Marriage Act." Government Accounting Office website: www.gao.gov (31 January 1997).

Bozett, F. W. 1993. "Gay Fathers: A Review of the Literature." In *Psychological Perspectives on Lesbian and Gay Male Experiences,* edited by L. D. Garnets and D. C. Kimmel. New York: Columbia University Press.

"*Donovan v. County of Los Angeles and State Compensation Insurance Fund:* California's Recognition of Homosexuals' Dependency Status in Actions for Workers' Compensation Death Benefits." 1986. *Journal of Contemporary Law* 12(151): 159–160.

Goldstein, J., A. Freud, and A. Solnit. 1973. *Beyond the Best Interests of the Child.* New York: Free Press.

Goodman, B. 1977. *The Lesbian: A Celebration of Difference.* East Haven, CT: Out & Out Books.

Gostin, L. 1988. "Forum on Surrogate Motherhood." *Law, Medicine and Health Care* 16(1–2): 5–6.

Harvard Law Review staff. 1990. *Sexual Orientation and the Law.* Cambridge, MA: Harvard University Press.

Hunter, N. D. 1991. Marriage, Law, and Gender: A Feminist Inquiry. *Journal of Law and Sexuality* 1: 19.

Hunter, N. D., S. E. Michaelson, and T. B. Stoddard. 1992. *The Rights of Lesbians and Gay Men: The Basic ACLU Guide to a Gay Person's Rights.* 3d ed. Carbondale and Edwardsville, IL: Southern Illinois University Press.

Partners Task Force for Gay and Lesbian Couples. 2000. *What Rights Come with Legal Marriage?* Seattle, WA: Partners Task Force for Gay and Lesbian Couples.

Perkoff, G. T. 1985. "Artificial Insemination in a Lesbian: A Case Analysis." *Archives of Internal Medicine* 145(3): 527–532.

Robson, R. 1997. *Gay Men, Lesbians, and the Law.* New York: Chelsea House Publishers.

Strong, C., and J. Schinfeld. 1984. "The Single Woman and Artificial Insemination by Donor." *Journal of Reproductive Medicine* 29(5): 293–299.

U.S. Bureau of the Census. 1990. "Marital Status and Living Arrangements: March 1989." In *Current Population Reports, Population Characteristics Series* P-20, No. 445. Washington, DC: Bureau of the Census.

Waldron, M. 1979. "Homosexual Foster Children Sent to Lesbian Homes." *New York Times* (27 November 1979): B2.

FEDERAL EMPLOYMENT NONDISCRIMINATION ORDER On May 28, 1998, President Clinton signed Executive Order 13087 that amended Section 1 of Executive Order 11478 (1969). The order reaffirmed the executive branch's longstanding internal policy that prohibits discrimination based upon sexual orientation within executive branch civilian employment. This was the first time a specific directive from any president prohibited discrimination based on sexual orientation. The order did not create any additional enforcement rights, such as the ability to proceed before the **Equal Employment Opportunity Commission (EEOC),** nor did it authorize **affirmative action** programs.

FULL FAITH AND CREDIT CLAUSE The U.S. Constitution, Article IV, Section 1, reads: "Full Faith and Credit shall be given in each State to the public Acts, Records, and judicial Proceedings of every other State." This has been interpreted to mean that each state must treat the judgment of a court in another state as the judgment would be treated in the state in which it was made. The clause is a "nationally unifying force" (*Magnolia Petroleum Co. v. White*) that recognizes that states are required to "sacrifice particular local powers as the price of membership in a federal system" of government (*Sherrer v. Sherrer*).

There are limits to the powers that the federal government can exert over states to accept another state's laws. Judgments of other states do not need to be respected if they are (1) "obnoxious" to the public policy of the state, or (2) if the state can show there are important, rather than merely legitimate, state interests in rejecting the other state's judgment. When courts are faced with competing state interests this becomes a choice of law.

Choice of law is a notoriously murky area. It is sometimes difficult to determine which state's laws apply to a particular situation. In general, the Supreme Court explained that "if a state has only an insignificant contact with the parties and the occurrence or transaction, application of its law is unconstitutional" (*Allstate Insurance Co. v. Hague,* 310–311). Further, courts have recognized that frequently the laws of one state and the contrary laws of another state may apply equally. Although one would think that the U.S. Supreme Court would have stepped in to help clear up the confusion over full faith and credit, this has not been the case. The Court believes such conflicts are "unavoidable" and has left it for each court to "determine for itself the extent to which the statute of one state may qualify or deny rights asserted under the statue of another" (*Allstate Insurance Co. v. Hague,* 547). The Court has decided that the alternative to this confusion is worse.

Marriage and divorce are two areas of full faith and credit that are fairly well developed legally. The state has a fundamental interest in marriage. If a couple marries in one state and lives in the same state, then only that state's laws apply in determining the validity of the marriage. In cases in which a couple marries in one state (state of celebration) but resides in another state (state of domicile), the laws from the states of celebration and domicile potentially apply, but no marriage laws from other states apply. In general, the laws of the state of celebration apply unless the marriage violates an important public policy of the state of domicile.

In those cases, the laws of the state of domicile apply and the marriage may not be valid.

It is important that a divorce granted in one state be recognized in other states so as to avoid the potential for bigamy. If a couple obtains a divorce decree from the state in which they both reside, the laws of that state apply and all other states will recognize the decree. If a couple obtains a divorce decree from a state in which neither of them resides, then the divorce will not be valid and all other states will not recognize the decree. Problems arise when a divorce is obtained from a state in which only one of the couple resides. Here courts have to determine if the decree-granting state was in fact the domicile of one of the couple. This may seem like a small difference in how marriage and divorce are evaluated, but it has radical implications for the enforcement of the federal **Defense of Marriage Act (DOMA)**.

The prospect of same-sex marriages has set off a storm of controversy nationwide. Confusion over the full faith and credit clause led Congress to enact the federal Defense of Marriage Act (DOMA). It was clear from the debate in Congress that there was no understanding of how the current system works. The DOMA (as well as legislation enacted in many states) defines marriage as being between one man and one woman, and allows states to not recognize same-sex marriages of couples who move within their borders. This was unnecessary because states already possessed this power. Legal theorists believe that when the federal DOMA is tested in court, it will be declared unconstitutional for a number of reasons.

G

GAY The preferred term for reference to a same-gender orientation is *gay*. Out of respect, a social group should be identified by the name that its members prefer. *Gay* rather than *homosexual* is the preferred term and is comparable to the distinction between *black* or *African American* and *Negro*. *Gay* is preferred to *homosexual* because homosexual implicitly emphasizes the sexual and diminishes the other aspects of gender orientation. Some people would like to see the word *homosexual* banished (Dynes 1985). Stylistically, *gay* is often paired with *straight*, meaning "heterosexual." Similarly, *homosexual* is paired with *heterosexual*. The history of the word *gay* is confused. It is thought that the word *gay* was used in eighteenth-century England to connote the conduct of a playboy. Later, in the nineteenth century, *gay* when applied to women came to mean "of loose morals; a prostitute." By the early twentieth century in the United States, the use of *gay* as applied to male homosexuals had been circulating and was first printed in 1933 in Noel Ersines's *Dictionary of Underworld and Prison Slang* as "geycat." English writer Peter Wildeblood (1955) defined *gay* as "an American euphemism for homosexual." (See also **Sexual Orientation**.)

References

Dynes, W. 1985. "Homolexis: A Historical and Cultural Lexicon of Homosexuality." *Gai Saber Monographs* 4. New York: The Scholarship Committee of the Gay Academic Union.

Ersine, N. 1933. *Dictionary of Underworld and Prison Slang*. Upland, IN: Freese.

GAY AGENDA It is often claimed that lesbians, gays, bisexual, and transgendered people are seeking "special rights." That is not true. As seen throughout this book and other resources, lesbians and gays are seeking protection for themselves as workers, homeowners, and citizens—rights that all other Americans have. These are not special rights, but rather equal rights. Unfortunately, the term *gay agenda* has been used to misinform the public and steer public opinion into believing that lesbians and gays are seeking legal rights over heterosexuals, **affirmative action**, or both. None of the national gay rights organizations, community services centers, college resource centers, or academic writers have ever made claims for special rights. (See also **Criminal Law**; **Family**.)

GAY BASHING

See **Hate Crimes**

GAY FATHERS Men who are gay and are involved in raising children are gay fathers. Frederick W. Bozett (1993) conducted a thorough review of academic literature concerning gay fathers. Although the samples and studies reviewed were nonrandom, small, and of primarily white, middle- to upper-class men with high levels of education, a few generalizations can be made concerning gay fathers and their unique situation.

A large percentage of gay fathers are married, or have once been married. Some of these men remain married because they: (1) believe there are no other alternatives; (2) are fully committed to their children; (3) believe their standard of living would decline; or (4) a combination of these reasons. Although gay fathers are involved in their traditional opposite-sex marriages, there often is much animosity and discord between partners. Coming out and forming same-sex relationships bring important psychological relief to the gay father.

Gay fathers usually describe their **family** backgrounds as generally positive. No differences have been found in the relationships between gay and nongay fathers and their parents. Gay men who father children are no more or less masculine than gay men who do not father children. On average, men who marry and then come out became aware of their homosexuality at a later age. Gay fathers seem to have greater difficulty in acknowledging their homosexuality and in telling their children that they are gay than do lesbian mothers. Also, gay African American men seem to have the greatest difficulty overall in telling their children of their homosexuality.

Having children still living at home makes coming out more difficult for gay fathers. Overall, most children do not react to or are tolerant and understanding of their fathers telling them of their sexual orientation. However, children seem to have greater difficulty in accepting a father's homosexuality than a mother's homosexuality. The earlier children are told of their father's homosexuality, the easier it is for them to accept and integrate it into their family model. Similarly, children seem to have few, if any, long-term problems with accepting their father's homosexuality.

Given that having a gay father does not adversely affect the emotional health of a family, it is discouraging that gay fathers more so than heterosexual fathers usually do not receive physical custody of their children.

Being gay is compatible with effective parenting. Studies show that gay fathers try harder to create stable home lives and positive relationships with their children than would be expected from traditional heterosexual parents. Contrary to stereotype, gay fathers make significant efforts to provide opposite-sex role models for their children and do not try to make their children into homosexuals. (See also **Adolescence; Lesbian Mothers**.)

Reference

Bozett, F. W. 1993. "Gay Fathers: A Review of the Literature." In *Psychological Perspectives on Lesbian and Gay Male Experiences,* edited by L. D. Garnets and D. C. Kimmel. New York: Columbia University Press.

GAY PANIC DEFENSE

See **Homosexual Panic Defense**

GENDER-MOTIVATED VIOLENCE ACT (GMVA)

This is a subsection of the federal Violence Against Women Act of 1994. Legislators and courts have often confused the concepts of sex, gender, and gender identity. (See also **Sexual Orientation**.) Until recently, courts have interpreted **Title VII** of the Civil Rights Act of 1964 as *not* applying to cases involving people between the sexes (**intersexed**) or transitioning from one sex to another (**transsexuals**).

Douglas Schwenk, a self-identified preoperative transsexual who went by the name of "Crystal" and dressed as a woman, received repeated unwanted sexual overtures from prison guard Robert Mitchell. Mitchell attempted to rape Crystal anally in her prison cell. She filed a federal lawsuit claiming violation of her civil rights under the Eighth Amendment ("cruel and unusual punishment") of the Constitution and the Gender-Motivated Violence Act (GMVA) (*Schwenk v. Hartford* [2000]).

Judge Stephen Reinhardt of the Ninth Circuit Court of Appeals concluded that Schwenk was protected under the Eighth Amendment because precedent had been set in prior transsexual prisoner cases (*Farmer v. Brennan*). He also rejected Mitchell's argument that the GMVA did not apply to the case because it was part of the Violence Against Women Act and Schwenk was a man. Reinhardt noted that members of Congress made statements that supported the interpretation of the GMVA as protecting all residents of the United States from gender-motivated violence.

Reinhardt went on to consider if "gender identity" came within the meaning of gender-motivated violence. Reinhardt reviewed the previous cases testing Title VII. He believed the limitations transsexuals faced in achieving standing to sue were effectively swept away by the Supreme Court's 1989 decision in *Price Waterhouse v. Hopkins*. In that case, a woman was denied a partnership in an accounting firm because she was perceived to be inadequately feminine in her appearance and behavior. The Supreme Court ruled that discrimination using sexual stereotypes about gender roles violated the ban on sex discrimination. Reinhardt found that the Supreme Court had, in fact, collapsed the concept of sex and gender into one broad category—gender identity.

Because Title VII had treated sex and gender separately, this was a groundbreaking conclusion. Reinhardt concluded that under Title VII, and, by extension, under the GMVA, discrimination or violence aimed at a person because of his or her gender identity would violate those statutes. In effect, this decision gives transsexuals and the issue of gender identity federal protection—something lesbians and gay men have failed to achieve.

Because Schwenk's case was brought on grounds of the Eighth Amendment and the GMVA, Reinhardt's discussion on Title VII is not technically binding, but it has alerted the courts under the Ninth Circuit that discrimination against transsexuals in employment and other areas may violate Title VII. Likewise, this decision makes it unnecessary to add "gender identity" to the Employment Nondiscrimination Act (ENDA) as it will already be covered under Title VII. It is expected that Mitchell's lawyers will appeal the decision and other judges will look closely at this controversial extension of Title VII. Also, this decision does not address people who do not conform to gender roles.

Hate Crimes Hate crimes encompass bias-motivated violence aimed at individuals because of their inherent characteristics or membership in particular demographic groups. Lesbians, gay men, the transgendered, or those perceived to be nonheterosexual are often the victims of hate crimes. Frequently referred to as *fag bashing* or *gay bashing,* hate crimes against nonheterosexuals are both commonplace and increasing in American society. The **homophobia** that is at the root of these acts of violence manifests itself not only at the individual level, but also at the institutional level, through the media, religious organizations, schools, scientific and medical associations, and the legal system.

American society is currently a patchwork quilt of conflicting laws and social mores. Almost one-third of the states still have sex statutes (often referred to as **sodomy** laws). These laws are rarely enforced; however, psychologically they function to intimidate gays and lesbians. At the same time, other states have reversed this historical tide of bias and instituted new laws that offer protection against hate crimes based on sexual orientation.

The civil rights movement helped to identify and propose solutions to the issue of hate crimes. Supervisor John Anson Ford of the Los Angeles County Commission on Human Relations was the first to use the term *hate crimes* in 1975. In 1988 sexual orientation was added to the hate crime statutes. In the *Hate Crime in Los Angeles County* report, hate crimes were defined as violent "acts directed at an individual, institution, or business expressly because of race, ethnicity, religion or sexual orientation."

Hate Crime Statistics Act

Much of the national awareness of hate crimes has come from the efforts of the Anti-Violence Project of the National Gay and Lesbian Task Force. In 1987 Connecticut became the first state to implement a hate crime statistics act. Later, in 1990, the U.S. Congress passed its Hate Crime Statistics Act. This act provided for the collection of statistics on the incidence of hate or bias-based crimes around the United States. It looked for crimes that "manifest evidence of prejudice based upon race, religion, sexual orientation, or ethnicity." Unfortunately, not all politicians were supportive of ending hate crimes. Jesse Helms effectively blocked passage of the federal Hate Crime Statistics Act in its first form in 1986 by claiming that "studying hate crimes against homosexuals is a crucial first step toward achieving homosexual rights and legitimacy in American society" (Yeoman 1996). Ultimately, he was overruled when the act passed in 1990.

The act included language in support of the family and specifically stated that the act was not intended to promote homosexuality. It also stated that "Nothing in this section creates a right to bring an action, including an action based on discrimination due to sexual orientation" (Robson 1997, 86). It is ironic that an act designed to assess the level of violence toward a stigmatized group would, itself, implicitly approve of discrimination against that group. Although the act contained these and other flaws, it was important because it focused attention on the national problem of antigay violence, provided a mechanism for determining the extent of the problem, marked the first time the term *sexual orientation* was included in any federal legislation, and was the first time openly gay men and lesbians were invited to the White House. Hopefully, the act will be modified in the future to address these problems and to include bisexual, transsexual, transgendered, and intersexed people.

Two Perspectives on Hate Crime Statutes

Two different perspectives concerning the creation and enforcement of hate crime statutes dominate discussion in the opening days of the twenty-first century. Some people believe some crimes are worse than others and, therefore, require special consideration. This "special model" is the approach taken by the Hate Crime Statistics Act and most hate crime statutes. Laws created using the special model impose greater penalties for crimes committed in which bias or hate is a major motivation. Thus, judges can impose stiffer fines and longer sentences for hate crimes that, for example, involve robbery, rather than for robbery itself. However, some lesbian and gay legal advisors argue against such a model. Instead, they propose a "neutral model" that requires rigorous enforcement of already existing criminal laws and penalties regardless of who the victim is. They argue that the primary problem facing lesbians and gays is the long history of courts showing leniency toward persons who commit crimes against nonheterosexuals or prosecutors who refuse to prosecute those who commit such crimes. Also, enacting hate crime laws possibly encroaches upon First Amendment rights to free speech. Lesbian and gay activists and legal thinkers understand the importance of free speech and are hesitant to impose limitations in this area for fear the limitations could be used against gay liberation.

HATE SPEECH

Hate crime statutes typically include restrictions on the use of language that intimidates, interferes, or oppresses another person. Determining when speech crosses over into criminalized hate is difficult. For example, Kenneth W. Rokicki of St. Charles, Illinois, did not like having his pizza handled by a homosexual employee of Pizza Hut. On previous visits to the restaurant, Rokicki complained loudly that there was a homosexual employed there. On October 20, 1995, he entered the restaurant and yelled "Mary," "faggot," and "Molly Homemaker" at the employee cutting his pizza, whereupon he pounded the counter and wagged his finger at the employee. The restaurant manager gave Rokicki his money back and asked him to leave. Rokicki left the restaurant and went to the South Elgin Police Department to complain because a homosexual was working at the restaurant. He wanted someone "normal" to touch his food. The restaurant employee who was threatened by Rokicki felt frightened for several days after the incident. Rokicki could have been charged with disorderly conduct, but instead, he was charged with the more serious hate crime. The courts agreed that Rokicki committed a hate crime. The court stated that "[t]he defendant is not being punished merely because he holds an unpopular view on homosexuality or because he expressed those views loudly or in a passionate manner, the defendant was charged with a hate crime because he allowed those beliefs to motivate unreasonable conduct" (*People of Illinois v. Rokicki*). Judges Lawrence D. Inglis and John J. Bowman concurred, saying that the "[d]efendant's conduct exceeded the bounds of spirited debate, and the First Amendment does not give him the right to harass or terrorize anyone" (Hanna 1999, 3).

Many **hate speech** statutes have been deemed unconstitutional due to their infringement on free speech guaranteed in the First Amendment.

RATE OF INCIDENCE

The reported incidence of antilesbian and gay violence increased nationally almost 400 percent between 1988 and 1996. Although reports of other violent crimes showed a decrease in rates, hate crimes continue to increase for all categories of victims. Of those antigay hate crimes that were reported, 50 percent of all victims sustained some injury, 25 percent received serious injuries, and 2 percent were killed (New York City Gay and Lesbian Anti-Violence Project 1996).

> Contrary to the conventional belief that most bias crimes are directed at property (such as graffiti and vandalism), a great majority of the violence against lesbian and gay men continues to be directed at individuals. Of the incidents reported (1996), 95 percent were

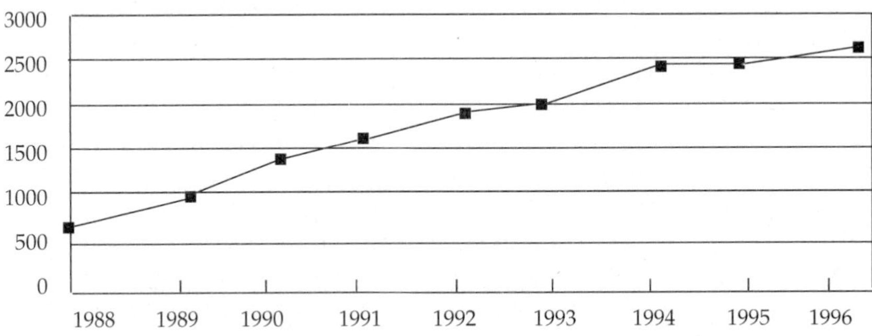

> directed at individuals, while only 5 percent targeted property. . . . Bats, clubs and blunt objects were the most frequently used weapons [24 percent of incidents involved weapons], followed by bottles, bricks and rocks. . . . The rate of the use of firearms in anti-Lesbian/Gay incidents is alarmingly high [14 percent of incidents involved weapons]. . . . [1996—6 percent increase] and indicates an increase in both the viciousness of the attacks, and the premeditation in the commission of anti-Lesbian/Gay crimes from last year. (New York City Gay and Lesbian Anti-Violence Project 1996, 1)

INTERSEX AND TRANSGENDERED ISSUES

Only recently have hate crime statutes begun to address the needs of **transgendered** people. The transgendered include **transsexuals,** the **intersexed, transvestites,** and others who do not identify with traditional gender or sexual roles. For example, based on California's hate crime statutes, Hector Bautista was convicted of murdering Mari Mar—a transgendered woman associated with Bienestar's Transgenderos Unidas, a support group for Hispanic transgendered people. This was the first time a hate crime statute was used in the United States to protect transgendered persons ("First sentences handed down . . ." 1999).

CIVIL RIGHTS—CALIFORNIA: A MODEL CODE

The California Hate Crime statutes are typical of hate crime statutes found nationwide. The guidelines used to determine if a crime is a hate crime include the following: (1) the crime involves a specific target; (2) bigotry must be the central motive for the attack; (3) assaults must be started with epithets; and (4) no other motive is present. In addition the Los Angeles County Commission on Human Relations in 1988 excluded actions such as writing graffiti on freeway overpasses and public phone booths that are not directed at a specific target; interracial crime not motivated by race, ethnicity, religion, or sexual orientation; name calling not accompanied by assault; and rallies and leafleting by hate groups. Not all hate crime ordinances have included sexual orientation as a protected status, thus comparing data from different locales is difficult.

The California hate crime law (Penal Code Title 11.6, Section 422.6) is fairly extensive and well planned. It is given here in detail and can serve as a model for a hate crime law in your location.

> *Subsection A:* No person shall, whether or not acting under color of law, by force or threat of force, willfully injure, intimidate, or interfere with, oppress or threaten any other person in the free exercise or enjoyment of any right or privilege secured to him or her by the constitution or laws of this state, or by the Constitution or laws of the United States, because of the other person's race, color, religion, ancestry, national origin or sexual orientation.
>
> *Subsection B:* No person shall, whether or not acting under color of law, knowingly deface, damage, or destroy the real or personal property of any other person for the purpose of intimidating or interfering with the free exercise of any right or privilege.
>
> *Punishment:* Any person convicted of violating California Penal Code, Section 422.6 may be punished by
>
> a. up to six months in jail,
> b. up to $5,000 in fines,
> c. or both.
>
> Aggravated circumstances: If the violator commits a Hate Crime and
>
> a. the victim is physically injured or the violator has the present ability to commit a violent (injurious) act,
> b. there is property damage in Excess of $1,000,
> c. the criminal is a repeat Offender who has been previously convicted of hate crimes,
>
> Then the crime becomes a felony and the punishment doubles to
>
> a. up to one year in prison,
> b. up to $10,000 in fines,
> c. or both.
>
> *Examples of hate crimes:*
>
> Verbal Harassment (name calling)
> Bomb Threat (targeting)
> Graffiti (swastikas on temples)
> Arson (Molotov cocktail, auto)
> Hate Mail (threats, derogatory statements)
> Assault and Battery (even murder)
> Vandalism (window smashing, etc.)

PROSECUTION ISSUES

A concern for prosecutors of crimes committed against lesbians and gay men is the prejudice of courts and juries upon learning of the sexual orientation of the victims. It is well documented that courts have a history of being lenient toward the perpetrators of antigay violence ("Gays Say Murderer Set Free" 1986; Moore 1989; "Panel to Examine Remarks" 1988; *Parisie v. Greer;* Valente 1984b). Sometimes it has been claimed that the homosexual made a pass at the defendant, who then responded with violence. This "gay advance defense" has been successfully used to reduce the sentence for convicted defendants of antigay violence ("Does a Gay Pass Justify Murder?" 1983; *Gilvin v. State;* Rangel 1987). (See also **Homosexual Panic Defense**.)

As we enter the new millennium, a number of states are entertaining the idea of empowering victims of wife beating, gay bashing, and other violence based upon gender or sexual orientation to sue their attackers. The Illinois state legislature was the first to consider such legislation in February 2000.

CHARACTERISTICS OF PERPETRATORS OF ANTIGAY VIOLENCE

Perpetrators of antigay and lesbian violence tend to be younger males who are unknown to their victims. Gay men and lesbians of color experience significantly more victimization by white perpetrators. In the general population, usually lone perpetrators attack single victims. In antigay hate crimes, it is usually small groups of perpetrators who attack small groups of gays and lesbians. During the attack, the perpetrators often verbally condemn the victim based on religious grounds. Courts have tended to be lenient toward perpetrators of antigay and antilesbian violence. Defense attorneys and judges have let perpetrators of antigay violence off by claiming they were "average boys exhibiting typical behavior" or that the homosexual victim naturally provoked them.

Studies have found that antigay feelings and the potential to be a gay basher result from learned beliefs and religious biases against gays and lesbians, sometimes combined with a latent fear of being homosexual (Adams, Wright, and Lohr 1996). For example, Winfield Mowder and Gary Matson were brutally murdered in their bed in their Happy Valley home in northern California in 1999 by Benjamin Williams and his brother James Williams. Investigators also found evidence linking the brothers to three bombings of synagogues in Sacramento that occurred a few weeks before the murders. In an interview, Benjamin Williams stated that "I'm not guilty of murder. I'm guilty of obeying the laws of the Creator. You obey a government of man until there is a conflict, then you obey a higher law. So many people claim to be Christians and complain about all these things their religion says are a sin, but they're not willing to do anything about it. They don't have the guts" ("Brother Admits Shooting Gays" 1999). (See also **Perpetrators of Antigay Violence**.)

COPING WITH HATE-MOTIVATED VIOLENCE

How do people react to hate-motivated violence? Research has shown that victimization creates psychological distress for the following reasons:

1. People maintain a sense of security and invulnerability through the daily process of denial. Hate-motivated violence makes the victim aware of his or her vulnerability. Lesbians and gay men may feel the need to return to the "closet" for safety.
2. Violence interferes with the perception of the world as an orderly and meaningful place. Victims may conclude that it was somehow their fault (characteristic self-blame stemming from internalized homophobia). This increases feelings of low self-esteem, depression, and hopelessness. Lesbians and gays may feel they are being "punished" for being homosexual, which reinforces internalized homophobia.

Three important stages in the psychology of victims have been identified (Bard and Sangrey 1979):

> (1) the *impact* phase, in which victims typically feel vulnerable, confused, helpless, and dependent on others for even the simplest decisions; (2) the *recoil* phase, which is characterized by mood swings and a "waxing and waning" of fear, rage, revenge fantasies, and displacement of anger (for example, arguing with loved ones); and (3) the *reorganization* phase, in which survivors assimilate their painful experience, are able to put the experience into perspective, and get on with their lives. (Garnets, Herek, and Levy 1993)

ROOTS AND ENFORCEMENT

Many groups experience bias hatred and violence, yet many are reluctant to make reports. Among other reasons, this stems from a historical fear of police and the belief that law enforcement will not take their reports seriously.

The psychological origins of hate crimes are complex and extensive. They are thought to stem from an irrational fear of someone who is different, accompanied by a feeling of inferiority. Hate crime, like other forms of prejudice, manifests itself between the haves and the have-nots, the educated and the uneducated, the powerful and the weak. Often the beginnings of hate come from a perpetrator's own home, where parents and other family members use discriminatory words and display discriminatory attitudes. Once these bias beliefs are incorporated into the psyche of children, they carry these beliefs with them into their own group settings (sometimes known as gangs). Gangs are an extension of a person's family and exacerbate the feelings of "we" versus "them." In this case, we are discussing gangs of "normal" kids who exhibit antigay sentiments. Adding alcohol and drugs lowers inhibitions against attacking one's perceived enemies and violent behavior often results. Hate crimes typically begin with negative epithets that lead to violence. (See also **Perpetrators of Antigay Violence**.)

UNDERREPORTING

There are five major reasons many victims and witnesses are unwilling to report hate crimes:

1. Personal shame. Many victims have internalized homophobia and feel a personal shame about who they are. They may feel that they "deserved it" and decide not to report the incident.
2. Fear of police abuse. Historically, police have been one of the major abusers of lesbians and gay men. Thus, victims often fear police abuse and do not report hate crimes. They feel that they would be discredited or verbally and possibly physically accosted.
3. Fear of being discovered to be gay. Many lesbians and gay men are not "out" about their sexual orientation. Reporting a hate crime creates a public document, leading to a possible subpoena and public appearance. To file a report of a hate crime could jeopardize the carefully constructed world of closeted lesbians and gay men. This may lead to family turmoil, loss of a job, loss of a security clearance, excommunication from church, and so on.
4. Belief that it isn't important. Many lesbians and gay men minimize the severity of hate crime incidents with a range of excuses: they are too busy to make a report; insurance will fix the damage; the attack produced only minor cuts and bruises; the police will never catch the violator; or it is cowardly to call the police department.
5. Alcohol. Hate crimes often occur near bars. Witnesses and victims may be under the influence of alcohol and fear that police will treat them as suspects rather than as victims.

STOPPING HATE CRIMES

To counteract the surge in hate crimes, the following actions are recommended:

1. Be part of the solution. Care enough to take an active role.
2. Know about hate crimes:
   a. Be able to identify and discern when a crime is motivated by hate or bias,
   b. Know how to report a hate crime,
   c. Follow up after filing a report.
3. Talk about hate crimes:
   a. Spread the word to family, friends, and community leaders,
   b. Get the word out to the community.
4. Take self-defense classes. People need to know how to protect themselves if attacked. It would be even better for them to learn how to avoid dangerous situations.
5. Use local government agencies. Police are only one limited source of protection. It is necessary to get local government involved and committed from the top down.
6. Improve media coverage. Both gay and nongay media should publish regular reports about the incidence of hate crimes. This includes reporting both the attack and court results.
7. Make a report. Tracking will be ineffective if no one reports.

MILITARY HATE CRIMES

Lesbians and gay men have always served in the U.S. military. The expulsion of homosexuals from the military comes in waves of persecutions related to conservative political changes. In 1993 President Clinton signed a compromise executive order better known as the **"Don't Ask, Don't Tell"** policy. Instead of reducing the identification and expulsion of lesbian and gay military personnel, it greatly increased the persecution, expulsion, and fear of homosexuals. A number of gruesome gay murders occurred that brought unwanted media attention to the problem of violent antigay hate crimes in the military. President Clinton signed an executive order on October 6, 1999, that amended the *Manual for Courts-Martial* to provide for (1) sentence enhancement in hate crimes, including antigay hate crimes, and (2) a limited psychotherapist privilege for service members, besides other provisions.

As with all hate crime statutes, the military order viewed bias-motivated crimes as very serious and deserving of greater punishment. Also, it was hoped that enhancing the sentences for antigay hate crimes would help discourage and deter violence motivated by hate. The second rule of limited psychotherapist privilege brings military procedures into closer compliance with the Supreme Court's ruling in *Jaffee v. Redmond,* which cleared up the extent of the psychotherapist privilege. However, the new order still allows psychotherapists to reveal service members' sexual orientation. Thus, commanders may use the private conversations between patients and psychotherapists to initiate or substantiate an administrative separation. Many organizations, such as the Servicemembers Legal Defense Network (SLDN), have encouraged the military to close this loophole and provide a safe space for service members to discuss their sexual orientation or harassment experiences.

The new order followed new antigay harassment guidelines released by the Pentagon a few months earlier in August 1999. These guidelines required commanders to investigate those who are alleged to have committed antigay harassment, not those who report it or are the victims of it. (See also **Military Expulsion**.)

References

Adams, H. E., L. W. Wright, and B. A. Lohr. 1996. "Is Homophobia Associated with Homosexual Arousal?" *Journal of Abnormal Psychology* 105(3): 440–445.

Bard, M., and D. Sangrey. 1979. *The Crime Victim's Book.* New York: Basic Books.

"Brother Admits Shooting Gays." (7 November 1999). Associated Press website: www.wire.ap.org/APnews.

"Does a Gay Pass Justify a Murder?" 1983. *Montrose* (Texas) *Voice* (1 April 1983): 14.

"First Sentences Handed Down under Law Boosting Penalties for Crimes against Transgendered." 1999. *Frontiers* 18(11): 23.

Garnets, L. D., G. M. Herek, and B. Levy. 1993. "Violence and Victimization of Lesbians and Gay Men: Mental Health Consequences." In *Psychological Perspectives on Lesbian and Gay Male Experiences,* edited by L. D. Garnets and D. C. Kimmel. New York: Columbia University Press.

"Gays Say Murderer Set Free." 1986. *Kalamazoo News* (14–20 February 1986): 1.

Hanna, J. 1999. "Court Rules Homosexual Slurs Were Hate Crime." *Chicago Tribune* (4 October 1999): 3.

Los Angeles County Commission on Human Relations. 1988. *Hate Crime in Los Angeles County.* Los Angeles: Los Angeles County Commission on Human Relations.

Moore, R. 1989. "Justice Is Not Blind for Gays." *San Diego Union* (10 January 1989): B7.

New York City Gay and Lesbian Anti-Violence Project. 1996. *Anti-Lesbian, Gay, Bisexual, and Transgendered Violence in 1996.* New York: New York City Gay and Lesbian Anti-Violence Project.

"Panel to Examine Remarks by Judge on Homosexuals." 1988. *New York Times* (21 December 1988): A16.

Rangel, B. 1987. "Brooklyn Youth Acquitted in Slaying of Catholic Priest." *New York Times* (5 February 1987): B3.

Robson, R. 1997. *Gay Men, Lesbians, and the Law.* New York: Chelsea House Publishers.

Valente, J. 1984b. "Gay Community Seeks Judge Nunzio's Ouster." *Washington Post* (19 May 1984): B1.

Yeoman, B. 1996. *Out.* Available at www.out.com/out-cgi-bin/article?a=9605/hesse.htm.

HATE CRIME STATISTICS ACT

See **Hate Crimes**

HATE SPEECH

Hate speech is speech intended to intimidate or harass individuals because of their membership in a particular demographic group. A number of cities and universities have implemented statutes and behavior codes to limit the use of hate speech. Often these have emerged from or are part of **hate crimes** statutes. Hate speech statutes represent the intersection between the concept of "fighting words," the linguistic structure of pejoratives and epithets, and public safety.

"Fighting words" are certain words or phrases that are intended to provoke violent physical responses. Examples would be "Come on, you bastard!" and "you son of a bitch!" The intention is to challenge and incite a fight between those exchanging the words. Often fighting words are linked with prejudice to form a challenge directed at particular groups. For example, the phrase "bull dyke" is a combination of the pejorative *bull* and the epithet *dyke.* The adjective *bull* is meant to demean, whereas the term *dyke* is a negative substitution for *lesbian.* This linguistic structure is true for many other antigay phrases such as "flaming queen," or "butch dyke." When these are combined into phrases such as "Come on, you butch dyke!" they form a challenge and intend to incite a fight.

Many organizations try to restrict the use of fighting words in order to maintain public safety. It is not socially acceptable and is illegal to yell "Fire!" in a crowded movie theater when there is no fire because of the possibility of injury to people caught in the stampede to get out. For the same reason, yelling "God hates faggots!" at participants at a gay festival could incite a riot and cause many injuries. However, some cities and universities that have implemented hate speech guidelines and statutes have run afoul of First Amendment rights to free speech. Defining when hate speech crosses the line into a public safety concern is difficult.

Here are examples of increasingly negative speech that indicate the difficulty in identifying when speech becomes an issue of public safety:

1. "I believe homosexuality is a sin." This is a statement of religious conviction and does not intended to intimidate or incite violence.
2. "Homosexuals are sick and homosexuality is a sin." The first part of this statement is simply not true as defined by the American Psychiatric Association. The second part is a moral condemnation of homosexuality to which not all people ascribe. There is a marked difference between saying "Homosexuality is

a sin" and "I believe homosexuality is a sin." Saying "Homosexuality is a sin" implies that this is universally accepted by all people. It is not. Many people and many religions do not classify homosexuality as a sin. When a speaker implies that all people believe a particular way and that you do not, they are attempting to intimidate you. Thus, if this statement were directed toward a lesbian or gay person, it would be considered to be inaccurate and negative and somewhat intimidating, yet not intended to incite violence.

3. "Fags should burn in hell." This statement uses the epithet *fags* and is very negative, yet it is not intended to incite violence. However, if this same statement was said or used on a placard at a gay and lesbian festival, it could incite violence. This demonstrates how the same words take on different emphasis in different settings.
4. "Die, you fag!" This statement is very negative and intends to be intimidating. Depending on the response by the lesbian or gay person, this could lead to violence.
5. "You're going to get it, faggot." This is very negative, intends to intimidate, and is a precursor to attack.

The hate crime statutes that include hate speech usually classify Example 5 above as criminalized speech; however, most police agencies would not act unless there was also physical violence. If the epithets used in Examples 3 and 4 were said while someone physically attacked another person, the violence could be classified as a hate crime. Remember that few states have hate crime laws that include sexual orientation and police virtually never cite for hate speech alone. Police typically cite or arrest only when hate speech is accompanied with violence to persons or destruction of property.

Many hate speech regulations have been deemed unconstitutional due to their infringement on free speech guaranteed in the First Amendment. For example, St. Paul, Minnesota, attempted to criminalize the placing of symbols, graffiti, or objects known to arouse "anger, alarm, or resentment" on the basis of "race, color, creed, religion, or gender" (Robson 1997, 89). The courts determined this to be unconstitutional. Similarly, courts have declared a number of university hate speech regulations to be unconstitutional. At this time it seems difficult to construct speech regulations that provide for the public safety and, at the same time, maintain the rights to free speech.

Reference

Robson, R. 1997. *Gay Men, Lesbians, and the Law.* New York: Chelsea House Publishers.

HERMAPHRODITE

See **Intersexed**

HETEROSEXISM

Heterosexism is the assumption, both explicit and implicit, that everyone is heterosexual. Heterosexism is "the continual promotion by major social institutions of heterosexuality and the simultaneous subordination" of lesbians, gay men, and bisexuals (Neisen 1990). For example, offering medical and other benefits to the spouses of married employees denies the fact that gay employees have significant partners. **Homophobia** is the strong negative emotional attitude toward gay people, whereas heterosexism is the conscious or unconscious bias that heterosexuals are more important than gay people, or that gay people do not exist, or both. (See also **Sexual Orientation**.)

Heterosexism creates invisibility for lesbians and gay men. Heterosexism keeps gay kids from learning about themselves. Parents assume their children are heterosexual and direct them to heterosexual experiences such as attending school dances with opposite-sex partners, associating with opposite-sex persons for the purposes of dating and marriage, and forcing children to attend religious training that enforces heterosexual beliefs. To the gay or lesbian child, these experiences are confusing and distasteful and reinforce feelings that their sexuality is not only invisible, but also a problem. These feelings are similar to what Jews, Muslims, Buddhists, or other non-Christians feel in predominantly Christian cultures during the celebration of Christmas or Easter. They feel invisible and may begin to believe their religious beliefs are not as important or "correct" as the dominant Christian dogma. Heterosexism creates feelings of isolation and incompetence. These feelings are similar to what a person in a wheelchair feels in a city that has only steps instead of ramps on sidewalks or into buildings. These feelings are similar to what a non-English-speaking person is confronted with in a society that uses only English. These feelings are similar to what an African American feels when seeing media personalities, police, government officials, and others that have only white faces. These are the feelings elderly people have in a society that recognizes, promotes, and rewards youthfulness.

Heterosexism is often not overt or direct. Yet, its subtlety is an insidious form of discrimination with attendant psychological consequences for homosexuals and heterosexuals alike. When homosexuals begin to notice their same-sex feelings (which marks the beginning stages of coming out), they also become aware of homophobia and heterosexism in others. No longer are fag jokes funny. No longer are antigay slurs said at school, on TV, or on the radio simply negative words, rather they are attacks felt personally by the person coming out as lesbian or gay. Coming to terms with one's homosexuality puts a person in touch with the oppressiveness of heterosexism.

Because heterosexism is so pervasive, heterosexuals are often ignorant of the terrible persecution experienced by lesbians and gay men. Heterosexuals tend to look upon sexual "minorities" as unfortunate people who "can't help being the way they are." When lesbians and gay men attempt to break through heterosexism and become visible, societal and institutional norms lash back with overt discrimination. For example, when a lesbian couple buys a house, the community usually ignores their relationship, deceiving themselves into believing that the "ladies" down the street are just "friends," if they think about it at all. But if the lesbian couple becomes involved in the community, for example, if they have children and insist on participating in school functions as an open, visible couple, then a community backlash often occurs. Legal actions may be initiated to take their children away from them.

Crossing the line from being invisible to being open about one's homosexuality puts one at risk of overt attack. Defining that line is difficult and varies with location and time. The subtlety of heterosexist actions frequently makes them extremely insidious and difficult to define and combat. (For an in-depth analysis of the processes used to subordinate homosexuals, see **Prejudice.**)

Reference

Neisen, J. 1990. "Heterosexism or Homophobia?" *Out/Look* 3(2): 36.

HIV

See **AIDS**

HOMOPHOBIA Homophobia is fear or other emotional aversion, often including prejudice or bigotry, toward lesbians and gay men. Homophobia shares many characteristics with other forms of prejudice, such as racism and sexism. Lesbians, gay men, and transgendered people are denied access to the rights and privileges enjoyed by others in our society. As such, they are, therefore, sometimes considered a "minority" group. Many lesbians and gay men are also members of other minority groups as well, and thus suffer multiple oppression. (See also **Criminal Law**.)

Two components make up the phenomenon of homophobia. The first is prejudice (from Latin, "to prejudge"), which is to hold an adverse belief or opinion about a group without justification or before acquiring sufficient knowledge. When people act upon their prejudicial feelings or beliefs, the result is the second component, discrimination. Discrimination prevents different people from being treated equally. Homophobia discriminates against homosexuality and therefore denies equality between heterosexuality and homosexuality.

Homophobia manifests itself in four ways: overt homophobia, institutional homophobia, societal homophobia, and internalized homophobia. Here are a few examples:

OVERT HOMOPHOBIA

Overt homophobia includes character assassination, name calling, use of defamatory words, verbal abuse, and violence. Violence directed against homosexuals is a growing national problem. Studies by the National Gay and Lesbian Task Force (1989) revealed that over 90 percent of respondents experienced some form of victimization on account of their sexual orientation, with more than one in three having been threatened directly with violence. (See also **Hate Crimes**.)

INSTITUTIONAL HOMOPHOBIA

Major social institutions—laws, customs, religious orders, schools, and so forth—work together to reinforce existing prejudice and discrimination. This constitutes institutional discrimination. Governments, schools, businesses, and religious groups create policies to dictate codes of behavior. These codes reinforce attitudes and values, and, in heterosexist societies, this means reinforcing antigay attitudes and values. Through the application of penalties and rewards, these powerful bodies create conformity to social norms through the use of incentives. Few U.S. institutions have policies supportive of homosexuals; many actively work against gay civil rights.

Examples of institutional homophobia include: (1) housing discrimination; (2) statutes in many states that make same-sex activity illegal and punishable by life imprisonment; (3) denial of child custody; (4) invalidation of personal unions; (5) exclusion from job protections; (6) denial of immigration; (7) discrimination in public accommodations; (8) denial of security clearances; (9) disinheritance; and (10) denial of police protection. Often same-sex couples or individuals are denied the right to adopt or serve as foster parents by state statutes or private agency regulations. Lesbian mothers and gay fathers have repeatedly lost custody of their children in the courts because of their sexual orientation. (See also **Adolescence**; **Family**.)

Military institutions discriminate against open gays and lesbians by barring them from enlisting and serving. Furthermore, the military is one of the largest employers in the United States and indirectly sets antigay attitudes for contractors and others. The harassment of lesbians and gays increased significantly after the implementation of the **"Don't Ask, Don't Tell"** policy. (See also **Military Expulsion**.)

Although there has been progress in obtaining equal rights for lesbians and gay men, there have been legal backlashes that are visible and clear indications of homophobia. For example, Congress conferred preferred legal status to heterosexuals with the **Defense of Marriage Act (DOMA)**. This act defined *marriage* as "a legal union between one man and one woman as husband and wife." A review of federal laws found that at least 1,049 regulations involved marital status, thus giving special rights to heterosexuals (Bedrick 1997).

More difficult to change are less obvious social codes of behavior. These are not written into law but nonetheless work within a society to legitimize oppression. (See also **Marriage**.)

Until 1973 the medical and psychiatric professions labeled homosexuality a pathology needing to be cured. The **American Psychiatric Association (APA)** has made it official policy that homosexuality and heterosexuality are equally valid, yet many practitioners still attempt to convert homosexuals to a heterosexual orientation. Physicians usually assume their patients are heterosexual. As such, they fail to ask questions or perform tests that are unique to homosexual needs. Homosexuals often are denied hospital visitation rights to their partners or lovers because hospitals sometimes limit visits to blood relatives. Until the 1970s, lesbians and gay men had been forced to undergo medical procedures, including electroshock treatment or lobotomies to cure their "disease." (See also **Reparative Therapy**). Likewise, relatives have had the right to commit homosexual family members to mental institutions solely because of their sexual orientation. And, finally, many therapists still consider homosexuality unacceptable, although it has been thirty years since the depathologization of homosexuality.

SOCIETAL HOMOPHOBIA

Until recently, the media kept homosexuals and issues of homosexuality hidden. This was the most effective way of invalidating the existence of lesbians and gay men in society. Schools also failed to include information about the homosexual orientation of people and the homosexual orientation of events discussed in English, history, and other classes. In fact, an active effort has been made to falsify and hide historical accounts of same-sex love. For example, Michelangelo's grandnephew changed the wording of his uncle's sonnets to make them more acceptable to the public (Boswell 1980). Similarly, the famous picture of Nazis burning books never explained that the first books confiscated and burned (as seen in the famous photo) were from the Magnus Hirschfeld Institute of Sexual Research—the world's leading library on homosexuality, women and gender issues, and cross-cultural accounts of human sexuality (Stewart 1999, 249). Television personalities and politicians often make antigay derogatory comments. This is tolerated, if not encouraged, while at the same time the struggle for equality by gays and lesbians is often trivialized as excessive or overindulgent. Sexual minorities are forced to keep their personal lives to themselves because it is claimed to be "not important." What is really being asked is that lesbians and gay men remain invisible. Societal homophobia is also described as **heterosexism**.

INTERNALIZED HOMOPHOBIA

When lesbians and gay men believe and accept the negative stereotypes, myths, and attitudes concerning homosexuality and the gay community, they are said to have internalized the culture's homophobia. Internalized homophobia manifests itself through a number of mechanisms. Examples of the self-destructive nature of internalized homophobia include contempt for "open" and "obvious" members of the community, attempts to "pass" as heterosexual, distrust of other gay people, the projection of prejudice onto another minority group, increased fear and withdrawal from friends and relatives, denial of one's sexual orientation, dating or marrying someone of the opposite sex in order to gain approval, and, in some instances, suicide. (See also **Coming Out**.)

AIDS has had a major impact on homophobia, and particularly internalized homophobia. As AIDS marched its way through the gay community, the religious right responded by claiming that AIDS was "God's punishment" for engaging in a "deviant lifestyle." Many lesbians and gay men accepted this condemnation and felt they deserved to die for being homosexual. They kept their secret life to themselves. For some, telling their family that they had AIDS was also the first time they told their family that they were homosexual. Recently, it was reported that Roman Catholic priests in the United States are dying from AIDS at a rate four times higher than the general population, yet the church has been quiet about the problem ("Dying in Silence" 2000). For example, Bishop Emerson Moore of the New York Archdiocese went to Minnesota in 1995 and died in a hospice for AIDS-related illnesses. His death certificate listed his death as due to "unknown natural causes" and his occupation was listed as "laborer" in the manufacturing industry. Thus, this man who spent his life helping others and being a respectable member of the community, died in obscurity to avoid the stigma of having AIDS. (See also **Religious Right Agenda**.)

References

Bedrick, B. R. 1997. "Report on The Defense of Marriage Act." Government Accounting Office website: www.gao.gov (31 January 1997).

Boswell, J. 1980. *Christianity, Social Tolerance, and Homosexuality: Gay People in Western Europe from the Beginning of the Christian Era to the Fourteenth Century.* Chicago: University of Chicago Press.

"Dying in Silence." 2000. *Frontiers* 18(21): 33.
National Gay and Lesbian Task Force. 1989. *Antigay and Lesbian Victimization.* Washington, DC: National Gay and Lesbian Task Force.
Stewart, C. 1999. *Sexually Stigmatized Communities—Reducing Heterosexism and Homophobia: An Awareness Training Manual.* Thousand Oaks, CA: Sage.

HOMOSEXUAL PANIC DEFENSE

The homosexual panic defense is a legal defense strategy used by perpetrators of antigay violence in which they claim to have panicked and reacted with violence toward a gay person who came onto them (also known as a "gay advance"). Homosexual panic was considered a psychological disorder based on the Freudian theory that persons with latent homosexual tendencies would react with extreme and uncontrollable violence when propositioned by a homosexual (Chuang and Addington 1988). No court has ever acquitted a defendant based solely on the homosexual panic defense. However, the defense has been instrumental in obtaining reduced sentences in murder cases involving gay victims.

In 2000 a Michigan jury reduced a murder charge to manslaughter after the defendant claimed that the teenager he killed made a pass at him. Anthony Larson, one of the jurors, reported that during deliberations the other jurors became obsessed with the sexual orientation of the victim. "They said, 'faggot got what he deserved. He shouldn't have grabbed him.'" Larson held out for two days and was threatened by the other jurors for not agreeing with them to reduce the charge. Ultimately, Larson caved in and agreed to the reduced charge. Larson said to the press, "The whole thing's perverted. I'm actually ashamed of myself" ("I'm Just Ashamed" 2000).

The homosexual panic defense is based upon two theories. First, homosexual panic is a mental defect and a form of insanity. As an insanity defense, defendants are absolved of criminal responsibility because they did not know the nature, quality, or wrongfulness of their act. Some courts have accepted that there is an "irresistible impulse" to homosexual panic that negates the ability of perpetrators to control their conduct. Second, homosexual panic is considered a diminished capacity.

As a mental defect theory, the homosexual panic defense has a number of problems. Accepting the mental defect theory requires the assumption that mental illness can be associated with sexual orientation. With the declassification of homosexuality as a mental illness by the **American Psychiatric Association (APA)** in 1973, there is no theory or evidence to explain why someone who has latent homosexual tendencies would be considered mentally ill, whereas someone who openly declares his or her homosexual sexual orientation would not.

The homosexual panic defense depends on proving the latent homosexual tendencies of the perpetrator. Human sexual orientation is viewed to be a continuum in which people are neither entirely heterosexual nor homosexual. According to this view, everyone who is not acting upon his or her homosexual tendencies could be classified as a "latently homosexual"; thus, anyone who commits violence against lesbians and gay men could claim a homosexual panic defense. Furthermore, proving a person has latent homosexual tendencies is as problematic as proving someone has latent heterosexual tendencies. One review of the literature concluded that the homosexual panic term "should be permanently assigned to the junkyard of obsolete psychiatric terminology" (Chuang and Addington 1988). Homosexual panic is not a mental disorder, but rather a culmination of our culture's homophobic attitudes. (To understand the psychology of those who respond with violence toward lesbians and gay men, see **Perpetrators of Antigay Violence**.)

Finally, accepting the homosexual panic defense relieves individuals of responsibility for committing such crimes and, in fact, blames the victim. It is more instructive to recognize that homosexual panic is the result of learned antigay bias and prejudice—which is homophobia. Homosexual panic is neither a mental defect nor diminished capacity, but rather the product of culturally imposed values that can be unlearned. Thus, homosexual panic is not a valid defense and perpetrators of antigay violence should be held accountable for their actions.

Although there is a long history of courts accepting the homosexual panic defense, most courts now reject the use of this strategy (*Commonwealth v. Carr*). Psychiatrists and courts have recognized that homophobia is the cause of antigay attacks and perpetrators are to be held accountable for their acts of violence.

With the inclusion of sexual orientation as a protected class in a few state **hate crime** statutes, a new phenomenon has developed. Gay bashers are attempting to avoid the increased sentencing that is imposed when the crime is classified as a hate crime by claiming that the crime was something else—such as a robbery or burglary that went wrong and included violence. However, if during the investigation and trial it looks as if their story will not be accepted and they will be charged with a hate crime, they sometimes attempt to use the homosexual panic defense. Fortunately, courts now rarely accept such a fallacious claim.

References

Chuang, H. T., and D. Addington. 1988. "Homosexual Panic: A Review of Its Concept." *Canadian Journal of Psychiatry* 33(7): 613–617.

"I'm Just Ashamed." 2000. *Frontiers* 18(22): 36.

HOMOSEXUALITY Homosexuality is a primary sexual attraction to members of the same gender. For men, the preferred terms are *gay man* or *gay male*. For women, the preferred terms are *gay woman, gay female,* or *lesbian*. It is acceptable to use the term gay to mean both men and women in the context of the *gay community,* but the term should not be overused. Instead, writers should use both *lesbian and gay* and the *gay community* in order to bring visibility to women. Also, it is important not to overlook bisexual, transgendered, transsexual or intersexed people. Using the all-encompassing term *gay community* does not provide recognition of their important issues. Writers are encouraged to use the appropriately specific terms. (See also **Sexual Orientation**.)

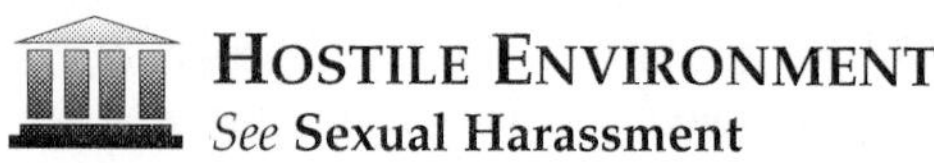

HOSTILE ENVIRONMENT
See **Sexual Harassment**

HOUSING Lesbians, gay men, and transgendered people often face discrimination when renting or buying a house, condominium, apartment, or other domicile. Some states and cities have enacted antidiscrimination ordinances to protect the rights of homosexuals to procure housing. An infamous 1977 case in New York illustrates the degree to which landlords and sellers can legally act capricious. A black, divorced woman who was a lawyer sued a landlord over his refusal to rent a unit to her. She claimed three areas of discrimination—race, sex, and marital status. In court, the landlord responded by saying that he refused to rent to lawyers because they tended to assert their rights. The court accepted his response and denied her claims (*Kramarsky v. Stahl Management*). Thus, landlords may act irrationally as long as they do not violate any prescribed statutes. Without specific protections, landlords may refuse to rent to lesbians and gay men (Hunter, Michaelson, and Stoddard 1992).

Lesbians and gay men may be able to protect themselves from discrimination using claims other than sexual orientation. Many of the fair housing ordinances provide protection based upon marital status, which includes protection for single people or nontraditional families besides those who are married. For example, a landlady in Washington state was found to have violated antidiscrimination statutes when she refused to rent to two gay men who were a couple. The Washington statute provided protection for single people besides those who were married. (See, for example, Colo. Rev. Stat. § 24–34–502 [1997]; N.Y. Exec. Law § 296 [McKinney 1982]; Or. Rev. Stat. § 659.033 [1989].) However, the Ninth U.S. Circuit Court of Appeals ruled in October 1999 that two Anchorage,

Alaska, landlords had the right to discriminate against tenants as a consequence of the landlords' right to freedom of religion. In this case, the landlords believed it to be a sin for two people to cohabit without being married. In previous cases, the supreme courts of Alaska and California had upheld their state discrimination laws against challenges by religious landlords. At the time of this writing, the Ninth Circuit has set aside the ruling and is planning a rehearing. If this court sides with the landlords, federal judges could bar enforcement of state antidiscrimination laws throughout the circuit against any property owners whose sincere religious beliefs forbid renting to unmarried couples. "The court said the state and city discrimination laws unconstitutionally forced landlords to choose between their businesses and their religious beliefs. The court also said prohibiting landlords from asking about a prospective tenant's marital status violates freedom of speech" (Egelko 1999).

Leases can provide some level of protection for lesbian and gay tenants, but they can also be used to discriminate. Many leases contain clauses that limit how tenants may use their units and who can share the space. Some leases restrict occupancy to those who are related by "blood or marriage." Sometimes landlords use these clauses to attempt to evict both the tenant and his or her lover or roommate. But not all clauses in a lease are enforceable. All states and most cities have laws regulating rental property. Leases are to be written to comply with the law. Items within a lease that conflict with the law may be challenged in court.

Rent control or rent stabilization statutes are often strict in their protection of renters' rights. For example, a New York City gay man was faced with eviction from his apartment when his lover of eleven years died from **AIDS**. The survivor's name did not appear on the lease. Rent control provisions precluded landlords from evicting "either the surviving spouse of the deceased tenant or some other member of the deceased tenant's **family** who has been living with the tenant" (*Braschi v. Stahl*, 212–213). The man argued that he was "family" and the New York Court of Appeals agreed with that position (*Braschi v. Stahl Associates Co.*). This was precedent setting and helped to establish the idea that lesbians and gay men could form legitimate families.

Regardless of the setting, landlords may evict tenants only after a formal legal hearing process. Tenants are always afforded legal notice and opportunity to present their side of the dispute. Federal housing antidiscrimination statutes provide protections based on race, color, religion, sex, national origin, "handicap," or family status (related to having children). A few states have also included sexual orientation as a protected status for housing. (See **Appendix A: State and Local Laws**.)

Lesbians and gay men who buy property also face potential discrimination. Except in those few states with specific antidiscrimination protections, sellers, mortgage companies, and others can refuse to sell to homosexuals. Although the personal life of applicants for home mortgages should be irrelevant, banks and other lenders have sometimes accepted the antigay stereotype that homosexuals are inherently unstable and, thus, financially unreliable. Other federal and state laws that prohibit discrimination, such as those based on gender or marital status, may be used to protect lesbians and gay men in specific circumstances.

Condominiums, in which members own their own apartments and have obligations to the common areas of the building, and cooperative apartments, in which members own stock in a corporation that manages the building, present additional challenges to lesbian and gay male couples. Because both of these housing arrangements involve ownership of common property with others, the prejudice and bias of the other owners can play an important role in the use of the property. Typically, there is a board or members' association that manages the common areas of the building and regulates the use of the building. The wants and desires of the members ultimately determine the living environment.

Buyers and sellers of condominiums and cooperative apartments are treated by law similarly to buyers and sellers of ordinary houses. Without specific ordinances outlawing discrimination based upon sexual orientation, there is little lesbians and gay men can do to challenge discrimination by sellers toward them. Similarly, when lesbians and gay men attempt to sell or transfer their property, difficulties may arise from the governing board, which often has the right to review all such transactions. For example, sometimes a lesbian or gay man cannot leave the property to his or her partner as part of a will without the approval of the board—even if the partner is living there. The best way around such a problem is to attempt to make the partner a joint owner while they are both alive.

Public housing gives preference to married couples and people with children. As such, lesbian and gay male couples are, for all practical purposes, denied participation in these programs because they are classified as single people who happen to occupy the same housing. As single people, they fall to the bottom of the waiting list for such public support (Public Health and Welfare Act, § 1437b[3]). Thus, the discrimination occurs because of their unmarried status, not because they are lesbian or gay. As seen in the *Braschi* case, it is expected that lesbian and gay male couples will begin to be seen as family units and obtain equality with married couples in public housing.

References

Egelko, B. 1999. "Court to Reconsider Ruling on Religious Landlords." (19 October 1999). Associated Press website, www.wire.ap.org/APnews.

Hunter, N. D., S. E. Michaelson, and T. B. Stoddard. 1992. *The Rights of Lesbians and Gay Men: The Basic ACLU Guide to a Gay Person's Rights.* 3d ed. Carbondale and Edwardsville, IL: Southern Illinois University Press.

HUMAN RIGHTS CAMPAIGN Founded in 1980, the Human Rights Campaign (HRC) is the nation's largest political organization fighting for the rights of lesbians, gay men, and bisexuals. With more than 300,000 members and a staff of forty, it lobbies Congress on issues that affect the lesbian and gay community, fights antigay ballot initiatives, and supports candidates who support antidiscrimination policies based on sexual orientation. Its political action committee (PAC) provides financial support for candidates who agree with **AIDS** funding, women's health issues, and choice. More than $1 million was used in 1998 to help elect fair-minded candidates at the federal level. Of the 200 political candidates to whom the HRC contributed money in 1998, 91 percent won their respective races. The HRC helped citizens defeat antigay measures in Oregon and Idaho in 1994 and in Maine in 1995. The HRC was the largest single financial contributor to the legal challenge to Colorado's **Amendment 2**. (See also **National Coming Out Day; *Romer v. Evans*.**)

I

IMMIGRATION Immigration by lesbians, gay men, and transgendered people into the United States has been virtually impossible in the past. Before 1990 homosexuals were officially banned from coming to the United States. A foreign national on any kind of visa whose homosexual activities became known to the Immigration and Naturalization Service (INS) would be immediately expelled. In 1990 Congress decriminalized homosexuality and the ban was lifted. However, it is still difficult for homosexuals to obtain permanent visa status.

People may legally immigrate to the United States through three means: (1) family sponsorship, (2) sponsorship through employment or profession, and (3) asylum.

Same-Sex Partner Sponsorship

As of this writing, the U.S. citizen partner of a same-sex couple cannot sponsor his or her foreign partner for immigration. In March 2000, U.S. Representative Jerrold Nadler introduced a bill—the Permanent Partners Immigration Act—into Congress to provide same-sex couples with all the privileges that currently accrue to legal spouses under federal immigration law. This would include a U.S. citizen sponsoring his or her foreign national husband or wife to immigrate on the basis of the spousal relationship. "This legislation finally brings the United States into line with the thirteen other countries that currently provide immigration rights to same-sex partners," said Lavi Soloway, chair of the Board of Directors of the Lesbian and Gay Immigration Rights Task Force (LGIRTF) ("Nadler Fights Homophobic Immigration Law" 2000, 17). Congress did not accept this bill, but it began the discussion process that might lead to a fairer immigration policy for same-sex couples.

Asylum

Asylum is not granted to persons solely on the basis of social discrimination or ostracism in their home countries. Asylum is granted only when the discrimination comes from the asylum seeker's own government or when that government is unable or unwilling to protect the seeker from persecution by nonstate actors (such as death squads or guerrilla armies). Also, the asylum seeker must apply under one of the five protected grounds—race, religion, nationality, membership in a particular social group, or political opinion.

The Refugee Act of 1980 specified that "members of a particular social group" are eligible for asylum in the United States. The meaning of that phrase had to be decided in practice. The first case of a gay male refugee to be considered under the 1980 Act was *In re Toboso-Alfonso.* Judge Robert Brown agreed in 1986 not to return Fidel Armando-Alfonso to Cuba because of the documented mistreatment of homosexuals by the communist government there ("Gay Refugees Tell of Torture, Oppression in Cuba" 1980). The Board of Immigration Appeals upheld the decision in 1990 and Attorney General Janet Reno in 1994 designated this decision as precedent for all other requests for asylum by homosexual applicants. As such, lesbians and gay men who are persecuted by their governments may be eligible to remain in the United States. To date, only a few lesbians and gay men have secured asylum in the United States through this process. This is because meeting the criteria for asylum is extremely difficult. Applicants need to show that returning to their home country would be hazardous to their well-being. They also need to prove that persecution of homosexuals occurs in their country—something difficult for the average person to document.

Applying for asylum based on persecution due to sexual orientation is the same as any application for asylum. The application is adjudicated on a case-by-case basis and requires rigorous standards of proof. Simply because the United States extends asylum to a lesbian based on her sexual orientation does not mean that all lesbians from the same country are granted automatic asylum. Every application for asylum requires specific evidence relevant to the specific case.

In 1996 President Clinton signed into law the Illegal Immigration Reform and Immigrant Responsibility Act. This act was fueled by the anti-immigration sentiments sweeping the nation as evidenced in California's Proposition 187, a statute that denied undocumented aliens access to medical aid, education, and other public services. The act stripped judges of the discretion they had in determining cases of asylum. This left even sympathetic judges without the means to humanize the punitive adjudication process. Once it became known how the act changed judicial discretion, legislators began work to overhaul the law.

HIV

In general, those with communicable diseases and HIV are routinely denied entry into the United States—whether as visitors or immigrants.

Congress recognized the potential problem of immigrants who were granted asylum, later contracted HIV, and were then forced to return to the dangers of their home countries. In 1993 legislation was passed that addressed this issue and allowed a waiver of HIV exclusion based on humanitarian grounds.

The waiver is not automatic and the guidelines are strict. Applicants for HIV waiver must show (1) that they have private health insurance and will never use U.S. publicly funded health services, and (2) that they have been counseled on HIV and give assurances that they will not spread the disease. For many poor immigrants coming from countries with socialized medicine, private health insurance is a foreign concept. Making HIV sufferers promise never to use Medicaid keeps far more people out of the United States than it allows in. Of the 24,500 people granted asylum in the United State in 1995–1996, two or three people received asylum from persecution solely because of HIV status.

References

"Gay Refugees Tell of Torture, Oppression in Cuba." 1980. *The Advocate* (27 November 1980): 15.

"Nadler Fights Homophobic Immigration Law." 2000. *Fab* (3 March 2000): 17.

INCIDENCE OF HOMOSEXUALITY

Estimating the number of lesbians, gay men, or bisexuals is impossible. Many gay activists claim that approximately 10 percent of the population is homosexual. Conservative religious leaders claim a much lower number. Why is it so difficult to determine the number of people who are homosexual or gay within a culture?

UNDERREPORTING

"[Homosexuality] is one of the most difficult things to measure," says Tom Smith, director of General Social Survey at the National Opinion Research Center (NORC). "It's personal and intimate, some people won't admit to it, and its practice is [legally] questionable in some states. Many people won't give a true response, which leads to underreporting" (Giger 1991, 43). Research by Clark and Tifft (1966) attempted to gauge possible underreporting discrepancies. The respondents in a study conducted on undergraduate students at the University of Illinois initially reported same-gender sexual contacts only 7 percent of the time. Later, students confronted with contrary information (polygraph tests) changed their answers to report homosexual contact 22.5 percent of the time. This is a substantial difference (more than 200 percent) and indicates the difficulty in making reasonable estimates (Clark and Tifft 1966).

DEFINITION

One difficulty in assessing the incidence of homosexuality is defining precisely what it means to be homosexual. Just exactly what is being measured—the number of people who have a gay identity or the number of people who engage in homosexual sex? How many times does someone have to engage in homosexual sex before he or she is considered homosexual? Do childhood experiences count, or do only adult experiences result in being categorized as gay? Is a gay identity the same as homosexual behaviors? What about feelings? Are people who have homosexual fantasies and feelings—yet never act upon them—gay? Are people who masturbate to same-sex images gay, even if they engage only in opposite-sex sexual behaviors? As you can see, how one defines gay and homosexual drastically changes research results. Likewise, what is sex? The scandal involving President Clinton and Monica Lewinsky demonstrated that there are varying views about what constitutes sex and what does not. Thus, how one defines sex also affects research results.

The famous study of sexuality in the 1930s and 1940s by Kinsey, Pomeroy, and Martin (1948) addressed some of these issues and helped to devise language to better define the problems. First, the researchers realized that human sexuality was not black and white, with people being either heterosexual or homosexual. Instead, human sexuality spanned a continuum, from being completely heterosexual to being completely homosexual. They also chose a behavioral model for their definition; that is, sex was defined as achieving orgasm, and sexual orientation was defined as the ratio of heterosexual to homosexual behaviors. Although the research was flawed, it represented an important milestone in sex research and is the source of the oft-quoted 10 percent figure to represent the number of people who are mostly homosexual.

The term *gay* is a modern word and reflects the politics of people who identify with other homosexuals in their fight to obtain equality with heterosexuals within a heterosexist society. Being gay is not synonymous with engaging in homosexual behaviors. Similar to the coming out process, many people are aware of their feelings, know the group to which they belong, and know which group oppresses them, sometimes years before they act sexually upon their feelings. Identification as *gay* reflects a political awareness of the oppression of homosexuals, as well as a sexual orientation. Most people who engage in homosexual behaviors do not eventually take on a gay identity. Thus, research that attempts to measure the number of gay people is not reflective of the number of homosexuals.

SETTING

Our Western culture is heterosexist and homophobic. Until recently, people accused of engaging in homosexual sexual behaviors faced prison terms or even death. Lesbian and "fag" bashings are on the upswing. One-third of the states still have sex statutes that make homosexual behaviors illegal. Very few cities or states have laws that provide protection in employment, housing, child custody, and other areas based upon sexual orientation. Considering these extremely negative environments, it is reasonable to assume that many, if not most, people who engage in homosexual behaviors will not be truthful to researchers. (See also **Hate Crimes**.)

Thus, measuring the incidence of homosexuality is dependent upon the definition of terms, the negativity of the environment in which the research is conducted, and the truthfulness of the respondents. Estimates as to the incidence of homosexuality (usually 10 percent or lower) should be suspected to be underestimates (Friedman and Downey 1994; Michael, Gagnon, Laumann, and Kolata 1995; Tremblay 1995).

The incidence of homosexuality is more than an item of curiosity. Corporations, cities, counties, and states are considering offering domestic partnership benefits to same-sex couples. During planning for these extended benefits, the question of additional cost comes up. So far, the experience of businesses and governmental agencies that have granted these benefits has shown the costs have been minimal. Very few same-sex couples take advantage of the programs. In fact, often more opposite-sex couples avail themselves of the programs than same-sex couples. Similarly, conservatives sometimes block research into lesbian and gay concerns because they believe it may lead to **affirmative action** and quotas in hiring. No national or major lesbian and gay organization has called for affirmative action. Thus, the conservative concerns are unfounded and this reason should not be used to block legitimate research.

References

Clark, J. P., and L. L. Tifft. 1966. "Polygraph and Interview Validation of Self-Reported Deviant Behavior." *American Sociological Review* 31(4): 516–23.

Friedman, R. C., and J. I. Downey. 1994. "Homosexuality." *New England Journal of Medicine* 331(14): 923–930.

Giger, B. 1991. "Is 10 Percent Too High?" *Frontiers* 10(4): 43.

Kinsey, A. C., W. B. Pomeroy, and C. E. Martin. 1948. *Sexual Behavior in the Human Male.* Philadelphia: W. B. Saunders Co.

Michael, R. T., J. H. Gagnon, E. O. Laumann, and G. Kolata. 1995. *Sex in America: A Definitive Survey.* New York: Little, Brown.

Tremblay, P. J. 1995. "The Homosexuality Factor in the Youth Suicide Problem." Paper presented at the meeting of the Sixth Annual Conference of the Canadian Association for Suicide Prevention, 11–14 October 1995, Banff, Alberta, Canada.

INDECENT EXPOSURE

See **Lewd Conduct**

INTERSEXED

Intersexed people have partially or fully developed genitalia, gonads, or chromosomes that are not distinctly male or female but are some combination of both. The archaic term *hermaphrodite* is inaccurate because it implies that an intersexed person has genitalia that are equally male and female. Intersexed persons are born between (inter) the sexes. There are roughly eight classifications and forty subclassifications of intersexuality. It is estimated that from 1 to 4 percent of the population (Fausto-Sterling 1993) has a hermaphroditic condition. That is approximately 2.8 to 12 million intersexed persons in the United States alone.

LAW

Many state and federal regulations and statutes differentiate between persons by their sex and gender. Surprisingly, these terms—*male, man, female, woman, sex, gender*—are not defined in law (Valdes 1995). Sex is viewed as a binary system composed of male or female and thought to be determined by biological factors. The sex of a person is determined at birth by inspection and recorded on the birth certificate for legal purposes.

Gender is thought of as the attitudinal or cultural qualities that are characteristic of a particular sex, that is, being feminine or masculine. Gender is a socially constructed attribute. Most laws and regulations use the word *sex,* yet many courts, legislators, and administrative agencies use the word *gender* in place of *sex* when interpreting these laws (Capers 1991). Thus, there is confusion over the terms and they are often used interchangeably.

The U.S. legal system distinguishes only two sexes and two genders. As a binary system, it excludes people who are not clearly male or female, or forces them into one of the two categories. As such, there are significant legal and ethical issues concerning **transgendered** and intersexed people and how they are treated by society.

Transgendered and intersexed people are treated differently within different legal jurisdictions. Some jurisdictions allow individuals to amend their official documents to better reflect the their self-identification (Diamond 1997). In other jurisdictions, official documents cannot be changed, and the sex of a person is determined biologically without regard to the person's self-identification. These types of decisions affect **marriage** for intersexed people, their employment, antidiscrimination policies, and more.

DOCUMENTS

Because so much of our lives is defined by our legal sexual identification, the ability of documents to accurately reflect intersexed and transgendered status is crucially important. Birth certificates, drivers' licenses, and passports are used for a variety of purposes, such as proof of citizenship, social security, life insurance, security clearances, and selective service registration. If the sex designation on the documents does not match the apparent sex of the bearer, embarrassment, misunderstanding, and rejection are possible. In many cases the sex indicated on a passport did not match the apparent sex of the passport's holder and he or she was not able to cross national borders. Many other cases can be found of police harassing intersexed and transgendered people because their identification did not match what the officers saw with their own eyes.

Birth certificates are the first documents to indicate sex and are used to obtain all other documents. If an error is made on the original document, the document can be reissued or amended in some states. However, changes due to later surgical or other alterations in sex are problematic. A number of states allow birth certificates to be reissued, indicating the new sex status as the result of a request or court order (Arizona, California, Hawaii, Illinois, Iowa, Louisiana, Michigan, Mississippi, North Carolina). Other states amend birth certificates only by court order (Alabama, Georgia, Oregon, Utah, Virginia, Wisconsin) or a doctors' notice (Massachusetts). At least one state actually forbids altering a birth certificate as the result of a sex change (Tennessee). New York, Oregon, and Ohio courts have ruled against **transsexuals** requesting changes to their birth certificates.

Some people go to court to change their names. There is no federal name change statute (*Moskowitz v. Moskowitz*). Some courts have allowed name changes as long as there was no attempt to commit financial fraud. Other courts have required transsexual applicants to complete all operations and submit documentation. As recently as 1995, Pennsylvania became the first state to issue a name change for a preoperative transsexual (*In re McIntyre* 1998). California is the only state to have reissued a birth certificate upon the request of an intersexual who had no reconstructive surgery (Harris 1988).

A survey of motor vehicle bureaus (Erikson Education Foundation 2000) found that thirty-four of them would issue new licenses with new sex indicators for postoperative transsexuals. However, a majority required a notarized letter from a treating physician attesting that the surgery was performed. In general, states are reluctant to issue new licenses unless there is proof of surgery. This, of course, poses a problem for unoperated or unaltered intersexuals or transgenderists.

States and courts give the following reasons to deny changing birth certificates, drivers' licenses, and other legal documents: (1) prevention of fraud; (2) fear that the new documents may be used for other purposes not sanctioned by society, such as same-sex marriage; (3) the belief that the legal system should not be used to help "psychologically ill" people to socially adapt; and (4) the belief that legal documents, particularly birth certificates, should be left in their original state (or wording) in order to preserve the accuracy of historical documents.

The argument that changing the sex of a person on legal documents encourages fraud is incorrect. In fact, intersexed people point out that denying a change of sex on birth certificates, passports, licenses, and other documents to better reflect the sex and gender of the holder, in fact, may lead to fraud. By disallowing such a change, there will be a greater discrepancy between outward appearance and official documents. This discrepancy causes miscommunication and could be used for fraudulent purposes.

The fear that changing a person's sex on legal documents may lead to same-sex marriage is not valid. Same-sex marriages already exist (see *Marriage* below in this entry). If the goal of some legislatures is to prevent same-sex marriage, then they need to consider new language, for not changing sex on legal documents does not achieve this end. Texas is a good example of the problem. Typically, only drivers' licenses are needed as proof of identity for the purposes of obtaining a marriage license. In Texas, unoperated transsexuals can obtain a new driver's license to better match their gender presentation or identity. Thus, in Texas, a transsexual can marry someone with dissimilar genitals by using his or her passport for identification or someone with similar genitals by using his or her driver's license. However, in 1999 Christie Littleton was denied the spousal right to sue in the case of her husband's death because the courts ruled that she was not a woman and, therefore, was never the legal wife of the deceased. This judgment occurred even though Littleton had gone through surgery more than twenty-five years earlier, had changed her name and all documents twenty-two years earlier, and was lawfully wedded for seven years to the man who died ("Transgender Legal Complications Abound" 2000). This shows the importance of being allowed to change all documents together to reflect the new sex designation and how laws are constantly under flux.

To claim that the legal system should not be used to help "psychologically ill" people is incorrect. Intersexuality is not a mental illness and gender dysphoria (confusion) may never come into play. Current medical research shows that transsexuals are also not psychologically ill. Finally, regardless of whether the legal system shows support for intersexed people and transsexuals, they will continue to find ways to live and adapt to a rather hostile culture. (See *Sexual Identification* in this entry for a detailed explanation of how sexuality is determined.)

Finally, the argument that legal documents should not be changed to preserve historical records is contrary to the fact that legal documents are changed all the time. These include adoptions, changes of name for minors, and verifications of paternity. Intersexuals and transsexuals should be afforded the same right.

MARRIAGE

Most states and the federal government define marriage as the union of one man and one woman. This same assumption of one man and one woman exists for those states that do not specify who can be married (*Baker v. Nelson; Jones v. Hallahan*). Sometimes there is language related to procreation or to the purpose of begetting offspring (*B. v. B.*). However, none of the states specifies by law or by opinion who is male, man, female, woman, or what constitutes sex. Even the **Defense of Marriage Act (DOMA)** failed to define these terms.

Because these terms have not been specified in law, it has been left to courts to define them. Same-sex couples have filed numerous suits to have their unions recognized as marriages. The courts have held that if one (or both) of them is transgendered, they have no valid claim toward marriage. There have been a few cases brought forward by transgendered individuals. Typically these cases involve an opposite-sex couple's marriage in which one partner later underwent sexual reassignment surgery and either the nontransgendered partner sued for divorce or annulment or the transgendered partner was the survivor when his or her partner died.

One of the earliest and precedent-setting cases was *Corbett v. Corbett*, in which a postoperative male-to-female transsexual married a man in England. After only fourteen days together, the man filed to have the marriage annulled because he claimed that (1) the marriage was between two persons of the same sex, and (2) the marriage could not be consummated because the transsexual had an "artificial vagina." England does not allow birth certificates or other legal documents to be altered. The woman was considered to be a man and the courts agreed that it was a marriage between two men. Also, the courts decided that the woman was incapable of "true intercourse." One court stated, "[S]exual intercourse, using the completely artificial cavity [cannot be described as] ordinary and complete intercourse. When such a cavity has been constructed in a male, the difference between sexual intercourse using it, and anal or intracrural [between the thighs] is, in my judgment, to be measured in centimeters" (*S. v. S.*, 55). The court annulled the marriage.

Although this was an English case, it was cited widely and, therefore, influenced many other transsexual cases. For example, the court used only three factors to determine sex for the purpose of marriage determination: chromosomes, gonads, and genitalia. These guidelines have been adopted by many other courts. Courts in New Jersey and California have allowed postoperative transsexuals to assume their postoperative sex, whereas courts in New York and Ohio have followed *Corbett* and disallowed the legal change of sex on documents and in marriage disputes.

The confusion over the right to change sex designation on legal documents has resulted in a number of "same-sex" marriages being legally allowed. For example, in Ohio, Paul Smith, a preoperative male-to-female transsexual who is identified as a lesbian, was granted a marriage license to marry a woman. Even though Paul dresses as a woman, intends to have sexual reassignment surgery, and legally changed her name to Denise, the courts viewed the couple as being of opposite sex—although the world will view them outwardly as two women (Scruggs 1996).

As we see, the binary sex system embedded in our legal system does not know how to deal with people who are transgendered. Trying to limit marriage to opposite-sex couples sometimes fails when intersexed and transsexual couples are involved. If legislatures try to specify what constitutes man and woman with no provisions for an in-between status, they will exclude the millions of intersexuals from having the opportunity to marry. There is no "opposite" sex for the intersexed. Laws allowing any two people to marry will not only help lesbian and gay male couples, but also the millions of intersexuals for whom there is no opposite to marry.

Employment

Many city and state statutes and Title VII of the federal Civil Rights Act of 1964 disallow discrimination based upon sex. However, the term *sex* is never defined and its legislative history is confused. Congress never discussed sexual categories other than male and female. As such, the courts have been reluctant to extend Title VII to homosexuals, intersexuals, and transsexuals. Likewise courts have refused to include intersexed and transgendered people as a protected class because they do not assert "traditional notions of sex" (*Holloway v. Arthur Anderson*).

In *Ulane v. Eastern Airlines,* Ulane was fired from Eastern Airlines after undergoing sexual reassignment surgery. Although Ulane had been a male pilot for many years before the male-to-female (MTF) surgery, the courts said Title VII protected sex—not changes in sex. In the only case of intersexual discrimination to be tried, the court found in *Wood v. C. G. Studios Inc.* that discrimination against hermaphrodites did not constitute sexual discrimination. The court claimed that Congress considered only the "plain" understanding of sex when it wrote Title VII. Thus, employers are free to discriminate against intersexed people because they do not fit the category of either male or female. Implicit in this finding is that intersexed people do not have a sex. This is incorrect. Intersexuals have a sex, just not within the binary system that requires all individuals to be either male or female. It is time to review our legal system to incorporate hybrid human sexuality, just as the medical community has done. Very few cities and states have included language to provide protection from discrimination to transsexuals and intersexuals.

SURGICAL ALTERATIONS

One of the ongoing controversies concerning intersexed individuals is the use of "corrective" surgery on intersexed babies to make them conform to sex norms. When a child is born with ambiguous genitalia, that is, either a too-large clitoris or too-small penis, since the 1960s doctors have recommended corrective surgery. Consequently, 90 percent are assigned as females and 10 percent are assigned as males with surgery including clitorectomy, vaginal construction, or destructive penile plastic surgery. This has often resulted in destroying the person's reproductive system and capacity to feel sexual pleasure (Dreger 1998).

One of the most famous cases of so-called corrective surgery involved a male baby whose penis was accidentally ablated when he was eight months old. The doctors decided to surgically alter the baby into a female and encouraged the parents to raise the child as a female and to hide all evidence that the child was born male. The parents did as recommended. In 1973 the case made headlines because the doctors reported that the parents and child had adapted normally—indicating that sex and gender are not inborn, but rather are surgically and socially constructed. For more than twenty years, the scientific literature reported this case as a success. However, in 1997 it was revealed that at the age of twelve the child refused to continue on hormone treatments and felt that she was really a male. The doctors agreed and remasculinized him using hormone shots, mastectomy, and reconstruction of his penis at age fifteen. He was accepted by the other boys and eventually married and helped his wife raise the wife's children.

What was learned from this case was that sex and gender identity are not easily manipulated. Sometimes it is claimed that intersexuals can be created surgically. This is not true. In this case, the boy was born male, attempts were made to surgically alter him into a female, these failed, and the boy was then resurgically altered back to a male. This is transsexualism, not intersexualism.

There has been a recent wave of lawsuits brought by intersexed adults who were surgically altered as children to conform to one sex. They complain of loathing their genitals, being sexually dysfunctional, and exhibiting other emotional scars (Kessler 1990). Case histories compiled between 1930 and 1960, before doctors began reconstructive surgeries on babies, show that intersexuals were well adjusted (Dicks and Childers

1934; Ghabrial and Girgis, 1962). With new evidence that people are not psychosexually neutral from birth as once thought, and that many surgically altered intersexuals show dissatisfaction with the procedures, medical experts are questioning the soundness of these interventions.

SEXUAL IDENTIFICATION

Medical science has identified eight factors in sexual identification: (1) genetic or chromosomal sex—XY (male) or XX (female); (2) gonadal sex (reproductive sex glands)—testes (male), ovaries (female), ovo-testes (intersexed); (3) internal morphological sex (determined after three months gestation)—seminal vesicles/prostate (male) or vagina/uterus/fallopian tubes (female); (4) external morphological sex (genitalia)—penis/scrotum (male) or clitoris/labia (female); (5) hormonal sex—androgens (male) or estrogens (female); (6) phenotypic sex (secondary sexual features)—facial and chest hair (men) or breasts (female); (7) assigned gender through rearing; and (8) sexual identity.

These factors are congruent in most people, and males and females are obvious from their looks. For intersexuals, these factors could be ambiguous, incongruent, or both—and the law must determine how to weigh the eight factors in the determination of sex. It has been proposed that the law could ignore sex completely, being not only gender neutral but gender blind.

Even if seven factors are congruent with being a particular sex, the person may not identify with the sex with which they were born. This is the eighth factor—sexual identity. Transsexuals have the feeling that they were born into the wrong body. They too may select reconstructive surgery so that their physical selves better conform to their emotional selves.

SEXUAL DIFFERENTIATION

Because the law presumes a binary sexual system, it is important to understand how sexual differentiation comes about so as to create laws that are more inclusive and fair.

All human embryos are sexually undifferentiated during the first seven weeks of growth after conception. At the seventh week, the testes-determining factor ("master switch") on the Y chromosome turns on and signals the embryonic gonads to form into testes. Embryos with XY chromosomes begin the path of becoming a male human. Because the typical female has twenty-three pairs of X chromosomes, the master switch is not turned on and the embryo continues along a typical female path. Many individuals have chromosome patterns different from either XX or XY, which may include XXX, XXY, XXXY, XYYY, XYYYY, and XO (a condition called Turner's Syndrome, in which half of the chromosomes are missing). These other patterns can affect the development of sex-determining hormones. It is important to realize that although chromosomes determine which hormones are produced, it is hormones that affect sexual development. Thus, courts that have relied upon chromosomes to determine sex are only partially correct and often are wrong.

Many factors can interrupt or interfere with the developmental path toward becoming male or female. Medical science has labeled some of them. These include chromosomal sex disorders, gonadal sex disorders, internal organ anomalies, external organ anomalies, hormonal disorders, and gender identity disorder. Many people who look like a particular sex from outward appearances do not meet the eight factors. For example, Maria Patino, a Spanish hurdler at the World University Games in 1985, was barred from playing when she failed the chromosome verification test. She had male chromosomes (XY), but had the external morphological sex, phenotype, and self-identification of a female. She had androgen insensitivity syndrome (AIS) and was unaware of it. (See Greenberg 1999 for a more detailed discussion of these disorders.)

Sex differentiation can also change at puberty. In several villages in the Dominican Republic and Papua, New Guinea, there are children born with external female genitalia who, at puberty, have their testes descend, their clitoris enlarge and become a penis, and their voices deepen. This occurrence is common enough that anthropologists report the villagers have given these children special names—*guevodoche* ("balls at twelve") or *machihembra* ("male female").

Many other cultures recognize people who are between the two sexes and form a third category. Many Native American cultures accepted and recognized a third gender called "two-spirit" (previously known as *berdache,* a term used by French explorers to describe Native Americans who violated gender and sexual norms). They were neither male nor female and enjoyed a special and revered status. Similar beliefs were found in India where transgendered people were known as *hijras.* A third sex is found in ancient cultures and religious texts, including the Jewish Tosefta and Talmud.

Even English law recognized three categories of humans. The 13th century British jurist Bracton stated in *On the Laws and Customs of England,* "(m)ankind may also be classified in another way: male, female, or hermaphrodite" (31). The law recognized three classifications of humans and one set of legal doctrine for all. Bracton further wrote "(a) hermaphrodite (wa)s classed with male or female according to the predominance of the sexual organs" (32). Later, in the 16th century, the renowned jurist Lord Coke wrote, "Every heire is either a male, or female, or an hermaphrodite, that is both male and female. And an hermaphrodite (which is also called Androgynus) shall be heire, either as male or female, according to that kind of the sexe which doth prevaile" (Coke, 1812).

IMPLICATIONS

The issues surrounding intersexuals may trigger a future wave of scientific and legal thought. The process of overcoming prejudice is the process of deconstructing a social bias. African Americans went from being nonpersons and property when slavery was legal, to becoming second-class citizens when segregation was legal, to finally having all legal differences abolished when *Brown v. Board of Education* ruled that the concept of "separate but equal" was inherently unequal. This process deconstructed the concept of race and the allocation of rights and privileges associated with that attribute.

Lesbians and gay men are entering the second phase of overcoming their stigmatization. Until the beginning of the civil rights movement, homosexual behavior was illegal and lesbians and gays were routinely arrested, prosecuted, and imprisoned and were constantly at risk of losing their jobs, homes, and children. With the possibility of recognition of same-sex marriages, a terrible backlash is occurring at the federal and state levels to define and defend marriage as an exclusive heterosexual institution. Some states are attempting to ameliorate the situation by providing domestic partnership for same-sex couples while retaining marriage for heterosexuals. Thus, lesbians and gay men are entering the "separate but equal" phase of civil rights. Ultimately, gay liberation will render sexual orientation legally irrelevant, much as African American liberation deconstructed race and the women's movement is deconstructing gender as a legal basis for discrimination.

Intersexed and transgendered people are still legal nonentities. Following the same civil rights process, we could predict that some laws and courts will attempt to define a third sex. But, with existing laws specifying, for example, that only one man and one woman can be legally married, intersexed people will have only achieved a status located between the first stage of being nonpeople with no rights and the second phase of being separate but supposedly equal. Ultimately, intersexual liberation will deconstruct sex. This will be achieved when we no longer have to list sex on a birth certificate, driver's license, and other documents, and no law favors one sex over another. (See also **Sexual Orientation**.)

References

Bracton, H. 1968. *On the Laws and Customs of England.* Translated with revisions and notes, by Samuel E. Thorne. Cambridge: Published in association with the Selden Society, the Belknap Press of Harvard University Press.

Capers, B. 1991. "Sex(ual Orientation) and Title VII." *Columbia Law Review* 91(5): 1158–1187.

Coke, E. 1812. *The First Part of the Institutes of the Laws of England.* Institutes 8.a.

Diamond, M. 1997. "Sexual Identity and Sexual Orientation in Children with Traumatized or Ambiguous Genitalia." *Journa of Sex Research* 199: 34.

Dicks, G. H., and A. T. Childers. 1934. "The Social Transformation of a Boy Who Had Lived His First Fourteen Years as a Girl: A Case History." *American Journal of Orthopsychiatry* 4(4): 508–517.

———. 1944. "The Social Transformation of a Boy Who Had Lived His First Fourteen Years as a Girl II: Fourteen Years Later." *American Journal of Orthopsychiatry* 14(3): 448–452.

Dreger, A. D. 1998. "When Medicine Goes Too Far in the Pursuit of Normality. One Person's Abnormality Is Another Person's Life." *New York Times* (28 July 1998): B10.

Erikson Education Foundation. 2000. *Information and Guidelines for Transsexuals*. Erikson Education Foundation (now renamed Renaissance Transgender Association) website: www.ren.org.

Fausto-Sterling, A. 1993. "How Many Sexes Are There? Intersexuality Is a Biological Condition, Not a Disease, and Medical Policy toward It Should Be Reevaluated." *New York Times* (12 March 1993): A15.

Ghabrial, F., and S. M. Girgis. 1962. "Reorientation of Sex: Report of Two Cases." *International Journal of Fertility* 249 (July–September): 7.

Greenberg, J. A. 1999. "Defining Male and Female: Intersexuality and the Collision between Law and Biology." *Arizona Law Review* 41(2): 265–328.

Harris, L. 1988. Reprint. "The Lynn Harris Story." *Social Issues Resources Series* 3(19) [cover story]. Originally appeared in *Los Angeles Herald Examiner* (28 November 1988): B1.

Kessler, S. J. 1990. "The Medical Construction of Gender: Case Management of Intersexed Infants." *Signs* 16(1): 3.

Scruggs, A. 1996. "Tying Legalities into Tangled Knots." *Cleveland Plain Dealer* (7 October 1996): 1B.

"Transgender Legal Complications Abound." 2000. *Lesbian/Gay Law Notes* (April).

Valdes, F. 1995. "Queers, Sissies, Dykes, and Tomboys: Deconstructing the Conflation of 'Sex,' 'Gender,' and 'Sexual Orientation' in Euro-American Law and Society." *California Law Review* 83(1): 1–378.

J

JURY DUTY Lesbians and gay men may serve as jurors without restriction. The process of questioning prospective jurors for competency is referred to as *voir dire.* It is during voir dire that both the defense and prosecution in a trial have the right to disqualify a predetermined number of prospective jurors without explanation (known as a peremptory strike). Recently, courts have determined that sexual orientation cannot be used as grounds for a peremptory strike, and, thus, lesbians and gay men cannot be excluded from the jury for that reason (Chiang 2000). Also, a juror cannot be disqualified for cause because of homosexuality (*State v. Viggiani*).

In cases in which sexual orientation is involved, particularly antidiscrimination cases, it is important that the jury be representative of a cross section of society and include people of differing sexual orientations. However, during voir dire, prospective jurors cannot be asked their sexual orientation. This eliminates the possibility of prejudice. Prosecutors and defense lawyers need to restrict all questions concerning sexual orientation to the jurors' beliefs and attitudes, not their personal practices or identity. (See also **Criminal Law**.)

Reference

Chiang, H. 2000. "Ruling Protects Gay Juror Rights." *San Francisco Chronicle* (3 February 2000): A1.

L

LAMBDA LEGAL DEFENSE AND EDUCATION FUND Founded in 1973, the Lambda Legal Defense and Education Fund is a national organization that aims to help achieve the full recognition of civil rights for lesbians, gay men, and people with **AIDS** through litigation, education, and public policy work. Lambda has been successful at challenging discrimination based on sexual orientation in employment, housing, public services, public accommodations, and the military. Lambda advocates for parenting rights, domestic partnership benefits, and equal marriage rights, and works to protect privacy, equal protection, and First Amendment rights.

Lambda was born out of rejection by a New York court of its application for incorporation. In 1973 New York's highest court overturned the ruling and Lambda took legal form. Initially, Lambda was a completely volunteer organization. By 1977 Lambda began to expand and change with the adoption of a governing board of directors and a paid executive director. In 1979 an office was opened in space at the New York Civil Liberties office. Lambda doubled in size by 1982, as it became a national organization with half of its members coming from outside New York.

Lambda fought and won the nation's first AIDS discrimination lawsuit in 1983. Since then Lambda has been at the forefront of many of the most influential lawsuits concerning issues that affect lesbians, gay men, and people with AIDS.

LESBIAN *Lesbian* is the term for a female with a same-gender orientation. The regular and conscious use of *lesbian,* as in "lesbians and gay men," affirms the equality and independence of women within the gay community. Reference to *gay people* and the *gay community* as inclusive of lesbians and gay men is acceptable if not relied upon exclusively. Many lesbians prefer the term *gay woman.* (See also **Sexual Orientation**.)

LESBIAN MOTHERS Women who are lesbian and involved with raising children are lesbian mothers. Child custody is the primary concern for lesbian mothers. Antigay stereotypes have played a major role in the legal denial of lesbian mothers' rights toward their children.

It is estimated that there are 1.5 million lesbians in the United States who are mothers (Henry 1990). The stereotypes courts have considered in child custody cases involving lesbian mothers faced with divorce include: (1) homosexuals are mentally ill; (2) lesbian women are less maternal than their heterosexual counterparts; (3) children raised by lesbian mothers are more likely to develop psychological or mental problems; (4) children raised by lesbian mothers are more likely to be sexually molested by the custodial parent, her partner, or her acquaintances; (5) "the gender role development of the child will be significantly impaired" (Falk 1993); (6) gender or sexual development will be influenced toward homosexuality; and (7) children in lesbian households will be stigmatized by the society and their peers. None of these stereotypes is true, yet courts have relied upon them to remove children from the custody of mothers who are lesbian.

Research by Bernice Goodman (1977) into the child-rearing practices of lesbian mothers found the following:

1. The personalities and attitudes of lesbian mothers concerning child rearing were as diverse as those found among heterosexual mothers.
2. Lesbian mothers are ambivalent about their children to the same degree as heterosexual mothers.
3. The lifestyles of lesbian mothers have a range equal to that of heterosexual mothers with two significant differences:
   a. Many lesbian mothers have an overwhelming sense of guilt and shame about their choice of a woman as a lover.
   b. The lesbian mother is at a greater advantage than the heterosexual mother in being less likely to have a man in her life out of need.

Recent research has reaffirmed the initial work of Bernice Goodman. Surveys of lesbians have revealed that one-third have been in heterosexual marriages and of these one-half have had children (Kirkpatrick 1987). There are great similarities between lesbians and divorced heterosexual mothers concerning marital history, pregnancy history, child-rearing attitudes, and lifestyle (Golombok, Spence, and Rutter 1983; Hoeffer 1981; Kirkpatrick, Smith, and Roy 1981; Mandel and Hotvedt 1980). The only difference these studies have found is the special fears lesbian mothers have of custody battles that might result from public disclosure of their homosexuality and the potential loss of their children. Attendant with these fears is the mother's personal concerns about whether her lesbianism may affect the development of her child, how and when to divulge her sexual orientation to her child, and the introduction of a lover into the household. (See also **Child Custody and Visitation Rights; Gay Fathers**.)

It is the sense of guilt and shame that interferes with many lesbian mothers' interactions with their children. Questions of "proper" behavior constantly come up and frequently within a heterosexist context. How is the lesbian mother to answer her child when the child informs the mother that he or she is being picked on at school for having a "dyke" mom? During the late 1970s, the feminist and lesbian movements were primarily concerned with consciousness raising. Although little direct political action was taken against schools, the psychological process of accepting the child's feelings of being in a position of difference evolved from the mother's challenge to her inner feelings of guilt and shame.

Other research has shown that lesbian mothers are virtually indistinguishable from heterosexual mothers in their parenting skills, except in their relationships to their partners (Hanscombe and Forster 1982; Kweskin and Cook 1982; Pagelow 1980; Shavelson et al. 1980). Additionally, lesbian mothers tend to be more self-confident (Green et al. 1986), to be more egalitarian in the distribution of household chores and **family** decision-making (Patterson 1995), and to report greater satisfaction in their relationships than heterosexual mothers (Pagelow 1980). Motherhood did not change the woman's desire to be a lesbian, if anything it reinforced her desire to establish relationships with other women, and these other women, in turn, discovered buried maternal longings to have children of their own.

The research on children raised by openly lesbian mothers has shown that there are no differences between children brought up by lesbians and children brought up by heterosexual single parents. Children of lesbians exhibit no greater incidence of homosexuality than the society at large (Green 1978). When closeted lesbian mothers reveal to their children that they are lesbians, the children do "experience shock and surprise at the disclosure of a mother's lesbian relationship . . . and do defend their mother against criticism, especially from the father" (Kirkpatrick 1987, 210). In these cases, it is suggested that peer counseling of children with similar experiences may be very valuable (Kirkpatrick 1987, 211). Therapeutic techniques should deal more with the usual issues of family intimacy and trust than the "deviance" of the lesbian mother. (See also **Child Molestation Stereotype; Children of Homosexual Parents**.)

Overall, the concern courts have expressed about lesbian mothers and their ability to be good mothers to their children is unfounded. Many courts now reject the old antilesbian stereotypes.

References

Falk, P. 1993. "Lesbian Mothers: Psychosocial Assumptions in Family Law." In *Psychological Perspectives on Lesbian and Gay Male Experiences,* edited by L. D. Garnets and D. C. Kimmel. New York: Columbia University Press.

Golombok, S., A. Spence, and M. Rutter. 1983. "Children in Lesbian and Single-Parent Households: Psychosexual and Psychiatric Appraisal." *Journal of Child Psychology and Psychiatry* 24: 551–572.

Goodman, B. 1977. *The Lesbian: A Celebration of Difference.* East Haven, CT: Out & Out Books.

Green, R. 1978. "Sexual Identity of 37 Children Raised by Homosexual or Transsexual Parents." *American Journal of Psychiatry* 135(6): 692–697.

Green, R., J. B. Mandel, M. E. Hotvedt, J. Gray, and L. Smith. 1986. "Lesbian Mothers and Their Children: A Comparison with Solo Parent Heterosexual Mothers and Their Children." *Archives of Sexual Behavior* 15(2): 167–184.

Hanscombe, G., and J. Forster. 1982. *Rocking the Cradle—Lesbian Mothers: A Challenge in Family Living.* Boston: Alyson Publications.

Henry, W., III. 1990. "The Lesbians Next Door." *Time,* special fall issue, 78.

Hoeffer, B. 1981. "Children's Acquisition of Sex-Role Behavior in Lesbian-Mother Families." *American Journal of Orthopsychiatry* 51: 536–544.

Kirkpatrick, M. 1987. "Clinical Implications of Lesbian Mother Studies." *Journal of Homosexuality* 14(1–2): 201–211.

Kirkpatrick, M., A. Smith, and R. Roy. 1981. "Lesbian Mothers and Their Children: A Comparative Study." *American Journal of Orthopsychiatry* 51: 545–551.

Kweskin, S. L., and A. S. Cook. 1982. "Heterosexual and Homosexual Mothers' Self-Described Sex-Role Behavior and Ideal Sex-Role Behavior in Children." *Sex Roles* 8: 967–975.

Mandel, J., and M. Hotvedt. 1980. "Lesbians as Parents." *Husarts and Praktijk* 4: 31–34.

Pagelow, M. D. 1980. "Heterosexual and Lesbian Single Mothers: A Comparison of Problems, Coping, and Solutions." *Journal of Homosexuality* 5(3): 189–204.

Patterson, C. J. 1995. "Sexual Orientation and Human Development: An Overview." *Developmental Psychology* 31: 3–11.

Shavelson, E. S., M. K. Biaggio, H. H. Cross, and R. E. Lehman. 1980. "Lesbian Women's Perceptions of Their Parent-Child Relationships." *Journal of Homosexuality* 5(3): 205–215.

LEWD CONDUCT Lewd conduct statutes criminalize public sexual behaviors. These are sometimes known as indecent exposure, vagrancy, or disorderly conduct statutes. There is a long history of abuse of the lesbian and gay community through the use of lewd conduct statutes. For example, in the 1940s and 1950s the police would enter lesbian bars, pick out the most masculine-looking lesbian, take her outside to the street, and make her strip off most of her clothes. They were looking to see if she was wearing men's boxer shorts. Laws at that time in many cities did not allow people to wear more than three articles of clothing appropriate for the other gender. Wearing "inappropriate" clothing was criminalized under the lewd conduct statutes. These same tactics were used against feminine-acting men. Similarly, many cities did not allow people of the same gender to touch or dance together. If a man tried to remove his shirt on the dance floor of a gay bar in Michigan in the mid-1980s, the house lights were turned on and the DJ would publicly admonish the dancer to put his shirt back on.

Lewd conduct statutes found in the United States today are more narrowly focused on the public exposure of one's genitals or engaging in public sex. There is wide variance between states as to what constitutes "public" space. Mostly these statutes are enforced in parks, bars, public bathrooms, adult bookstores, and movie theaters. Sometimes the distinction between public and private is unclear and the police raid private parties held at a bar or facility that is closed to the public.

Many lewd conduct statutes include language defining a public place as an area without a "reasonable expectation of privacy" and the prohibited behaviors as being offensive to a "reasonable person." The courts have struggled to decide whether a bar attracting a particular clientele, for example a leather bar with a back room where sex takes place, is truly public or if the particular public that enters the bar would be offended by the sexual behaviors to be found there. This is related to the existence of public nudity at beaches and rivers. Most cities tacitly accept the existence of such areas, as long as they are relatively confined and remote. Usually such areas are ignored unless criminal activities occur or conservative politicians take up the issue for political reasons.

Police often arrest men for engaging in sex with other men in public parks. Are these men gay? Research indicates that 54 percent of those arrested for lewd conduct are married and almost all do not identify themselves as gay, but rather as heterosexual (Humphreys 1970). Thus, the problem of public sex is not directly a gay issue, but rather a problem of inappropriate behavior by mostly heterosexual men that inadvertently reinforces lesbian and gay male stereotypes.

Although lewd conduct laws are usually gender and sexual orientation nonspecific, they have nevertheless been used disproportionately against men engaged in homosexual activity. Across the nation, lesbian and gay organizations report a disparity in police action: heterosexuals receive a warning not to engage in public sex, whereas same-sex couples are arrested and convicted for engaging in the same activity. Police have not been forthcoming with reviews of their arrest records. For example, for three years the Lambda Legal Defense and Education Fund attempted to obtain lewd conduct arrest records from the Los Angeles Police Department (LAPD). Finally, in January 2000, Lambda was forced to sue the LAPD for the records (Lambda Legal Defense and Education Fund 2000). As of this writing, the records have not been released. Without the records, it is impossible to determine the extent of the problem. The long delays give the impression that the police are purposely hiding discriminatory practices.

A favorite tactic of police is to conduct sting operations in which officers pose as gay men on the prowl for sex at notable cruising areas. Pop singer George Michael was arrested in such a sting in 1998 while using a Beverly Hills park bathroom. Police claim they arrest far more heterosexual men engaging in lewd conduct. But these are not the same situations. The filing of lewd conduct charges against heterosexual men usually stems from arrests for solicitation of female prostitutes. These are weak cases. Here, the charge of lewd conduct is a last resort and easy conviction when a prostitution conviction is unlikely. Police, however, make most of their lewd conduct arrests against gay men by targeting sting operations.

Bruce Nickerson, a lawyer from San Carlos, California, has been successful at shutting down police sting operations in Modesto and several San Francisco Bay area communities. He was the lawyer who sparked the 1996 California Supreme Court ruling (*Baluyut v. Superior Court*) that found police lewd-conduct practices in the city of Mountain View to discriminate against gays. He contends that decoy operations are invalid as decided in a state high court ruling in 1979. Here, the court agreed that, for someone to be charged with lewd conduct, he or she should have known that there would be people present who would be offended by the conduct. When decoy officers invite someone to have sex, whether verbally or through their actions, there is no violation of the law because the invitee reasonably believes that the decoy officers won't be offended by his or her acceptance of the invitation. Using this defense, Nickerson rarely lost a case. Many communities have stopped decoy or sting operations rather than face civil suits. Instead, increased patrol and police presence in known cruise areas reduces the number of inappropriate behaviors.

In lieu of permanent records for lewd conduct violations, some law enforcement agencies have attempted to implement diversion programs. Sometimes, lewd conduct statutes include language that also addresses **solicitation and loitering**. (See also **Criminal Law; Police Abuses**.)

References

Humphreys, L. 1970. *Tearoom Trade*. Chicago: Aldine.

Lambda Legal Defense and Education Fund. 2000. "Lambda Back in Court for Lapd Lewd Conduct Arrest Records." 2000. Press release on Lambda Legal Defense and Education Fund website: www.lldef.org/cgi-bin/pages/documents/record?record=555. Accessed 20 January 2000.

M

MARRIAGE The idea that gays and lesbians should be allowed to marry has polarized the United States. Hawaii came close to legalizing same-sex marriages in 1993. The Vermont Supreme Court required the Vermont legislature to create equality between same- and opposite-sex couples, either by allowing same-sex couples to marry or by creating a new category that provided all the same legal benefits. In April 2000 Vermont created **civil unions** for same-sex couples that conferred these rights. Other states reacted with panic and passed legislation to deny recognition to such unions. At this time, no state allows same-sex couples to marry. The **Defense of Marriage Act (DOMA)** established the union of one male with one female as the legal definition of marriage with respect to federal laws and programs, and specified that states could legally ignore same-sex marriages performed in other states.

CONCERNS OVER SAME-SEX MARRIAGES

Religious conservatives have expressed a number of recurring concerns over allowing same-sex marriages. These include:

- Marriage should be reserved for monogamous male-female attachments to further the goal of raising psychologically, emotionally, and educationally balanced offspring.

Counterpoint: This belief is based on two false concepts. The first is that the primary purpose of marriage is reproduction. If this were true, then people who by reason of age or infertility cannot have children or who choose not to have children should not be able to marry—yet they can. In addition, most of the time that heterosexuals engage in sex, it is nonreproductive (that is, no offspring are produced). Also, many people have children outside of marriage. Reproduction and marriage are not inseparable. Second, the belief that only heterosexual parents provide emotionally stable environments for children is false. **Lesbian mothers**, **gay fathers**, and same-sex couples provide equally healthy **family** environments for children.

- Government policy should encourage marriage and intact families because they are the basic units of social order, stability, and growth.

Counterpoint: Many lesbians and gay men agree with this statement. However, there is an underlying assumption that healthy families can be structured only along traditional lines. This is not true. Families can take many different forms. Same-sex marriages help create legal stability for children of lesbian and gay couples. Government policies that encourage families should recognize same-sex marriages.

- Even domestic partnerships, as legalized by the city of San Francisco, are a reason for alarm. The apparent evenhandedness of the law is deceptive. Heterosexuals, who have the option of marriage, will not use domestic partnership registration. Instead, this is a homosexual rights ordinance and it promotes behavior that increases the likelihood of transmission of **AIDS**.

Counterpoint: Many leaders of the religious right are alarmed at the adoption of domestic partnership programs. They see this as a step toward final recognition of same-sex marriage. This is probably true, but it should not cause alarm. Domestic partnership is a gay rights stopgap provision. Gays and lesbians should be afforded the option to be married as a matter of justice. Congress conferred preferred legal status for heterosexuals with the Defense of Marriage Act, in which *marriage* was defined as "a legal union between one man and one woman as husband and wife." At least 1,049 federal laws and regulations involve marital status, and thus give special rights to heterosexuals (Bedrick 1997).

It is often claimed that domestic partnership programs are homosexual rights ordinances in disguise. Cities that have enacted such programs have found that a majority of enrollees are opposite-sex couples, not lesbian or gay male couples. (See also **Domestic Partnership**.) Finally, the belief that a homosexual "lifestyle" promotes disease is false and suggesting that it is true is one of the strategies used by the religious right to smear the gay community.

- This is part of the gay agenda. From asking that persecution end to demanding recognition, gays are asking for domestic partnership, marriage, or both as a means for preferential treatment to counter historic discrimination.

Counterpoint: The **gay agenda**, if there is such a thing, is to obtain equal rights, not special rights. (See also **Religious Right Agenda**.) No gay activist organization, lesbian and gay student group, or gay academic has ever requested **affirmative action** or preferential treatment based upon sexual orientation. Linking the drive for equal rights with affirmative action is misleading.

- Approving of gay marriage will lead to the sanction of **polygamy** or worse.

Counterpoint: Again, this is a scare tactic used to imply that approving same-sex marriages will create a domino effect, thus allowing all kinds of marriages. This is faulty logic, yet this and other similar accusations were used in the debates over interracial marriages. Allowing interracial marriages has not led to the downfall of society nor an abandonment of marriage as once alleged by white supremacists. Allowing same-sex marriages is not related to the issue of polygamy or to the sanction of other family forms, which will be debated on their own merits or lack thereof.

There are striking parallels between the arguments once used against interracial marriage and the arguments now given against same-sex marriages.

FOUNDATION OF MARRIAGE

Sometimes it is claimed that same-sex marriage is simply impossible because it is barred by definition. This takes on a number of arguments:

- Contradiction in terms. Same-sex marriage is often considered a contradiction in terms because marriage is defined as the holy and legal union of one man and one woman. However, whether something is a contradiction in terms depends upon the definition used to characterize the term. For example, interracial marriages were not legal in many states until the U.S. Supreme Court in 1967 in *Loving v. Virginia* declared such marriages legal. Before then, the concept of interracial marriages was a contradiction in terms. Even so, sixteen states still have antimiscegenation laws on their books and the Uniform Marriage and Divorce Act allows the denial of interracial marriage. In other countries, people of different religions have been legally prohibited from marrying. In those situations, interreligious marriage would be a contradiction in terms. Thus, claiming that same-sex marriage is a contradiction in terms depends upon which particular definition of marriage is used.

  The problem is finding definitions that are reasonable and enforceable. Definitions are a mix of common usage, formalized speech (as found in the dictionary), legal and legislative terminology, and court interpretation. There can be wide variances among these sources of definitions and they can have different meanings in different cultures and change over time through social forces. It is common today to hear same-sex couples refer to their relationship as a marriage. Journalists and others often discuss and review same-sex marriage issues. However, *Black's Law Dictionary* defines *marriage* as the "[l]egal union of one man and one woman as husband and wife" (1990, 779). *Black's* definition is based upon the 1974 court ruling in *Singer v. Hara* that relied upon the "usual and ordinary" use of words for its definition. Times have changed and possibly the same case today would come up with a definition of marriage that includes same-sex couples.

The legislatures of many states and the federal government, through the Defense of Marriage Act (DOMA), have attempted to preempt same-sex marriages by defining marriage as the legal union of one man and one woman. They leave in place state prohibitions of marriages to blood or adoptive relatives, underage persons, and someone who is currently married (polygamy). At one time, interracial marriages were also disallowed. The very act of explicitly refusing to permit same-sex couples to marry acknowledges these relationships. Thus, same-sex marriages are not a contradiction in terms in both the common and legislative use.

- Nature. Another approach is to claim that the definition of marriage is so authoritative that legislatures cannot redefine it. For example, in *Jones v. Hallahan,* the Kentucky Supreme Court in 1973 concluded that the state of Kentucky was not discriminating against two women who wanted to be married because it was their "own incapability of entering into a marriage as that term is defined" that prevented the union. On some occasions legislatures cannot change a definition through the adoption of law. For example, states cannot pass laws that deprive citizens of their fundamental rights unless there is a compelling state interest, that is, they cannot create definitions that violate already accepted definitions. However, the fifty states, the District of Columbia, and other jurisdictions are constantly forming law and redefining conditions. Through court cases these are compared to existing law and legislative goals. Together, definitions, such as the definition of marriage, continue to evolve. As such, the definition of marriage is not obvious by "nature," but rather reflects the social mores of the time—and that now includes the possibility of same-sex marriages.
- God's will. Sometimes it is claimed that God's will precludes same-sex marriage. This rests on two assumptions. First, that *all* religions believe same-sex marriages are a violation of moral

> codes. This is not true. Many religions perform same-sex commitment ceremonies, including some sects of Christianity. As of March 2000 the national's largest Jewish movement announced that their members were free to officiate at same-sex unions (Stammer 2000).
>
> There is no consensus as to "God's will" concerning same-sex marriages. To impose one view would be tantamount to adopting a state religion. This violates the U.S. Constitution's principle of separation of church and state. Second, even if all religions agreed about the issue of same-sex marriages, U.S. law does not require the government to adopt this position. Thus, the claim that God's will precludes acceptance of same-sex marriages is unsubstantiated.

The U.S Government has a fundamental interest in marriage. A number of court cases have affirmed this position. In *Loving v. Virginia* (1967), the Supreme Court said, "[The] freedom to marry has long been recognized as one of the vital personal rights essential to the orderly pursuit of happiness by free men . . . [and is] one of the 'basic civil rights of man,' fundamental to our very existence and survival" (12). This position is supported in *Griswold v. Connecticut.* Likewise, in *Santosky v. Kramer* (1982) the Court stated that marriage "is a fundamental liberty interest protected by the Fourteenth Amendment" (753). As dealing with a fundamental interest, marriage laws receive heightened scrutiny when they are challenged in the courts.

What is not clear is why—if marriage is a fundamental right—same-sex couples are not afforded that right. A few lower courts have addressed this issue with a mixture of results. The *Singer v. Hara* court denied same-sex marriage because "it is apparent that no same-sex couple offers the possibility of birth of children by their union" (1195). In *Zablock v. Redhail,* the Supreme Court linked the right to marry to procreation and the raising of families.

Procreation seems to be a predicate for marriage. Is this necessary? Even the *Singer* court recognized that "married couples are not required to become parents and . . . some couples are incapable of becoming parents and . . . not all couples who produce children are married" (1195). Still, the Court claimed that each of these reasons was an exception to the rule and was not, in itself, an argument invalidating the link between procreation and the right to marry. The decision was faulty on a number of grounds. First, the belief that it was the exceptional married couple who did not have children is false. Many married couples do not have children (those who are sterile, married after menopause, or those who elect not to have children), and this is very common as evidenced by our census numbers. Even if this were not true, it is not a persuasive argument. Second, same-sex couples do have children—either from previous opposite-sex marriages, **artificial insemination**, or adoption. The argument that marriage provides stability for children applies equally for opposite- and same-sex couples. Thus, court decisions in the area have been confused and indicate an unwillingness on the part of the courts to treat same-sex relationships fairly and in good faith.

In *Turner v. Safley,* the Supreme Court came to a number of important conclusions about marriage. It determined that prisoners had a right to marry while they are in prison because: (1) marriages are expressions of emotional support and public commitment; (2) there may be the exercise of religious faith; (3) most marriages are formed with the expectation that they will be consummated; and (4) marriage is often required in order to receive government benefits. The Court did not mention the need for procreation as a predicate to marriage. Likewise, it said *most,* but not *all,* marriages are formed with the expectation of consummation. Considering this ruling, it seems contradictory that courts will not allow same-sex couples to marry because they meet all the stated conditions.

It has been suggested that sex statutes would preclude same-sex marriages. The Supreme Court in ***Bowers v. Hardwick*** upheld Georgia's right to impose **sodomy** statutes upon its citizens. However, Georgia's law, as written, limited sodomy to sex between unmarried persons, whether same- or opposite-sex couples. Thus, if same-sex couples were allowed to be married, the Georgia sodomy statute would not apply. There is great variation among states as to what constitutes sodomy. Most would not affect the ability of same-sex couples to marry. (See also **Criminal Law**.)

Finally, it is sometimes claimed that allowing same-sex couples to marry would give the impression that the state encourages or condones homosexual behavior. In ***Romer v. Evans,*** the Supreme Court analyzed this charge. The state of Colorado claimed that if **Amendment 2** (which denied legal protection from discrimination based upon sexual orientation) was not upheld, then it would give the impression that Colorado encourages homosexuality. The Court decided that allowing intrasexual or interracial marriages does not become an endorsement of those marriages. Thus, allowing same-sex marriages does not mean that the state morally approves of them, only that they are legally allowed.

The state has a fundamental interest in marriage. The courts have linked marriage and procreation, yet recent cases suggest that this link may be weakening. If unbiased standards are applied, all the conditions that have been set to enable opposite-sex couples to marry have been met by same-sex couples. Therefore, the state's position on marriage should apply to same-sex couples.

EQUAL PROTECTION

Besides approaching marriage as a fundamental right, same-sex marriage can be analyzed by courts under the equal protection clause of the U.S. Constitution. The Supreme Court has determined that legal discrimination against specific groups requires closer scrutiny to determine its constitutional validity. When determining the constitutionality of legislation aimed at specific groups, the Court uses a three-tiered analysis: (1) strict scrutiny; (2) heightened scrutiny; or (3) the rational basis test. Under strict scrutiny, the state must show a narrow and compelling interest for enacting the legislation. Heightened scrutiny requires the state to demonstrate that the statute is substantially related to an important state interest. The rational basis test simply requires that the statute be rationally related to a legitimate state goal. At this time, only religion, race, ethnicity, and national origin are considered suspect classes requiring strict scrutiny. Gender and illegitimacy have merited a quasi-suspect class status and statutes impacting these people come under heightened scrutiny. Sexual orientation has not achieved a suspect or quasi-suspect class status. Laws affecting people based on sexual orientation are evaluated under the rational basis test. (See also **Suspect Class**.)

Many legal experts believe that laws specifying sexual orientation should be evaluated with strict scrutiny as a suspect class. Such a designation was almost achieved in *Romer v. Evans,* but the Court found sexual orientation failed one aspect of the test for suspect class. Will suspect class be achieved for sexual orientation? In *Massachusetts Board of Retirement v. Murgia* (1976), Justice Marshall noted that the Court has "apparently lost interest in recognizing further . . . 'suspect' classes" (318–319). The entire subject of suspect class may be redefined by the courts so that sexual orientation will achieve legal protection.

Another approach is to view laws that discriminate based on sexual orientation as a form of sex or gender discrimination. In ***Baehr v. Lewin,*** the Hawaii Supreme Court agreed with this interpretation. Because the Hawaii constitution made sex a suspect class, the statute preventing same-sex couples from marrying came under strict scrutiny. The state could not show a compelling interest for maintaining the statute. Before the court could make a final ruling allowing same-sex couples to marry, the voters of Hawaii passed a constitutional amendment defining marriage in terms of opposite-sex couples only. Thus, the issue became moot.

The Vermont Supreme Court reviewed this same connection in ***Baker v. Vermont.*** The Vermont constitution made gender discrimination a suspect class subject to strict scrutiny. The state could not make a compelling argument as to why same-sex couples could not be legally married. The Vermont legislature crafted a new category—civil union—to give same-sex couples the same legal rights and responsibilities available through opposite-sex marriage.

If sexual orientation ever achieves suspect class status with the U.S. Supreme Court, a host of discriminatory laws against lesbians and gay men should fall. The logic found in *Loving v. Virginia* would demonstrate that antigay legislation is virtually identical to racial and anti-interracial marriage discrimination. However, this is not anticipated. Instead, more courts are expected to see the connection between sexual orientation and gender or sex, and apply the equal protection clause accordingly. Ultimately, discrimination against lesbians and gay men is based on bigotry and bias. The *Romer* Court made that clear when it stated that "[it] seems inexplicable by anything but animus toward the class that it affects . . . [and antigay statutes] lack a rational relationship to legitimate state interests" (1627).

FULL FAITH AND CREDIT CLAUSE

With the prospect of same-sex marriage becoming accepted in Hawaii and Vermont, many states enacted preemptive legislation defining marriage as the union of one man and one woman and specifying that they would not legally recognize same-sex marriages celebrated in other states.

The federal government became involved in the debate. It was feared that if one state allowed same-sex marriage, there would be a rush of lesbian and gay couples flying to that state, getting married, and then going back to their home states and demanding that those states recognize their marriages. Many people believed that the **full faith and credit clause** of the U.S. Constitution would force states to accept these marriages. To avoid this, Congress passed the Defense of Marriage Act (DOMA), which defined marriage as the union of one man and one woman for federal purposes, and allowed states to refuse to recognize same-sex marriages performed in other states.

It was obvious from the debate in Congress that legislators were ignorant about how the clause and choice of law process works. The DOMA was unnecessary because states already possessed the legal power to deny same-sex marriages.

The full faith and credit clause of the U.S. Constitution (Article IV, Section 1) requires that the states accept the "public acts, records, and judicial proceedings" of other states. The purpose of the law is to help unify laws throughout the United States. For example, it is important that a divorce decree obtained in one state be honored in other states, otherwise a person who remarries may not be legally divorced and therefore may enter into polygamy. Likewise, it is important for child custody and other reasons that marriage be respected from state to state.

States generally respect marriage contracts from other states, although there are a number of conditions and exceptions. Marriages from other states do not need to be recognized if they are (1) "obnoxious" to the public policy of the state, or (2) if the state can show that their acceptance conflicts with important state interests.

The American Law Institute is an organization that reviews legislation and court cases and develops generalized statements of the law as it develops in the United States. These *Restatements,* as they are called, are highly influential, but not legally binding. Many states have adopted the *Restatements* into their legal codes.

Restatements have been issued on the topic of marriage and the acceptance of marriage between states. The *First Restatement of the Conflicts of Law* suggests that a marriage is valid everywhere if the marriage is valid in the state in which it was celebrated. However, a number of marriages are declared void by law and invalid everywhere in the domicile state. These include polygamous marriages, incestuous marriages, marriages between persons of different races (which have not been deleted from the restatements despite the U.S. Supreme Court decision in *Loving v. Virginia*), and marriages that are declared void by the domicile state even if they are legal in the states in which they were celebrated.

Further, Comment *b* of the *First Restatement* declares marriages void if they offend a strong public policy of the domicile state. Comment *c* of the *First Restatement* describes "odious" marriages as those that not only are prohibited by the state, but that also offend a deep-rooted sense of morality in the state. The *Second Restatement of the Conflicts of Law* suggests a similar policy. It states that a marriage will be recognized as valid everywhere unless it violates the strong public policy of the state that has the most significant relationship to either partner at the time of the marriage. Thus, both *Restatements* suggest that a marriage that is valid where celebrated will be valid everywhere unless the marriage would be considered void in the domicile state.

For example, Bob and Jim wish to marry and their domiciliary state does not allow same-sex couples to marry. A nearby state allows same-sex marriage. Bob and Jim travel to that state, get married, return to their domiciliary state, and adopt children. After a few years together, they decide they want to go their separate ways. Bob files for divorce in their domiciliary state. Jim decides to fight the divorce as a way to avoid paying child support. Jim claims in court that they were never married because their domiciliary state forbade same-sex couples from marrying. The court in their domiciliary state should uphold their marriage since where they were married, the celebration state, allowed such marriages. The domiciliary state may declare Bob and Jim's marriage void only if it was obnoxious to an important state policy.

What constitutes grounds for voiding a marriage varies from state to state. Courts have also recognized numerous validly celebrated marriages that have been allegedly extremely offensive to the public policy of the domicile state. For example, what constitutes an incestuous marriage is different in different states and some courts have accepted marriages between first cousins, even though the domicile state declared such unions void. Polygamy is another example. Several courts have recognized Native American polygamous marriages for the purpose of succession and foreign polygamous marriages for the purpose of probate. Likewise, interracial marriages were once illegal in many states, but this became moot when the U.S. Supreme Court in *Loving v. Virginia* struck down antimiscegenation marriage laws. Thus, some kinds of marriages that have a long history of being void by state law have now been accepted as legal.

Another tactic taken by a few states is the enactment of evasion statutes. These statutes are directed toward couples who purposefully travel to other states to get married because their own states will not recognize their marriages, and then return to their own states. Evasion statutes clarify the legislature's intent and, thus, make it much less arguable in court that an otherwise voided marriage should be allowed. For evasion statutes to have direct influence on same-sex marriages, they have to be directly named.

States without evasion statutes have to decide which marriages, void in the domicile state but celebrated in another state, to legally recognize. They need to decide what is odious to public policy. Sometimes it has been claimed that a particular marriage was shocking to community standards. But courts long ago noticed that the mere claim that something shocks a community does not make it true.

Another approach is to claim that same-sex marriage violates natural law. But what does this mean? Natural law is a vague term that takes on different meanings within different religious systems. Many conservative Christians make the claim that same-sex marriage violates natural law, yet some Christian sects perform same-sex commitment ceremonies (for example, the Metropolitan Community Church and Unitarian Universalist Church). Interracial marriages were once claimed to violate natural law, yet such marriages are now legal. Overall, the natural law argument has not been given much consideration by the Supreme Court (*Rochin v. California*). Finally, many states have enacted antidiscrimination policies based upon sex, gender, and sexual orientation. These give evidence of the changing U.S. social norms toward the acceptability of same-sex marriages.

Overall, the full faith and credit clause and choice of law process allow states not to recognize same-sex marriages conducted in other states. However, the civil union statute enacted by the state of Vermont in 2000 brings up a host of untested legal questions. For example, if one of the partners of a lesbian couple has a child and the couple obtains a civil union in Vermont and then moves to another state, what is their relationship status? If the biological mother should die, who is the legal parent of the child and who inherits the deceased person's property? These are not abstract legal issues but real concerns for lesbian and gay male couples.

DEFENSE OF MARRIAGE ACT

The federal Defense of Marriage Act (DOMA) was signed into law in September 1996. It was designed to prevent states from being forced by the full faith and credit clause of the U.S. Constitution to recognize same-sex marriages validly celebrated in other states, and to define marriage for federal purposes as the union of one man and one woman.

The debate in Congress over this act revealed that most legislators were unfamiliar with the laws governing marriage and divorce in the United States. Family law, including marriage and divorce, are functions of state law and not federal law or the full faith and credit clause. It is individual state laws and the choice of law procedures that regulate how states recognize out-of-state marriages and divorces. The DOMA added no new rights for states to deny same-sex marriages and, in some situations, still would be unable to prevent some states from being forced into recognizing same-sex marriages. Interestingly, the DOMA may impact same-sex divorce. If so, the DOMA will modify state laws in ways that are most likely unconstitutional.

The act is also the antithesis of the full faith and credit clause, lacks sufficient generality, was constructed without adequate justification, encroaches upon state law, restricts interstate travel, and was motivated by animus toward a disfavored group. For these reasons, it is expected that the DOMA will be found to be unconstitutional when tested in court.

BENEFITS FOR LESBIANS AND GAY MEN THROUGH MARRIAGE

When the issue of same-sex marriage is debated, reasons are often given as to why marriage should be restricted to opposite-sex couples. However, every reason given could apply equally to same-sex couples.

Same-sex couples want marriage because they want the stability of knowing their legal rights in situations of child custody, property ownership, property succession, medical decisions, financial investments, child rearing and education, government and employment benefits, access to public accommodations and housing, and more. Same-sex couples want social validation for their unions. Same-sex couples have the same reasons for desiring marriage as opposite-sex couples.

SIMILARITIES TO PAST RESTRICTIONS ON INTERRACIAL MARRIAGE

It is mostly tradition that precludes gay marriages. For example, laws prohibiting marriage between persons of different races (miscegenation) are still on the books in sixteen states. However, the Supreme Court in 1967 struck down the remaining miscegenation statutes, saying that it was clear the only purpose of those laws was to "maintain white supremacy" (*Loving v. Virginia,* 163). It is informative to review the court history of miscegenation.

Before *Loving v. Virginia,* most courts upheld state laws voiding interracial marriages that were validly contracted in other states. Yet some courts were willing to legally recognize such marriages. These exceptions stem from the *First Restatement of the Conflicts of Law,* which allows states to determine if interracial marriages are odious to state policy. Comment *c* of this *First Restatement* further explains that to find a marriage odious, it must not only be prohibited by statute, but must offend a deep-rooted sense of morality that is predominant in the state.

This "deep-rooted sense of morality" clarification allowed courts wide discretion. Courts sometimes upheld their state bans on recognizing out-of-state interracial marriages, whereas other times they would conclude that such marriages did not deeply offend. Even as far back as 1847, a Vermont court declared "the most serious minded, earnest, and strenuously religious of our citizens" cannot be thought to represent the views of everyone. This court further stated that when "making inquiry into the state of the moral feeling of the whole community, we must not forget that . . . it is almost infinitesimally divided" (*Adam v. Gay,* 367). The court suggested that the fact that a practice shocks some community members is not sufficient cause to label it odious. A practice is odious not because a simple majority opposes it, but because there is strong and uniform community disapproval of the practice.

Slowly, more and more states overturned their antimiscegenation laws. But there were still a few holdouts. It took a Supreme Court decision to finally strike down these discriminatory laws. We should expect the same process for same-sex marriages. First a few states will allow same-sex marriage. Same-sex validly married couples will move to other states, some that do not allow same-sex marriages. Court cases will be filed. These states will have to decide on the validity of these out-of-state marriages. Some courts will not find same-sex marriages odious to state policy and will allow them, whereas other courts will uphold their state bans on recognizing the unions. Given a generation or two, same-sex marriages will probably gain full legal recognition.

We must not forget how offensive interracial marriages were to many Americans. The arguments used against miscegenation are the same arguments being fielded against same-sex marriage today. They were not true then; they are not true now. Marriage should be afforded to same-sex couples.

DIVISION WITHIN THE GAY COMMUNITY

The gay community is divided over the issue of marriage. There are those who believe lesbians and gay male relationships are "just like" heterosexual ones and should be extended the same rights and responsibilities as obtained through heterosexual marriage, and those who believe lesbian and gay male relationships are "different" from traditional heterosexual ones and seek reforms broader than obtaining marriage. From a practical standpoint, the "just like" camp argue that it is unfair that heterosexual spouses can obtain health insurance and other benefits from being married to someone who works for a corporation that provides such benefits, whereas a same-sex spouse cannot because they cannot marry. The "different" camp argues that the basic system is wrong when important needs such as health insurance and other benefits are tied to being the spouse of someone who works for a corporation that provides such benefits. Politically, the "just like" proponents are often derided for being assimilationist or naive in believing that heterosexism and its attendant oppression will disappear the day same-sex marriage is approved. Those of the "different" perspective are also derided for being politically correct, radical separatists who often advocate decoupling monogamy, relationships, home ownership, and child care. "Assimilationists" and "separatists" are two political camps that are further separated by such other considerations as race, class, gender, age, and ability. Thus, a consensus on marriage within the gay community is unlikely.

INTERNATIONAL STATUS

Contrary to popular opinion, no country in the world allows same-sex marriages. Some countries allow same-sex couples to register their relationships, but they do not confer the same rights and responsibilities given to opposite-sex marriage. The Netherlands provides the closest thing to actual marriage to same-sex couples, which is very similar to Vermont's civil union status. These are super domestic partnership arrangements, but still are not marriage. However, on December 21, 2000, Queen Beatrix signed bills that would allow same-sex couples to marry and adopt. Both bills became law on January 11, 2001, but have a few obstacles to clear they go into effect on April 1, 2001. The Netherlands may become the first nation to sanction same-sex marriage and adoption.

References

Bedrick, B. R. 1997. "Report on The Defense of Marriage Act." Government Accounting Office website: www.gao.gov (31 January 1997).

Black's Law Dictionary. 1990. 6th ed.

Stammer, L. B. 2000. "Gay Unions Affirmed by Reform Rabbis." *Los Angeles Times* (30 March 2000): 1.

MATTACHINE SOCIETY The Mattachine Society is considered the founding organization of the gay civil rights movement. Harry Hay (previously known as Henry Hay and who wrote under the pseudonym Eann MacDonald) spearheaded the Mattachine Society and the homophile movement. When Hay was seventeen years old in 1930, he came to Los Angeles and met Champ Simmons who had recently been involved with one of the members of the Chicago **Society for Human Rights**—the first homophile organization in the United States. Simmons spoke about the Society, which encouraged Hay to begin a similar organization.

Hay was a communist organizer and sought-after teacher of communist theory in Los Angeles in the 1930s. He realized his homosexuality after being married, and in 1948 conceived the idea of organizing a gay group. He believed political organizing was the key to political power and self-protection. He discussed the idea with friends at the University of Southern California (USC). Two years later he assembled enough friends to launch the group—International Bachelors Fraternal Orders for Peace and Social Dignity (sometimes referred to as Bachelors Anonymous). The goals of the group included the following: to fight encroaching American fascism, to help save employment of "androgynous civil servants" (androgynous was Hay's term for gay and lesbian), to protect and improve conditions for the "androgynous minority," and to collaborate and help attain full-class citizenship for all minorities. The group was initially set up as underground separate guilds. This way no one would know everyone involved. A secret society structure was thought to be necessary in light of the police harassment that lesbians and gay men faced in the Los Angeles of the 1950s. Also, a secret society structure was a method used by the old left and was employed by Algeria in its successful liberation from France.

In April 1951 the group refocused and incorporated itself in California as the Mattachine Society. The goals of the group were to unify homosexuals, to educate homosexuals and heterosexuals about how the homosexual rights movement would parallel other minority rights movements, and to lead the "whole mass of social deviants" (Katz 1976, 412). The name *Mattachine* was inspired by the *Société Mattachine,* a secret fraternal organization in thirteenth- and fourteenth-century France and Spain of unmarried townsmen who performed music, dances, and rituals while wearing masks, sometimes in protest against oppression. At the formation of the Mattachine Society, Hay severed his eighteen-year tie with the Communist Party to devote himself completely to homosexual emancipation. The Mattachine Society was seen as a vehicle to assist homosexuals to explore in discussion groups basic questions such as "Who are we?" "Where have we come from?" and "What are we here for?" A separate entity, the Mattachine Foundation, provided a legal front for the Society.

Several members of a discussion group within the Mattachine Society decided to publish a monthly newsletter to be distributed nationally. The new organization, **ONE, Incorporated,** began publication in January 1953. Soon, the newsletters were seized by the U.S. Post Office on grounds that they were "obscene, lewd, lascivious and filthy." ONE editors went to court, and ultimately, the U.S. Supreme Court overturned the lower courts in 1958 (*One, Inc. v. Olesen*). This was a "legal and publishing landmark" (*Gay Almanac* 1996, 13). Homosexual materials were no longer automatically deemed obscene and the mail service could be used to distribute them. (See also **ONE, Incorporated**.)

In 1953 a number of forces came together to change the direction of the homophile movement. Joseph McCarthy called Fred M. Snyder, Mattachine Foundation legal advisor, to testify before the House Un-American Activities Committee. McCarthy branded Snyder an unfriendly witness and attempted to defame and humiliate him. The investigation caused grave concern for Mattachine members. At the same time, President Dwight Eisenhower issued Executive Order 10450, which expanded President Truman's loyalty and security program to exclude from government employment those who engaged in "sexual perversion." Historian John D'Emilio estimated that approximately 1,000 homosexuals were fired from federal employment each year during the 1940s, approximately 2,000 per year during the 1950s, and over 3,000 per year during the 1960s.

Within this climate, the Mattachine Society held a convention in Los Angeles on April 11, 1953. More than 500 representatives participated in the largest such gathering of homosexuals in U.S. history. A power struggle ensued between the founders who were leftist and those who wanted a more moderate, liberal organization. The liberal factions won out and the old Mattachine Foundation board resigned.

The newly incarnated Mattachine Society was open and democratic. Its goals were primarily educational. It believed that legal change could be accomplished through education, not necessarily political action. The organization was increasingly concerned with being "respectable" and adhered to a basic homophile outlook.

As the years passed, a multitude of people and forces helped shape the Mattachine Society and ONE, Incorporated. Jim Kepner, one of the leaders of the Mattachine Society after the resignation of the board in 1953, went on to found the International Gay and Lesbian Archives. ONE Publication was the premier homophile newsletter until 1972 and continues to this day. By the mid-1990s, the Mattachine Society had been completely enveloped by ONE, Incorporated and merged with the International Gay and Lesbian Archives (ONE/IGLA). ONE/IGLA is now located on the campus of the University of Southern California with over 1,000,000 items in the collection—making it the largest collection in the world of homophile art, books, articles, and other items and the premier academic research facility of queer history.

Reference

Gay Almanac, The. 1996. Complied by the National Museum and Archive of Lesbian and Gay History. New York: Berkley Books.

Katz, J. 1976. *Gay American History: Lesbians and Gay Men in the U.S.A.* New York: Thomas Y. Crowell.

MILITARY Homosexuality is considered incompatible with military service. There has been a long history of harassing and persecuting homosexuals in the military. With the issuance of the **"Don't Ask, Don't Tell"** policy by President Clinton on July 19, 1993, the debate came to the forefront of the American consciousness. A number of lawsuits against this policy have been filed with mixed results. (See also **Military Expulsion**.)

DEBATE OVER LESBIANS AND GAYS IN THE MILITARY

Here are the major arguments against and for the inclusion of homosexuals into the military.

Arguments against Accepting Homosexuals into the Military

Allowing homosexuals to serve in military units will have detrimental effects on troop morale and military readiness.

There will be a misuse of power by gay noncommissioned officers. They will hit on soldiers, give combat awards to lovers who have never been on the line, have affairs with ambitious teenage soldiers in exchange for kicking up their test scores, and they will corrupt and destroy the fighting spirit and gut effectiveness of U.S. combat forces.

Polls show a majority of American citizens favor allowing gays into the military. However, others feel that the majority is acting upon ignorance. They believe that if the majority understood the realities of war and the military, they, too, would argue against allowing homosexuals into the military.

Yes, it is discrimination, but "civilian standards of fairness and equality don't apply down where the body bags are filled" (Hackworth 1993, 104).

"Sex between service members undermines those critical factors that produce discipline, military orders, spirit and combat effectiveness" (Hackworth 1993, 104).

Arguments for Accepting Homosexuals into the Military

It is estimated that almost 200,000 homosexuals are currently serving in U.S. forces.

The military's policy each year expels about 1,000 able-bodied women and men (ten women to every one man), wasting approximately $27 million in training costs.

Integrating gays and lesbians into the military has been successful in other countries such as Britain, Denmark, Holland, Sweden, Norway, Switzerland, and Israel. These programs use educational seminars to teach sensitivity toward minorities in the military, in particular women, blacks, and gays. The United States is the only NATO country that still excludes lesbians and gays from the military.

The fear that gays are targets for blackmail has been discounted even by Secretary of Defense Dick Cheney in 1991: "If the Pentagon were willing to supply the effort, gays could be integrated with no more upheaval than when blacks were integrated decades ago" (Konigsberg 1993, 100).

PARALLELS TO DESEGREGATION

When candidate for president Bill Clinton announced in 1991 that he would lift the ban on gays in the military, there was a terrible backlash in Congress and across the nation. Instead, President Clinton implemented a half-way measure termed "Don't Ask, Don't Tell" in 1993. The policy has been a disaster and persecution and harassment of lesbian and gay service members has increased. Many writers and analysts have noted that Clinton should have modeled his action after President Harry Truman, who issued the executive order ending segregation in the military in 1948. Within a few short years, known racists were no longer allowed to hold positions of authority and were eventually weeded out. Within a few decades, the military had more black managers than found in the civilian sector.

Before Truman issued the order, a military panel suggested that white soldiers would never accept blacks as commanders or comrades in arms. The panel suggested using a quota system to keep black numbers down and to limit blacks to troop support and other duties in which they could be kept from integrating. Truman rejected this piecemeal approach and, in one swift action, began the process of desegregating the military. Perhaps this approach would have been successful in integrating lesbians and gay men into the military.

HATE CRIMES AND HARASSMENT IN THE MILITARY

On July 5, 1999, Private First Class Barry Winchell was murdered at Ft. Campbell, Kentucky. Winchell faced daily harassment for four months prior to his murder, based on rumors that he might be gay. Instead of interceding and stopping the harassment, Winchell's supervisors testified that they investigated his sexual orientation and asked him directly if he was gay. Their actions violated the "Don't Ask, Don't Tell" policy. Private

Calvin Glover, Winchell's murderer, confessed that he had been drinking and was goaded by another service member to use a baseball bat to hurt Winchell, otherwise Glover feared being teased repeatedly by others for having had "his ass kicked by a faggot" in a fight the previous day. Glover used the baseball bat to kill Winchell. Glover was reported to have said after the murder, "[T]he one thing I hate is faggots and niggers" (Servicemembers Legal Defense and Education Network 1999).

Winchell's murder was only one of many hate crimes committed in the military. The Servicemembers Legal Defense Network reported that antigay harassment increased by 142 percent in 1999 over 1998 (Servicemembers Legal Defense and Education Network 2000). In response to the growing problem of hate crimes and harassment in the military, President Clinton signed an executive order amending the military criminal code in October 1999 to add stiffer penalties for crimes motivated by hatred based on the victim's race, religion, ethnicity, or sexual orientation. The order also created confidentiality privileges for service members' conversations with psychotherapists during criminal matters. It has long been a complaint of lesbian and gay service members that military therapists do not keep their conversations confidential. Now, during criminal investigations, there is some level of confidentiality.

References

Hackworth, D. 1993. "The Military Should Not Accept Homosexuals." In *Homosexuality: Opposing Viewpoints,* edited by W. Dudley. San Diego, CA: Greenhaven Press.

Konigsberg, E. 1993. "The Military Should Accept Homosexuals." In *Homosexuality: Opposing Viewpoints,* edited by W. Dudley. San Diego, CA: Greenhaven Press.

Servicemembers Legal Defense Network (SLDN). 1999. "Soldier Pleads Guilty to Non-Premeditated Murder in Murder of PFC Barry Winchell." Press release on Servicemembers Legal Defense Network website: www.sldn.org/templates/press/index.html?section=2&record=102. Accessed 7 December 1999.

———. 2000b. "Antigay Harassment in Military Surges Even after Pentagon Announces 'Zero Tolerance' for Harassment." Press release on Servicemembers Legal Defense Network website: www.sldn.org/templates/press/index.html?section=2&record=21. Accessed 9 March 2000.

MILITARY EXPULSION Expulsion from the U.S. military for being homosexual or engaging in homosexual behavior is standard procedure. The military finalized regulations banning homosexuality in 1943, which led to the 1950 establishment by Congress of the Uniform Code of Military Justice (UCMJ). The UCMJ set down the policies and procedures for discharging homosexual service members. In 1957 a 639-page navy report, the **Crittenden Report,** concluded that there was no sound basis to the belief that homosexuals posed a security risk. However, the Pentagon denied the existence of this report for twenty years.

In 1975 Sergeant Leonard Matlovich sued the air force to be reinstated after being dismissed for homosexuality. His story made the cover of *Time* magazine and was later made into an NBC television movie. His suit dragged on until 1980, when a federal judge ordered Matlovich reinstated. However, instead of reentering the air force, Matlovich settled for financial restitution and became a gay rights activist. In late 1988 Matlovich died. He had engraved on his tombstone "The Air Force pinned a medal on me for killing two men and discharged me for making love to one" (*Gay Almanac* 1996, 69).

In 1981 the military revised its policy on homosexuality and not only barred gay people from serving, but required questions about recruits' sexual orientation to be asked. Another important chink in that discriminatory armor was achieved in 1989 when Perry Watkins was reinstated into the army under orders of a federal court (after a ten-year court battle). He had been discharged because he was gay. He demonstrated in court that he had been open about being gay during his entire distinguished military career, was allowed to reenlist three times, and that throughout his career his supervisors knew he was gay. Thus, he argued that there was an implicit acceptance of him by the military. Instead of reentering the army, Watkins too settled for financial restitution and became a gay rights activist.

The *Watkins* case did not directly challenge the military right to separate personnel from service due to homosexuality. An ongoing concern for the courts was the distinction between status as a homosexual and homosexual conduct. Ben-Shalom, a reserve sergeant, proclaimed that she was homosexual and was dismissed from the military. The military court found no evidence of homosexual conduct but claimed that it was reasonable to infer from her status as a homosexual that she had engaged, or probably would engage, in homosexual conduct. The Seventh Circuit Court agreed with this logic (*Ben-Shalom v. Marsh*) and cited ***Bowers v. Hardwick*** in concluding that homosexual conduct did not enjoy constitutional protection and, thus, the military was justified in discharging personnel who openly proclaimed their homosexuality. Similarly, in *Pruitt v. Cheney,* the Ninth Circuit Court decided that declaring one's homosexual sexual orientation was not a First Amendment issue since such a declaration inferred conduct.

However, not all courts agreed with these assessments. Both in *Cammermeyer v. Aspin* and *Meinhold v. U.S. Dept. of Defense,* the courts declared that statements admitting to homosexual sexual orientation did not demonstrate a propensity to commit homosexual acts. Furthermore, in *Meinhold,* the courts accepted arguments that the military could not justify its ban against homosexuality. The navy's principal counsel at the hearing admitted, "there is no scientific or sociological evidence that supports the Navy's position that homosexuals impair the military objective" (*Meinhold v. U.S. Dept. of Defense,* 22). The court found the navy's policy against homosexuals "bears no rational relationship to the Navy's stated objectives of protecting the accomplishment of the military mission" (*Meinhold v. U.S. Dept. of Defense,* 8). However, at the same time that these two cases were decided in favor of the plaintiffs, the District of Columbia Circuit Court reinforced *Ben-Shalom v. Marsh,* allowing the discharge of the service member, and declared that it was rational to infer homosexual conduct from statements of homosexual orientation (*Steffan v. Perry*).

Many gay organizations provided information to the military to try and change policy. The Defense Personnel Security Research and Education Center, a research arm of the Department of Defense, conducted its own research and issued two reports in 1988 and 1989 (also known as the PERSEREC reports) (Dyer 1990). Both reports found no reason to exclude homosexuals from the military or from obtaining security clearances. Attempts were made to bury the reports, but copies were leaked to the press, which then reported the findings. In 1991 *The Advocate* magazine outed Department of Defense spokesperson Pete Williams. In 1992 the Government Accounting Office reported that almost 17,000 service men and women were discharged for homosexuality between 1981 and 1990 at a cost of $500 million. Of course, this cost does not take into account the personal tragedy experienced by each of the discharged persons.

The policy against homosexuals seems to apply equally to men and women, but it has been used aggressively and disproportionately against women and blacks (Dyer 1990). For example, Pentagon policy against homosexuality falls disproportionately on women at almost a ten-to-one ratio (Lewin 1988), and the navy is the most aggressive service branch in discharging homosexuals. In addition, the Government Accounting Office (GAO) study (1992) found that enlisted men and women make up almost all homosexual discharges, because officers are allowed the option of resigning ("Pentagon Cost of Discharging Gays Put at $500 Million" 1997).

When Bill Clinton was running for president, he promised to lift the ban on gays in the military. When he was elected and brought the issue to Congress, wide disagreement almost paralyzed that body. Ultimately, Clinton took a compromise position and in 1993 implemented the "Don't Ask, Don't Tell" policy, which did not significantly alter the previous ban and which ultimately increased the surveillance and discharge of lesbian and gay military personnel. Most importantly, the new policy included a requirement that the service member declaring him or herself as homosexual must rebut the presumption of homosexual conduct; that is, demonstrate that he or she is not a person who engages in, attempts to engage in, has a propensity to engage in, or intends to engage in homosexual acts (Don't Ask, Don't Tell § 654[b][2]).

Lieutenant Richard P. Watson came under investigation from the United States Navy after delivering to his commanding officer a one-page document in which he stated that he had a homosexual orientation and that he did not intend to rebut the presumption. During the review process, he submitted a document stating that he denied engaging in any homosexual conduct with any military student or service member during the performance of military duty or while on any military installation, and that he denied any intent or propensity to engage in the described conduct. His statement was considered deficient to refute the presumption required under §654 (that also applied to off-base and off-duty behaviors with nonmilitary personnel) and he was discharged. He sued in district court and was not successful (*Watson v. Perry*).

First Lieutenant Charles Andrew Holmes sent a memorandum to his commanding officer at the California Army National Guard (CANG) informing him that he was gay. The commanding officer initiated an investigation. Holmes presented evidence of his excellent service record; however, he did not present any evidence to refute the presumption. He was discharged from the CANG for violation of "Don't Ask, Don't Tell." He sued in district court, which upheld his claim of violation of his constitutional rights to equal protection and free speech (*Holmes v. California Army Nat'l Guard*).

The two cases were combined and heard by the Ninth Circuit Court (*Holmes/Watson v. California Army National Guard*). Both Watson and Holmes challenged the constitutionality of the "don't ask, don't tell" policy's presumption of homosexual conduct (§654) that is created solely by a statement of homosexual sexual orientation. The court concluded that §654 and its implementing regulations were constitutional on their face as applied to Watson and Holmes (see *Richenberg v. Perry, Able v. United States, Thomasson v. Perry*). The court believed the policy is not discriminatory because it treats homosexuals and heterosexuals equally since neither are allowed to say they are gay without proving that they will not engage in homosexual conduct.

Again, the Department of Defense ordered another study into the suitability of allowing homosexuals to participate in the military. Rand Corporation issued their research in 1993, stating that they could find no justification for discrimination against homosexuals. As usual, the military tried to suppress the report. In 1999, in response to a number of terribly gruesome gay bashings in the military, President Clinton signed an executive order amending the military criminal code to add stronger penalties for hate-motivated crimes based upon the victim's race, religion, ethnicity, or sexual orientation. In March 2000 the Pentagon inspector general released a report based upon the responses of 72,000 troops stationed around the world. The survey found "disturbing" levels of gay harassment in the U.S. military. Defense Secretary William S. Cohen said the survey shows that additional efforts are needed to end the terrible harassment (Richter 2000).

Most people feel it is only a matter of time before the military lifts its entire ban on homosexuality. Conservatives such as Barry Goldwater and others understood that the military has always had homosexuals fighting bravely and performing professionally with the other personnel. With the lifting of the ban on homosexuals in the military by Britain in the year 2000, all countries of the NATO alliance, with the exception of the United States, now accept homosexual personnel in the military. These countries reported that integrating lesbians and gays into their militaries was successful. There are extreme costs associated with excluding and discharging specific groups. Since the prohibition on gay men and lesbians in the military was instituted in 1943, over 100,000 men and women have been discharged for alleged homosexuality (Berube 1990). (See also **"Don't Ask, Don't Tell"**; **Hate Crimes**.)

References

Berube, A. 1990. *Coming Out Under Fire: The History of Gay Men and Women in WWII.* New York: Plume.

Dyer, K. 1990. *Gays in Uniform: The Pentagon Secret Report.* Boston: Alyson Press.

Gay Almanac, The. (1996). Complied by the National Museum and Archive of Lesbian and Gay History. New York: Berkley Books.

Lewin, T. 1988. "Gay Groups Suggest Marines Selectively Prosecute Women." *New York Times* (4 September 1988): 1.

"Pentagon Cost of Discharging Gays Put at $500 Million." 1992. *Los Angeles Times* (19 June 1992): A14.

Richter, P. 2000. "Armed Forces Find 'Disturbing' Level of Gay Harassment." *Los Angeles Times* (25 March 2000): A1.

U.S. General Accounting Office. 1997. *Defense of Marriage Act Report.* OGC 97–16: 58. Washington, DC: Government Printing Office.

N

National Coming Out Day

National Coming Out Day The **Human Rights Campaign** designated October 11 as National Coming Out Day in 1988. This day has grown into thousands of events held nationally to encourage people to come out to **family**, friends, neighbors, and fellow employees about being lesbian, gay, bisexual, transgendered, transsexual, or intersexed. It has been found that visibility—that is, being seen and known to be homosexual—is the most effective way to effect societal changes toward the acceptance of homosexuality. However, there are many legal questions about what constitutes being openly gay and what behaviors are legally protected. (See also **Speech and Association.**)

National Gay and Lesbian Task Force Founded in 1973, the National Gay and Lesbian Task Force (NGLTF) has been one of the major organizations to help increase the acceptance of lesbians and gay men in society. It was influential in educating the **American Psychiatric Association (APA)** about the normalcy of homosexuality. This led the APA to remove homosexuality from its list of mental disorders in 1974.

The NGLTF is the national progressive organization working for the civil rights of gay, lesbian, and bisexual, and transgendered people. It serves as a national resource center to many other organizations and legislatures. It publishes a number of reports available online, including the *Hate Crime Report;* the *Domestic Partnership Organizing Manual for Employee Benefits; Gay, Lesbian, Bisexual and Transgender Civil Rights Law in the United States; Calculated Compassion—How the Ex-Gay Movement Serves the Right's Attack on Democracy; Legislating Equality—A Review of Laws Affecting Gay, Lesbian, Bisexual, and Transgendered People in the United States.*

The NGLTF often works in conjunction with the **Lambda Legal Defense and Education Fund**, the American Civil Liberties Union, the National Conference of Black Lawyers, the National Organization for

Women's Legal Defense and Education Fund, and the **Human Rights Campaign**, among others.

NECKTIES AS PHALLIC SYMBOLS Every culture differentiates between genders and indicates status through the use of clothing. Courts have been divided on the right of businesses and governments to specify dress codes. (See also **Dress and Grooming Codes**.)

Even in cultures that do not typically wear clothing, men can be found using materials to bring attention to their penises. For example, Claude Levi-Strauss, who spent several seasons among the Bororo of central Brazil, observed, "The men were quite naked except for the little straw corner covering the tip of the penis and kept in place by the foreskin, which is stretched through the opening to form a little role of flesh on the outside" (Levi-Strauss 1977, 237).

In other cultures, an actual sheath is applied over the penis to bring attention to it. As British anthropologist Somerville observed with several groups in the New Hebrides (now Vanuatu):

> The natives wrap the penis around with many yards of calico, and other materials, winding and folding them until a preposterous bundle of eighteen inches or two feet long and two inches or more in diameter is formed, which is then supported upwards by means of a belt, in the extremity decorated with flowering grasses, etc. The testicles are left naked. (Rudofsky 1971, 58)

Similarly phallic sheaths, or phallocrypts, are found among the peoples of the Pacific, Africa, and the river valleys of South America. These may be made of twisted leaves, shells, gourds, or bamboo—depending upon local materials. Evidence indicates that such practices have a long history, and have been seen on 9,000-year-old African rock carvings.

In one of the more in-depth analyses of the reasons for phallic sheaths, J. C. Flugel maintained:

> [I]t has been manifest to all serious students of dress that of all the motives for the wearing of clothes, those connected with the sexual life have an altogether predominant position. . . . Among savage peoples, clothing and decoration start anatomically at or near the genital region, have frequently some definite reference to a sexual occasion (puberty, marriage, etc.). Among civilized peoples, the overtly sexual role of many clothes is too obvious and familiar to need more than a passing mention. . . . Their ultimate purpose, often indeed their overt and conscious purpose, is to add to the sexual attractiveness of their

> wearers, and to stimulate the sexual interest of admirers and the opposite sex and the envy of rivals of the same sex. (Flugel 1971, 26)

With increasing wealth, human cultures developed greater involvement with clothing. Clothing became much more than protection from the elements: it became symbolic of wealth, status, and sexuality. Over the years, men have exaggerated their shoulders with padding (an adornment still retained in the epaulets of military officer uniforms and hotel doormen), their stature through the use of hats and other devices, or their valor with the use of fur, skins, feathers, fangs, or other animal items.

Headgear of any shape or size has a direct relation to men's phallic character (Strage 1980, 258) and stature. James Laver noted:

> In the nineteenth century it is possible to plot the rise of the curve of feminine emancipation from the height of men's hats. Absolute male domination of, say, 1850, was certainly accompanied by extremely tall hats [as seen worn by Abraham Lincoln]. With the advent of the New Woman in the 1880s many men adopted the boater, which might be thought of as a very truncated top hat. And towards the end of the century men began to wear, so to speak, the very symbol of their base in authority: the trilby. (Laver 1969, 122)

As we end the twentieth century, men in Western societies have virtually ceased wearing hats (except for occupational reasons—such as hard hats), which corresponds to the greater degree of women's liberation.

But the most distinct form of displacement is evident in another common article of masculine clothing. The necktie can trace its origin—and its more formal name—to a cloth ribbon worn underneath the open-necked shirts of Croatian mercenaries who served in the armies of Louis XIV in the eighteenth century. It then became the cambric or linen stock meticulously folded and ironed according to the dictates of Beau Brummell in the nineteenth century, and later still evolved into its present form—a length of cloth that is tied around the neck and allowed to hang loosely down the middle of the chest. It serves no purpose other than to call attention to itself. Significantly, it was for a long time—and still is for many men—the only article of attire that could be brightly colored or strikingly patterned. Men who wear the same drab uniform year after year—blue or gray suits, black shoes and socks, white or blue shirts—often lavish tender attention on the selection of a necktie. For many boys, the first wearing of a necktie has become an even more distinct rite of passage than their first pair of long pants (Strage 1980, 260).

A few critics have objected to the analysis that connects neckties to the phallus, instead saying that the wearing of particular neckties was to help identify their possessors with some particular group—such as educational, military, or social groups. However, two examples cannot be explained in terms other than a connection with the phallus. First, male religious leaders of orders that require celibacy do not wear neckties. Their clothing is designed with their collars turned around in order to present to the world an unbroken surface to which no tie could be attached. The lack of a necktie is a symbol of celibacy. Second, women do not wear neckties. Women do sometimes defy tradition and wear neckties, but it is considered extremely aggressive in the business world to do so.

Neckties are probably the last vestiges of male clothing that bring direct attention to the male penis and men's power. Many people object to neckties because of the association with power and sexual nature conferred by such symbolism. Likewise, neckties have become a symbol of wage slavery and subjection to the corporate order. Some feminists and others of similar political beliefs refuse to wear neckties, whereas some women feminists wear neckties to usurp the power conferred upon men through this symbol. We look forward to a time when status and sex are no longer projected through the clothing we wear and neckties are abolished. Wearing neckties is an overt sexual action. (See also **Sexual Orientation**.)

References

Flugel, J. C. 1971. *The Psychology of Clothes.* London: Woolf.

Laver, J. 1969. *Modesty in Dress.* Boston: Houghton Mifflin.

Levi-Strauss, C. 1977. *Tristes Tropiques.* New York: Atheneum.

Rudofsky, B. 1971. *The Unfashionable Human Body.* New York: Doubleday.

Strage, M. 1980. *The Durable Fig Leaf.* New York: Morrow.

O

ONE, INCORPORATED Door Legg, an early board member of the **Mattachine Society** and some of his fellow members decided to publish a national monthly newsletter under a new organization, called ONE, Incorporated. Its goals were liberal instead of leftist and it derived its name from a line by the nineteenth-century essayist Thomas Carlyle: "A mystic bond of brotherhood makes all men one" (Blumenfeld and Raymond 1993, 293). The newsletter began publication in January 1953 and served as the voice of the homophile movement during its early years. (It is still published today in conjunction with the International Gay and Lesbian Archives located at the University of Southern California.) The members of ONE kept themselves separate from the Mattachine Society, primarily because many Mattachine members were having reservations about the group's secrecy and leftist politics.

In 1954 the Los Angeles postmaster seized copies of *ONE* magazine and refused to mail them on the grounds that they were "obscene, lewd, lascivious and filthy." *ONE* editors challenged the seizure in court. Two lower courts upheld the actions of the postmaster, but, ultimately, the U.S. Supreme Court overturned the lower courts in 1958 (*One, Inc. v. Olesen*). This was a "legal and publishing landmark" (*Gay Almanac* 1996, 13). Material containing homosexual themes and information was no longer automatically deemed obscene and could be distributed through the mail service. (See also **Speech and Association.**)

ONE, Incorporated and the International Gay and Lesbian Archives merged in the late 1990s. The library moved to the University of Southern California.

References

Blumenfeld, W. J., and D. Raymond, eds. 1993. *Looking at Gay and Lesbian Life.* Rev. ed. Boston: Beacon Press.

Gay Almanac, The. 1996. Complied by the National Museum and Archive of Lesbian and Gay History. New York: Berkley Books.

P

Perpetrators of Antigay Violence Professor and Reverend Gary Comstock (1991, 201) conducted extensive research into antigay violence. Perpetrators of violence toward lesbians and gays had the following characteristics:

Perpetrators of antigay and lesbian violence tend to be younger males who are unknown to their victims, as compared with national crime statistics for perpetrators of all violent crimes. Lesbians and gay men of color experience much more victimization by white perpetrators. In addition, often small groups of perpetrators attack small groups of gays and lesbians. This is in contrast to attacks in the general population where a lone perpetrator targets single victims. In cases of verbal harassment of lesbians and gays, 39 percent of the harassers made explicit statements about God, the Bible, or some other religious reference (Comstock 1991, 142).

Historically, courts have tended to be lenient toward perpetrators of antigay and lesbian violence. Defense attorneys and judges typically have claimed that the perpetrators were "average boys exhibiting typical behavior" and that boys would naturally be provoked by a homosexual advance. Even in a case of murder, one defense attorney observed that queer bashing was common practice: "[Teenage boys] go down to the park, roll the queers down the hill and have a good laugh and so on. It's a phenomenon" (Shein 1986). (See also **Criminal Law**.)

Are gay bashers themselves gay? Are they in denial, or trying to compensate, or both? Light is shed on this common belief by two studies. Professor Gregory Herek found that 40 percent of persons hostile to homosexuals were defensive about their own sexuality (Goleman 1990). A second study, at the University of Georgia, experimentally showed that latent homosexuality was a factor in antigay sentiments. White heterosexual male volunteers from the school's Psychology Department were first selected if they indicated an exclusive heterosexual arousal. These men were then given the Index of Homophobia Test, a measure of feelings toward homosexuals and about homosexuality (Hudson and Rickets 1980). This allowed researchers to divided the group into two groups:

Characteristics of Perpetrators	Victims Gay/Lesbian	Victims General Population
Relationship—perpetrator was a stranger to victim	66%	56%
Gender of perpetrator—male	94%	87%
Age of perpetrator(s)—under age 22	46%	29%
Race of perpetrator—white	67%	69%
Among victims of color, race of perpetrator—white	54%	17%
Victims—single	53%	87%
Perpetrator—working alone	52%	73%

those who were homophobic and those who were not homophobic. Next the men were shown erotic videotapes. But before the tapes were shown, a rubber circumferential strain gauge was placed around each man's penis that would indicate if there was swelling. The men were first shown heterosexual and lesbian sex scenes. Both groups of men responded with penile swelling. Next, the men were shown erotic videotapes featuring males only. Very few of the nonhomophobic men exhibited penile swelling, whereas most of the homophobic men did. After seeing the videotapes, the men were asked if they were aware of any sexual arousal. Interestingly, none of the subjects reported being aware of their arousal during the tapes of male erotica. Thus, the homophobic men were either unaware of, in denial of, or purposely lied about their homosexual feelings. These two findings support the belief that antigay feelings and the potential to develop into a gay basher are often combined with latent fears of being homosexual (Adams, Wright, and Lohr 1996). (See also **Hate Crimes**; **Homosexual Panic Defense**.)

References

Adams, H. E., L. W. Wright, and B. A. Lohr. 1996. "Is Homophobia Associated with Homosexual Arousal?" *Journal of Abnormal Psychology* 105(3): 440–445.

Comstock, G. D. 1991. *Violence Against Lesbians and Gay Men.* New York: Columbia University Press.

Goleman, D. 1990. "Studies Discover Clues to the Roots of Homophobia." *New York Times* (10 July 1990). Available at youth.org/loco/PERSONProject/Resources/ResearchStudies/homophobia.html.

Hudson, W., and W. Ricketts. 1980. "A Strategy for the Measurement of Homophobia." *Journal of Homosexuality* 5(4): 357–372.

Shein, B. 1986. "Gay-bashing in High Park." *Toronto Life* (April): 65.

POLICE ABUSES Police abuse toward homosexuals has a long history. Before the 1970s, when all states still had sex statutes outlawing homosexual sexual expression, the police routinely raided gay bars and meeting places. As the gay civil rights movement took hold and antigay laws were overturned, police abuses were reduced. Still, concerns over police abuse of lesbians and gay men persist. (See also **Criminal Law**; **Sodomy**.)

Some communities have begun to question the fairness of the enforcement of **alcoholic beverage control (ABC)** regulations. Lawsuits in the 1990s have revealed that police typically inspect gay and lesbian bars much more frequently than they inspect bars that cater to predominantly heterosexual clientele. Police claim they are responding to community complaints and that these complaints mostly involve gay bars. It will be seen how this overenforcement of ABC regulations is resolved so that homosexuals are not disproportionately targeted.

Another concern is the disparity in enforcing **lewd conduct** laws. Police arrest men engaging in public sex in disproportionate numbers. Lawsuits on this issue show a pattern of police arresting men who engage in public sex with other men, whereas heterosexuals engaging in the same behavior receive only a warning and are sent home. It is believed that sexual stereotypes may be responsible for this unfair behavior by police. Research conducted by the Los Angeles Police Department concerning enforcement of lewd conduct in Griffith Park revealed that a majority of the men arrested were married and that very few of these men identified themselves as gay. Thus, lewd conduct is a problem of inappropriate sexual behavior, not a gay problem per se. Laws aimed at lewd conduct need to be equitably applied.

Finally, the police environment is still antigay. Research has shown that as many as 30 percent of all police officers advocate violence toward lesbians, gay men, and transgendered people (Stewart 1995). Thus, there is a problem with an organizational culture that allows, if not encourages, the very people who are vested with the power to protect homosexuals to express violent contempt for them.

Reference

Stewart, C. 1995. "The Efficacy of Sexual Orientation Training in Law Enforcement Agencies." Ph.D. dissertation, University of Southern California, UMI Dissertation Services, 9614075.

POLYGAMY

Polygamy is marriage to more than one partner at the same time. In the debate over legalizing gay marriage, it is often claimed that if same-sex couples are allowed to marry, then other forms of prohibited marriage, such as polygamy, will follow. Such arguments are a non sequitur. Same-sex marriage needs to be discussed on its own terms. Polygamy is a separate issue.

The prohibition against polygamy stems from a number of sources, including a social, religious, and governmental backlash to the formation of the Church of Jesus Christ of Latter-Day Saints (Mormons). Originally, the Mormons approved of polygamous marriages, but the U.S. government made banning such marriages a condition of statehood for Utah. Utah codified bans on polygamous marriage in its constitution and Mormon Church doctrine changed to no longer condone its existence. However, polygamous marriages are still known to exist without legal or religious sanctions. The debate over polygamous marriages is a conflict between religious beliefs and is not related to same-sex marriage.

Historically, the context of polygamous marriages occurred within patriarchal societies. Men took on many wives as a symbol of wealth and power. There are many feminist arguments against arrangements that restrict women to second-class status. Same-sex marriages are not related to the power differential associated with polygamy. Thus, allowing gay marriages does not pave the way for other forms of prohibited marriages. Polygamy must be debated on its own merits or lack thereof.

PREJUDICE

Prejudice is a preconceived and unfounded belief or attitude (in Latin, "prejudgment") concerning a class of people. Every society has in-groups and out-groups. The in-group has rights and privileges that are denied members of the out-group. The out-groups are sometimes called minorities (even if they are a majority in numbers). Although some groups reject the term *minority* and are developing their own names, this term will be used here.

Two processes are responsible for keeping minorities subjugated to the dominant culture. First is prejudice, which is adverse opinion or belief without just grounds or before acquiring sufficient knowledge. Second, discrimination denies people equality of treatment. When prejudice and discrimination are reinforced through social institutions, they are said to constitute institutionalized discrimination (Eitzen 1980, 107). Furthermore, discrimination may result in the segregation of populations by two means: (1) *de jure* segregation, which is formalized segregation mandated by law, and (2) *de facto* segregation, which is informal segregation that comes about through social customs and business practices. (See also **Homophobia**.)

THE ORIGINS OF PREJUDICIAL STEREOTYPES

Stereotypes structure prejudice and allow for discrimination. Stereotypes are characteristics, usually negative, that are attributed to a class of people. Stereotypes may have originally contained a small grain of truth, but they are exaggerated and distorted out of context. Usually, stereotypes are based upon false generalizations about a group of people. Once negative stereotypes are attached to a group of people, the people are subjected to discrimination from members of the dominant group. This process of transferring negative attributes onto a group of people, and then attacking the stigmatized group is called scapegoating.

Scapegoating is documented in the Book of Leviticus (16:20–22). There it is explained that on the Day of Atonement, a live goat is selected by a high priest who places both of his hands on the head of the goat. He then prays and confesses the sins of the people, which are "transferred" to the goat. The animal is then slaughtered or cast into the wilderness. This process is believed to cleanse the people of their sins and feelings of guilt (Blumenfeld and Raymond 1993, 222–223).

Why are certain people selected for scapegoating? Saenger (1953, 110) identified three conditions for choosing certain people as scapegoats:

1. A prejudice must already exist against the people.
2. The group must appear to be too weak to fight back successfully.
3. Social institutions must sanction the scapegoating.

Although some cultures have valued lesbians and gays, others have demonized and scapegoated them. Religious beliefs form the backbone from which social norms, and social and legal institutions, grow. In societies dominated by antigay religious prejudice, those who are exclusively homosexual become the perfect scapegoats due to their small numbers and apparent weakness.

THE FUNCTION OF PREJUDICE

Beliefs and prejudices, whether true or false, are created for psychological reasons. Jamie Wurzel (1986) identified four basic functions of prejudice:

1. Utilitarian function. Prejudicial attitudes are created and maintained to avoid some punishment or to gain particular rewards.
2. Self-esteem, the protective function. Prejudice allows self-esteem to be protected from conflicts and weaknesses arising from feelings of limitation.
3. Value-expressive function. People prefer their own values and modes of living, thus groups that challenge one's values are perceived to be inferior and threatening.
4. The cognitive function. People divide reality into separate categories in order to comprehend the world. Stereotypes provide such categories and prejudice becomes a shortcut for interrelating with others.

Prejudice against gays in American culture fulfills these four functions. First, many legal discriminations are still enforced against homosexuals. These restrictions fulfill the utilitarian function by punishing homosexuals and rewarding heterosexuals. Second, people who feel threatened by the demands of gender roles may find it to their benefit to be prejudiced against people who challenge gender roles (lesbians and gays). Thus, being prejudiced against homosexuals provides a protective function for heterosexual self-esteem. Third, the modern gay movement is seen as a threat to American dominant values. Prejudice against lesbians and gays attempts to preserve modes of living and is, therefore, a value-expressive function. Finally, American society attempts to keep lesbians, gays, and homosexuality hidden. Gay stereotypes serve a cognitive function for maintaining order in the heterosexual dominant view of the world.

Overall, prejudice and discrimination are tools used consciously and unconsciously by the dominant group to maintain its control and power over minorities. The most significant action lesbians and gays can take to challenge prejudice is being out at all levels—at school, in the workplace, and with their families and friends. However, threats and violence from the dominant culture are often made against visible minorities.

RESPONDING TO OPPRESSION

How do people respond to prejudice, stigmatization, scapegoating, and oppression? Gordon Allport (1954) enumerated the varieties of negative responses to stigmatization: (1) obsessive concern resulting in feelings of deep anxiety, suspicion, and insecurity; (2) denial (from both oneself and others) of actual membership in the minority group; (3) social withdrawal and passivity; (4) clowning, being the "court jester" in an effort to be accepted by the dominant group; (5) slyness and cunning—often for mere survival; (6) identification with the dominant group—a sign of self-hate; (7) aggression against and addressing blame to one's own group; (8) directing prejudice and discrimination against other minorities; (9) excessive neuroticism; (10) internalizing and acting out the negative social definitions and stereotypes—the self-fulfilling prophecy; and (11) excessive striving for status to compensate by substitution for the feelings of inferiority.

Some members of minority groups react as listed above. These negative responses are not inevitable, but are, rather, understandable defenses to discrimination. But when these responses occur, they often lead to reinforcement of negative stereotypes and beliefs. By contrast, some minority members react positively in response to discrimination against them by: (1) strengthening ties with minority-group members; (2) sharing sympathy with and support for other minorities; (3) showing enhanced striving and assertiveness, that is, seeing oppression as merely an obstacle or challenge to be surmounted; and (4) challenging the status quo in a variety of ways and refusing to "take it any longer," which often brings about progressive social change (Blumenfeld and Raymond 1993, 263).

Almost everyone has been subjected to prejudice and discrimination at some time during his or her life. Gays, lesbians, and bisexuals continue to be despised, although certain conditions have improved, particularly in democratic political systems. It is difficult to determine if prejudice toward lesbians and gay men is decreasing. On the one hand, laws are slowly changing and antidiscrimination statutes are being passed that include protections based upon sexual orientation. But, on the other hand, hate crimes are increasing and there is a terrible conservative backlash occurring, as demonstrated by the swift passage of "defense of marriage" legislation in many states.

References

Allport, G. 1954. *The Nature of Prejudice.* Reading, MA: Addison-Wesley.

Blumenfeld, W. J., and D. Raymond, eds. 1993. *Looking at Gay and Lesbian Life.* Rev. ed. Boston: Beacon Press.

Eitzen, D. S. 1980. *Social Problems.* Boston: Allyn & Bacon.

Saenger, G. 1953. *The Social Psychology of Prejudice.* New York: Harper.

Wurzel, J. 1986. "The Functions and Forms of Prejudice." In *A World of Difference: Resource Guide for Reduction of Prejudice.* Boston: Anti-Defamation League of B'nai B'rith and Facing History and Ourselves National Foundation, Inc.

PUBLIC ACCOMMODATIONS

Public accommodations are services, goods, or benefits offered to the general public at large. They commonly include hotels and motels, restaurants, stores, and other businesses or organizations catering to the public. The legal definition of public accommodation varies from jurisdiction to jurisdiction. A business subject to ordinances against discrimination in one jurisdiction may be exempt in other jurisdictions. For example, two gay organizations sued a newspaper in Green Bay, Wisconsin, in 1990 for refusing to carry their ads. The newspaper convinced the appellate court that newspapers in that state do not offer "accommodations" to the public as specified in the state's civil rights laws and therefore the newspaper was legally able to refuse the ads (*Hatheway v. Gannett Satellite Information Network, Inc.*).

Offices of physicians, dentists, lawyers, and other highly trained professionals are often not deemed "places of public accommodation" by state law. However, the federal statutes designed to protect people with HIV have designated physicians' offices as places of public accommodation. Thus, there can be conflicting rules concerning what constitutes public accommodation within a single jurisdiction (Hunter, Michaelson, and Stoddard 1992).

Likewise, certain professions are excluded from state definitions of public accommodation. For example, those who sell insurance are excluded. However, they are regulated under special state commissions that may have their own provisions protecting lesbians and gay men in obtaining services.

Private organizations and clubs are exempt from complying with public accommodation statutes. Private operators are able to restrict membership, to establish dress codes, and to regulate decency, noise, and other behaviors of their members. However, what constitutes a "private" club is an area of continuing litigation in our society. For example, the **Boy Scouts** have been sued for excluding gay members. Many cities and school districts have removed their support from the Boy Scouts because of their discriminatory policies. The guiding rule to determine whether a private social club or private business is in actuality public is its relative lack of selectivity in choosing its membership and, in some cases, the receipt of public funding.

Only a few cities and states have antidiscrimination policies that include sexual orientation. In all other places stores, restaurants, movies, bars, motels, and other public businesses may refuse service to lesbians and gay men. But laws other than antidiscrimination statutes may be used to provide access. For example, Disneyland in Anaheim, California, was sued in the 1980s for refusing to let two men dance together. Because of California's Unruh Civil Rights Act, the couple prevailed. However, soon afterward, Disneyland tried to stop two men from touching while dancing together. They claimed that the previous suit applied only to "fast dancing." The courts agreed with the gay couple and Disneyland had to let lesbian and gay couples engage in both kinds of dancing (Kane 1999).

Federal law prohibits discrimination based upon race, color, religion, national origin, or disability. All attempts to include sexual orientation in the federal list have languished in Congress since 1975. Interestingly, sex and gender are also missing from federal statutes related to public accommodation.

If lesbians or gay men are refused service in a jurisdiction that provides protections based upon sexual orientation, they are able to file complaints with that city, county, or state commission entrusted with the enforcement of its antidiscrimination statutes. Once the complaint is taken, an investigation is conducted by the agency. If there is probable cause that impermissible discrimination took place, the agency may conduct a full hearing. The particular steps and time limits are specific to the jurisdiction.

In jurisdictions that do not have antidiscrimination polices based upon sexual orientation, there are still potential ways for lesbians and gay men to combat acts of discrimination. Perhaps the discrimination falls under other class protections such as gender, race, or marital status. If the act of discrimination occurred on government property, then claims that equal protection under the law (as required by the Fourteenth Amendment) was violated are sometimes successful.

References

Hunter, N. D., S. E. Michaelson, and T. B. Stoddard. 1992. *The Rights of Lesbians and Gay Men: The Basic ACLU Guide to a Gay Person's Rights.* 3d ed. Carbondale and Edwardsville, IL: Southern Illinois University Press.

Kane, R. 1999. "An Incomplete History of Gay and Lesbian OC." *Orange County Weekly* (13–19 August 1999) website: www.ocweekley.com/ink/99/49/news-kane.shtml.

PUBLIC SAFETY Public safety statutes are designed to maintain the safety of the public. For example, **alcoholic beverage control (ABC)** regulations monitor bars (including gay and lesbian bars) against overcrowding, serving alcohol to underage patrons, or serving alcohol to patrons who are inebriated. Public safety also includes monitoring crowds and protest demonstrations. All persons in the United States have the right to express their beliefs through legal free speech. When police officers must act to disperse an unlawful assembly or stop civil disobedience, safety considerations are of utmost importance. This includes the safety of the officers, civilian bystanders, property, and the demonstrators. Applying stereotypic characteristics to the demonstrators must be avoided because it can lead to oversimplification and overreaction, thereby aggravating the situation. Police officers should not use pejorative language or other denigrating comments toward the demonstrators; this can only inflame an already volatile situation. (See also **Criminal Law; Speech and Association.**)

Q

QUEER *Queer* was probably the most common mid-twentieth-century American abusive slang term for homosexual. The word is most likely rooted in the use of the word for counterfeit money and coins, as in "queer as a three-dollar bill." Queer implies not being authentic. When applied to male homosexuals, queer implies that the man is not an authentic male and not normal. Queer was rarely applied to women.

In the early 1990s, the term queer began to be appropriated by the lesbian and gay community. Queer Nation was an activist anarchist group that staged in-your-face confrontations with political, business, and educational leaders. Similar to ACT-UP, which brought media attention to the problem of **AIDS**, Queer Nation brought attention to the problems of homophobia and heterosexism.

Queer became assimilated into mainstream academic parlance. Instead of writing the phrase lesbian, gay, and bisexual, and transgendered, transsexual, and intersexed people, the word queer became a shorthand way of referring to all people who were not heterosexual. Many college and academic conferences on lesbian and gay issues became queer conferences. However, the lesbian and gay community has not wholeheartedly embraced the term. For many, the term is still negative in much the same way that the word *faggot* is.

The process of appropriating epithets by stigmatized groups is well documented. For example, the word *black* was an epithet that Negroes and colored people once detested. The Black Panthers appropriated the term in the 1960s. Now, black no longer has the sting it once had and can be used neutrally to refer to African Americans. This same process may happen with the word queer, but at this time, it is not universally accepted by the lesbian and gay community and still should not be used by heterosexuals in reference to homosexuals.

R

Relationships, Lesbian or Gay

Relationships, Lesbian or Gay Because marriage is unavailable for lesbian or gay male couples, measuring simple things like the length of a relationship is problematic. Letitia Anne Peplau (1993) conducted a thorough review of the literature concerning gay and lesbian relationships. She found over 5,000 citations from the social sciences, humanities, and popular press concerning relationships, but these were almost exclusively heterosexual in nature. Of those citations, only thirty-six were classified as involving gay or lesbian "couples." This is in contrast with 362 citations mentioning homosexuality that dealt with psychiatry, "cures," or law enforcement. Therefore, only a handful of academic research sources exist that look at gay and lesbian relationships without bias.

Common Myths

There are four common myths about lesbian and gay relationships:

1. *Homosexuals don't want enduring relationships and can't achieve them anyway.* The data sharply counter this stereotype. Lesbian couples and gay male couples form enduring relationships. Contrary to stereotypes, lesbians do not necessarily form *more* enduring relationships than either heterosexuals or gay men.
2. *Gay relationships are unhappy, abnormal, dysfunctional, and deviant.* When queried, most gay men and lesbians report that their relationships are happy and satisfying. Heterosexual and homosexual relationships are indistinguishable concerning levels of love, satisfaction, and complexity (Nava and Dawidoff 1994). Unfortunately, some research has looked into the "abnormal" or "deviant" nature of homosexual relationships. These are value-laden terms and not applicable to the scientific description of any relationship. Such research should be immediately dismissed. With the declassification of homosexuality as a pathology by the **American Psychiatric Association (APA)** in 1973, the

normality of any sexual orientation is not questioned. Homosexuality and heterosexuality are considered equally sound sexual orientations and relationships that are either homosexual or heterosexual are equally valid.

3. *"Husband" and "wife" roles are universal in intimate relationships.* Role-playing along gender lines has decreased among lesbians and gay men. Instead, they frequently form "dual-worker" or "companionate" relationships. Many lesbians and gay men pattern their relationships on friendship or peer structure with an emphasis on companionship, sharing, and equality.
4. *Gays and lesbians have impoverished social support networks.* Lesbians and gay men have social support networks similar to heterosexuals. If anything, lesbians and gay men have learned to create strong supportive links because they are often estranged from their biological families.

Until the late 1990s courts in the United States have viewed lesbian or gay male relationships as being deviant or somehow not as good as heterosexual relationships. Courts have ordered children removed from biological parents if they entered a homosexual relationship. Likewise few **housing** ordinances provide protection for lesbian or gay male couples. The realization that homosexual relationships are virtually indistinguishable from heterosexual relationships should help reverse the tide of legal discrimination against homosexual couples. (See also **Child Custody and Visitation Rights**.)

References

Nava, M., and R. Dawidoff. 1994. *Created Equal: Why Gay Rights Matter to America.* New York: St. Martin's Press.

Peplau, L. A. 1993. "Lesbian and Gay Relationships." In *Psychological Perspectives on Lesbian and Gay Male Experiences,* edited by L. D. Garnets and D. C. Kimmel. New York: Columbia University Press.

RELIGIOUS RIGHT AGENDA Writers for the so-called religious right often describe the movement toward recognizing equal rights for lesbians and gay men as an attempt to secure "special rights." They portray this as being part of a "**gay agenda**." But what is seldom mentioned is the agenda of the religious right and its impact on the U.S. legal system.

In July 1998 full-page paid advertisements were placed in major national newspapers promoting the "ex-gay" movement. The ads were purchased through a coalition of fifteen Christian right organizations and represented a reframing of their longstanding condemnation of homosexuality. In addition to condemning homosexuality as a sin, emphasis was given to curing homosexuality as an act of religious affirmation.

Frightening people with homosexual stereotypes has been a long-standing tactic of the religious right. In 1977 fundamentalist singer and orange-juice industry spokesperson Anita Bryant led a successful campaign to repeal a gay rights law in Dade County, Florida. She tied child molestation to homosexuality with the campaign slogan "Save Our Children."

Robert Billings, the first executive director of the Moral Majority (a Christian nonprofit organization that spearheaded much of the religious right's political activity during the 1980s and 1990s), recognized the solicitation potential in using homosexuality. He stated to the members at one of the first meetings of the Moral Majority, at which the press was present, "I know what you feel about these queers, these fairies. We wish we could get in our cars and run them down when they march. . . . We need an emotionally charged issue to stir up people. . . . I believe that the homosexual issue is the issue we should use" (Young 1982, 78).

But scaring people about homosexuality did not always work. A similar attempt to bar lesbians and gay men from teaching in California public schools failed with the defeat of the Briggs Initiative in 1978. Significant advances toward gay rights were achieved in the 1980s. The religious right reacted and began to provide voting advice to their constituents and published pamphlets on how to fill local political offices with fundamentalist candidates. Because these political actions violated the U.S. tax code for religious tax exemptions, the nonprofit religious status of the Christian Coalition was revoked.

In the early 1990s an increased number of Republicans were elected to office, so much so that they issued a document, called the "Contract for America," outlining the future of America as it was to be molded by right-leaning politicians. Confidence was high in this plan, as exhibited by Patrick Buchanan's bid for the presidency in 1996. While running for office he stated, "You just wait until 1996, then you'll see a real right-wing tyrant" (Corn 1995, 915). At the same time, there were attempts to repeal **affirmative action** statutes by the same groups that fought against gay and lesbian civil rights. Again, Buchanan best summarizes the position held by the religious right. In his 1988 autobiography, *Right from the Beginning,* Buchanan wrote about race relations in the 1940s and 1950s, "There were no politics to polarize us then, to magnify every slight. The 'Negroes' of Washington had their public schools, restaurants, bars, movie houses, playgrounds and churches; and we had ours" (131). Statements like these demonstrate the connection between the desire to "ghettoize" people who are minorities because of their skin color and to ostracize people who are different because of their sexual orientation.

Yet, even with the U.S. political shift to the right, lesbian and gay civil rights made great strides. It became apparent to leaders of the religious right that if lesbians and gay men were allowed to marry and form legally recognized families that included child custody as well as other rights, the religious right would have lost their "culture war." So, they initiated other strategies:

- They increased the use of homophobic rhetoric to raise money and recruit followers (Berlet 1998; Mookas 1998). The homophobic rhetoric reinforced antigay stereotypes and played upon the fears of fundamentalists.
- They continued to fund and disseminate misinformation on human sexuality. The primary source of antigay statistics originates with Paul Cameron of the Family Research Institute. When his teaching contract in the Department of Psychology of the University of Nebraska was not renewed in 1980, Cameron began to publish hysterical pamphlets alleging that gays were disproportionately responsible for serial killings, child molestation, and other heinous crimes. The other psychologists whose work he referenced charged Cameron with distorting their findings. When the American Psychological Association (APA) investigated Cameron, it found that he not only misrepresented the work of others, but also used unsound methods in his own studies. For this ethical breach, it expelled Cameron in 1983. In 1987 Cameron founded the Family Research Institute to continue his antigay agenda. He has been a virtual one-man propaganda press, periodically revising his brochures and distributing them to policymakers. He continued to use unsound survey techniques and unrepresentative samples (Pietrzyk 1994). Yet despite all these problems of poor science, the religious right latched onto and helped fund Cameron's work to substantiate their religious agenda. When challenges are made concerning Cameron's ethical breaches, unsound research methodology, and misinformation, the religious right holds him up as a martyr and continues to promote his work.
- They forged an alliance between the Christian right and the ex-gay movement. By doing so, they hoped to overcome scientific and academic research that demonstrated that lesbians and gay men are really no different than heterosexuals. It is this objective research, tied with gay activism, that has influenced the development of gay rights. (See also **Reparative Therapy**.)
- They reinvigorated their old message of "no special rights" for homosexuals. This created the impression that lesbians and gay

men seek rights above and beyond those enjoyed by heterosexuals. This is not true. However, the "no special rights" ploy has been effective at stopping the legalization of gay marriages, gay adoptions, and other rights held by heterosexuals. (See also **Gay Agenda**; **Heterosexism**.)

- They continued to try to place into political office people who conform to their agenda and to squash those who are against them. For example, the Christian Coalition gave up its fight for tax-exempt status, and, instead, split into two groups: the Christian Coalition International, which openly endorses candidates and makes campaign contributions, and the tax-exempt Christian Coalition of America (formerly the Christian Coalition of Texas), which continues with the original organization's activities. In another example, the U.S. Justice Department was requested by Jesse Helms and other senators to investigate Americans United for Separation of Church and State (AU). It was the AU that provided information to the IRS concerning illegal political behaviors by the Christian Coalition. Also, the AU sent letters to churches advising them that their own tax-exempt status could be jeopardized if they distributed the Christian Coalition's voter's guide. Two weeks after the senators met with Christian Coalition founder Pat Robertson, the request was submitted to the Justice Department. The Justice Department rejected the request. Americans United Executive Director Barry L. Lynn stated, "With absolutely no evidence, these six men asked the top law enforcement official in the land to undertake a criminal investigation of my organization. This grotesque abuse of power should alarm every American" ("Case Dismissed" 2000, 32).

The religious right's goal is to create a theocratic state, a "nation whose laws are based on fundamentalist's interpretation of the Bible" ("We've come a long way . . . maybe" 2000, 12). Pat Robertson, founder and director of the Christian Coalition, stated on his television show, *The 700 Club,* "The country was founded by Christians. It was founded as a Christian nation. They're trying to sell us this nonsense about separation of church and state. And that's what it is, it's a fanatical interpretation of the First Amendment. . . . We're going to win this battle but we've got to stand together, all the Christians in America need to join hands together and say we've had enough of this utter nonsense" (White 1997). This opinion is also held by Gary Potter of the Catholics for Christian Political Action. He stated, "When the Christian majority takes control, pluralism will be seen as evil and the state will not allow anybody the right to practice evil" (White 1997). And one of the major evils the religious right wants to eliminate is homosexuality. As Dean Wycoff, director of the Moral Majority of Santa Clara County, California, stated, "I agree with capital punishment and I believe that homosexuality . . . could be coupled with murder. . . . It would be the government that sits upon this land who will be executing the homosexuals" (Young 1982, 77). Similarly, Reverend Dr. Rousas John Rushdoony of Chalcedon, Inc., an extremist Christian organization in Vallecito, California, advocates the death penalty for homosexuals, believes that democracy is a heresy and the enemy of Christianity, that women need protection and not equal rights, that slavery is acceptable in modern societies, and that judges should be representatives of God (Rushdoony 1973). Thus, it appears that the not-so-hidden agenda of such conservatives is to take control of the United States and use state power to discriminate, incarcerate, and kill those who do not agree with them—particularly homosexuals.

LEGAL IMPLICATIONS OF THE RELIGIOUS RIGHT

"The ex-gay movement poses a significant new threat to efforts to secure civil rights legal protections for gay/lesbian/bisexual/transgender people. Potentially, it is the most damaging manifestation of an ongoing backlash against this community" (Khan 1998, 17).

Lesbian, gay, and bisexual, and transgendered, transsexual, and intersexed people have made many legal strides: the elimination of most sex statutes; increased positive media coverage of major issues; passage of the federal Employment Non-discrimination Act (Executive Order 13087); and the growing number of state, county, and city antigay discrimination ordinances. The religious right has mobilized against these gains and continues to promote the belief that homosexuality is deviant and sinful. Objective scientific inquiry into homosexuality continues to show that it is not a mental illness, nor a psychological, social, or cultural deficit. To counter the loss of ground, the religious right has claimed that homosexuality is a chosen lifestyle and is alterable. Based on their beliefs that homosexuality is a deviancy and is chosen, then logically those who choose it deserve pain, stigmatization, and legal restrictions. They claim that all lesbians and gay men need to do is choose heterosexuality and they will receive all the legal protections afforded that status. Accepting the ex-gay movement's position undermines lesbian and gay men's claim to civil rights. (See also **Appendix A: State and Local Laws; Criminal Law; Sodomy**.)

This is a repackaging of the "no special rights" strategy and has been effective. For example, the 1998 "family values" campaign by the Christian right in Maine resulted in the successful referendum and reversal of antidiscrimination law in that state. A similar strategy by the Christian right was successful in achieving congressional denial of federal funds to municipalities that required domestic partnership benefits to same-sex couples.

"The long-term goal of the Christian right in using the ex-gay movement to convince people that lesbian, gay, and bisexual people can become heterosexual is to create a restrictive legal environment in which equal rights are only accorded to heterosexual men and women" (Khan 1998, 18).

References

Berlet, C. 1998. "Who Is Mediating the Storm? Right-Wing Alternative Information Networks." In *Media, Culture, and the Religious Right,* edited by L. Kintz and J. Lesage. Minneapolis, MN: University of Minnesota Press.

Buchanan, P. 1988. *Right from the Beginning.* Boston: Little, Brown.

"Case Dismissed." 2000. *Frontiers* 18(22): 32.

Corn, D. 1995. "Buchanan Rages on a Potent Trinity—God, Country and Me." *The Nation* (26 June 1995): 915.

Khan, S. 1998. *Calculated Compassion: How the Ex-Gay Movement Serves the Right's Attack on Democracy.* Washington, DC: Political Research Associates, the Policy Institute of the National Gay and Lesbian Task Force, and Equal Partners in Faith.

Mookas, I. 1998. "Faultlines: Homophobic Innovation in Gay Rights/Special Rights." In *Culture, Media, and the Religious Right,* edited by L. Kintz and J. Lesage. Minneapolis: University of Minnesota Press.

Pietrzyk, M. E. 1994. "Queer Science." *The New Republic* (3 October 1994).

Rushdoony, R. J. 1973. *The Institutes of Biblical Law.* Phillipsburg, NJ: Presbyterian Reformed—A Chelcedon Publication.

"We've Come a Long Way . . . Maybe." 2000. *Frontiers* 18(22): 12.

White, M. 1997. *The 700 Club. The Justice Report.* Video. Laguna Beach, CA: Soulforce.

Young, P. D. 1982. *God's Bullies: Native Reflections on Preachers and Politics.* New York: Holt, Rinehart, and Winston.

REPARATIVE THERAPY

The attempt to change sexual orientation through a number of therapies is known as "reparative" therapy (that is, "to repair that which is broken").

In the late nineteenth and early twentieth centuries, the medical profession almost universally regarded homosexuality as an illness that required a cure. Among the methods attempted to make homosexuals heterosexual were castration, hysterectomy, lobotomy, and electroshock therapy. By the mid-twentieth century psychotherapy had become the most common method of "curing" homosexuality. Many homosexuals spent years in analysis attempting to change their sexual orientation.

> In the 1950s and 1960s a growing number of psychiatrists began to question whether such efforts were misguided. What mental and emotional problems homosexuals faced, they reasoned, stemmed from coping with society's antigay prejudices rather than from homosexuality itself. . . . In 1973 the American Psychiatric Association removed homosexuality from its official list of mental disorders. Other medical institutions soon followed the APA's example, and health practitioners began to focus on helping gays and lesbians accept and affirm their homosexuality rather than change it. (Dudley 1993, 125)

Homosexuality as a mental disorder was replaced with the confusing "ego-dystonic homosexuality" diagnosis in 1973. This diagnosis was dropped in 1988, completing the official depathologization of homosexuality. However, efforts to "cure" or convert homosexuals into heterosexuals persist. Can this be done?

PSYCHOANALYSIS

Therapists using standard psychoanalysis report conflicting results. Most therapists report being unsuccessful at achieving a change from homosexuality to heterosexuality. Those who claim success face methodological problems that make their claims difficult to interpret. For example, most of the subjects of these efforts to change sexual orientation are usually bisexual, with only a few who are exclusively homosexual. A further problem faced by these attempts is the definition of "success." For example, Birk claimed that 38 percent of his patients achieved a "solid heterosexual shift," yet he cautioned that "[m]ost, if not all, people who have been homosexual continue to have some homosexual feelings, fantasies, and interests. More often than not, they also have occasional, or more than occasional, homosexual outlets, even while being 'happily married'" (Birk 1980, 376–390).

What was achieved here? A change in sexual orientation? No! The person engaged in more heterosexual behavior but still engaged in "more than occasional" homosexual behavior. Reports that pertain to exclusively homosexual patients report no change. This is further illustrated by Joseph Nicolosi, one of the leaders in the religion-based reparative therapy movement. He acknowledges that he never "cured" a client of homosexuality. His most "successful" client married and had three children, yet reported "homosexual fantasies that lingered 'like a gnat buzzing around your ear'" (Buie 1990, 20–21).

CONVERSION AND AVERSION THERAPY

These therapies originated in the science of behaviorism. Therapists attempt to form a contingency between a negative stimulus (like an electrical shock) and homosexual fantasies. These therapies have failed to change a person's sexual orientation. Instead, they only reduced sexual interest and response (Burr 1996, 126; Cabaj and Stein 1996, 530–531; McConaghy 1981).

"DEPROGRAMMING"

Another psychotherapy is called "deprogramming." Here, a series of punishments and rewards are thought to change emotional programming. As an example of "deprogramming," a nineteen-year-old Ohio lesbian was kidnapped by her father and three other men, deprived of sleep and food, and repeatedly raped. The sensory depravation was thought to lower her resistance, and the rape was to initiate her into heterosexual sexual behaviors. When she was released, she filed charges against her parents and the male deprogrammers who kidnapped and raped her. In court, the parents admitted to paying $8,000 for the "service" and were fully aware of the techniques to be used. The judge dismissed all charges of sexual battery, assault, and kidnapping. He further deleted all references to rape and, instead, redefined this horrific experience as "heterosexual activity meant to sway [her] from her lesbianism" (Comstock 1991, 201).

RELIGION-BASED CONVERSION PROGRAMS

In the 1990s the primary proponents of sexual orientation conversion programs have been pastors and religiously oriented lay persons. Persons with strong doctrinaire religious practices are more likely to view their homosexuality as a "sin." As such, they are vulnerable targets for the "ex-gay" ministries. There are many such ministries and they publicly promise "change." However, they "acknowledge that celibacy is the realistic goal to which homosexuals must aspire" (Haldeman 1991, 156). None of these groups has published their results in peer-reviewed journals, nor will they allow researchers access to their files.

Leaders of these ministries have a history of engaging in sex with their clients. This has led to the demise of many groups and attempted cover-ups by the religious organization (perhaps the most notorious of these is by Colin Clark of the Seventh Day Adventist Church) (Lawson 1987). "The tradition of conflicted homosexual pastors using their ministries to gain sexual access to vulnerable gay people is as longstanding as the conversion movement itself" (Haldeman 1991, 157). And, as reported by another prominent "ex-gay" ministry, Exodus International, "[the program was] ineffective . . . not one person was healed" (Newswatch Briefs 1990, 43). These religion-based programs often exacerbated already prominent feelings of guilt and personal failure among those seeking counseling; many were driven to suicidal thoughts as a result of the failed "reparative therapy" (Haldeman 1991, 159).

The American Psychological Association's (APA) "Fact Sheet on Reparative Therapy" states that "no scientific evidence exists to support the effectiveness of any of the conversion therapies that try to change sexual orientation." Perhaps bisexuals can be shifted toward more heterosexual behaviors, but homosexual fantasies, feelings, and behaviors cannot be extinguished. "These interventions do not shift sexual orientation at all. Rather, they instruct or coerce heterosexual activity in a minority of subjects, which is not the same as reversing sexual orientation" (Haldeman 1991, 151).

All the conversion therapies, and particularly the religion-based "reparative" therapies, violate ethical standards:

> Psychological ethics mandate that mental health professionals subscribe to methods that support human dignity and are effective in their stated purpose. Conversion therapy qualifies as neither. It reinforces the social stigma associated with homosexuality. . . . It now makes sense to discontinue focusing on conversion attempts and focus instead on healing and educating an intolerant social context. . . . Mental health and paraprofessional practitioners who engage in conversion therapies may be likely to harm such clients, and in addition may also commit consumer fraud, as this damaging practice simply does not work. (Haldeman 1991, 159–160)

LEGAL IMPLICATIONS

Reparative therapy or any other conversion therapy that claims to be able to change sexual orientation is consumer fraud. Mental health practitioners who engage in any of these therapies only exacerbate feelings of inadequacy and failure in clients. Counselors could be sued or reported to state commissions and have their professional licenses revoked for using these techniques.

However, most conversion programs are promoted and supported by religious organizations. They skirt the law by claiming that they are not engaging in psychotherapy (which would require state licensing and oversight), but instead are providing "religious counseling." As seen in the tragic case of the nineteen-year-old Ohio lesbian, who was kidnapped and raped by "deprogrammers," the courts have not been willing to prosecute the perpetrators of such actions. Someday the psychotherapy profession and the criminal law system may be able to stop these fraudulent and dangerous practices. (See also **Religious Right Agenda**.)

References

Birk, L. 1980. "The Myth of Classical Homosexuality: Views of a Behavioral Psychotherapist." In *Homosexual Behavior: A Modern Reappraisal,* edited by J. Marmor. New York: Basic Books.

Buie, J. 1990. "'Heterosexual Ethic' Mentality Is Decried." *American Psychological Association Monitor* 21(3): 20–21.

Burr, C. 1996. *A Separate Creation: The Search for the Biological Origins of Sexual Orientation.* New York: Hyperion.

Cabaj, R. P., and T. S. Stein. 1996. *Textbook of Homosexuality and Mental Health.* Washington, DC: American Psychiatrist Press.

Comstock, G. D. 1991. *Violence Against Lesbians and Gay Men.* New York: Columbia University Press.

Dudley, W., ed. 1993. *Homosexuality: Opposing Viewpoints.* San Diego, CA: Greenhaven Press.

Haldeman, D. C. 1991. "Sexual Orientation Conversion Therapy for Gay Men and Lesbians: A Scientific Examination." In *Homosexuality: Research Implications for Public Policy,* edited by J. C. Gonsiorek and J. D. Weinrich. Newbury Park, CA: Sage.

Lawson, R. 1987. "Scandal in the Adventist-Funded Program to 'Heal' Homosexuals: Failure, Sexual Exploitation, Official Silence, and Attempts to Rehabilitate the Exploiter and His Methods." Paper presented at the meeting of the American Sociological Association, Chicago, Palmer House, 17–21 August 1987.

McConaghy, N. 1981. "Controlled Comparison of Aversive Therapy and Covert Sensitization in Compulsive Homosexuality." *Behavior Research and Therapy* 19(5): 425–434.

Newswatch Briefs. 1990. *Gay Chicago Magazine,* 22 February, 43.

RESEARCH ON SEXUAL ORIENTATION It is difficult, if not impossible, to correctly identify gays, lesbians, and bisexuals in our heterosexist and homophobic society. Lesbians and gay men can be legally fired from their jobs, lose their housing, lose rights to their children, and much more, simply for engaging in homosexual behavior. Thus they have a vested interest in not being identified. Accordingly, research that attempts to describe the majority of lesbian and gay people in the United States should be questioned and scrutinized.

Much of the research is tainted by the use of biased samples (that is, samples that are not representative of the entire population). For example, the stereotypes that gays are alcoholic, criminal, and mentally unbalanced came from the psychological studies performed in the 1940s and 1950s. These studies were biased by problems with population sampling. The practical problem researchers faced then, as now, is where to find homosexuals. Homosexuals had no safe public gathering places before the modern gay liberation movement. Researchers relied upon convenient locations such as bars, prisons, and mental hospitals in which to conduct their studies. Is it any wonder their research found a high proportion of participants who were alcoholics (from bar samples), criminals (from prison samples), and mentally unbalanced (from mental hospital samples)?

Furthermore, the definition of *gay* or *homosexual* affects research outcomes. Is gayness or homosexuality based on sexual behavior, sexual and affectionate feelings, socialization patterns, or something else? There is also the problem of defining frequency. How often or when does such behavior occur in a person's life? Often, lesbians and gay men do not come out until later in their lives, sometimes after engaging in heterosexual behavior that includes marriage and producing children. Is behavior the same as identity? Interestingly, many people who do engage in same-sex sexual behaviors do not identify themselves as gay and vice versa. Similarly, most people have same-sex sexual desires but do not act on those desires. Are these people identified as homosexual, gay, bisexual, or what? (Laumann et al. 1994). Thus, the definition of homosexuality that a researcher chooses will influence all subsequent attempts to identify its common characteristics.

There are important legal implications regarding sexual orientation research. When the field of psychology began in the late 1800s, Victorian and Christian morals strongly influenced definitions of sexuality, **family**, and social order. Thus, homosexuality was deemed immoral and subsequently medicalized as a mental disorder and worse. By the mid-1900s, a revolution occurred in psychology in which old definitions and theories were reevaluated for bias and validity was required to be shown through empirical evidence. Many archaic terms were dropped or reformulated in ways that enabled them to become testable. Homosexuality is a prime example of this process. Originally it was presumed to be a mental disorder and disease because of Christian dogma. Research into homosexuality always attempted to confirm this definition. But as researchers demanded the use of representative samples, the antigay stereotypes were found to be false. Ultimately, the very foundation of the deficit model of homosexuality was challenged. Once the Christian condemnatory root was removed, researchers were able to engage in legitimate research. More than forty years of academic research has revealed that there really are no differences between heterosexuals and homosexuals. These findings are having an impact on the courts.

Cases involving gay issues, such as Colorado's **Amendment 2**, gay marriage, child custody, and others bring forth a flood of legal briefs for both sides. Conservatives and religious right leaders bring forth the same arguments against granting homosexuals the same rights enjoyed by heterosexuals. However, the research on sexual orientation is countering antigay arguments and courts have slowly begun to recognize the legal flaws limiting gay rights. (See also **Child Custody and Visitation Rights; Defense of Marriage Act (DOMA)**; ***Romer v. Evans*.**)

Sometimes antigay forces try to counter new research that does not find problems with homosexuality. They claim that the new research is either flawed because it was conducted by lesbian and gay researchers and thus is biased, or, is just as flawed as the old research, thereby demonstrating how no one can rely upon science to solve the problem. The first argument is not true. Most of the researchers into human sexuality are heterosexuals. Also, even if a researcher is homosexual, the process of peer review and ensuring validity through scientific review removes much of the bias. Before the 1950s, there was no balance and all research was severely biased.

Understanding how science works is important to counter the first and, particularly, the second claim. Science makes definitions and constructs relationships between definitions. Then experimentation attempts to validate them. If they do not work, new definitions and relationships are devised. The process is continually reviewed and if new evidence challenges an old idea, the process begins again to bring us closer to clearly defining an objective reality.

Religious conservatives quoted psychological research as long as it agreed with their antigay agenda. The new research does not affirm their antigay beliefs; thus they discredit all academic research. As a last resort, they have founded their own research organizations like the Family Research Institute, and others. These organizations publish pamphlets for their own membership that contain hyperbolic antigay claims. None of these organizations will submit its work for peer review, nor will they report details about how they obtained their findings.

Similar to the long civil rights process for African Americans, courts are beginning to separate the moral condemnation of homosexuality from the academic research. With the demise of antigay stereotypes, lesbians and gay men are slowly obtaining some of the rights enjoyed by heterosexuals.

Reference

Laumann, E. O., J. H. Gagnon, R. T. Michael, and S. Michaels. 1994. *The Social Organization of Sexuality: Sexual Practices in the United States.* Chicago: University of Chicago Press.

Romer v. Evans

In *Romer v. Evans,* the U.S. Supreme Court in 1996 overturned Colorado's **Amendment 2**, which attempted to bar protection against discrimination based upon sexual orientation. This was one of the pivotal U.S. Supreme Court decisions of the 1990s and has had a major influence on other antigay cases.

Similar to other states, Colorado saw a rise in gay activism from the 1970s and a corresponding backlash from the religious right and others. In 1974 the Colorado Gay Alliance signed an agreement with the Denver Police Department as part of a court settlement to eliminate police harassment and selective enforcement of public indecency laws. The settlement stated that the police would stop going to gay bars and stop arresting people for simply holding hands or kissing. However, instead of reducing arrests, arrests doubled within a year after the settlement. Similarly in 1974 the city of Boulder enacted the first law prohibiting discrimination based on sexual orientation. However, the voters overwhelmingly rejected it and the law was repealed. Later, in 1987, Boulder citizens were asked the same question and this time they approved an antidiscrimination ordinance based on sexual orientation.

This political seesaw of approving antidiscrimination laws, backlash, then reaffirmation occurred in other Colorado cities. By 1989 Colorado governor Roy Romer issued an executive order prohibiting discrimination against people with **AIDS**. In 1991 the Colorado Civil Rights Commission recommended that the state adopt antidiscrimination statutes based on sexual orientation.

In response to these changes, three religious right activists—David Noebel, Tony Marco, and Kevin Tebedo—formed a new organization called Colorado for Family Values (CFV). Their goal was to repeal the governor's executive order and the antidiscrimination laws that were in force in the cities of Aspen, Boulder, and Denver, and to prevent any future efforts to pass antidiscrimination laws aimed at protecting lesbian and gay people elsewhere in the state.

The CFV modeled its efforts on strategies used by Lou Sheldon's Traditional Values Coalition, James Dobson's Focus on the Family, the antifeminist Eagle Forum, and those listed in the Concerned Women for America's guidebook *How to Defeat Gay Rights Legislation.* The CFV drafted an amendment to the Colorado constitution, gathered signatures, and had it placed on the ballot. Amendment 2 sought to repeal any existing law or policy that protected persons with "homosexual, lesbian, or bisexual orientation" from discrimination in the state and any of its cities, towns, counties, and school boards and to prohibit future adoption or enforcement of any such law or policy. The primary argument the CFV gave for passage of the amendment was that policies that prohibited discrimination based upon sexual orientation provided "special rights" to lesbians, gay men, and bisexuals that they neither "deserved" nor "needed." Those who opposed Amendment 2 claimed that such a law would make lesbians, gay men, and bisexuals extremely vulnerable to discrimination and that it would begin the process of eliminating similar protections extended to other minorities.

The "special rights" argument has a long history. Originally used by opponents of laws prohibiting discrimination based upon race, the slogan infers that this class of people would receive rights or privileges that the majority would not get. "In truth, the laws simply ensured that minorities would have the same rights the majority already had, to participate in society without fear of discrimination" (Keen and Goldberg 1999, 10). Even so, the "special rights" slogan took hold in the minds of the voters. Brain McCormick, staff counsel for Pat Robertson's National Legal Foundation, coached the CFV to keep the phrase "special rights" out of the initiative, but to use it in all campaign promotions. As McCormick explained in his June 13, 1991, letter to Colorado for Family Values founder Tony Marco, "If language denying special privileges to homosexuals is in the amendment it could possibly allow homosexuals to argue that they are not asking for special privileges, just those granted to everyone else. [However] I believe that 'No Special Privileges' is a good motto for the amendment's public campaign" (Keen and Goldberg 1999, 11).

On November 3, 1992, Colorado voters passed the amendment with 53 percent in favor and 46 percent against. Because this was an initiative passed by the people, any challenges to the law would be defended by the state of Colorado. Lesbians, gay men, and bisexuals could not count on the state to defend their rights and, therefore, organized an activist team of attorneys to mount a lawsuit against the measure. Nine days later, this group of activists filed their lawsuit in the Colorado District Court for Denver.

Thus, the clash between the Constitution's principle of majority rule and its protections for the rights of oppressed groups was placed into the hands of the judiciary to referee. Throughout the history of the United States, courts have shown that there are limits to both positions. Absolute majority rule is limited by legitimate or compelling reasons by the state. For example, a ballot initiative passed in the 1960s attempted to discriminate against African Americans (*Hunter v. Erickson*). The U.S. Supreme Court ruled that "people may retain for themselves the power over certain subjects" but that the people themselves had put limits on majority power through the Constitution.

At the first hearing, a temporary injunction was granted to the plaintiffs, barring the state from implementing Amendment 2. Six months later, the case was heard by the Colorado District Court for Denver, Judge Bayless presiding. The state gave six reasons why Amendment 2 was constitutional: (1) it promoted statewide uniformity by eliminating city-by-city and county-by-county battles over the political issue of homosexuality and bisexuality; (2) it recognized the power of the people to put into place laws through the initiative process; (3) it allowed states not to expend resources on protecting the rights of individuals not considered to be from a **suspect class**; (4) it prevented the government from interfering with personal, familial, and religious privacy; (5) it prevented the government from subsidizing the political objectives of a special interest group; and (6) it promoted the physical and psychological well-being of children. Using these six reasons, the state attempted to show that there were compelling interests to uphold the will of the people.

As part of its legal strategy, the plaintiffs' legal team decided to attempt to prove that homosexuals should be afforded legal protection from discrimination because they form a suspect class. This was a big gamble with major implications. If they were able to convince the court of this position, it might set precedent to strike down all antigay statutes and ordinances nationwide. To prove suspect class status, the legal team believed it necessary to prove that sexual orientation was immutable and not a choice, that there was a history of discrimination against people based on homosexual sexual orientation, and that lesbians and gay men had little political power to ensure that their rights were protected.

To prove sexual orientation to be immutable and not a choice, they brought in experts in the field of human sexuality. They were able to show that **sexual orientation** is mostly biologically based and is set by an early age. Choice is not related to sexual orientation, however, sexual behaviors can involve some level of choice. Interestingly, the state declined to call the primary providers of antigay "research"—Paul Cameron or Charles W. Socarides. Instead, they cross-examined the academic researchers in an attempt to discredit them, but failed. (See also **Religious Right Agenda**; **Reparative Therapy**.)

Again, calling on a long list of academic historians, the plaintiffs easily showed that gay people have had a long history of persecution and oppression. While presenting the history of lesbian and gay oppression, the plaintiffs were able to demonstrate that the real purpose of Amendment 2 was to allow discrimination against lesbians, gay men, and bisexuals. The arguments and political processes used by the CFV were virtually identical to those used to deny prohibitions to discrimination based on race, sex, and other characteristics.

The more difficult task for the plaintiff was to quantify the lack of political power by lesbians and gay men. The state used data from market survey companies that reinforced the stereotype that lesbians and gay men have higher incomes than the general population. They also pointed at the steady progression in antidiscrimination ordinances and other gains made by the gay community as evidence that lesbians and gay men were not politically disenfranchised. The plaintiff countered by showing that the market research data was not from representative population samples and that academic research of census data showed that lesbians and gay men are, in fact, economically disadvantaged. Furthermore, the steady improvements in laws protecting employment and housing still reached a minority of Americans and had much further to go. Ultimately, this issue of political power would be the one aspect of suspect class determination that the courts would not accept.

Judge Bayless issued a sixteen-page ruling adhering closely to the six justifications and the evidence introduced at trial. He rejected the state's first claim. He felt that there was a more compelling state interest in maintaining competition in ideas than in reducing factionalism. He rejected the second claim, saying that the state failed to provide evidence that a "militant gay aggression" endangered state political functions, and, as such, the people could not enact such legislation. When Denver enacted antidiscrimination ordinance protections based upon sexual orientation, it did not experience an increase in cost. Thus, Judge Bayless denied the third claim that the amendment was needed to preserve limited financial resources for discrimination claims against legally recognized suspect classes. The fourth claim contended that the amendment was necessary to maintain people's right to discriminate against gay people for any reason—whether personal, familial, or religious. Judge Bayless said that antidiscrimination laws could be narrowly tailored to exempt religious organizations from compliance, but it could not deny the fundamental rights of lesbians, gays, and bisexuals to participate in the political process. Furthermore, the court rejected the narrow definition of family that the state claimed needed protection from lesbians and gays, and said family values would be achieved by pro-family actions, not actions against some other group. Overall, Bayless rejected the privacy defense mounted by the state. Bayless identified the fifth claim as the state's "strongest" argument, that is that Amendment 2 served a compelling interest by preventing the government from subsidizing "special interests." However, Bayless stated that the state failed to cite authority or support it, and rejected the fifth claim. Finally, Judge Bayless rejected the sixth claim because the state failed to provide sufficient evidence to support the claim that Amendment 2 was necessary to protect children.

Besides rejecting all six claims by the state, Judge Bayless went further and analyzed the plaintiffs' contention that laws based on sexual orientation should require a heightened level of judicial scrutiny. First, Bayless noted that no federal appellate court had ever granted homosexuals and bisexuals a suspect or "quasi-suspect" class status. Bayless wrote that whether sexual orientation is inborn or freely chosen, the case would be decided in another court or forum, not his court. He agreed that lesbians and gay men have experienced a history of discrimination. He disagreed with the plaintiffs that gay people are relatively powerless and cited the ability of a few homosexuals to influence 46 percent of Coloradans to vote against the measure as evidence for their political power. As such, Bayless decided that gay people failed to meet the elements needed to obtain suspect class status under the law.

The state appealed Judge Bayless's decision to the Colorado Supreme Court, asking that court to reverse the fundamental rights analysis. By doing so, the state hoped to lower the burden of proof from a compelling one to a rational relationship justification. The state supreme court rejected this approach and reiterated its view that Amendment 2's ultimate effect was to infringe upon the fundamental rights of the plaintiffs by prohibiting the adoption of laws, regulations, ordinances, and policies against discrimination based on sexual orientation. The state supreme court provided a step-by-step analysis similar to that prepared by Judge Bayless (*Evans v. Romer* [*Evans II*]).

The state then introduced a new argument in the brief stating that even if the court struck down Amendment 2's restrictions on antidiscrimination protections based upon sexual orientation, it should uphold the restrictions on "conduct, practices, or relationships." The state relied upon the 1986 U.S. Supreme Court decision in *Bowers v. Hardwick,* which upheld Georgia's sex statutes restricting homosexual **sodomy**. The Colorado Supreme Court rejected this argument and concluded that sexual orientation, conduct, practices, or relationships are different ways of identifying the same class of people—that is, lesbians, gay men, and bisexuals. Although the government had the right to specify behaviors, it could not deny the rights of an identifiable group to participate equally in the political process as Amendment 2 attempted to do. (See also ***Bowers v. Hardwick.***)

In 1995 the U.S. Supreme Court agreed to review the Colorado Supreme Court's decision. Besides the two primary parties involved, the Court accepted more than two dozen friend-of-the-court (amicus curiae) briefs from almost 100 organizations, cities, and individuals. The debate before the Court was similar to the arguments before the lower courts. The Supreme Court characterized Amendment 2 as "unprecedented in our jurisprudence" in that it identified "persons by a single trait and then denies them protection across the board. . . . A law declaring in general that it shall be more difficult for one group of citizens than for all others to seek aid from government is itself a denial of equal protection of the laws in the most literal sense." Also, Amendment 2 "inflicts on [gay people] immediate, continuing, and real injuries that outrun and belie any legitimate justifications that may be claimed for it" (*Romer v. Evans* 1996).

The Court ruled six to three (Scalia, Thomas, and Rehnquist dissented) that Amendment 2 appeared to violate the fundamental right of lesbians, gay men, and bisexuals to participate in the political process on an equal basis with other Coloradans. Writing for the majority Justice Kennedy stated, "We conclude that Amendment 2 classifies homosexuals not to further a proper legislative end but to make them unequal to everyone else. This Colorado cannot do. A state cannot so deem a class of persons a stranger to its laws" (*Romer v. Evans* 1999, 1629).

Reference

Keen, L., and S. B. Goldberg. 1999. *Strangers to the Law: Gay People on Trial.* Ann Arbor, MI: University of Michigan Press.

S

Safe Sex

Safe Sex Safe sex involves specific sexual practices that reduce the transmission of sexually transmitted diseases (STD). With the advent of **AIDS**, health professionals developed safe-sex guidelines to reduce the risk of contracting the HIV virus that causes it. The publication and distribution of these guidelines resulted in much controversy. Because of the concerns of Congress, many of the safe-sex pamphlets were heavily edited before they were released. AIDS activists proceeded to create their own, more explicit, instructions for distribution to the public and schools. On occasion, parents and others complained that the explicit instructions were pornographic and obscene.

Safe-sex campaigns have proved effective. The rate of HIV infection for gay men has dropped significantly. "Gay males have changed their behavior on an unprecedented scale" (Gonsiorek and Shernoff 1991, 237). It is important that explicit safe-sex information reaches the general population and young adults. (See also **AIDS**.)

Reference

Gonsiorek, J. C., and M. Shernoff. 1991. "AIDS Prevention and Public Policy: The Experience of Gay Males." In *Homosexuality: Research Implications for Public Policy*, edited by J. C. Gonsiorek and J. D. Weinrich. Newbury Park, CA: Sage.

Saint Patrick's Day Parade

Saint Patrick's Day Parade Boston's Saint Patrick's Day Parade, sponsored by the South Boston Allied War Veterans Councils, became a U.S. Supreme Court test case involving the First Amendment and the expression of gay rights. A gay marching contingent applied to participate in the parade and wanted to carry a banner indicating gay pride. The organizers refused their application and barred them from the event because of their intent to express a message in the parade contrary to that of the parade organizers. The gay contingent sued. In *Hurley v. Irish-American Gay, Lesbian, and Bisexual Group of Boston*, the U.S. Supreme Court upheld the First Amendment right of the organizers to exclude gays from their event, not because they were gay but rather because they intended to promote a political belief contrary to the beliefs of the private organizers of the event. The Court said parades are a "form of expression" and private sponsors cannot be forced to include groups that "impart a message the organizers do not wish to convey."

Since the refusal by some Saint Patrick's Day Parade organizers to allow lesbians and gay men to march under their banner, alternative parades have been launched that are more inclusive. (For discussion of the legal arguments concerning this conflict between free expression and public accommodations, see also **Boy Scouts**.)

SCHOOL CURRICULA There is much disagreement over including lesbian and gay topics in school curricula. School curricula are regulated by federal, state, and local school boards and influenced by teachers and parents. Some localities give teachers wide discretion in deciding what is included in the curriculum, while other school districts tightly regulate what is taught. Sexuality, and particularly lesbian and gay sexuality, is a very volatile issue. For example, a book is just as likely to be removed from a reading list or library for heterosexual sexual expression as it is for containing information on homosexual sexual expression.

When disagreement occurs over curricula, both sides typically claim that their First Amendment rights were violated. For example, in the early 1980s, David Solmitz was a social studies teacher who helped organize a Tolerance Day at Madison High School in Maine, after there had been a series of antigay violent acts there. He invited a prominent lesbian to come and speak. The principal and school superintendent disapproved because they thought that including the lesbian speaker would be too controversial. Some parents protested and bomb threats were received by the school. The school canceled Tolerance Day over worries of security. Solmitz and a student sued, claiming that their First Amendment rights relating to academic freedom were violated (*Solmitz v. Maine School Administrative District No. 59*). Maine's highest court reviewed the case and noted that the school district chose to cancel the entire day, not just the lesbian speaker, and, thus, did not violate Solmitz's First Amendment rights. Ironically, Dale McCormick, the lesbian who was asked to speak at Tolerance Day and was considered to be too controversial was, in 1990, elected to Maine's state legislature and spoke to another high school in 1992.

In 2000, five Lexington, Massachusetts, residents, with the help of lawyers from a conservative group, filed suit against the school district to stop a program called "Respecting Differences: Creating Safer Schools and a More Inclusive Community for Gay and Lesbian People and Their

Families." The program was to take place on a weekend in conjunction with some of the events taking place in a few churches on Sunday. All churches and religious organizations in town were invited to participate. The plaintiffs argued that the schools were supporting a religion, which is impermissible under the First Amendment's constitutional separation of church and state. The court ruled against the plaintiffs since the event involved no government funding and the message or content of the program contained no religious activities. ("Judge Refuses to Block" 2000).

Those who object to the inclusion of lesbian and gay materials into the curriculum claim that their First Amendment rights are being infringed by the imposition of certain ideas. Sometimes they claim their religious beliefs that homosexuality is immoral are being trampled on by schools. These arguments are similar to those who object to sex education programs. In response to these objections, "opt out" procedures are sometimes implemented for parents to keep their children out of such programs. (See also **Sex Education**.)

Reference

"Judge Refuses to Block Lexington Program on 'Respecting Differences.'" (12 October 2000). Associated Press website: www.wire.ap.org/APnews.

SCHOOL FACULTY MEMBERS' RIGHTS

The United States Constitution is the primary source for the legal rights of public school lesbian and gay teachers. These rights do not apply to truly private schools.

Lesbian and gay teachers are afforded protection in their profession by the Fourteenth Amendment's guarantees of both due process before being deprived of life, liberty, or property, and equal protection of the laws. Courts have interpreted these clauses to mean that government actions must be rationally related to a legitimate government purpose; that is, the government may not act capriciously, nor may its objectives be illegitimate.

Courts have been inconsistent in applying these principles to lesbians and gay men. Beginning with the 1969 case of *Norton v. Macy*, courts required the reinstatement of a gay man to his federal job at the National Aeronautics and Space Administration after he was terminated for being homosexual. The government claimed that his sexual orientation impaired the efficiency of governmental operations. However, the government was not able to demonstrate this connection and lost the case. This established the legal precedent that employees must be judged individually based on their performance rather than on the supposed characteristics of all homosexuals.

In 1969 the California Supreme Court applied the *Norton* principles to a case involving a schoolteacher. Here, Marc Morrison's teaching credentials were revoked because he engaged in noncriminal same-sex conduct that the Lowell Joint School District of California deemed "immoral." The court in *Morrison v. State Board of Education* held that teaching credentials cannot be revoked because of homosexual conduct unless school authorities can demonstrate an "unfitness to teach." Importantly, the court required factual evidence of unfitness rather than mere speculation about immorality.

Even though these two cases were based on sound analysis, other courts have capitulated to antigay hysteria. For example, in *Gaylord v. Tacoma School District No. 10* (1977), the Washington Supreme Court agreed with the Tacoma School District, which contended that being known as a "gay teacher" automatically impaired the efficiency of the teacher. The court resorted to encyclopedias, including the *New Catholic Encyclopedia,* to conclude that homosexuality was implicitly immoral. Therefore, the court concluded that James Gaylord could not be trusted to teach students about morality and his presence was considered disruptive, even though he had been a successful teacher for the previous twelve years. This court's opinion about the immorality of homosexuality was contradictory to the conclusions reached by the state, which had repealed its sodomy law by the time of the trial.

The U.S. Supreme Court ruled in *Tinker v. Des Moines Independent Community School District* (1969) that "It can hardly be argued that either students or teachers shed their constitutional rights to freedom of speech or expression at the schoolhouse gate" (736). Teachers do not forfeit their basic constitutional rights on the job. However, the First Amendment rights in schools are not as comprehensive as in other settings. This stems from the uniqueness of school settings. One of the goals of schools is to inculcate morals and values. This gives school districts control over what is said. However, neither teachers, students, nor school boards have absolute rights in every situation. Courts often look to find a balance between the First Amendment rights of teachers and students and the interest in schools as educators and employers.

Although the climate is better now for teachers who come out as homosexuals, the sodomy statutes still make employment by lesbian and gay teachers problematic. Approximately one-third of the states still have sex statutes that prohibit sexual conduct engaged in by homosexuals. State education credentialing requirements often exclude persons who engage in illegal conduct because they are considered to be poor role models for students. Homosexual teachers are faced with being labeled immoral and denied teaching credentials in those states with sodomy statutes because of their illegal behaviors. As such, they may be denied employment or fired from their jobs.

TEACHERS' RIGHT TO ASSOCIATE

School districts commonly ask applicants to disclose the groups or organizations to which they belong. Lesbian and gay teachers are often hesitant to list lesbian and gay organizations for fear of not being hired or being fired. The Supreme Court ruled in *Shelton v. Tucker* that school authorities may not require complete disclosure. But this can become a trap for the unwary. For example, in the case of *Ancafora v. Board of Education* (1974), the court ruled for the board of education when it transferred Joseph Ancafora to an administrative position away from teaching, leading to his eventual dismissal when they discovered that he left off his membership in "Homophiles of Penn State" from his teaching application. The court agreed that his intentional misrepresentation was sufficient grounds to justify the board's decision for the transfer and dismissal. It is difficult for teaching applicants to be truthful about membership in lesbian and gay organizations, especially since anti-sodomy statutes presumably make lesbian and gay teachers "inappropriate" role models for students.

TEACHERS' RIGHT TO PARTICIPATE IN THE POLITICAL PROCESS

Teachers have the right to express themselves as citizens about public matters as long as this expression does not affect the efficiency of the workplace. In *Pickering v. Board of Education* (1969) the Supreme Court agreed that Marvin Pickering, a teacher at Township High School in Will County, Illinois, had the right to write a letter to a local newspaper that was critical of tax increases and its use by the school board. The Court clearly specified that as long as his statements were not knowingly false or malicious, he had a right to criticize his employer.

This has carried over into situations in which gay and lesbian teachers advocated fair treatment for homosexuals. In *National Gay Task Force v. Board of Education* (1985), lesbian and gay teachers in the Oklahoma City school system brought suit against the state to rescind a state law permitting punishment of teachers for "public homosexual conduct." This conduct was defined as advocating, soliciting, imposing, encouraging, or promoting public or private homosexual activity in a manner that may bring it to the attention of school children or school employees. Advocacy, the Supreme Court ruled, is squarely within the protection of the First Amendment. Teachers have the right to take political action, including advocating for lesbian and gay rights.

TEACHERS' RIGHT TO RAISE HOMOSEXUALITY AS A TOPIC IN CLASS

The United States Supreme Court has never directly addressed the First Amendment rights of teachers in the classroom. In *Keyishian v. Board of*

Regents (1967), the Court overturned New York laws that forbade teachers from engaging in subversive activities or that prohibited hiring teachers who belonged to subversive organizations. Later, in *Solmitz v. Maine School Administrative District No. 59* (1985), the Maine Supreme Court carefully noted that school boards cannot prohibit teachers from discussing "tolerance [of] or prejudice against homosexuals, whether in Solmitz's classes or otherwise within [the school]" (813). As such, discussing homosexuality should be legal if it is related to the curriculum.

In general, schools have the administrative authority to control the content, manner, and ambiance in which education takes place. Regulating speech must be reasonably related to "legitimate pedagogical concerns" (*Hazelwood School District v. Kuhlmeier,* 271). Speech regarding sexuality is also protected. In *Hosford v. School Committee of Sandwich,* a special education teacher responded to a student's inquiry about the meaning and use of certain vulgar words. The teacher, who was recognized as a "no-nonsense" instructor, used what she believed to be educationally appropriate explanations based on factual definitions, without becoming provocative. She admonished the student to avoid using the words. However, the school district terminated her employment. She sued and the state supreme court of Massachusetts ordered the school committee to reinstate Hosford and compensate her for lost income.

Sometimes even just saying the word homosexual can lead to detrimental effects. In March, 2000, an elementary school teacher of six years was place on administrative leave by the school principal after just one parent complained that he used the word homosexual in a sex education class. The teacher, who wanted to remain anonymous, was a certified "Family Life" instructor in the Denver Public Schools (DPS) and had previously taught the curriculum without incident. However, a student in his last class asked a question about "homosexual families." The teacher responded simply as he or his wife would have done to his or her own children. The next day, an irate parent of one of the children in his class contacted the teacher, principal, lawyers, the media, and the administrative offices regarding the teacher's use of the word homosexual in class. The teacher was put on administrative leave, which he initially wanted to fight, but after seeing a month-long interrogation of his friends, fellow teachers, students, and investigation into his past teaching record, he agreed to a negotiated settlement in return for his resignation from his teaching position. He stated, "sometimes you must evaluate the cost of winning what would be a very public battle. I did, and the cost was too high" ("Denver Public Schools" 2001).

Two new cases, *Godkin v. San Leandro School District* (1999) and *Berrill v. Houde* (1997), illustrate a current trend in First Amendment arguments. In both cases, parents complained that teachers made progay comments in class and that this violated their religious liberty. The courts saw through the argument and said that the teachers' discussion of homosexuality could not be legitimately characterized as the imposition of a theology. In Veronica Berrill's case, the teacher told her Brookfield High School homeroom class in Connecticut that students were not allowed to use derogatory terms about gay people in her room. Parents of one of the girls in the class complained, writing the Brookfield Board of Education contending that Berrill's remarks constituted "homosexual recruiting" and a promotion of a "homosexual agenda." Berrill sued the parents for defamation and settled out of court. Thus, it seems courts and school districts are occasionally supporting teachers' rights to discuss homosexuality as a topic in class.

Until recently, teachers have been able to make antigay statements with impunity and, in some cases, with support of their school district. That is beginning to change. For example, the Los Angeles Unified School District (LAUSD) declared June to be "Gay and Lesbian Awareness Month" in Memorandum No. 111 adopted by the school board on May 18, 1992. The memorandum stated that its goal was to insure all students equal access to quality education and that school policies and practices were to foster a climate that reduced fears related to difference and deterred name-calling and acts of violence or threats motivated by hate and bigotry. Posters and materials provided to schools were designed to eliminate hate and help create safe school environments for all students. The school board was aware of the possible controversy concerning the materials, but wanted to promote tolerance for diversity. During the month of June, bulletin boards inside school buildings were to be made available to faculty and staff to post materials related to Gay and Lesbian Awareness Month along with materials provided by the district office.

At Leichman High School (a special education school), some of the staff created a bulletin board in May 1997 that contained posters illustrating the themes of the civil rights movement; diversity; differently constituted families; the rainbow flag and other gay and lesbian symbols; and the problems of name-calling and hate crimes. They also displayed a newspaper article regarding LAUSD Board approval of domestic partnership benefits; a board resolution regarding discrimination; a Los Angeles County Human Relations Commission brochure against gay bashing; a listing of famous lesbian and gay people; and more. Robert Downs, teacher for twenty years in LAUSD, objected to the materials and the designation of June as Gay and Lesbian Awareness Month. He created his own bulletin board next to his room entitled "Redefining the Family." He posted the Declaration of Independence, newspaper articles, various school district memoranda, and four excerpts: (1) an opinion poll showing that 60 percent of Americans hold that homosexuality is immoral and that most mainline religions in American condemn homosexual behavior; (2) quotes from the Bible (Leviticus 18:22–24); (3) a statement that physiology determines that heterosexual sex is natural and homosexual sex is unnatural and; (4) documents recording that the U.S. Supreme Court has upheld antigay sex statutes (sodomy).

In both 1997 and 1998, faculty members complained to the principal, who ordered Downs to removed the materials due to their "disrespectful," "offensive," "upsetting," "objectionable," and "derogatory" nature. Downs received several letters over the next two years from his principal and LAUSD's legal counsel informing him that the bulletin boards were not "free speech zones," and that his bulletin boards had nothing to do with school work, student work, or district-approved information.

Downs sued LAUSD on November 30, 1998. The lower court and Ninth Circuit Court ruled against Downs. The court agreed with the school district that the bulletin boards were not a public forum and, thus, under the school's control for content. As such, Downs's claim of infringement of his First Amendment right to free speech was not applicable. Furthermore, since Downs included Bible citations in his own bulletin boards located on school property, the school district insisted he remove the materials; otherwise the school district would have opened itself to charges of promoting a particular religious viewpoint and thus legal problems with the Establishment Clause of the U.S. Constitution. The court emphasized that Downs had the right to promote his ideas on sidewalks, in the parks, through chat-rooms, at his dinner table, and countless other locations. However, he could not do so when he was speaking as a "government representative" unless the school district authorized him to do so.

The court determined that "tolerance" was a legitimate pedagogical concern. Downs argued that the school district was not neutral in its viewpoint. The court found otherwise and ruled that "Gay and Lesbian Awareness Month" did not advocate the gay and lesbian lifestyle, but instead engaged in the legitimate pedagogical interest of teaching tolerance. Also, the court stated, "just as a school could prohibit a teacher from posting racist material on a bulletin board designated for Black History Month, [LAUSD] may prohibit [Downs] from posting intolerant materials during 'Gay and Lesbian Awareness Month'" (*Downs v. Los Angeles Unified School District*).

TEACHERS' RIGHT TO COME OUT AT SCHOOL

Federal law has not made a simple statement of coming out as protected speech. In both *Van Ootegehm v. Gray* (1980) (federal employee), and *Ancafora v. Board of Education* (1974) (teacher), courts have upheld the right of lesbian and gay employees to come out. However, the exact opposite position was taken by the court in *Rowland v. Mad River Local School District* (1985). Here, Marjorie Rowland confided to a school secretary that she was bisexual and had a female partner. She later disclosed her bisexuality to the school principal and several teachers. She was suspended and then reassigned to a position with no student contact. Her one-year contract was not renewed when it expired. The court dismissed her suit, saying that her speech was personal only and not protected by the First Amendment, even though there was no evidence that her actions interfered with her duties at the school.

Some school districts still try to keep teachers from sharing information about their sexual orientation with others at school. In *Weaver v. Nebo School District, et al.* the school threatened Wendy Weaver with charges of insubordination and possible termination if she continued to share her "homosexual orientation and lifestyle" with students, staff members, and parents. The school district placed a gag order on her speech about her sexual orientation. She sued and the federal district court in Utah struck down the gag order in 1998.

Although the right of lesbian and gay teachers to be open about their sexual orientation is gradually being upheld by courts, the battles can result in devastating personal costs. For example, Gerry Crane was hired by the Byron Center in Michigan in 1993 to revive a floundering music program. Crane was a gay, tenured music teacher described as one of the best teachers on the staff and a good role model for students. He rebuilt the music program to a high quality. Two years later, in 1995, Crane and his partner Randy planned for an October commitment ceremony. Before the event took place, someone at the center learned of the impending ceremony and spread word to staff, parents, and students. At the December school board meeting, a few angry parents out of the 700 people who attended demanded that Crane be fired. The school board took no immediate action but issued a scathing statement that said "individuals who espouse homosexuality do not constitute proper role models as teachers" (Yared 1997, 2). The board warned Crane that they would "investigate and monitor" the situation.

In the months that followed, many parents removed their children from Crane's class and he became the center of media attention. A school official released the names and addresses of Crane's students to implement a propaganda campaign. The parents of Crane's students received a booklet and video entitled "Gay Rights/Special Rights: Inside the Homosexual Agenda." This antigay film was produced by a group promoting the religious right agenda. More parents removed their children from Crane's class. Crane made it through the school year but decided to accept one year's salary, health benefits, and a letter of reference to leave the school district. Five months later, on December 27, 1996, Crane collapsed, went into a coma, and died seven days later at age thirty-two. The forensic pathologist concluded that he died from a floppy heart valve that was a congenital condition, but not usually fatal. The doctor added that the stress from his public struggle contributed to his death.

Thus, teachers are cautioned to realize that different communities will react differently to the news that a teacher is lesbian or gay. In states that have antidiscrimination laws, coming out is safer than in states that do not have such protections. Sometimes, teachers can turn to unions to help protect their right to come out.

References

"Denver Public School Escapes Legal Battle with Teacher." 2001. Colorado Legal Initiative Project website: www.clipcolorado.net. Accessed January 13, 2001.

Yared, C. (1997). "Where Are the Civil Rights for Gay and Lesbian Teachers?" *American Bar Association Human Rights*, 24(3): 1–6.

SCHOOL LIBRARIES

In the 1982 case of *Board of Education v. Pico*, the Supreme Court decided that school boards cannot remove books from a school library just because they do not agree with the content. However, schools certainly have the right to select books they think have the greatest value for their students and to reject those that they think have very little value. Between limited budgets and community pressures from religious groups and other groups to censor schoolbooks, libraries and school administrators are under heavy pressure to comply. Consequently, school libraries tend to purchase noncontroversial material that often does not include any content on lesbian and gay issues. The struggle over censorship of school libraries also affects public libraries. For example, in Wichita Falls, Texas, the city council enacted a policy that allowed "objectionable" books to be removed from the public library if 300 library-card holders signed a petition. This took place after some citizens complained about the library placing *Heather Has Two Mommies* and *Daddy's Roommate* on the library's shelves. The first book portrays a lesbian couple who raises a daughter, and the other book describes a son who meets his father's boyfriend. U.S. District Judge Jerry Buchmeyer declared the resolution unconstitutional and labeled the issue an "unfortunate story of the censorship of two children's books." ("Judge Nixes" 2000).(See also **Speech and Association.**)

Reference

"Judge Nixes Book-Removal Resolution." (20 September 2000). Associated Press website: www.wire.ap.org/APnews.

SCHOOL PROGRAMS FOR LESBIAN AND GAY STUDENTS

Many schools have programs that give support to lesbian and gay students. These include school-sponsored counseling programs such as Project 10 of the Los Angeles Unified School District, and student-initiated programs, including curricular and extracurricular clubs (Uribe 1992). There is still much controversy over these programs and many lawsuits have been filed. Courts are slowly recognizing the needs these programs fulfill in creating safe places in schools for lesbians and gay students.

SCHOOL-SPONSORED PROGRAMS

Counseling programs, such as Project 10, aim at keeping high-risk lesbian and gay students in school. This is achieved by raising the self-esteem of gay youths and helping make schools safer by reducing homophobia. Besides counseling students, the programs often provide information to teachers and administrators about lesbian and gay issues, and materials that can be integrated into school curricula.

Arguments against Project 10

Although programs such as Project 10 are designed to help students stay in school and make the educational environment safe for all students, many members of the religious right have complained about the programs. The religious right often claims:

- Project 10 is built upon false assumptions: The school district's 10 percent estimate for the number of gays and lesbians in the student population is not accurate and suggests normalcy for this orientation. The program uses prohomosexual authority figures and acceptance of the gay lifestyle to strongly influence youth toward homosexuality and reinforce students' gay identity.
- Project 10 advocates homosexuality as an "alternative lifestyle": The program presents homosexuality as a neutral, value-free choice instead of informing youths about the negative facts about homosexual behavior and its deadly, disease-ridden lifestyle.
- Project 10 increases the risk of disease by encouraging homosexual contacts and behavior.
- Project 10 uses sexually explicit materials, offensive to most students and parents: One of the books used by Project 10 includes graphic descriptions of unnatural sexual behavior.
- Project 10 violates parent-child privacy: Schools supporting Project 10–type programs often invite homosexuals to speak at schools without giving prior notice to parents, in violation of many state sex education laws.

- Project 10 recruits vulnerable young teens into homosexuality: Information about gay and lesbian organizations, including their addresses and phone numbers, is made available to all students. This encourages teenagers who feel different to accept the homosexual lifestyle and to call these numbers. Blatant recruiting!
- Project 10 exists as part of a larger gay agenda: Dating back to 1972, the gay rights platform advocated teaching sex education courses that presented homosexuality as a valid and viable alternative to heterosexuality, and the National Education Association (NEA) has joined these leftist political agendas with their endorsement at the 1990 NEA convention of homosexual teaching (Smith 1993).

"Yes, all students deserve freedom from name calling, whether the name be 'queer' or 'homophobe.' All students deserve the opportunity to attend school without discrimination or abuse. But it is cruelty, rather than compassion, which encourages people to take pride in behavior that is destroying them" (Smith 1993, 119).

Arguments for Project 10

Programs such as Project 10 (Los Angeles Unified School District) and the Hetrick-Martin Institute (New York City) each evolved as a drop-in counseling program for gay and lesbian students experiencing severe harassment. Los Angeles created the EAGLE Center and New York created Harvey Milk High School as special high schools for the most at-risk gay and lesbian students. These are small schools with only a few teachers and fewer than 100 students. The intent of these programs is to provide a supportive, homophobia-free environment to enable gay and lesbian students to successfully complete school. In these special schools, students' sexuality is accepted without judgment and it is hoped they will return to regular school within a short time. Homosexuality, bisexuality, transgenderism, intersexualism, and heterosexuality are all viewed as valid sexual and gender identities without preference given to one over another. Antigay stereotypes are untrue, as are the other contentions made by the religious right about these programs. Homosexuality is not considered to be "unnatural," "disease-ridden," or in any way a deficit—reflecting the **American Psychiatric Association's (APA)** judgment that homosexuality is as valid a sexual behavior and identity as heterosexuality. These programs believe that "problems gay and lesbian teens have are not a result of their sexuality, but come from the homophobia that permeates the society around them" (Mirken 1993). (See also **Adolescence**; **Child Molestation Stereotype**; **Family**; **Incidence of Homosexuality**; **Research on Sexual Orientation**; **Sexual Orientation**.)

STUDENT-INITIATED PROGRAMS

In many high schools and colleges, controversy surrounds the formation of lesbian and gay student clubs.

Gay-Straight Alliances

One of the most successful techniques used by lesbian and gay high school students has been to start a Gay-Straight Alliance (GSA) organization. Students obtain coordinating information and help from the Gay, Lesbian, Straight Education Network (GLSEN) and petition their school for recognition. Within one year, the number of grassroots student GSA groups registered with the GLSEN rose from 99 to 600 (1998), and the number is still increasing. The GLSEN has been helpful in aiding students in filing complaints and lawsuits against schools that refuse to recognize their applications.

The Salt Lake City School District exemplifies the fear and hysteria some school districts have over allowing gay students to organize. In 1995 a group of lesbian and gay students at East High submitted an application to form a gay-straight alliance on campus. The school denied the application. The students sued, citing the **Equal Access Act (EAA)**. This act requires federally funded public schools that provide access to noncurricular clubs to extend the same opportunity to all clubs without discrimination. In April 1996 the school board terminated forty-six school clubs not directly linked to the curriculum in an effort to block the GSA from meeting on school property. The clubs that were terminated included the Students Against Drunk Driving and the Young Republicans. Many in the community blamed the gay students and a "gay agenda" for the cancellation of the extracurricular activities. The lesbian and gay students still met, but off campus. However, it was learned that at least one noncurricular club was allowed to meet on school property in the 1997–1998 school year. The lesbian and gay students sued again. Federal District Judge Bruce S. Jenkins ruled that the school district violated the federal Equal Access Act and the student's First Amendment rights (Lambda Legal Defense and Education Fund 1999). A few months later, a federal judge dismissed the student lawsuit against the Salt Lake City School Board because school officials produced definitive policy guarantees that allowed the right to express progay opinions (*East High Gay/Straight Alliance v. Board of Education*). However, the lesbian and gay students still wanted to meet on campus. Thus, they reorganized their original GSA club to link directly with the curriculum. In February 2000 the students petitioned the school to form the People Respecting Important Social Movements (PRISM) academic club. The goal of the club is to discuss history through gay and lesbian issues and expand and enhance the study and understanding of American history and government. The school denied their application. The students sued. U.S. Judge Tena Campbell granted PRISM a preliminary injunction because school officials violated their own policy and the Constitution.

Student Fees

Many universities use student fees to fund diverse student services and activities. With the growth of university-funded lesbian and gay student groups, some students with antigay religious convictions sued their universities to stop funding such groups. They claimed that their money was being used to fund organizations of which they morally disapproved, and, thus, that this violated their First Amendment right to free speech and association. In a unanimous decision, the U.S. Supreme Court upheld university funding systems that use student fees for all student groups. Because students contributed to a neutral fund that supported all viewpoints rather than a particular ideology, the Court ruled that the university did not compel any speech nor violate the First Amendment (*Board of Regents v. Southworth*). However, the Supreme Court said that a university must provide some First Amendment protection to students who object to certain groups. The case was sent back to federal court to determine if the system used by the University of Wisconsin to distribute the money (by a majority vote of the student body) represented a "viewpoint neutral" way of doing so. On December 15, 2000, the federal court ruled such a system in violation of the First Amendment and said the university must devise another plan. As of this writing, it is uncertain how universities will proceed to create a system of student fee distribution to student groups while at the same time protecting students' First Amendment rights.

References

Lambda Legal Defense and Education Fund. 1999. "Gay/Straight Alliance's Lawsuit to Proceed Against Salt Lake School Board." Press release on Lambda Legal Defense and Education Fund website: www.lldef.org/cgi-bin/pages/documents/record?record=485. Accessed 8 October 1999.

Mirken, B. 1993. "School Programs Should Stress Acceptance of Homosexuality." In *Homosexuality: Opposing Viewpoints,* edited by W. Dudley. San Diego, CA: Greenhaven Press.

Smith, P. 1993. "School Programs Should Not Stress Acceptance of Homosexuality." In *Homosexuality: Opposing Viewpoints,* edited by W. Dudley. San Diego, CA: Greenhaven Press.

Uribe, V. 1992. "Homophobia—What It Is and Who It Hurts." In *Project 10 Handbook.* Los Angeles: Friends of Project 10, Inc.

SCHOOLS, PRIVATE The First Amendment and Title IX of the federal Civil Rights Act of 1964 are not applicable to lesbian and gay student groups seeking recognition or funding from private schools, colleges, and universities. Some student groups have relied upon state or local laws that prohibit discrimination based on sexual orientation to force recognition by private schools. However, private schools, particularly religiously affiliated schools, claim the First Amendment right to reject lesbian and gay student groups because the endorsement of homosexuality conflicts with their religious beliefs. Courts have had a difficult time with these conflicts of interest. For example, a lengthy lawsuit involving the Gay Rights Coalition against Georgetown University (a Jesuit institution) pitted the District of Columbia's antidiscrimination ordinance against the university's claim of freedom of religion. The court found a compromise position based upon interpretations of "endorsement," "recognition," and "support" for the student group. Ultimately, an out-of-court settlement was reached that allowed the lesbian and gay student organization to exist.

SCHOOLS, PUBLIC Public schools are under the control of federal and state governments and local school boards. Addressing the needs of lesbian and gay students and including gay topics into the curriculum have been met mostly with negative responses.

GROUPS DENIED ACCESS TO PUBLIC SCHOOL FACILITIES

State and local laws that prohibit discrimination based upon sexual orientation have influenced public schools to exclude particular groups. These include some employment recruiters, the Reserve Officers Training Corp (ROTC) and other military units, and the **Boy Scouts**. Many high schools, colleges, and universities allow employers to come onto campus to recruit and interview students as potential employees. Likewise, the ROTC and other military units are sometimes allowed to recruit on campus. However, several law student groups have been successful at preventing access to schools for the purpose of recruitment if the recruiter discriminates against employees based upon sexual orientation. Some businesses and the military discriminate against lesbian and gay men. Courts have ruled that state and local ordinances prohibiting discrimination based upon sexual orientation apply to military recruitment. Thus, educational institutions that are covered by antidiscrimination statutes cannot allow the military, businesses, or other organizations that discriminate against lesbians or gay men to use their facilities to recruit. Pitzer College in Claremont, California, was the first college to ban the ROTC in 1990 over protest of the military's antigay policies. Similarly, the antigay policy of the Boy Scouts has resulted in many schools denying access to their facilities for Scouting functions.

SEX EDUCATION

Most school districts have sex education programs. Courts have clearly stated that parents have the right to opt their children out of attending these programs. The inclusion of homosexuality has put many sex education programs under severe pressure. (See also **Sex Education**.)

COLLEGE STUDENT FEES

Some religious conservative students have objected to their student fees being used to fund student groups they oppose—particularly lesbian and gay student groups. In *Board of Regents v. Southworth*, the U.S. Supreme Court upheld university funding systems that use student fees for all student groups. Students do not have the right to withhold or specify where their fees are used. (See also **School Programs for Lesbian and Gay Students**.)

SECURITY CLEARANCE

Lesbians and gay men have suffered a long history of being denied access to confidential and secret information, and being denied security clearances by the Department of Defense and other intelligence agencies. Stereotyping has been one of the major tools used to classify homosexuals as unfit to serve or work in certain areas. Such stereotypes represent institutionalized homophobia and heterosexism. The primary antigay stereotypes involve the following beliefs: (1) gays and lesbians are mistaken in their gender identity; (2) gays and lesbians are pervasive, sinister, conspiratorial, and corruptive; and (3) gays and lesbians are alcoholics, mentally ill, and criminals. The belief that homosexuality is a mental deficit (including a supposed confusion over gender identity) was reinforced by medical researchers of the early 1900s. Sex researchers went to bars, mental hospitals, and jails to find subjects because that is where homosexuals could be easily found. Is it any wonder that they found this subpopulation had higher incidences of alcoholism (from bar samples), mental disorders (from mental hospital samples), and criminal behavior (from prison samples)? The revolutionary studies conducted by Evelyn Hooker (1963) showed that these stereotypes were wrong and that the psychiatric labeling of homosexuality as a deficit was also inaccurate. Eventually, the **American Psychiatric Association (APA)** removed homosexuality from its list of mental disorders in 1973. (See also **Research on Sexual Orientation**.)

Historically, the anticommunist cold war hysteria of the late 1940s and early 1950s resulted in a concerted effort to exclude lesbians and gay men from important jobs in the federal government. The common explanation was that gays formed secret societies (the conspiratorial stereotype) and were subject to blackmail. As such, they were viewed to be poor security risks (*High Tech Gays v. Defense Industry Security Clearance Office*). These concerns were unfounded. A Pentagon study, "Homosexuality and Personnel Security" (Sarbin 1991), concluded that lesbians and gay men are not security risks; that "sexual orientation is unrelated to moral character" (1). The thirty-nine-page study focused exclusively on the issue of security clearances and sexual orientation. It examined case histories of people who committed or attempted to commit breaches of security since 1945. The study found that monetary gain, and not sexual orientation, was the chief reason a person was disloyal to the United States. There were no instances in which homosexuality was a factor in a security breach. This report followed two previous Pentagon-commissioned studies by the Personnel Security and Education Center (PERSEREC) (Dyer 1990). These earlier studies advocated that homosexuality be eliminated as a factor in granting security clearances. It also urged the Pentagon to repeal its directive barring gays and lesbians from the service. (See also **Military Expulsion**.)

Currently, the Department of Defense (DOD) no longer denies security clearances because of sexual orientation. However, it is unclear if the Department of Energy (DOE) (which handles CIA clearances) continues to exclude gays and lesbians. In 1995 President Clinton signed an executive order barring discrimination in the processing of security clearances. However, there have been continuing political fights in Congress over this issue and it is not certain if the policy is being enforced. This is similar to the military's continued enforcement of its irrational **"Don't Ask, Don't Tell"** policy. Since the implementation of this policy, the numbers of gays and lesbians dismissed from the military have increased.

References

Dyer, K. 1990. *Gays in Uniform: The Pentagon Secret Report.* Boston: Alyson Press.

Hooker, E. 1963. "The Adjustment of the Male Overt Homosexual." In *The Problem of Homosexuality,* edited by H. M. Ruitenbeed. New York: Dutton.

Sarbin, T. R. (1991). *Homosexuality and Personnel Security.* Monterey, CA: Defense Personnel Security Research and Education Center (PERSEREC).

SEX EDUCATION

The history of sex education is long and labored. In the early twentieth century, Margaret Sanger, who opened the first U.S. birth control clinic in Brooklyn, New York, and began publishing the *Birth Control Review* in 1917, promoted the idea of sex education. The National Education Association endorsed sex education in 1912. Getting sex education into public schools has been a slow process. With the advent of **AIDS**, sex education in public school gained widespread support from both conservatives and liberals alike. However, the crisis became an opportunity to promulgate a new message advocating chastity among the nation's youth.

Many parents who hold strong conservative religious convictions object to sex education programs. Courts have upheld their right to keep their children out of these courses. Thus most schools have forms that can be completed by parents requesting that their children be excused from attending sex education programs.

Because of the negative response to sex education programs, some school districts have decided to eliminate these programs. Some people hold the belief that if you don't tell children about sex, they will not engage in sex. Other schools use a "controlled" approach by which students are told certain things at certain times. Still other schools use a facts-only approach (also known as the "plumbing" approach) that provides only anatomical facts, but ignores information on values, attitudes, feelings, and relationships. "Those of us who received our sex education through these approaches may have developed feelings of guilt, shame, anger, and fear, as well as an undying curiosity and a low self-concept with respect to sexuality. We learned that our bodies were taboo" (Reed and Lang 1987, 158).

The inclusion of homosexuality into the sex education programs has made religious conservatives even more adamant about controlling or eliminating sex education programs, often using legal means.

Reference

Reed, R., and T. A. Lang. 1987. *Health Behaviors.* New York: West Publishing Company.

SEXUAL HARASSMENT

SEXUAL HARASSMENT Sexual harassment is unwelcome, illegal harassment that is sexual in nature, which occurs in workplaces and schools.

HISTORY OF SEXUAL HARASSMENT

Primarily, sexual harassment lawsuits have originated in situations where men sexually pursued women in workplaces or classrooms. For most of this nation's history, sexual harassment was considered normal, resulting from a natural biological attraction of males to females. However, the scholarly works of Catharine MacKinnon, professor at the University of Michigan Law School, and Susan Brownmiller, an activist, shifted the perception of sexual harassment from an issue of sex to an issue of power. These scholars argued that sexual behaviors in the workplace or the classroom were not natural or normal, but were instances of discrimination against women. They noted that the women suffering these unwelcome sexual advances were lower in the workplace or school hierarchy than their harassers and that the behavior often served to reinforce women's "inferior" status.

Slowly the focus on the issue of sexual harassment shifted from "sexual" to "harassment." This change occurred not only among academic and legal scholars, but in the courts and the general public as well. Throughout the 1980s and 1990s, a number of court decisions helped clarify the rights and responsibilities of employers and employees alike regarding sexual harassment.

SUMMARY OF SEXUAL HARASSMENT LEGISLATION AND COURT DECISIONS

Sexual harassment in federal law is defined as unwelcome sexual advances, requests for sexual favors, and other verbal and physical conduct of a sexual nature when:

- submission to such conduct is made either explicitly or implicitly a term or condition of an individual's employment;
- submission to or rejection of such conduct by an individual is used as the basis for employment decisions affecting such an individual; or
- such conduct has the purpose or effect of unreasonably interfering with an individual's work performance or creating an intimidating, hostile, or offensive working environment.

Conduct that could be defined (under specific circumstances) as sexual harassment includes:

- pressure for sexual activity;
- asking about a person's sexual fantasies, sexual preferences, or sexual activities;
- unwelcome patting, hugging, or touching of a person's body, hair, or clothing;
- repeatedly asking for a date after the person has expressed disinterest;
- sexual innuendoes, jokes, or comments;
- making sexual gestures with hands or body movement;
- making disparaging remarks to a person about his or her gender or body;
- making suggestive facial expressions such as licking the lips or wiggling the tongue; and
- sexual graffiti or other visuals.

There are two legally recognized types of sexual harassment: tangible employment action harassment and unlawful hostile environment harassment.

TANGIBLE EMPLOYMENT ACTION HARASSMENT

Tangible employment action harassment (previously called quid pro quo harassment) occurs when an individual's submission to, or rejection of, sexual advances or conduct of a sexual nature is used as the basis for employment decisions affecting the individual, or the individual's submission to such conduct is made a term or condition of employment.

To prove tangible employment action sexual harassment, it is necessary to show:

- The victim was a member of a protected class (legally defined groups protected by law including gender, race, age, and religion).
- The victim was subjected to unwelcome harassment. EEOC policy guidelines in March 1990 made it clear that a single sexual advance many constitute harassment if it is linked to the granting or denial of employment benefits. Thus, multiple instances of harassment are not required.
- The harassment was based on sex.
- The victim's reaction to the harassment affected tangible aspects of her or his compensation, terms, conditions, or privileges of employment. Unfulfilled threats are insufficient.

The courts have held employers strictly liable for tangible employment action sexual harassment initiated by supervisory employees. If a supervisor undertakes or recommends a tangible job action based on a subordinate's response to unwelcome sexual demands, the employer is liable and cannot raise the affirmative defense. (Following common sense, the courts have stated that an "affirmative defense" against liability is for employers to adequately construct policies and procedures for preventing and handling sexual harassment in the workplace.)

An employer is liable for this kind of sexual harassment whether the employee rejects the demands and is subjected to a tangible adverse employment action or submits to the demands and consequently obtains a tangible job benefit. Also, consensual sexual relationships between a supervisor and a subordinate employee can result in tangible employment action sexual harassment if the subordinate changes his or her mind, refuses further sexual relations, and the supervisor continues with unwelcome sexual advances. If a challenged employment action is not "tangible," it may still be considered, along with other evidence, as part of a hostile environment claim that is subject to the affirmative defense.

UNLAWFUL HOSTILE ENVIRONMENT HARASSMENT

Unlawful hostile environment harassment occurs when unwelcome sexual conduct unreasonably interferes with an individual's job performance or creates a hostile, intimidating, or offensive work environment, even though the harassment may not result in tangible or economic job consequences.

To prove unlawful hostile environment harassment, it is necessary to show:

- The harassment was unwelcome.
- The harassment was based on membership in a protected class.
- The harassment was sufficiently severe or pervasive to create an abusive working environment. The victim must subjectively perceive the environment to be abusive. However, the courts have not directly addressed the question of whose viewpoint should be used in assessing the work environment. The courts have used the "reasonable person" standard to assess the severity or pervasiveness of a hostile working environment.
- The employer had actual knowledge or constructive knowledge of the environment, but took no prompt and remedial action. *Constructive knowledge* is a legal term that means that under the circumstances the employer should have known about the hostile working environment. Employers cannot simply ignore the situation and later claim they did not know about it (*Meritor Savings Bank v. Vinson*).

The Supreme Court has held that profanity or other language that offends someone can create a hostile environment depending on the frequency of the conduct, the severity of the conduct, whether the conduct is physically threatening or humiliating, and/or whether the conduct unreasonably interferes with anyone's work performance. The 1999 EEOC enforcement guidelines specified that unlawful hostile environment harassment can be either a pattern of offensive conduct—that is, the behavior, although not physically threatening, that is continuous; or a single or unusually severe incident of harassment, such as rape (Equal Employment Opportunity Commission 1999).

For example, the Supreme Court let stand a California Supreme Court decision that a company had the responsibility to stop an employee from using bigoted words to harass coworkers. John Lawrence, an employee with Avis Rent-A-Car System, Inc., routinely harassed only the Latino drivers at San Francisco airport facility by calling them derogatory names and demeaning them on the basis of their race, national origin, and lack of English language skills. Lawrence also appeared to have engaged in uninvited touching of the Latino drivers. A group of drivers sued Lawrence and Avis under California's Fair Employment and Housing Act (FEHA). The court awarded each respondent $25,000 and issued an injunction against Lawrence requiring him to cease and desist from using derogatory racial or ethnic epithets directed at, or descriptive of, Hispanic/Latino employees of Avis Rent-A-Car System, and that Avis must take efforts to stop Lawrence from committing these acts. The case was appealed but the U.S. Supreme Court refused to hear the case, stating that there was a paucity of lower court decisions to guide them about the conflict over First Amendment rights to free speech and workplace harassment law. (See *Avis Rent-A-Car System, Inc. v. Aguilar.*)

Two conditions determine employers' liability in cases of hostile environment sexual harassment: (1) the employer knew or should have known about the harassment, and (2) the employer failed to take appropriate corrective action. An employer can be held liable for a hostile environment created by a supervisor, by nonsupervisory personnel, or by the acts of the employer's customers or independent contractors if the employer has knowledge of such harassment and fails to correct it.

The EEOC enforcement guidelines say an employer may be expected to know about the hostile environment if:

- There was a complaint to management.
- Management failed to establish a policy against sexual harassment.
- The harassment was openly practiced or well known among employees.

Current Update

Sexual harassment continues to persist, primarily because employees are reluctant to complain and employers are reluctant to respond. In *Burlington Industries, Inc. v. Ellerth* and *Faragher v. City of Boca Raton* (1998), the Supreme Court addressed both of these issues in terms of Congress's intent in Title VII of the 1964 Civil Rights Act to "encourage forethought by employers and saving action by objecting employees." For employers to mount a defense against hostile environment sexual harassment charges, they must (1) exercise reasonable care to prevent and promptly correct any sexually harassing behavior, and (2) prove that the plaintiff employee unreasonably failed to take advantage of any preventive or corrective opportunities provided by the employer or to avoid harm otherwise.

Significantly, the two cases cited above have made it clear that the law requires employees to make reasonable use of an employer's complaint procedure. However, there are still defensible reasons why a plaintiff may not use the complaint procedures. The burden now falls on the employee, however, to demonstrate those reasons.

Same-Sex Sexual Harassment

Oncale v. Sundowner Offshore Services, Inc. was another landmark sexual harassment case. A male claimed sexual harassment by his male supervisor and two male coworkers on an offshore oil rig. All parties in the case represented themselves as heterosexual, thus indicating that inappropriate behavior is not related to sexual orientation. The Supreme Court ruled that:

> There is no justification in Title VII's language or the Court's precedents for a categorical rule barring a claim of discrimination "because of . . . sex" merely because the plaintiff and the defendant (or the person charged with acting on behalf of the defendant) are of the same sex. Recognizing liability for same-sex harassment will not transform Title VII into a general civility code of the American workplace . . . the objective severity of harassment should be judged from the perspective of a reasonable person in the plaintiff's position, considering all the circumstances. (75–81)

The Court continued:

> The conduct that is not severe or pervasive enough to create an objectively hostile or abusive work environment—an environment that a reasonable person would find hostile or abusive—is beyond Title VII's purview. . . . We have always regarded that requirement as crucial, and as sufficient to ensure that courts and juries do not mistake ordinary socializing in the workplace—such as male-on-male horseplay or intersexual flirtation—for discriminatory conditions of employment. . . . In same-sex (as in all) harassment cases, that inquiry requires careful consideration of the social context in which particular behavior occurs and is experienced by its target. A professional football player's working environment is not severely or pervasively abusive, for example, if the coach smacks him on the buttocks as he heads onto the field—even if the same behavior would reasonably be experienced as abusive by the coach's secretary (male or female) back at the office. The real social impact of workplace behavior often depends on a constellation of surrounding circumstances, expectations, and relationships which are not fully captured by a simple recitation of the words used or the physical acts performed. (80)

CONCLUSION AND FUTURE QUESTIONS

In what may be a surprising view, the Seventh Circuit Court in *Holman v. State of Indiana* concluded that a supervisor who sexually harasses both men and women could not be charged with sexual harassment under Title VII. Since the supervisor did not discriminate based upon the sex of his workers, he did not violate Title VII. Sstill, most state antidiscrimination statutes would apply against such an "equal opportunity" harasser. (See **Bisexual**.)

Sexual harassment must be sexually motivated or severe to be illegal.

Sexual orientation is not covered under Title VII. This was reinforced recently in a case of a postal worker severely harassed at work. Dwayne Simonton, an openly gay man who worked for the U.S. Post Office in Farmingdale, New York, suffered persistent harassment from his coworkers. They would make remarks to him about being subjected to anal sex, tape notes on the bathroom wall linking him to celebrities who had died from AIDS, post pictures of erect penises, and send to his home copies of erotic magazines. The Second Circuit Court of Appeals agreed that he had suffered appalling persecution that was morally reprehensible. Simonton did not make the claim that the discrimination was based on his gender, but on the fact that he was openly gay. The court ruled that the discrimination was not based on sex, but rather sexual orientation, and that Title VII did not clearly cover this type of harassment as evidenced by the refusal of Congress to pass bills aimed at prohibiting sexual orientation discrimination in the workplace ("Man Loses Sex Harassment Case" 2000).

Burlington Industries, Inc. v. Ellerth and *Faragher v. City of Boca Raton* helped clarify the responsibilities of employers and employees alike, but these cases left open the question of when it is acceptable for an employee not to avail himself or herself of the employer's complaint procedure. *Oncale v. Sundowner Offshore Services, Inc.* contained language that shows the U.S. Supreme Court is unaware of, or is insensitive to, lesbian and gay concerns when it hopes that "courts and juries do not mistake ordinary socializing in the workplace—such as male-on-male horseplay or intersexual flirtation—for discriminatory conditions of employment." "Male-on-male horseplay" is a prime example of the hyper-male environments that are offensive and hostile to both homosexuals and women. Finally, *Avis Rent-A-Car System, Inc. v. Aguilar* seems to suggest how state antidiscrimination statutes and enforcement may influence Title VII into becoming a general civility code, regardless of the fact that the Court specifically stated in *Oncale* that it would not. Thus, the courts will have to deal with these questions at a future date.

Reference

Equal Employment Opportunity Commission. 1999. *EEOC Enforcement Guidance: Vicarious Employer Liability for Unlawful Harassment by Supervisors.* Washington, DC: Government Printing Office.

"Man Loses Sex Harassment Case against Man." 2000. *Washington Blade* (8 September 2000): Legal Briefs.

SEXUAL HARASSMENT IN SCHOOLS The landmark court case *Nabozny v. Podlesny* (1996) and the August 1998 guidelines to Title IX have made it clear that sexual harassment of lesbian and gay students is illegal. (See also **Sexual Harassment**.)

SEXUAL HARASSMENT IN SCHOOLS

It is estimated that children hear twenty-five antigay remarks each day in public schools. These include words such as *faggot*, *dyke*, or the slang expression "That's so gay." And when slurs are made in front of teachers, 97 percent of those teachers make no effort to stop the attacks (Carter 1997, B3).

Too often, what begins as antigay remarks escalates into physical and sexual harassment of lesbian and gay students. Until the landmark case of *Nabozny v. Podlesny*, it was not clear what responsibilities schools bore in preventing such harassment.

Jamie Nabozny experienced terrible abuse from other students while attending an Ashland, Wisconsin, high school. He was wrestled to the classroom floor while his teacher was out of the room, and then two boys pretended to rape him while twenty other students watched and laughed. He was also urinated upon in a bathroom and kicked so badly that he required surgery to stop internal bleeding. His parents complained, but a school official told them that he "had to expect that kind of stuff" because he was a homosexual. Jamie eventually moved to Minneapolis, where he graduated with an equivalency degree, but he sued the Ashland School District in 1995. Initially the case was dismissed, but the Seventh U.S. Circuit Court of Appeals could not find any rational reason for permitting one student to assault another based on the victim's sexual orientation and thus allowed the suit to continue. A jury found that the school officials violated Jamie's rights under the Fourteenth Amendment's equal protection clause and the school district was forced to pay $900,000 in damages.

This case opened a floodgate of lawsuits and, perhaps more importantly, the threat of lawsuits from gay students who experienced sexual harassment in schools.

A second case, *Davis v. Monroe County Board of Education* (1999), further clarified that school districts may be liable if school employees are deliberately indifferent to complaints of peer-to-peer sexual harassment. In this case, Aurelia Davis was continually harassed by boys, the harassment taking the form of sexual comments and gestures. School employees ignored her complaints. She sued and won.

The Office of Civil Rights for the U.S. Department of Education in March 1997 released new guidelines for educators on Title IX. This is the federal statute that bars sex discrimination in public schools that receive federal funding. These guidelines make clear that one form of antigay harassment in schools—namely harassment that creates a sexually hostile environment—is illegal under Title IX.

TITLE IX

Title IX does not prohibit discrimination on the basis of sexual orientation. It does prohibit sexual harassment directed at gay or lesbian students.

For example, Title IX does not prohibit one student heckling another student with comments based on the student's sexual orientation (for example, "Gay students are not welcome at this school"). But if the actions or language involve sexual conduct, then Title IX applies (for example, when Nabozny was mock-raped in class, the boys alluded that he would "like it"). Such situations are termed creating a "sexually hostile environment."

The guidelines make it the responsibility of school districts to make students aware of their right to file complaints regarding sexual harassment. These rights now expressly include antigay sexual harassment. Also, schools have responsibility and liability toward the witnesses of antigay sexual harassment, including the gay friends or peers of a targeted student. Thus, schools have much greater responsibility toward lesbian and gay students than ever before.

Educators take Title IX very seriously because it can be a basis for legal liability for schools and payment of monetary damages. Complaints can be filed with the Office of Civil Rights (OCR) or in court. Because of the changes in Title IX and the *Nabozny* case, it is likely that educators in general will now consider antigay harassment more seriously than in the past.

Some state and local laws may prohibit discrimination on the basis of sexual orientation. Some school districts and teacher union contracts have included language providing antidiscrimination protections based on sexual orientation. Between court cases, Title IX, and antidiscrimination laws and policies, schools should be able to create a safe learning environment for all students, including lesbian and gay students.

Reference

Carter, K. 1997. "Group Monitors Pervasiveness of Comments: Gay Slurs Abound, Students Say." *Des Moines Register* (7 March 1997): B3.

SEXUAL ORIENTATION

Commonly, in laws and elsewhere, sexual orientation is limited to one of three possibilities: homosexual, heterosexual, or bisexual. However, how someone expresses himself or herself sexually is much more complex than this. Human sexual expression is the outcome of the interplay of biological sex and gender roles (which includes gender identity, social sex roles, and sexual orientation).

Biological sex is a concept based on chromosome factors (XX—female, XY—male). These factors help to determine our external genitalia, hormonal states, and secondary sexual characteristics. However, many people are born without clear chromosomal indicators. Likewise, the internal and external genitalia, hormonal states, and secondary sexual characteristics of many people are not exclusively male or female. (For a detailed analysis on this development and the eight characteristics used to define sexual identity, see **Intersexed**.)

The physical makeup of a person is only part of human sexuality. When a baby is born, the very first question asked by the parents is "Is it a girl or a boy?" This begins a life-long path of social reinforcements for being either a female or male. These gender roles are perceived to be natural and innate. For example, many people and our educational system believe that boys are naturally more rambunctious, better at perceiving spatial relationships, and better at math than girls. Likewise, girls are believed to be naturally more reserved, better at languages, and better at social interactions than boys. However, Maccoby and Jacklin (1974) found that "there is very little evidence to prove that the psychological differences commonly attributed to each sex are essentially inherent [and not learned]" (Blumenfeld and Raymond 1993, 43).

Children are raised with specific role expectations associated with their sex. Gender roles have three components: (1) gender identity, which is the core feeling of being a male or female; (2) social sex roles, which are the culturally prescribed behaviors for females and males (that is, acting feminine or masculine); and (3) sexual orientation, which is the erotosexual attraction (including physical or sexual attraction and affectional attraction) to persons of the same sex or opposite sex, or both sexes. Within these three categories, women and men can comply closely or vary widely from cultural definitions. Also, these three categories are not necessarily interconnected. For example, **transsexuals** are people who "gender transpose" on their gender identity and social sex roles, whereas gay males, **lesbians,** and **bisexuals** gender transpose on their expected sexual orientation but not usually on all three categories. (For example, a female-to-male transsexual is born a biological female but does not conform to a female gender identity or feminine social gender roles. Instead, she transposes her gender identity and social gender role to the male norm.)

Regrettably, the entire topic of sex and gender often implies polar opposites. Many researchers suggest that the term *other sex* instead of *opposite sex* be used because *other* signifies difference without the negative values associated with *opposite.* Yet even *other* seems insufficient because people who are intersexed have neither *opposite* nor *other.*

Understanding these concepts is important. The original Civil Rights Act (1964) included *sex* as a protected class. Antidiscrimination laws are beginning to include the term *sexual orientation* and a few are including the term *gender.* Most laws and regulations use the word *sex.* However, many courts, legislators, and administrative agencies use the word *gender* in place of *sex* when interpreting these laws. To them, sex and gender are interchangeable concepts (Capers 1991). Thus, there is mass confusion in the legal world about these concepts and, therefore, it often fails to provide protection to those most in need. For example, a number of court decisions have shown that antidiscrimination provisions that provide protection based upon sexual orientation do not apply to transsexuals or **intersexed** people. (See also **Gender-Motivated Violence Act (GMVA)**.)

References

Blumenfeld, W. J., and D. Raymond, eds. 1993. *Looking at Gay and Lesbian Life.* Rev. ed. Boston: Beacon Press.

Capers, B. 1991. "Sex(ual Orientation) and Title VII." *Columbia Law Review* 91(5): 1158–1187.

Maccoby, E. E., and C. N. Jacklin. 1974. *The Psychology of Sex Differences.* Palo Alto, CA: Stanford University Press.

SEXUAL PREFERENCE

Sexual preference should not be used as a synonym for sexual orientation. *Sexual preference* suggests that sexual orientation is a choice. No person would choose to become a stigmatized outcast of society. A better term is *sexual orientation.* (See also **Sexual Orientation**.)

SOCIETY FOR HUMAN RIGHTS

In 1924 the Society for Human Rights was formed, representing the first homosexual emancipation group in the United States. It was structured after the German Scientific Humanitarian Committee founded by Magnus Hirschfeld to alleviate persecution of homosexuals, and was granted a nonprofit corporation status from the state of Illinois. It was founded by Henry Gerber, a German American immigrant, along with a number of working-class homosexuals living in Chicago.

Their goals were to encourage homosexuals to join the Society, to give lectures pointing out the attitudes of society in relation to homosexuality, to launch a publication, and to educate legal authorities about the issues. Two issues of the Society's newsletter, *Friendship and Freedom,* were created and distributed. The newsletter got into the hands of law enforcement and all the Society's board members were arrested (without warrant). The men were jailed and brought to trial. Ultimately, the men were set free when the judge found out there was no arrest warrant, but the group disbanded and Gerber lost his Post Office job.

It is important to note Gerber's perspective on homosexuality. In twelve articles that he wrote for *Friendship and Freedom,* he not only urged the removal of laws that oppressed homosexuals, but he observed that oppression by church and oppression by state were the historical antecedents to the development of modern psychoanalysis. He believed that psychoanalysts were constructing a new set of taboos and myths about homosexuality and that these were having a negative effect on homosexuals. He did not believe homosexuals were neurotic, antisocial, or criminal, and rejected all notions of "curing" homosexuals. In the "nature versus nurture" debate, he aligned himself with neither position and maintained that both are responsible (Katz 1976, 393).

Champ Simmons had been involved with one of the members of the Society. Years later, Simmons met seventeen-year-old Harry Hay in Los Angeles. He spoke to Hay about the Society and its goals. This led to the founding of the **Mattachine Society** in Los Angeles in the early 1950s, which marks the beginning of the modern gay movement.

Reference

Katz, J. 1976. *Gay American History: Lesbians and Gay Men in the U.S.A.* New York: Thomas Y. Crowell.

SODOMY

Sodomy statutes are used by some states of the United States to control the sexual behavior of their citizens. The statutes are inconsistent in defining sodomy. In some states, sodomy is defined as sex between persons of the same sex, whereas in other states sodomy is defined as sex between anyone other than a spouse. Even what sexual acts are characterized as sodomy varies greatly from state to state (some limit it to anal penetration, others include mouth to genital contact, whereas others do not specify it at all, but vaguely state "detestable and abominable crime against nature").

Approximately 150 lesbians and gay men are convicted each year under sodomy and other archaic laws. These laws are used mostly against homosexuals (Richards 1991). The penalties can be severe. Rhode Island, which had a blanket prohibition against sodomy until 1998, mandated a prison sentence of not less than seven and not more than twenty years. In Mississippi, conviction for homosexual sodomy may result in ten years' imprisonment.

HISTORY

The term *sodomy* comes from the biblical city of Sodom. The Bible tells of the destruction of Sodom by God because of the evils practiced by its citizens. Genesis 19 of the Bible states, "God sends two angels, disguised as travelers, to find one just man. They come upon the house of Lot. When the Sodomites learn of the presence of the visitors, they demand, 'Where are the men, which came unto thee this night? Bring them out unto us, that we may know them.'" Based on the phrase "that [they] may know them" some people believe homosexual sex is condemned by God and punishable by death. Although most current Biblical scholars acknowledge that Sodom's sin was inhospitality, that has not stopped certain Jewish and Christian sects from interpreting the destruction of Sodom as God's wrath on homosexuals (Blumenfeld and Raymond 1993, 173).

Sodomy, which was not precisely defined, included all nonprocreative sex. Sex outside of marriage, masturbation, and oral and anal sex were considered to be "crimes against nature," "crimes against God," and thus immoral and illegal. During much of Europe's Middle Ages, sodomy was considered a religious offense. The religious courts tried many people for committing sodomy. Once found guilty by the Inquisition (as most surely was the case), the convict was turned over to the state for punishment. Punishment varied from simple public censure to execution—by burning at the stake, drowning, hanging, beheading, being buried alive, and other methods. Usually, all property was stripped from the convict and the convict's family.

Henry VIII of England made sodomy a crime punishable by death. The imprecision of the religious definition of sodomy was transferred over into the legal code, which used equally vague phrases as "lewdness," "impurity," "unnatural lust," and others. As colonists moved to the North American continent, they brought English law, including the death penalty for sodomy, with them. The Virginia Colony passed the earliest American sodomy law in 1610, requiring the death penalty for offenders. It did not mention women as potential "sodomites." In 1641 the Massachusetts Bay Colony adopted a body of law that included sodomy as a capital crime—and took on its first sodomy case against three men accused of having sexual contact with two female children. This code included women and defined sodomy as "man lying with mankind as he lies with a woman." The wording came directly from *Leviticus* 20:13 and shows the influence of Christianity on the construction of antigay sex statutes. Imprecise phrases such as "sodomy," "buggery," "unnatural copulation," and "crime against nature" became codified into state sex statutes (Katz 1976).

The earliest recorded execution in the Americas for sodomy was in 1646 of "Jan Creoli, a Negro" in New Netherland. He was executed by choking. In the same year, William Plaine was executed in New Haven, Connecticut, for committing sodomy twice in England and for corrupting "a great part of the youth of Guilford by masturbations" (*Gay Almanac* 1996, 7). The first women to be punished for committing "lewd behavior . . . upon a bed" were two married women in 1649 in Plymouth. It was not until 1682, in the Quaker colony of Province, Pennsylvania, that leniency was first shown toward sodomites with legislation that made sodomy by any person a noncapital offense. Later in 1777–1779, Thomas Jefferson was involved in revising Virginia law to reduce the death penalty for sodomy to "castration" (Katz 1976).

In 1955 the American Law Institute (ALI) revised the Model Penal Code and excluded sodomy. Illinois became the first state to follow these recommendations and in 1961 eliminated sex statutes against consensual homosexual sex. It took another ten years before another state eliminated its sex statutes (Connecticut). Before ***Bowers v. Hardwick*** (1986), when states considered removing their sex statutes, they obtained guidance from the decision in *Doe v. Virginia.* In that case, the court held "that 'since [sodomy] is obviously no portion of marriage, home or family life,' the state could punish sodomy in the promotion of morality and decency" (Selland 1998, 675).

In 1986 the U.S. Supreme Court in *Bowers v. Hardwick* refused to strike down a Georgia law criminalizing sodomy. In a five-to-four vote, the majority stated that there was no constitutional right to engage in homosexual sodomy. However, Justice Lewis Powell, who voted with the majority, conceded after his retirement that he "had made a mistake" (Marcus 1990, A3) and should have voted to strike down Georgia's sodomy law.

Since *Bowers v. Hardwick,* however, some prosecutors seem to be more willing to prosecute sodomy cases—and defendants find themselves without protection (Oliver 1989). Ironically, some of the first to suffer prosecution were heterosexuals. Particularly during divorce or rape proceedings, a number of men who may have been acquitted of the original charges were subsequently convicted of sodomy for having engaged in oral sex. As of 1996 there were approximately thirty men in Georgia prisons serving long sentences for engaging in oral sex.

In 1992 the Kentucky Supreme Court struck down its sex statutes in *Commonwealth v. Wasson.* This was an important decision because the court rejected many of the points made by the majority in *Bowers v. Hardwick,* and recognized that privacy extended to adult consensual sex regardless of whether it was homosexual. One by one, states began reviewing and eliminating their sodomy laws.

As of the second millennium, two-thirds of the states have eliminated sex statutes that criminalized homosexual sex. Even so, many people use the term *sodomy* to refer to sex that is exclusively homosexual in nature. For example, when Congress held hearings concerning the military's policy of excluding gays, Senator Strom Thurmond asserted that "heterosexuals don't practice sodomy" (Bruce 1996, A9). Even the courts have held this position, as evidenced in *Padula v. Webster,* where the court said that sodomy was the "behavior that defines the class" of homosexuals (103). Even with the elimination of sex statutes, other statutes, known as lewd conduct, solicitation, loitering, vagrancy, indecent exposure, or disorderly conduct statutes, still need to be reviewed for bias against homosexual contact. (See also **Stereotypes**.)

CURRENT STATUS OF SODOMY STATUTES

As of the year 2000, consensual sodomy was legal in thirty-three states and the District of Columbia. Some states are confused, having enacted legal protections outlawing discrimination based on sexual orientation, while at the same time retaining their sodomy laws.

As of 2000, sodomy is legal in the following places: Alaska, California, Colorado, Connecticut, Delaware, District of Columbia, Georgia (sodomy law found to violate consitutional right to privacy in *Powell v. State of Georgia* [1998]), Hawaii, Illinois, Indiana, Iowa, Kentucky, Maine, Massachusetts, Montana, Nebraska, Nevada, New Hampshire, New Jersey, New Mexico, New York, North Dakota, Ohio, Oregon, Pennsylvania, Rhode Island, South Dakota, Tennessee, Texas, Vermont, Washington, West Virginia, Wisconsin, and Wyoming.

In the following states sodomy is illegal between persons of the same sex: Arkansas, Kansas, and Missouri. Sodomy is illegal for all persons in the following states: Arizona, Florida, Idaho, Louisiana, Maryland, Michigan, Minnesota, Mississippi, North Carolina, Oklahoma, South Carolina, and Virginia. In two states sodomy is illegal with anyone other than a spouse: Alabama and Utah.

MAJOR ARGUMENTS ON SODOMY

There are a number of arguments used for the continued support of sodomy laws.

First, the right to engage in sodomy is not a fundamental right. As Chief Justice Burger wrote in *Bowers v. Hardwick,* "To hold that the act of homosexual sodomy is somehow protected as a fundamental right would be to cast aside millennia of moral teaching" (*Bowers v. Hardwick,* 197). Burger also noted that "homosexual sodomy was a capital crime under Roman law. During the English Reformation when powers of the ecclesiastical courts were transferred to the King's Courts, the first English statute criminalizing sodomy was passed" (*Bowers v. Hardwick,* at 196–197). Thus, supporters of sodomy statutes accept the moral imposition of certain religious beliefs upon the citizenry as a whole and use the power of the state to restrict these behaviors as a way to maintain a "decent" society.

Justice Blackmun, in his dissenting opinion, wrote that "[D]epriving individuals of the right to choose for themselves how to conduct their intimate relationships poses a far greater threat to the values most deeply rooted in our Nation's history than tolerance of nonconformity could ever do" (214).

The dissenting justices in *Bowers v. Hardwick* also noted that not all "religious groups condemn the behavior at issue" and the state has "no license to impose their judgments on the entire citizenry" (211). As seen, *Bowers v. Hardwick* demonstrated the continuing debate over the issue of separation of church and state.

A second argument in favor of retaining sodomy laws holds that the right of the state to regulate sodomy is not a violation of privacy. In dissent in ***Commonwealth v. Wasson*** Justice Wintersheimer said that the state has "a rightful concern for the moral welfare of all its citizens and a correct commitment to examining criminal activities wherever they may be committed, whether concealed in the home or elsewhere" (515). Justice Wintersheimer continued by saying that adhering to a protection of privacy "could result in constitutional protection being claimed for the private use of cocaine, consensual incest, suicide and prostitution" (514). Furthermore, the overturning of sodomy laws based upon privacy rights would "generate a tremendous amount of litigation in other criminal areas and would call into question the validity of existing statutes and case law dealing with search and seizure questions" (510–511).

However, there has been a continued expansion of the right to privacy. Previous Supreme Court decisions had extended rights of privacy not only to married couples, but also to unmarried couples. In *Griswold v. Connecticut* (1965), the Court held that the use of contraceptives by married couples was protected by the right to privacy. In *Eisenstadt v. Baird* (1972), the Court expanded the zone of privacy to include the use of contraceptives by unmarried adults. Also, in *Stanley v. Georgia* (1969), the Court expanded the zone of privacy to allow individuals to possess pornography in their own homes. But the Court in *Bowers v. Hardwick* did not accept these arguments for the expansion of privacy because "no connection between family, marriage, or procreation on the one hand and homosexual activity on the other has been demonstrated" (191). Thus, the Court in ***Bowers v. Hardwick*** maintained a nexus between procreation and the right to privacy.

A third argument sometimes raised for keeping sodomy statutes in place holds that sodomy statutes punish conduct and not status and are therefore desirable and permissible. Homosexuals, per se, are not criminalized, only homosexual behavior. In *Neville v. State* (1981), Maryland's highest court, the Court of Appeals, stated that it did not attempt to criminalize status by prohibiting sodomy, but instead "imposed a sanction for behavior it deems harmful or offensive to the sensibilities of a large segment of the community" (581). The problem with this perspective is that it denies that homosexual behavior is connected to gay identity, and thus criminalizing homosexual sodomy criminalizes lesbians and gays. The sodomy laws brand homosexuals as less than equal, which fosters hostility and violence toward them.

A fourth argument maintains that sodomy statutes are rationally related to the legitimate concerns of the government. Particularly with the emergence of **AIDS**, some believe the control of sodomy reduces the spread of this and other sexually transmitted diseases. However, when it is realized how infrequently sodomy laws are enforced, it is obvious that controlling disease is not the purpose of sex statutes. Likewise, focusing on sodomy as the cause for the epidemic spread of sexually transmitted disease denies many other sources.

As more and more states overturn their sex statutes, it has come apparent that the arguments used to support sodomy laws are a form of heterosexism mixed with homophobia. The existence of the sodomy laws has fostered hate and discrimination toward lesbians and gay men. For example, a Virginia court denied custody of a child to her lesbian mother because the mother was in a committed relationship with another woman, which meant that she was believed to be sexually active. In a state with sodomy statutes, this made her, by matter of law, a criminal and thus unfit to be a parent (*Bottoms v. Bottoms*). Also, Attorney General Michael Bowers (of *Bowers v. Hardwick* fame) used Georgia's sodomy statute to justify not hiring a qualified lesbian. Under Georgia law, the woman's behavior was criminal and, thus, it was not considered appropriate to have her work in a legal capacity. For years, security clearances have been denied gay applicants because engaging in sodomy was illegal and, consequently, they were disrespectul of the laws of society (*High Tech Gays v. Defense Industry Security Clearance Office*). (See also **Security Clearance**. For an analysis of the strategies used by the sex statutes, see **Criminal Law**.)

References

Blumenfeld, W. J., and D. Raymond, eds. 1993. *Looking at Gay and Lesbian Life.* Rev. ed. Boston: Beacon Press.

Bruce, T. M. 1996. "Doing the Nasty: An Argument for Bringing Same-Sex Erotic Conduct Back into the Courtroom." *Cornell Law Review* 81:1135–1151. Citing "Senators Loudly Debate Gay Ban." *New York Times* (8 May 1993): A9.

Gay Almanac, The. 1996. Complied by the National Museum and Archive of Lesbian and Gay History. New York: Berkley Books.

Katz, J. 1976. *Gay American History: Lesbians and Gay Men in the U.S.A.* New York: Thomas Y. Crowell.

Marcus, R. 1990. "Powell Regrets Backing Sodomy Law." *Washington Post* (26 October 1990): A3.

Oliver, C. 1989. "Georgia on My Mind." *Reason* 21(5): 14.

Richards, D. 1991. "Activism=Arrests." *The Advocate* (9 April 1991): 48–50.

Selland, D. 1998. "Will Maryland Enter the Twenty-First Century in the Right Direction by Rescinding Its Ancient Sodomy Statutes?" *Law and Sexuality* 8: 671–698.

SOLICITATION AND LOITERING

Solicitation statutes criminalize invitations, requests, or offers to perform illegal or improper acts. Loitering statutes criminalize staying in a public place for no apparent reason or for the purpose of engaging in immoral and illegal behaviors or the solicitation thereof. Solicitation statutes and loitering statutes are often used together to control same-sex socializing. These statutes are commonly enforced using police vice and entrapment schemes, and, as such, are universally despised by the lesbian and gay community.

In states with sex statutes (commonly known as sodomy laws), the very act of lesbian or gay people meeting and arranging to engage in sex is a violation of state law for which they could be charged with solicitation. Even in municipalities without specific solicitation statutes, the state sex statutes could be used to obtain an arrest for solicitation. Whether the couple had been dating for a while or were in a long-term relationship, the act of arranging to engage in sex could be considered solicitation. As such, the existence of sex statutes and solicitation statutes works to inhibit lesbians and gay men from meeting and forming relationships. In states that have abolished consensual sodomy as a crime, solicitation to engage in intimate sexual relations has been decriminalized and the solicitation statutes, if not eliminated, have been narrowed to focus on solicitation to engage in illegal public behaviors.

Loitering statutes, commonly known as vagrancy or disorderly conduct statutes, criminalize staying in a public place without apparent reason or for the purpose of engaging in illegal behavior. Loitering statutes have come under constitutional attacks (see, for example, *People v. Berck*). Because of the vagueness of solicitation and loitering statutes, they have been a primary tool used to target and to oppress lesbians and gay men. (See also **Criminal Law; Lewd Conduct; Sodomy**.)

SPEECH AND ASSOCIATION The First Amendment of the U.S. Constitution provides the fundamental basis for ensuring the right of citizens to engage in freedom of speech and association. Until the 1960s and into the 1970s, censorship of books, plays, and films with explicit homosexual content was common. Gay bars were regularly raided and homophile organizations were harassed. The 1969 Stonewall Inn raid, in which drag queens fought off New York City police for a number of days, acted as the catalyst for the modern gay liberation movement. Openly gay and lesbian organizations now demanded the end of discrimination through public discussion in the mass media. A backlash occurred in the 1980s during attempts by Congress to form **AIDS** legislation. Antigay attacks focused specifically on forms of speech whereby AIDS educators were not allowed to "promote or encourage" homosexuality or describe homosexuality as "normal," "natural," or "healthy." Likewise, funding for "controversial" gay and lesbian artists was rejected by the National Endowment for the Arts in the early 1990s. (See also **Police Abuses; Stonewall Riot**.)

A steady stream of lawsuits has reduced the discrimination experienced by lesbians and gay men. But not all progress has been forward. The conservative backlash has also formed court opinion. Whereas the First Amendment has been the gay movement's primary weapon against oppression, there are numerous examples of courts failing to protect lesbians' and gay men's freedom of expression and association.

Speech

Speech protected through the First Amendment encompasses more than just verbal comments. It also includes opinions written in newspapers, newsletters, and other pamphlets; the wearing of armbands and buttons; marching in parades; posting signs and flags; coming out; and other private and public acts.

Protest

People have the legal right to participate in peaceful demonstrations and picket in support of lesbian and gay rights. City permits may be required for public protest, but the conditions of the permit must apply equally to all groups and must be clear and neutral (*Shuttleworth v. City of Birmingham*). Police may limit the number of pickets in a congested area; specify the time, place, and manner in which the demonstration takes place; and specify other conditions for safety, but otherwise cannot interfere with peaceful actions.

Obscenity

At one time, all materials that contained information on homosexuality were deemed obscene. For example, the Post Office confiscated and refused to deliver the newsletter from **ONE, Incorporated** in 1954. ONE sued and the U.S. Supreme Court overturned the lower courts in 1958, declaring that materials containing homosexual themes and information were no longer automatically deemed obscene (*One, Inc. v. Olesen*). Thus, the U.S. Post Office was required to distribute the ONE magazine and other homophile publications.

Obscenity, as defined by the First Amendment and interpreted by the Supreme Court, is material that, when viewed through the lens of local community standards and taken as a whole, appeals to prurient interests; depicts or describes in a patently offensive way certain sexual conduct (as specified by state law); and as a whole lacks serious literary, artistic, political, or scientific value (*Miller v. California*).

For materials to be deemed obscene, they must meet all three criteria. This is difficult to do. For example, a Cincinnati museum sponsored an exhibition of Robert Mapplethorpe's photographs in 1990. Some of the photos were homoerotic. The museum was charged with showing obscene material. The jury acquitted the defendants because of the artistic value of the works. Still, every year, there are attempts by communities and religious conservatives to have books, music, films, and other art and literary works banned from public display or libraries. Such controversy has led to congressional attacks on the National Endowment for the Arts (NEA)—primarily over art with lesbian and gay themes. Although the NEA has weathered these attacks, its budget is often in limbo with threats of dissolution.

States may provide greater (but not less) protection of speech than the federal government. Some states, such as Oregon, have declared that there is no obscenity exception to the free speech provisions of their constitution.

Internet

Many parents, members of Congress, and conservatives desire to censor information from the Internet in the belief that some material is harmful to minors. Congress passed the Communication Decency Act (CDA) in 1996, which was struck down in *ACLU v. Reno I* as being an unconstitutional restriction of the First Amendment. Congress tried again and created the Child Online Protection Act (COPA) in 1998. Even though it was more narrowly focused, U.S. District Judge Lowell A. Reed Jr. issued a preliminary injunction that barred COPA from going into effect after determining that the American Civil Liberties Union (ACLU) was probably going to win the case against it (*ACLU v. Reno II*). Court discussion showed that there were major questions about enforcing the act. For example, the act claimed to protect children from "harmful" materials, yet no one could give a clear definition of what constituted "harmful," or give evidence that such material actually harmed. Second, the act required adults to divulge personal information such as credit card numbers to gain access to adult sites. The judges recognized that this would produce a "chilling effect" and radically reduce usage of the sites because some people would be reluctant to give that information. Third, the act specified that "contemporary community standards" would be used to delineate "offensive" material. However, the government could not clearly indicate which community standard would be used. Because the Internet is worldwide, is the community standard of a different country to be used? Or those in the United States? And of those in the United States, does one use liberal or conservative standards? Or is there a national standard that can be used universally? Judge Reed concluded that the government is relatively helpless in trying to solve the problem of children's access to material that may be harmful to them on the Internet.

The problem of government censorship of the Internet is of concern for lesbians and gay men. By trying to control sexuality, the government will inadvertently interfere with the transmission of material designed to educate on the political and social issues of homosexuality. For example, if someone types the word *gay* into any of the search engines, many pornography sites will come up, but so will many college and academic sites that contain important information. Screening for the word *gay* will thus interfere with First Amendment rights to disseminate information.

The Internet is a new technology to which our social and legal systems have not yet fully adapted.

Parade Participation

Marching in parades is a protected activity under the U.S. Constitution. Parades sponsored by private groups may restrict the message conveyed by the participants in the parade. For example, a gay and lesbian contingent applied to march in Boston's **Saint Patrick's Day Parade.** They planned to carry a banner identifying themselves as lesbian and gay. The parade organizers denied their application. The contingent sued, claiming that their First Amendment right to free speech was violated. The Court stated that the parade was a private event not subject to **public accommodation** laws and that the organizers had the right to promote a particular message that excluded the message that the lesbian and gay contingent desired to display.

Coming Out

In some cases, **coming out** is considered a political act protected by the First Amendment and the due process clause of the Fourteenth Amendment. For example, the California Supreme Court ruled in 1979 that a person's affirmation of homosexuality was analogous to expressing a political view, and, as such, was protected under the state labor code (*Gay Law Students' Association v. Pacific Telephone and Telegraph Co.*). Since this ruling, the labor code has been modified to specifically list sexual orientation as a protected class. (See also **Effectiveness of Antidiscrimination Statutes**.)

Federal cases in this area are mixed. Sometimes they uphold the right of gay employees to share information about their sexual orientation with other employees or with the public. Other times, lesbian and gay employees have been fired for the same acts. These cases sometimes pivot around the issue of "flaunting" behaviors. For example, courts have upheld the firing of gay employees who have attempted to obtain same-sex marriage licenses or to politically agitate to reform marriage laws. In *Singer v. U.S. Civil Service Commission,* the court ruled that Singer, by "publicly flaunting and broadcasting his homosexual activities" while attempting to legalize same-sex marriage, undermined the government's interest in maintaining public confidence in the agency for which he worked (255).

Courts often attempt to make a distinction between homosexual status versus homosexual conduct; that is, identity-based discrimination versus speech- or behavior-based discrimination. In *Bowers v. Hardwick,* the Court concluded that states have the right to pass and enforce laws that prohibited specific conduct; in this case, homosexual sodomy. The U.S. military in implementing "Don't Ask, Don't Tell" took the same route in saying that homosexuals are welcome to join and serve, but that they cannot engage in homosexual behaviors. The military believes that stating that one is homosexual presumes the person will engage in homosexual conduct. Service members who come out and declare their homosexuality, or are found out to be gay, must rebut the presumption they will engage in homosexual sex. Homosexual service members have fought the status/conduct distinction, claiming that the policy treats homosexuals and heterosexuals differently and thus violates the equal protection clause of the First Amendment. In *Holmes/Watson v. California Army National Guard,* the court concluded that the policy applied equally to heterosexuals and homosexuals—that either could say they were gay and both would be required to rebut the presumption that they would engage in homosexual sex. Many legal theorists believe the status/conduct analysis is flawed and no longer applicable. Even Judge Reinhardt, dissenting in *Holmes/Watson,* believed the "status/conduct distinction to be irrational and without substance" (1137).

In coming out, homosexuals are declaring who they are and seeking to be treated equally with heterosexuals. Courts are divided as to what it means to treat homosexuals equally with heterosexuals. For example, when Aaron Fricke wanted to take a same-sex date to his senior prom in 1980, it took court intervention to uphold his right to be treated the same as opposite-sex couples and be allowed to go with the date of his choice (*Fricke v. Lynch*). But when adult homosexuals attempt to engage in the same behaviors as do heterosexuals in rearing children, the courts often retreat into antigay stereotypes to justify their denial. Recently, the Georgia District Court ruled that a divorced lesbian mother was in contempt of court for allowing her female partner to share a home with her and her three children. The court believed this was in violation of her divorce decree because she agreed to maintain each child in a "morally and physically wholesome environment." Since her children were being "exposed" to her lesbian relationship, the court required her partner to move out or for her to move out with her children (Parvin 2000b, 27). Such a demand would not have been made if her partner were a man.

Adults seem also to have difficulty accepting lesbians and gay men when they act in similar ways to heterosexuals. Same-sex kissing upsets many people. On August 8, 2000, Danielle Goldey and Meredith Kott celebrated seventh-inning home runs by the Los Angeles Dodgers by kissing. The security guards of section 53 at Dodger Stadium, Los Angeles, descended upon the women and forced them to leave the stadium. Since the women came with another couple, they had to wait outside in the parking lot until the game was over. Fans videotaped the expulsion, hissed, and booed the guards. One of the guards reported that "Someone complained they didn't want their kids around those kind of people." A few days later, the Dodgers apologized to the women and to all other gays and lesbians, donated 5,000 tickets to lesbian and gay organizations, and implemented a sensitivity training program for the staff. Kott said, "I was scared. It reminded me of all the reasons I was so afraid to come out [as a lesbian]." (McDermott 2000, A2).

A similar situation occurred on a Delta Airline flight to Rome. Charles Mayfield and his boyfriend Ken Drooker began kissing in seats along the back row when the lights were dimmed. Soon, a female flight attendant came back and demanded they "knock it off." Mayfield asked the attendant what that meant, but she refused to say. Mayfield and Drooker resumed kissing in what Mayfield characterized as "pretty passionate," but not "making out" and there was no fondling—"Like we were sitting on the couch watching TV and kissing." The flight attendant again came back and demanded they knock it off. Mayfield again asked what behavior he was being asked to cease. The captain of the plane left the cockpit, marched down to Mayfield, shook his finger at Mayfield, and said that if Mayfield continued asking the flight attendants questions, he would land the plane in London and Mayfield would be arrested. Mayfield remained silent the rest of the trip but was detained by airport authorities in Rome. He was soon released and the next week, when he attempted to board the plane to return home, he was refused a boarding pass and told that he would not be permitted to fly Delta Airlines that day or in the future. When interviewed by the press, Mayfield said that he saw heterosexual couples kissing on the plane, but they were not asked to stop. Also, no one ever "told me what I was doing wrong." (Parvin 2000a, 14).

These are some of the scenarios homosexuals face while coming out. Homosexuals behaving in ways similar to heterosexuals infuriates and offends some heterosexuals, since heterosexuals perceive the behavior to be different. Homosexuals engaging in public kissing or holding hands or acting as a couple with their partner will be perceived as overt conduct. Often the conduct that is deemed inappropriate will not be named. Some heterosexuals feel it necessary to "protect" children from seeing homosexuals engaging in behaviors similar to those of heterosexuals because, when homosexuals do these same acts, they are considered to be "immoral."

Finally, the issue of identity has been blended with that of conduct. In *Boy Scouts v. Dale*, the U.S. Supreme Court concluded that the Boy Scouts had a legal right to exclude homosexuals from their organization. In this case, James Dale was a model troop leader. He was not open about being gay, but was the director of a college gay group. The Boy Scouts believed his mere presence sent a message about the acceptance of homosexuality that was not concurrent with the values they wanted to inculcate in their members. Even though Dale had not declared himself gay to the Boy Scouts nor made any mention of homosexuality, his mere presence was an act of coming out and the Court considered this to be an expressive act. Thus, the Court blurred the distinction between status and conduct. It is uncertain how the courts will resolve the issue of coming out, gay identity, and homosexual conduct as related to First Amendment rights.

AIDS

The production and distribution of AIDS-related materials cannot be stopped by government action unless the material is deemed obscene. Obtaining governmental funding is another story. Federal, state, and local agencies have different rules concerning the discussion of sexuality. As such, funding for AIDS-related materials is often hostage to policies that prohibit explicit discussion of the problem and its solutions. Private funding groups are not restricted by these rules and may be more or less accepting of explicit sexual descriptions.

Speech on College Campuses and in High Schools

Students have the right to ask questions, wear armbands and other political insignia, form lesbian and gay support organizations, attend proms and other social functions with same-sex partners, and more. Although teachers can be legally out and supportive of gay rights, depending on the beliefs of the community and the laws of their state, teachers may experience discrimination that courts will uphold. (See also **School Faculty Members' Rights**; **School Libraries**; **Students' Rights**.)

Speech in the Workplace

Many corporations and businesses have found themselves in the uncomfortable position of having to monitor and dictate behaviors appropriate for the workplace. Sometimes employees make antigay remarks to or around customers or other employees. If these remarks become hostile and sexual, the employee may establish a hostile environment form of **sexual harassment** that opens the corporation or business to potential harassment charges and lawsuits. (See also **Employment**; **Sexual Harassment**.)

An employee who is open about being lesbian or gay may antagonize other employees who hold antigay beliefs. Taking their direction from sexual harassment laws and cases, a few of these employees with conservative or fundamental religious beliefs have sued. They claim that based on the First Amendment they have the right not to have to associate with people they believe to be immoral, and that the company, by allowing homosexuals to work in the same workplace, has created a hostile work environment. So far, courts have rejected these arguments.

In *Avis Rent-A-Car System, Inc. v. Aguilar,* the U.S. Supreme Court left intact a California Supreme Court ruling that a company (Avis Rent-A-Car) could order an employee to stop using bigoted words. In this case, John Lawrence, a supervisor, used vulgar and derogatory ethnic slurs against his employees to degrade them. The judges ruled that the use of such epithets contributed to a hostile and abusive work environment. Words spoken with the intent to discriminate apart from their communicative impact, lose constitutional protection, just as does violence or other types of potentially expressive activities that produce special harms.

Antigay Speech

Protecting the speech of racists, bigots, and others who deeply offend our sense of morality is directly related to defending the speech of all people. For example, in the 1949 case of *Terminiello v. Chicago,* the ACLU successfully defended an ex-Catholic priest who had delivered a racist and anti-Semitic speech. This precedent became the basis for successfully defending the civil rights demonstrators of the 1960s and 1970s.

In 1942 the U.S. Supreme Court ruled in *Chaplinsky v. New Hampshire* that intimidating speech directed at a specific individual in a face-to-face confrontation constituted "fighting words" and that persons uttering such speech could be punished if "by their very utterance [the words] inflict injury or tend to incite an immediate breach of the peace" (571–572). However, over the past fifty years the Court hasn't found the "fighting words" doctrine applicable in any of the hate speech cases that have come before it.

Nonverbal symbols of hate—cross burnings, flag burnings, swastikas—are constitutionally protected if they are worn or displayed before a general audience in a public place (march or rally). However, they cannot be used to encroach upon, or desecrate, private property (for example, spray-painting a swastika on the wall of a synagogue or dormitory).

Historically, defamation laws have proved ineffective at best and counterproductive at worst. Remember, those who ultimately determine what is offensive are those in power—not the alleged victims of **hate speech**. Thus, for example, the eighteen-month experiment by the University of Michigan in 1988 to enforce speech codes resulted in twenty white students charging black students with offensive speech. Bigoted speech is symptomatic of the problems of the country. Speech codes simply deter people from being open about their beliefs and feelings. As a consequence, the real issues do not get addressed.

In the closing decade of the twentieth century some religious conservatives have sued cities and counties for sponsoring antidiscrimination policies based on sexual orientation. They claim that gay rights ordinances violate their religious liberty and that government is promoting one moral belief over another. For example, a number of landlords have filed lawsuits against cities challenging their ordinances that forbid discrimination in public housing. The landlords claim that it is against their religious beliefs to allow unmarried or same-sex couples to rent their property. They claim that forcing them to rent to "immoral" people violates their religious freedom. So far, courts have rejected this approach and maintained the right of government to enact antidiscrimination ordinances.

There is a distinction between hate speech and conduct. Hate speech stops being speech when it becomes conduct targeting specific individuals and when it forms a pattern of behavior that interferes with the ability of citizens to exercise their rights. Instead of speech codes, what are needed are regulations that penalize acts of violence, harassment, or intimidation, and invasions of privacy. Furthermore, the mere presence of speech as one element in an act of violence, harassment, intimidation, or invasion of privacy does not grant that act immunity from punishment. For example, threats, bias-inspired phone calls, or shouting racist epithets at a woman of color while following her—are clearly punishable acts.

ASSOCIATION

The freedom to associate with people of the same beliefs stems from the First Amendment freedom of speech and assembly, and from the due process clause of the Fourteenth Amendment to the U.S. Constitution.

Lesbian and Gay Organizations

The right to associate was validated by courts specifically for lesbian and gay organizations in *Gay Students Organization v. Bonner* (1974). Such organizations have the right to incorporate and obtain federal tax-exempt and tax-deductible status. Initially, when the Gay Activists Alliance sought to obtain corporate status in New York in 1972, their application was rejected because the secretary of state believed that the purpose of the organization was to promote activities that were illegal in the state. A New York court overruled the secretary of state, saying that it was not unlawful for individuals to peaceably agitate for repeal of any law (*Gay Activists Alliance v. Lomenzo*).

Lesbian and gay organizations have the right to keep the names of their members confidential in most circumstances. In general, the Supreme Court has recognized that forcing organizations to reveal the names of members could have a detrimental effect on the associational rights of the members. Exceptions to this rule include divulging sources of income or contributions to political candidates or political measures (*Buckley v. Valeo*).

Lesbians, gay men, and bisexuals, and transgendered, transsexual, and intersexed people usually do not need to reveal their association with organizations to prospective employers or the government. However, public school teachers are faced with a Catch 22 problem if they reveal an association with gay organizations. On the one hand, if lesbian and gay teachers reveal that they are gay or belong to gay rights groups, they often face overt discrimination. If lesbian and gay teachers try to hide their associations, they can be accused of falsifying employment applications. For example, in *Ancafora v. Board of Education,* a federal court upheld the school district's transfer and eventual dismissal of a gay teacher for failing to reveal on his application that he was involved with a gay activist group. (See also **School Faculty Members' Rights**.)

Sex Statutes

Sexual behaviors between same-sex partners have been regulated through the application of state sex statutes (also known as **sodomy** laws). Although none of them criminalized homosexuality per se, they had a chilling effect on the rights of lesbians and gay men. At one time, all states had sex statues that criminalized homosexual conduct. As of the year 2000, approximately one-third of the states still have such laws.

In states that criminalized homosexual behaviors through sex statutes, police routinely monitored or raided places where homosexuals met, such as bars. Homosexuals were intimidated from organizing. Much of the intimidation has ceased as lesbians and gay men organized openly to repeal the remaining sex statues and agitate on other civil rights issues. (See also **Criminal Law**.)

School Programs

Courts have upheld the right of high school and college students to form lesbian and gay support clubs and organizations in state-supported schools (*Healy v. James; Gay Students Organization v. Bonner*). These organizations must be provided with the same access and funding as other student organizations. (See also **Equal Access Act (EAA); School Programs for Lesbian and Gay Students; Schools, Public**.)

References

McDermott, T. 2000. "All Smiles after Kiss Commotion." *Los Angeles Times* (24 August 2000): A2.

Parvin, P. 2000a. "Kissing on a Delta Plane Lands Couple in Hot Water." *Southern Voice* (31 March 2000): 14.

———. 2000b. "Ruling against Lesbian Mom Appealed to Georgia Supreme Court." *Southern Voice* (27 April 2000): 27.

STEREOTYPES Stereotypes are preconceived notions about people that represent oversimplified opinions, affective attitudes, or judgments. Stereotypes have greatly influenced law.

Society holds primarily two groups of contradictory antigay stereotypes:

1. The idea that one can guess gender identity from appearances, attitudes, or actions. This includes the belief that lesbians are women that want to be, or at least look and act like, men (for example, bull dykes, diesel dykes) and that gay men are men who want to be, or at least look and act like, women (for example, queens, fairies, limp-wrists, nellies).
2. The idea that gays are a pervasive, sinister, sick, conspiratorial, and corruptive threat. Common permutations of this idea are beliefs that gay persons are mentally ill child molesters, sex-crazed maniacs, and destroyers of the family and civilization.

The early investigations into homosexuality were performed on a skewed sample of people who visited gay bars, patients in psychiatric hospitals, and prison inmates. Not surprisingly, these studies confirmed the societal beliefs and false generalizations that gays are alcoholics, crazed, and criminal. In the mid-1950s, UCLA psychologist Evelyn Hooker (1963) carried out the first rigorous nonclinical studies using gays. She presented the results of a standard psychological diagnostic test—but with indications of sexual orientation omitted—to a group of psychiatrists. They were unable to identify which test results belonged to lesbian and gay respondents. This was surprising because it was thought that lesbians and gay men were crazy and psychiatrists should have been able to easily identify them by their mental illnesses. These and similar studies proved to be a profound embarrassment to the psychiatric establishment. Psychiatrists made money "curing" allegedly insane gays and now it was shown they could not even identify them. Eventually the studies contributed to the dropping of homosexuality from the **American Psychiatric Association**'s **(APA)** registry of mental illness in 1973 (Bayer 1981). However, the stereotype of gays as sick continues in the minds of many Americans and in many courts. (See also **Criminal Law**; **Sexual Orientation**.)

False generalizations help maintain stereotypes, they do not form them. The origin of stereotypes lies in a culture's ideology. Stereotypes are transmitted across generations by diverse cultural devices, including slang and jokes. They are not the products of bad science, but are social constructions that perform central functions in maintaining society's conception of itself. (See also **Prejudice**.)

It is easy to see that antigay stereotypes surrounding gender identification are the chief means of reinforcing already powerful gender roles in society. "The stereotype of gays as child molesters, sex-crazed maniacs, and civilization destroyers functions to displace problems from their actual source to a foreign one. Thus, the stereotype of child molester functions to give the family unit a false sheen of absolute innocence" (Mohr 1988, 24).

The problem is not that society's usual standards of evidence and procedure in coming to judgments of social policy have been misapplied to gays: rather, when it comes to gays, the standards themselves have simply been disregarded in favor of mechanisms that encourage unexamined fear and hatred.

Science and academic research have disproved all antigay stereotypes. Lesbians and gay men are not mentally ill, are not child molesters, provide nurturing families, and homosexuality is a normal developmental path for some people. Yet antigay sentiments and stereotypes abound in our culture and **hate crimes** against lesbians and gay men are increasing. (See also **Adolescence**; **Child Molestation Stereotype**; **Family**; **Gay Fathers**; **Heterosexism**; **Lesbian Mothers**.)

Courts are faced with scientific findings that are contrary to the traditional antigay moral code. Therefore, there is wide variance in the acceptance of rights for homosexuals. Some states still have sex statutes that criminalize homosexual behaviors and use stereotypical language such as "deviant" in their laws. Other states have abolished sodomy laws and implemented domestic partnership statutes that all but mimic heterosexual marriage. Most likely, as antigay stereotypes fade away, legislatures and courts will follow suit and eliminate restrictions against lesbians and gay men. (See also **Criminal Law**; **Sodomy**.)

References

Bayer, R. 1981. *Homosexuality and American Psychiatry.* New York: Basic Books.

Hooker, E. 1963. "The Adjustment of the Male Overt Homosexual." In *The Problem of Homosexuality,* edited by H. M. Ruitenbeed. New York: Dutton.

STONEWALL RIOT The riot at Stonewall Inn in New York's Greenwich Village marks the beginning of the modern gay activists' movement. On the night of June 27, 1969, officers from the Public Morals Section of the New York City Police Department attempted to shut down this small local bar. The bar was a favorite meeting place for drag queens, street kids, dope heads, speed freaks, and other marginal people. As people were dismissed by the police and allowed to leave, they gathered across the street. Each time someone appeared in the doorway whom the crowd knew, they applauded, which encouraged the brassy individual to pose and make some flippant remark. This only infuriated the police even more. When the paddywagon came to take away the drag queens, bar owner, and bartender, a cry went up from the crowd to overturn the paddywagon. The wagon drove off, but then the crowd exploded by throwing bottles and stones at the police. The police had to retreat into the bar. A battle cry was heard throughout the Village and hundreds came out to participate. A small fire began in the window of the Stonewall. Soon after, more police arrived and the crowd scattered. (See also **Police Abuses**.)

For the next couple of nights, street demonstrations took place that were more political in nature. Groups of people milled around the streets yelling "gay power," holding hands, and kissing in public. A group of gay cheerleaders were heard singing "We are the Stonewall girls/We wear our hair in curls/We have no underwear/ We show our pubic hairs" (Marotta 1981, 75). After the first two days of disturbances, the **Mattachine Society** of New York handed out flyers in the Village christening the "Christopher Street Riots" as the "Hairpin Drop Heard around the World" (Marotta 1981, 77).

Before Stonewall, approximately a dozen gay organizations existed. Within three months of the riot, more than fifty lesbian and gay organizations formed throughout the United States. These organizations became more radical, with many cities hosting marches and festivals in June to commemorate the anniversary of the Stonewall Riots. It is these events more than any others that help bring unity to the gay community and influence their political and legal progress.

References

Marotta, T. 1981. *The Politics of Homosexuality.* Boston: Houghton Mifflin.

Mohr, R. D. 1988. *Gay Justice—A Study of Ethics, Society, and the Law.* New York: Columbia University.

STUDENTS' RIGHTS

In *Tinker v. Des Moines Independent Community School District* (1969), the Supreme Court held that students in public schools do not leave their First Amendment rights at the schoolhouse gate. Students may express themselves orally and in writing in the form of leaflets, buttons, armbands, T-shirts, or other forms of writing. The only restriction on the students is that expressing these opinions must not "materially and substantially" disrupt classes or other school activities. This often includes the use of "vulgar or indecent" words. There are a number of areas in which courts have affirmed what rights students enjoy in schools.

SCHOOL NEWSPAPERS

In public schools, if a paper is completely student run and paid for, the school may not censor or limit distribution as long as the content is not "indecent" and it does not "materially and substantially" disrupt school activities. However, the school may place "reasonable" limits on the "time, place or manner" of handing it out. These same rules apply to leaflets or buttons created and paid for by students.

If the paper is an official school publication in a public school, the 1988 Court decision, *Hazelwood School District v. Kuhlmeier,* gave power to school administrators to censor student speech in official school publications or activities (like school plays, art exhibits, newspapers, or yearbooks). School administrators decide what is "inappropriate" or "harmful," even if it is not vulgar and does not disrupt. However, schools may not censor one side of an issue. Thus, important but controversial issues like sex education, condom distribution, drug abuse, or lesbian and gay issues are often restricted from being mentioned at all in school-supported newspapers.

Some states, including Colorado, California, Iowa, Kansas, and Massachusetts, have high school free expression laws that give students more rights to free speech than the federal Constitution requires.

Many college newspapers are independent of their schools. For example, the Supreme Court held that the First Amendment did not apply to the *Daily Nebraskan* campus publication because the newspaper was not sufficiently connected to the government through the public university's administration. Although it was associated with the University of Nebraska, the paper was nevertheless independent and could refuse advertisements, such as "lesbian seeking roommate" and related ads.

SCHOOL DRESS CODES

Dress codes are covered by a patchwork quilt of state laws and school district policies. In some states, students may wear their hair any way they want or wear anything they wish as long as they do not create a safety hazard. In states that regulate hair length, there are also dress codes that typically regulate clothing along gender lines. Some school districts have become concerned about gang activity and have barred gang-related clothing. With the recent development of public schools returning to the use of uniforms, the issue of freedom of expression with regard to hair and clothing is not resolved.

These are particularly important issues for transgendered students who do not conform to gender stereotypes and do not want to do so. For example, a seventeen-year-old transgendered youth named Brian-Violet Peters was suspended from his Gresham, Oregon, high school after coming to class wearing a black velvet dress, low-heeled pumps, and a touch of red lipstick. The school claimed that he violated the school's dress code that bans "disruptive" or "distracting" clothing. Peters responded by saying that the effect of his actions was no different from what the first girl who wore pants to school must have experienced. Further, he claimed that the harassment, jeers, and hoots that he received at school were the problem, not his clothing ("Dressed Down" 2000).

The Massachusetts Superior Court ruled that a transgender student had the right to express her gender in middle school (*Doe v. Brockton School Committee*). The Brockton School Committee had blocked a fifteen-year-old student, who was born male, from wearing female clothing to school. Known in court records only as Pat Doe, she fought the school district for two years for the right to express her transgenderism. Doe argued that girls who wore the same clothing as she were not prevented from attending school or otherwise disciplined. The school justified its exclusion of Doe due to the discomfort of other students. The judge rejected this argument through the well-established principle set forth in *Cleburne v. Cleburne Living Center, Inc.:* laws and policies cannot give voice to mere "negative attitudes" toward others. Judge Jacobs stated "the stifling of plaintiff's selfhood merely because it causes some members of the community discomfort" is insufficient to stop Doe from wearing girls' clothing ("Brockton Court Rules" 2000).

EXTRACURRICULAR ACTIVITIES

Extracurricular activities comprise a major component of many student careers and can be the foundation of one's academic success. For example, athletic scholarships are used by many students as a means of attending college. But sports have been traditionally antigay. In a 1993 case, *Yost v. Board of Regents,* a female hockey player who received an athletic scholarship was told that her department wanted to portray "an image of heterosexuality" and she was ordered not to be seen with her girlfriend, not to participate in the lesbian and gay speakers bureau, and not to be seen at lesbian or gay events. Her scholarship was threatened if she did not comply with these rules. She sued after she completed college, which complicated the procedural issues of the suit, and, thus, the suit was never fully litigated. Yost's case charted ways the First Amendment could be used to protect other lesbian and gay athletes.

The prom is another example of an extracurricular activity that traditionally has excluded same-sex couples. When lesbians and gay students attempt to bring a same-sex partner to school proms, administrators often deny the request, citing fear of violence from the other attendees. In one celebrated case, Aaron Fricke wanted to bring his friend Paul Guilbert to the 1980 Cumberland High School senior prom in Sutton, Massachusetts. The principal denied the request, saying that there was a "real and present threat of physical harm" toward the two boys. Fricke sued. At the trial of *Fricke v. Lynch,* the judge acknowledged that the principal's fears were real but said that the school should have looked into ways of increasing security and other safety strategies rather than denying the couple the right to attend. The court recognized that attendance at a prom is "symbolic speech," much like marching in a parade, and thus merits First Amendment protection.

RIGHT TO ASK QUESTIONS

A few courts have made it clear that students have the right to ask any question in school. What is not clear is whether teachers have the right to answer. For example, students often ask personal questions of teachers—such as whether they are married, have children, or are engaged. Lesbian or gay teachers who answer truthfully may experience a backlash from parents and school administrators claiming that they are talking about sex or "promoting" homosexuality. (See also **School Faculty Members' Rights; Sex Education**.)

RIGHT TO FORM GAY-SUPPORTIVE ORGANIZATIONS

Since the passage of the **Equal Access Act (EAA)** in 1984, lesbian and gay students have had as much right to form noncurricular clubs and have access to publicly funded school facilities as do other noncurricular clubs. Students also have the right to form curriculum-oriented clubs that must be treated the same as all other curricular clubs. (See also **School Programs for Lesbian and Gay Students**.)

HATE SPEECH ON COLLEGE CAMPUSES

Many colleges have responded to hate speech by adopting codes or policies prohibiting speech that offends any group based on race, gender, ethnicity, religion, or sexual orientation. Courts have repeatedly struck these down as unconstitutional. The First Amendment to the United States Constitution protects speech virtually no matter how offensive its content. Speech codes adopted by government-funded colleges and schools amount to government censorship. (See also **Hate Crimes; Hate Speech; Speech and Association.**)

SEXUAL HARASSMENT

A child hears approximately twenty-five antigay remarks each day in public schools. These include word such as *faggot, dyke,* or the slang expression "That's so gay." And when slurs are made in front of teachers, 97 percent of those teachers make no effort to stop them (Carter 1997).

Until recently, lesbian, gay, bisexual, and transgendered students had no legal recourse from the terrible harassment they received in schools. This has now changed with the landmark case of *Nabozny v. Podlesny* in which Jamie Nabozny won the first lawsuit alleging antigay harassment in public schools. In 1997, new guidelines were released by the U.S. Department of Education clarifying that Title IX requires schools to provide a safe environment free of sexual harassment. Under specific conditions, such as what Jamie Nabozny experienced, lesbian and gay students have new legal tools to combat antigay harassment. (See also **Sexual Harassment in Schools**.)

References

"Brockton Court Rules in Favor of Transgender Student." (12 October 2000). Associated Press website: www.wire.ap.org/APnews.

Carter, K. 1997. "Group Monitors Pervasiveness of Comments: Gay Slurs Abound, Students Say." *Des Moines Register* (7 March 1997): B3.

"Dressed Down." 2000. *Frontiers* 18(23): 30.

SUSPECT CLASS

Courts have identified certain classes of people whose cases must receive "strict scrutiny" when evaluating the application of law. This does not confer additional or special rights to these people. Instead, it is the recognition that certain classes of people have historically been denied rights afforded all citizens.

Suspect classification stems from the famous footnote 4 in the 1938 Supreme Court ruling *United States v. Carolene Products Co.* The Court stated that "prejudice against discrete and insular minorities may be a special condition which tends seriously to curtail the operation of those political processes ordinarily to be relied upon to protect minorities, and . . . may call for a correspondingly more searching judicial inquiry." The Court recognized that laws often reflect the prejudices of society. Therefore, the Court declared that laws that single out certain groups should be carefully scrutinized for bias and prejudice.

A number of cases have signified that laws singling out people based upon race, ethnicity, or national origin are typically motivated by bias and must be treated as meriting suspect classification. The First Amendment also disallows the government from interfering with personal religious beliefs. Laws that target religion, race, ethnicity, or national origin are subjected to "strict scrutiny" by the courts and the state must show a "compelling interest" for them to be upheld. Other cases have found that gender and illegitimacy merit "quasi-suspect" classification. A lower standard of judicial review is used for laws that treat people differently on these bases and the state must show an "important" reason for upholding these laws. A third legal tier exists for groups not deemed suspect or quasi-suspect. Lesbians, gay men, and bisexuals, and transgendered, transsexual, and intersexed people occupy this lowest legal position. Government discrimination against these categories of people is allowed as long as the government can convince the court that the law is "rationally related" to a legitimate purpose.

The Supreme Court has never identified a single test for determining whether a group of people meets the suspect or quasi-suspect classification. However, it has identified three broad areas to test for additional judicial scrutiny. First, it needs to be shown that there is a history of "purposeful unequal treatment" (*Massachusetts Board of Retirement v. Murgia*) based upon the characteristics under consideration. Second, the characteristic needs to be "obvious, immutable, or distinguishing" (*Bowen v. Gilliard*). Third, an estimation is made concerning the political power the group has to ensure that its rights are protected and to defend against attacks from the mainstream political process (*Frontiero v. Richardson*).

Some legal analysts have argued that lesbians and gay men (that is, sexual orientation) should be afforded suspect classification. This was argued during the legal impasse over Colorado's enactment of **Amendment 2**. Here, Colorado attempted to eliminate all existing and future laws that granted antidiscrimination protections based on sexual orientation. Lawyers representing lesbian and gay plaintiffs provided the Supreme Court with convincing evidence demonstrating a long history of gay persecution. The Court also accepted the biological evidence that sexual orientation is mostly inborn and, thus, immutable. The Court, however, did not accept the arguments that lesbians and gay men are politically vulnerable and needing protection. Thus, ***Romer v. Evans*** did not establish a suspect classification based on sexual orientation.

The entire process of suspect classification is being reevaluated by legal theorists. Each of the three tests has definitional and methodological problems. For example, demonstrating a history of discrimination can become a game of one-upmanship. Whether it involves African Americans detailing their history of slavery, Jim Crow laws, lynching, and other acts of terrorism, or Jews detailing the Holocaust and rampant anti-Semitism, or women showing their historical second-class status by the denial of the right to vote or the "glass ceiling" in the workplace, or lesbians and gay men tracing the history of their imprisonment, execution, and exclusion from the workplace and family life, it becomes difficult to assess the level of discrimination warranting governmental protection.

Determining which features are "obvious, immutable, or distinguishing" is difficult. For example, race is considered obvious, immutable, or distinguishing by many people, yet it is not. Many nonwhite people can pass for white because of their light coloration and other features. America's pluralistic society has made distinctions based on race problematic. For example, an African American military serviceman weds a woman while stationed in Korea. Although the man's family history contains mostly African American ancestors, he has a white male plantation owner and a Native American woman in his family tree. The serviceman's wife was born in Japan and has a Japanese father and Korean mother. The serviceman and his wife are transferred to a base in South America where they give birth to a girl. They stay at that base for fifteen years before being permanently relocated to the United States. Is the child African American, Native American, White, Japanese, Korean, or Latino? Physically, she could look African, Native American, White, Japanese, Korean, or some combination. She may speak English with a Spanish accent. What would Americans consider her to be? What is her "obvious" race?

The "one drop" rule legally permits anyone who has bloodlines to someone who is not white, no matter how many generations removed, to be considered a member of the nonwhite race. According to this theory, one drop of nonwhite blood "pollutes" the purity of being white. This is offensive to nonwhites because it establishes white as the norm from which other races deviate. The "one drop" rule is used for such purposes as determining the race or ethnic origin for classification by the U.S. Census Bureau, qualifying children in public schools for special programs and many affirmative action programs.

Race is not immutable. The market is filled with products to help lighten skin tone and straighten curly hair. Plastic surgeons perform operations worldwide to alter eyes into oval shape and change lip, nose, and cheek proportions. Just as transsexuals can alter many of their characteristics to better conform to their self-image by changing their gender, racial characteristics can be altered. Race, like gender, once thought to be immutable, can be altered through modern technology. When the issue of slavery was discussed in Congress, some people contended that Africans were subhuman and quoted scientists of the time to support their position. Biologists and medical experts now conclude the concept of separate racial groups has no meaning. Any set of characteristics that are thought to represent a racial group do not hold up under scrutiny. There are always members of the group who violate the set.

Yet race, as a social construct, definitely holds sway on the American consciousness. People are aware of differences based on racial stereotypes. People are categorized by how they look, and are treated, or discriminated against, accordingly. Race does not conform to the legal requirement to be "obvious, immutable, or distinguishing" at the scientific level. As a cultural force, however, race is "obvious" and our legal system struggles to judge acts of racial discrimination with the highest level of judicial review.

Religious affiliation is strongly protected in the United States by the First Amendment to the Constitution, which states "Congress shall make no law respecting an establishment of religion, or prohibiting the free exercise thereof." As a Constitutional right, religion is granted strict judicial scrutiny at every step. Religion may not have achieved strict scrutiny status if it had to qualify as other suspect classes have done. Religious beliefs are learned and chosen. People often change their religious beliefs. People often wear items of clothing or jewelry associated with their religion in order to make obvious or distinguishing statements about their religious affiliation. Religion is not obvious, immutable, or distinguishing. As such, religion does not meet the guidelines for suspect class, yet is granted these protections during court review.

Gender may be perceived to be obvious, immutable, or distinguishing. For many people, this is not true. Intersexed people are born with some combination of external and internal genitals, chromosomal patterns, and other characteristics that are not definitively male or female. Likewise, transsexuals do not conform to strict gender definition and demonstrate the fluidity of sex and gender by changing their sex and gender. At this time, gender has achieved quasisuspect status, but intersexed and transsexual people are excluded from this definition.

Thus, many of the classes that have been granted suspect or quasisuspect classification do not, themselves, meet the very guidelines used to create their status. Sexual orientation faces the same difficulties in trying to meet the guidelines for suspect class. Some claim that sexual orientation, unlike race, is not obvious (or as obvious) unless the person comes out. This is partially true. Many lesbian and gay men spend their entire life hidden, often marrying to cover their true identity, or never becoming fully aware of their sexual orientation. But other gay people are "obvious" as children and as adults. It is these people who experience the brunt of society's displeasure. One measure is the level of hate crimes. Each year the number of hate crimes in the United States increases, and the number committed upon lesbian and gay men slightly exceed the number committed against racial minorities. Similarly, sexual harassment of gay kids has become a liability issue for school districts. There are a significant number of lesbians and gay men who are "obvious" and who cannot hide.

Sexual orientation as an immutable characteristic faces many problems. How sexual orientation is defined, how measurements are made, the population studied, and the climate in which the studies are conducted each modify the outcome of the results. Western scientific tools are pinpointing the part of the human chromosome believed to determine sexual orientation. But if we look at other cultures, such as southern New Guinea, all people are in homosexual relationships for the majority of their lives (Williams, 1992). In these cultures, homosexuality, heterosexuality, and bisexuality are words that have no meaning. Many lesbian and gay researchers are coming to the conclusion that the wrong question is being asked. Instead of trying to find out what makes homosexuals, perhaps it will be more instructive to learn why some people develop heterosexist and homophobic beliefs. Legally, trying to achieve suspect classification for lesbians and gay men may be as futile as continuing the status/conduct dichotomy. (See also **Incidence of Homosexuality**; **Prejudice**; **Sexual Orientation**; and **Speech and Association**.)

Feminist theorists have recognized that suspect classifications are an attempt to remedy the impingement by the politically powerful upon the politically weak. This power dynamics has been termed "moral slavery" and is related to identity formation. People form identities a number of ways. One way is through emulation. For example, before someone becomes a ballet dancer, football player, writer, teacher, baker, taxi cab driver, lawyer, computer programmer, sales representative, or other professional, he or she forms an image of themselves in that profession and associates with people in those fields. Identities can also be formed as a reaction to negative experiences (otherwise known as a reaction-formation).

Reaction-formation identities reveal cultural moral slavery. For example, African American children do not learn of their racial identity until they, or their family, are attacked by the racist white culture. Women do not learn of their gender identity until they are subjugated by patriarchy. Lesbians and gay men do not learn of their sexual orientation until the heterosexual majority bashes them. It is when society enforces its moral code upon people with characteristics deemed deficient that people take on a persecuted or victim identity. The culture condemns people with a particular characteristic and enacts laws against them. People with the characteristic become oppressed and form a persecuted or victim identity. There is nothing inherent about the characteristic—whether it be race, national origin, religion, gender, or sexual orientation—that forms an identity, but rather the individual's response to the social status of the characteristic. The way to attack moral slavery is to educate people about the moral issue involved and dispel stereotypes through accurate information, not to apologize or justify the characteristic deemed deficient. (See also **Coming Out; Sexual Orientation**.)

It was not the testimony of scientists in the 1800s to Congress about Africans that swayed them for or against slavery. Instead, it was the moral arguments that all humans are equal regardless of the color of their skin that eliminated slavery. It was not the testimony of scientists in the 1900s about the role of women with respect to men that swayed Congress one way or another to amend the Constitution granting women the right to vote. It was the moral arguments that all humans are equal regardless of their gender that changed the law. Lesbians and gay men are at the same historical juncture. Scientists were called into court to prove the immutability of sexual orientation during *Romer v. Evans.* They were partially successful. Many gay activists believe this is the wrong approach. Instead they see this as a moral slavery issue. The powerful heterosexual majority keeps homosexuals in a second-class status through a myriad of laws granting additional rights to heterosexuals. These are slowly changing as lesbians and gay men present their arguments about the moral issue of equal rights for all people regardless of sexual orientation. (See also **Heterosexism**.)

Reference

Williams, W. 1992. *The Spirit and the Flesh: Sexual Diversity in American Indian Culture.* Boston: Beacon.

T

TITLE VII Title VII is the section of the 1964 Civil Rights Act that prohibits discrimination in employment based upon race, color, religion, sex, and national origin. (For a copy, go to <www.eeoc.gov/laws/vii.html.) There have been numerous court cases initiated by lesbians, gay men, transsexuals, and intersexuals claiming discrimination under Title VII. Courts have consistently held that sex, gender, and sexual orientation are distinctive characteristics, and that Title VII applies only to sex discrimination (*Holloway v. Arthur Anderson Co.*). Some gay males have complained that they were discriminated against because they do not conform to gender role expectations or because they were "effeminate." Courts have rejected these claims under Title VII (see, for example, *Smith v. Liberty Mutual Insurance Co; DeSantis v. Pacific Telephone & Telegraph Co.*). Furthermore, a federal district court stated, "The term 'sex' in Title VII refers to an individual's distinguishing biological or anatomical characteristics, whereas the term 'gender' refers to an individual's sexual identity," or socially constructed characteristics (*Dobre v. Amtrak* 1993, 76). (See also **Gender-Motivated Violence Act [GMVA]; Intersexed**; **Transsexual**.)

However, in the year 2000, the Ninth Circuit Court of Appeals reanalyzed Title VII in a case entitled *Schwenk v. Hartford.* Judge Stephen Reinhardt believed that sex and gender had been collapsed into one category—gender identity—in the 1989 Supreme Court decision in *Price Waterhouse v. Hopkins. Hopkins* dealt with a woman who did not conform to traditional feminine norms. Ann Hopkins was a successful senior manager and a candidate for partnership at Price Waterhouse. When her nomination came up, many partners at Price Waterhouse reacted negatively and accused her of being "macho," said she "overcompensated for being a woman," and that she needed to take a "course in charm school." To improve her chances of becoming a partner she was told to "walk more femininely, talk more femininely, dress more femininely, wear makeup, have her hair styled, and wear jewelry." Hopkins sued and prevailed with the courts. The U.S. Supreme Court stated:

> An employer who objects to aggressiveness in women but whose positions require this trait places women in an intolerable and impermissible Catch 22: out of a job if they behave aggressively and out of a job if they do not. Title VII lifts women out of this bind. . . . She had proved discriminatory input into the decisional process, and had proved that participants in the process considered her failure to conform to the stereotypes credited by a number of decisionmakers had been a substantial factor in the decision. (257)

Using the logic in *Price Waterhouse v. Hopkins,* Reinhardt stated, "the Supreme Court held that Title VII barred not just discrimination based on the fact that Hopkins was a woman, but also discrimination based on the fact that she failed 'to act like a woman'—that is, to conform to socially constructed gender expectations" (*Schwenk v. Hartford,* 16). Thus, it follows that transsexuals and others not conforming to gender expectations are afforded federal protection from discrimination in employment under Title VII. This was a radical ruling and is sure to be challenged.

TRANSGENDERED A transgendered person is one whose outward gender presentation (being feminine or masculine) does not conform to his or her biological sex (being female or male). Transgendered persons may self-identify as Butch, Femme, Drag King, Drag Queen, **Intersexed** Person, **Transvestite,** Transgenderist, Androgyne, or **Transsexual**. (See also **Sexual Orientation**.)

TRANSSEXUAL A transsexual is a person deeply dissatisfied with the gender to which he or she was born. Transsexuals may seek to change their gender through surgery or hormonal therapy or both. A newer term, *pansexual,* has been adopted to include transsexuals and all other persons whose gender, sexual orientation, and affective orientation do not coincide with societal norms, thereby supporting their sexuality instead of classifying them as dysphoric. (See also **Intersexed; Sexual Orientation**; **Transgender**.)

Transsexuals are persons whose biological sex is not congruent with their gender identity (that is, they strongly desire to be a gender other than their biological sex). Transsexualism is not directly related to sexuality at all. Instead, the *sex* root of the word refers to gender rather than sexual orientation. This misconception has emerged from public confusion of transsexuals with two much larger groups: effeminate homosexuals or drag queens and transvestites. Drag queens are gay males who imitate feminine mannerisms or dress as an expression of their sexuality.

Transvestites are usually heterosexual males who enjoy wearing female clothing. Neither of these two groups has the body-identity gender conflict experienced by transsexuals. Transsexuals, both before and following what is called sex-reassignment surgery, may be heterosexual, bisexual, lesbian, gay, or celibate.

Tens of thousands of transsexual surgeries have been performed in the United States (Rutledge 1989). Until recently, male-to-female (MTF) surgeries were performed more often than female-to-male (FTM) surgeries. Now there are almost equal numbers of each (Devor 1997). Surgical sex reassignment is specified under the *Standards of Care: The Hormonal and Surgical Sex Reassignment of Gender Dysphoric Persons* and is justified under the terms of the *Diagnostic and Statistical Manual of Mental Disorders* (1994). Although transsexuals are dependent upon medical intervention, there is widespread animosity between mental health professionals and transsexuals. This distrust has fostered misleading stereotypes, such as the mental illness paradigm and the presumed homogeneity of transsexuals.

It is often believed and the medical literature reinforces the stereotype that male-to-female transsexuals are hyperfeminine. Bolin (1988) believes the stereotype exists because (1) transsexuals believe this is what medical doctors expect and if they do not give it to them, they will not be provided with the medical assistance they seek, and (2) the psychological assessment devices used to determine masculinity and femininity are probably not valid for this category of persons because transsexuals do not adhere to the concept of "total sex role" (Bolin 1988, 110).

THE SEX-REASSIGNMENT PROCESS

The Rite of Transition—A Becoming

Transsexuals are required to participate in a program of hormonal management prior to and after surgery. There is no consensus among medical experts over the kinds of hormones to be administered and with what frequency. Regardless, it is known that the use of either male or female hormones over a lifetime has the potential to adversely affect the kidneys and other organs.

Transsexuals must lead a double life during the transition period. They need to take on the physical and behavioral characteristics of the other gender and edit their biographies to remove all things from their past that remind them of their original gender (for example, drivers' licenses, other documents, and wardrobe). They do not want a destigmatized transsexual status. Rather, they want acceptance as a "normal" man or women. "Passing"—that is, being accepted without question at a club, in a store, in the gay and straight community, by children, and so on—is very important.

It takes a number of years of hormone treatment and cultural training before transsexuals can walk in public without ridicule. The "change-over" is intended to make the person feel better about himself or herself. Instead, it initially leads to desertion by friends, loss of job, vilification in the streets, ostracism from the **family**, and a severe loss of self-esteem.

Transsexuals "regard 'changing over' (transsexual argot for going full-time) while remaining in the same work situation as the worst possible strategy" (Bolin 1988, 95). Most quit their jobs and seek new employment under their new gender. "Landing a job [in the new sex] is an event of great significance in transsexual lives that is shared by others and is considered the ultimate test of making it" (Bolin 1988, 153). Not surprisingly, the "majority of transsexuals becoming a woman [experience] a reduction in income" (Bolin 1988, 158).

It takes a series of surgical procedures over a number of years for female-to-male (FTM) transsexuals to achieve the transformation. As such, FTM transsexuals are faced with even greater employment discrimination during this process. At the same time, many FTM transsexuals report improvements in their income, even if performing the same work, simply by becoming a man. Approximately 70 percent to 80 percent of preoperative FTM transsexuals are involved in lesbian relationships and, after surgery, most FTM transsexuals identify as heterosexual men (Devor 1997).

The Facts of Surgery

Surgery is the final stage in the sex-reassignment procedure. It can costs anywhere from $6,000 to $50,000. FTM surgeries costs two to three times more than MTF surgery. Transsexuals generally feel better about themselves after the surgery than before (Bolin 1988, 178). The particulars of the surgeries are as follows:

1. MTF surgery: The first step is removal of the testicles. The penis is then inverted and a vagina-like opening is created. The scrotum is then used to create the labia. Some of the penile tissue is used to create a clitoris. The nerve endings in the penis are left intact, so hopefully orgasm will be possible. There are other optional surgeries such as the removal of the Adam's apple, jaw scraping, breast implants, cheek implants, collagen injections, and liposuction. The urethra is not rerouted nor is the prostate gland removed.
2. FTM surgery: A mastectomy and repositioning of the nipples is the first step. This is fairly minor surgery. Next, a hysterectomy with a bilateral salpingooophorectomy (removal of uterus, ovaries, and fallopian tubes) is performed. At present there is no effective way to create a penis. Penile implants are often used, but unfortunately they rarely function adequately. Radical fore-

arm grafts and intestinal grafts are also widely used, but these leave scars on parts of the body.

TRANSSEXUAL LEGAL AND WORKPLACE ISSUES

The problems faced by transsexuals in the workplace reveal the depths to which gender impacts employment and the law. Some of the issues are reviewed here (Walworth 1998).

Legal Name/Sex Change

By consistently using a new name (called the usage method), a transsexual may establish legal recognition of the name change in many states. Name change can also be achieved by filing simple legal papers. There is no uniform method of changing federal documents, as each department has its own requirements. In most cases, a statement from a licensed therapist or surgeon is sufficient to have the name and sex changed on drivers' and other state licenses, Internal Revenue Service and Social Security Insurance Administration records, school records, and elsewhere. Former employers will often cooperate and change personnel records accordingly.

Until recently, only transsexuals who completed or nearly completed changing over, including surgery, could have their names changed (see, for example, *Anonymous v. Mellon; Frances B. v. Mark B.;* and *Hartin v. Director of Bureau of Records*). With the case of Robert Henry McIntyre (*In re McIntyre* 1998), the Pennsylvania Supreme Court granted permission to Robert to change his name to Katherine Marie McIntyre, even though he had not begun surgical reassignment. The justices followed the courts' reasoning in *Commonwealth v. Goodman* and *In re Grimes* that the main purpose of name change statutes were to prohibit fraud by those attempting to avoid financial obligations. Furthermore, in *In re Eck* the court determined that it was not a matter of governmental concern when someone wanted to change his or her traditionally female or traditionally male name. Thus, in *In re McIntyre,* the court found no public interest in denying McIntyre's request for name change and his transgenderism had no bearing on the matter.

Medical Insurance

Virtually all health insurance policies and government medical programs contain clauses that specifically exclude sex reassignment surgery and other services related to transsexualism. Only a few companies have arranged to include transsexual medical needs in coverage. A Suffolk Superior Court decision in 2000 forced the state of Massachusetts to pay for the breast reconstructive surgery of a transsexual woman who developed cancer. This is the first time the courts treated a transsexual woman as they would a nontranssexual woman in upholding her right to basic health care (Gay and Lesbian Advocates and Defenders 2000). (See also **Employment**.)

Transition on the Job

Historically, preoperative transsexuals were encouraged to quit their jobs, submit to surgery, then reemerge in their postoperative status with a new job. This has changed, with more and more transsexuals opting to keep their existing jobs while transitioning. Thus, employers have been faced with situations that they are often ill prepared to handle. Here are some guidelines:

- Recognize that transitioning is a stressful time for transsexuals and employers alike. Although the transsexual has contemplated and planned this for years, the employer often plays catch up to prepare the work environment to be safe for all persons.

- The transsexual may require some time off from work to prepare. Psychotherapy and doctors' appointments for hormonal monitoring are usually done after work for a few hours each month. Electrolysis is often done on weekends. Just before coming to work in their new gender, many transsexuals need a few days to get prepared. The time off for surgery is dependent upon the kinds of surgery involved. For example, a hysterectomy is major surgery and requires six to eight weeks to recover (just as it would in a nontranssexual woman).

- Some transsexuals prefer to be transferred to another location after they transition. However, other transsexuals prefer to remain with coworkers who are familiar and supportive. It is important that regardless of whether a transfer is involved, the transsexual is treated fairly and not demoted because of transitioning.

- Transsexuals are just as competent before and after transition. Some jobs may require special handling. For example, MTF transsexuals maintain their lower, male voice until they have retraining, surgery, or both. As such, transsexuals working jobs that require telephone use may confuse clients who hear the lower voice. Each transition is different and companies need to weigh the benefits of changing the transsexual's job duties with the effects on the transsexual's long-term career goals.

- Awkward moments might be anticipated when transsexual employees deal with the public. These occur mostly because the transsexual employee may present an ambiguous gender appearance. Interviews with many transsexuals and employers have found that most customers are not concerned about the gender (or sexual orientation) of the contact, rather they focus on conducting business. However, it is suggested that employers prepare and have ready a simple statement that the employee is a transsexual and will continue to perform her or his job as capably as before for those few situations in which a customer inquires.

Transsexuals and Children

Transsexuals should not be restricted from working with children. It is surprising to most adults that children have an easier time accepting transsexuals' change of sex. Very young children have not been taught that sex is not supposed to change and believe that simply changing the length of hair makes the person a member of the other sex. Children around ages six and seven are acutely aware of gender ambiguity. It is no use trying to tell the child that a transsexual woman is a woman because they won't believe it. However, children of this age are nonjudgmental and accept the transsexual as a person. The reaction of adolescents to transsexuals depends upon their upbringing and their response ranges from total acceptance to hatred and brutal attacks. A few final remarks: Having contact with transsexuals will not make children transsexual, or gay, or mentally disturbed, and transsexuals are no more likely to molest children than nontranssexuals.

Legal Protections

Title VII of the Civil Rights Act of 1964 protects employees based on race, color, religion, sex, and national origin. The courts, however, have interpreted Title VII as based on individuals' status as men or women, and that it does not extend protection to people who shift between these two categories. However, a recent decision by the Ninth Circuit Court of Appeals (*Schwenk v. Hartford* 2000), drawing authority from the 1989 Supreme Court decision in *Price Waterhouse v. Hopkins,* has collapsed the concepts of sex and gender into one broad category: gender identity. Under this interpretation, transsexuals are entitled to federal protection from discrimination in employment under Title VII. This radical interpretation gives transgendered and transsexual people greater protections than currently afforded lesbians and gay men. This decision is very controversial and expected to be challenged. (See also **Gender-Motivated Violence Act [GMVA]**.)

Ordinances that provide employment protections based upon sexual orientation are not applicable to transsexuals. Only a few states, counties, and city governments provide specific employment protections to transsexuals. Many corporations and governmental departments have enacted employment protections for transsexuals. In most locales, it may be legal to dismiss an employee for being transsexual.

A recent ruling by the federal district court in Boston determined that a transgendered customer who was discriminated against by a bank for the way she dressed might have violated the federal Equal Credit Opportunity Act (*Rosa v. Park West Bank & Trust Co.* 2000). This act forbids banks from discriminating in extending credit on the basis of sex. In this particular case, Lucas Rosa went to the Park West Bank & Trust Company in 1998 to seek an application for a loan. Rosa was dressed as a woman. All of her identification documents depicted her in male clothing. The loan officer refused to give her an application unless she went home and changed into male clothing. Citing *Price Waterhouse v. Hopkins* (1989), the court agreed that the discrimination Rosa experienced was due to gender role conformity and constituted sex discrimination ("First Circuit Court Gives Cross-Dresser a Day in Federal Court" 2000).

Disability

An amendment to the **Americans with Disabilities Act (ADA)** of 1990 specifically excluded transsexualism (along with transvestitism, pedophilia, exhibitionism, and voyeurism) from coverage. However, employees who have lost their jobs due to transsexualism have sometimes been successful in making claims for receiving Social Security disability income.

Dress Codes

Courts have upheld the rights of employers to specify dress codes for employees and to specify different codes for men and women as long as there is a "reasonable" justification for this difference (dress codes include clothing, facial hair, use of makeup, length of hair, and more). Once transsexuals transition to the other gender, they are legally the other gender and employers cannot force them to wear clothing specified for their original gender. Occasionally, an employee may show up at work wearing clothing appropriate for the other gender. This employee may or may not be transsexual. If this behavior concerns management, the employee's supervisor should inquire as to the reason for the attire, and if need be, enforce the dress code. Hopefully, rigid gender and social roles will relax in the near future and the issue of what constitutes "appropriate" attire will become moot.

Sexual Harassment

Because transitioning often includes changes to genitalia, some employers fear that conversations on these topics may constitute sexual harassment. This is not the case. If transsexuals are asked personal questions, they may answer to the degree that they feel comfortable. However, once the transsexual establishes the boundary of what is acceptable, persistent questions from other employees may constitute harassment. Likewise, not all coworkers will want to hear details of the transition from the transsexual worker. Thus, transsexual employees need to be aware of conduct boundaries and be held equally accountable. (See also **Dress and Grooming Codes**.)

Other Employees

Coworkers will react to the transsexual with varying amounts of support. Almost all will feel awkward around the transsexual at first. But with time and strong management support, the transsexual will be fully accepted. A few weeks before the transition, management should make an announcement that gives support to the transsexual. In meetings and memoranda the transsexual employee should be referred to by the pronoun appropriate for his or her new status. It is also the time to announce changes in restroom use, training sessions, and more. Many transsexuals prefer to meet individually with coworkers and management before a formal notice is announced. Most negative responses to the announcement come from ignorance. As such, it is important that management and coworkers obtain accurate information about transsexualism. There will be heightened curiosity during the first few weeks. After a few months, most transsexuals report being fully accepted as members of their target group.

Title

Transsexuals should be addressed by their newly chosen name and by the pronoun appropriate for their new gender. The deliberate use of "it" or "he-she" or the wrong pronoun should be considered malicious and a form of gender harassment.

Restroom

The use of the restroom is probably the most frequently expressed concern by employers. Legally, a transsexual under the care of a therapist is entitled to use the restroom appropriate for his or her transitioned gender role, whether genital surgery has been performed or not. However, not everyone is comfortable with this arrangement. The solution to this problem depends on the physical layout of the work environment. For those environments in which there are unisex restrooms (both males and females share the same facility) there are no problems. For larger facilities that have multiple restrooms, the transsexual could be assigned to use particular ones (that conform to his or her gender) and the other employees, who have the concern, could use the other restrooms. The most challenging situation is a small facility that has only one restroom that accommodates multiple people at the same time. Some employers have installed a reversible sign on the restroom door that indicates if it is being used by the transsexual or coworkers. This strategy is used by many fire stations to accommodate women firefighters. In making these arrangements, it is important to recognize that neither the transsexual nor the uncomfortable coworker is at fault. Once surgery is complete (if chosen), the transsexual should use the restroom appropriate to the new sex without restriction.

Uncomfortable Clients

This is a difficult question. It was often claimed that allowing women or people of color into management or sales would drive clients away. What we have learned over forty years of civil rights progress is that—yes, some clients are driven away, but not many, and that fairness and improved relations with other clients offsets the loss. This is true for transsexuals. Some clients may be intolerant working with transsexual employees. Accommodations can be made, but hopefully without trampling on the rights and dignity of the transsexual.

Coworkers with Religious Objections

Occasionally, some employees with restrictive religious beliefs are so uncomfortable working with transsexual employees that they either ask for a transfer or quit. Coworkers who harass transsexual workers should be warned and disciplined. Their open hostility exposes the company to a possible lawsuit.

Teasing

Coworkers will sometimes tease the transsexual. The transsexual may actually enjoy the gentle teasing or may be putting up a brave front. The only way to know is to ask. This conversation should be held in private and not repeated. Sometimes a memo will be sufficient to reduce or eliminate the teasing.

Benefits

A transsexual who was married before surgery and who continues to stay married may continue to list his or her spouse with the company's benefits package. Their legal marriage was conducted before sex reassignment surgery. Although this employee and his or her spouse would now be living as a same-sex couple, the courts have not considered this to be in violation of the **Defense of Marriage Act (DOMA).**

The most important thing an employer can do to make the transition as smooth as possible is to be supportive of the transsexual. (See also **Intersexed; Sexual Orientation**.)

References

Bolin, A. 1988. *In Search of Eve: Transsexual Rites of Passage.* New York: Bergin & Garvey.

Devor, H. 1997. *FTM: Female-to-Male Transsexuals in Society.* Bloomington, IN: Indiana University Press.

"First Circuit Gives Cross-Dresser a Day in Federal Court." 2000. *Lesbian/Gay Law Notes* (July/August 2000).

Diagnostic and Statistical Manual of Mental Disorders. 1994. 4th ed. Washington, DC: American Psychiatric Association.

Gay and Lesbian Advocates and Defenders. 2000. "Massachusetts Court Orders State to Provide Health Care to Transsexual Woman." Gay and Lesbian Advocates and Defenders press release on website: www.glad.org. Accessed 4 May 2000.

Rutledge, L. W. 1989. *The Gay Fireside Companion.* Boston: Alyson.

Walworth, J. 1998. *Transsexual Works: An Employer's Guide.* Westchester, CA: Center for Gender Sanity.

TRANSVESTITE

A transvestite is a person who chooses to wear clothing that society deems appropriate for the opposite gender. German sexologist Magnus Hirschfeld introduced the term in 1910. Transvestitism is prevalent among both heterosexuals and homosexuals. When transvestites completely dress in clothing of the opposite sex, they are attempting to "pass" as the opposite sex. Homosexual transvestites are popularly known as "drag queens." Mixing clothing and hair styles of both genders at one time is known as "camp." (See also **Sexual Orientation**.)

V

VAGRANCY

See **Lewd Conduct**

VICE

Vice involves a category of behaviors deemed morally wrong. Vice often includes prostitution, gambling, certain types of sex (for example, sodomy), pornography, drug use, and others. Because the definition of vice often is based upon religious convictions, what is deemed to be morally wrong runs the gamut of religious beliefs. The legal system of the United States is an outgrowth of the English legal system that incorporated the powers of the ecclesiastical courts during the English Reformation. As such, many statutes contain Protestant moral values and language. For example, most of the **sodomy** laws in the states contained direct reference to or language found in the Bible's Book of Leviticus.

The vice units of police departments are responsible for enforcing these moral codes. Homosexuals have been targeted by law enforcement through the use of vice squads. Historically, police officers would enter gay or lesbian bars and other meeting areas and harass patrons through the arbitrary enforcement of vice laws. At times, it has been illegal for homosexuals to gather in public, to dance together, to wear gender-nonconforming clothes, besides other behaviors. Thus, vice laws have been a major tool used to oppress lesbians, gay men, and bisexuals, and transgendered people. Slowly, these oppressive statutes have been lifted, but remnants remain. (See also **Criminal Law; Victimless Crimes**.)

VICTIMLESS CRIMES

Victimless crimes involve behaviors that are criminalized by society, yet that result in no harm to others. Prostitution, gambling, pornography, and drug use are just a few of the behaviors that are often categorized as victimless crimes. The issue of victimless crimes is important to lesbians, gay men, and bisexuals, and transgendered, transsexual, and intersexed people. Sex statutes used to criminalize nonheterosexual personal and private sexual acts are also sometimes classified as vice laws. When sex acts are consensual, many would believe there are no victims and no vice. However, others, particularly religious conservatives, claim that homosexuals, pornographers, prostitutes, and others are victims of their vices and that society needs to be protected from them and that they need protection or "saving" from themselves. (See also **Criminal Law**.)

Some religious beliefs condemn homosexual behaviors and these have influenced our legal system. These religious beliefs cast homosexuals as victims of vice and claim that they are hurting their souls and are a danger to society. They believe homosexuality is not victimless. Other religions, such as some Native American, neo-pagan, Unitarian, and reform religions, do not hold these beliefs and instead view homosexuals as special people with unique and deeply spiritual qualities. These people would not classify homosexual sex as a crime. They would consider our system of criminalizing homosexual behaviors as making homosexuals into victims of judicial abuse. (See also **Sodomy**.)

Deciding what constitutes crime is difficult for society. Although the United States has a civil code emphasizing the separation of church and state, religion has had a major influence on our legal system. But which religious beliefs does one choose from? There are over 1,100 recognized religions in the United States, with more than 300 different denominations of Christianity.

As an alternative to religion-based law, a secular model used to distinguish between victim and victimless crimes is the "harm principle" attributed to John Stuart Mills (Mills 1885). The harm principle expresses the belief that people should be allowed to do whatever they desire as long as they do not harm another person or intentionally create a situation that may harm another person. Law then should regulate only acts that infringe upon another's rights or liberties. Under such a scheme, consensual activities, such as sex between adults, would not be criminalized.

It is sometimes argued that decriminalizing victimless crimes would lead to the downfall of society. There is some research in this area:

- Gambling was once a highly restricted activity. Many cities and states have legalized gambling without a measurable increase in crime rates. A small percentage of people become addicted to gambling with dire consequences to families, but revenue from state gambling has also helped benefit public schools (Horn 1997, 34).
- Drugs are still tightly controlled in the United States. Because of this, the cost of illicit drugs is exceedingly high. There is significant organized crime involved in the distribution, sale, and pro-

tection of drugs. Drug enforcement accounts for a large portion of local, state, and federal police budgets. In contrast, many countries have less stringent drug laws. In both England and Denmark, the government dispenses drugs to addicts as a way of reducing their need to engage in crime to pay for their habit. These countries have not experienced an overall increase in drug use and their crime rates are much lower than those found in the United States.

- Homosexuality is often associated with the "demise" of civilization by religious conservatives. There is no evidence that the decline of a civilization is related to the sexual orientation of its members (Stewart 1999, 170).

Adopting the harm principle would provide benefits to society. It is estimated that 80 percent of law enforcement time and money is spent regulating private morals (Simon 1996, 211). By changing the focus in society away from victimless crimes, scarce resources could be better utilized to combat violence and real crime.

References

Horn, B. P. 1997. "Is There a Cure for America's Gambling Addiction?" *USA Today Magazine* 125(2624): 34.

Mills, J. S. 1885. *On Liberty.* New York: Holt.

Simon, D. R. 1996. *Elite Deviance.* Boston: Allyn & Bacon.

Stewart, C. 1999. *Sexually Stigmatized Communities—Reducing Heterosexism and Homophobia: An Awareness Training Manual.* Thousand Oaks, CA: Sage.

White Night Harvey Milk was a long-time gay activist in the city of San Francisco. After running for public office many times, he was elected to the Board of Supervisors in 1977. He was always aware of his responsibility in being gay and representing the predominantly gay district of the city. He drafted and submitted to the Board of Supervisors a landmark gay-rights ordinance. The ordinance ended antigay discrimination in employment, housing, and public accommodation. The Board passed the ordinance with only one dissenting vote by Supervisor Dan White. White and Milk often took opposing positions concerning the city.

A year later in 1978, Harvey Milk and Mayor George Moscone were gunned down in their City Hall offices. The murderer was Dan White. Three weeks earlier White had resigned from the Board of Supervisors, claiming that he could not live on the money paid for the half-time position. Five days later White asked for his job back, but the mayor refused, citing complaints from White's constituents to substantiate the denial. Just thirty minutes before the mayor was to announce the appointment of the new supervisor, White confronted the mayor and shot him. White, who was supported by conservatives and outspokenly antigay, then walked across the hall to the office of Milk and shot him. White left the building and later turned himself in to the police, where he confessed.

The city was stunned. On the evening of the shooting, more than 25,000 people conducted a candlelight vigil from the Castro District to City Hall. Later, White was convicted of second-degree murder. One of the claims made by the defense was that White was addicted to "junk food," such as Hostess Twinkies, and acted emotionally in response to the sugar rush (otherwise known as the "Twinkie" defense). The light sentence resulted in a massive riot in 1979 throughout San Francisco (also known as "White Night"). Many police vehicles were overturned and burned. White served a few years in prison before he was released. Soon after being released from prison in 1985 he committed suicide.

Since Milk's murder many organizations, high schools exclusively serving gay students, and gay community support funds have been named in his honor.

WILLS It is important for same-sex couples to write reciprocal wills. This has been a fairly successful technique to ensure property transference upon the death of a life partner. Without a will, there is no legal relationship between same-sex couples. The estate does not automatically go to the surviving partner, but instead is distributed to the parents of the deceased. If the parents are not alive, the estate is distributed to brothers, sisters, nieces, and nephews. If no relatives are alive, the estate goes to the state (*Max v. McLynn*).

Marriage laws and most domestic partnership statutes do not apply to same-sex couples for the distribution of property. Even when there is a will, relatives of the deceased have sometimes been successful in contesting it. In some cases, relatives have claimed that the will was written under duress or "with undue influence" by the life partner (see, e.g., *In re Kaufmann's Will*). To avoid having the will contested, some same-sex couples have resorted to a "no-contest" provision in the will. Such a provision attempts to preclude others from contesting the will under threat of being completely cut out of the will. Courts have sometimes ruled for relatives of the deceased even when wills contained a "no-contest" provision.

A few states have laws that recognize the reciprocal rights of couples who have cohabited for extended periods. The supreme court of Washington state in 1984 provided for "meretricious relationships." This concept grants property rights to the surviving partner for all "community property" as specified in the state's marriage laws. In 1995 the court in *Connell v. Francisco* established three tests to determine if a couple qualifies for meretricious relationship status: (1) the relationship must be "stable"; (2) the relationship must be "marriage-like"; and (3) the parties must "cohabit with knowledge that a lawful marriage between them does not exist." A gay man attempted to apply the test of meretricious relationship when his lover of twenty-eight years died without a will in 1995. Frank Vasquez applied to inherit the house, business, and financial assets the couple built together when his lover, Robert Schwerzler, died at age seventy-eight. The trial court agreed with Vasquez and awarded him virtually all of Schwerzler's property. However, two sisters of Schwerzler also filed claims and appealed the judgment. Judge Bridgewater from the court of appeals ruled against Vasquez and stated, "We find no precedent for applying the marital concepts, either rights or protections, to same-sex relations . . . [extending the law that governs unmarried, long-term couples to gays] is for the Legislature to decide, not the courts" ("Appeals Court Overturns Awarding of Estate to Gay Partner" 2000). (See also **Domestic Partnership**; **Family**; **Marriage**.)

Reference

"Appeals Court Overturns Awarding of Estate to Gay Partner." (17 February 2000). Associated Press website: www.wire.ap.org/APnews.

Appendix A: State and Local Laws

The laws related to lesbian, gay, and bisexual, and transgendered, transsexual, and intersexed people are rapidly changing in the United States. Slowly, discriminatory practices against nonheterosexuals are being replaced with laws that provide protection based upon sexual behaviors, sexual identity, and gender identity. Even still, a backlash from conservative political groups has brought forth a new round of discriminatory practices, for example, antimarriage legislation and constitutional amendments that prohibit people other than one man and one woman from obtaining legal marriage.

This appendix contains specific listings of laws, statutes, and ordinances for all fifty states, the District of Columbia, and major cities with populations over 80,000. Sex statutes, hate crimes, and antimarriage statutes are the creations of state legislatures. The issue of blanket protections against discrimination in employment (both public and private), union practices, public accommodations, education, credit, housing, and domestic partnerships are commonly addressed by counties and cities. Few states have looked at lesbian and gay civil right issues.

Sex Statutes

Sex statutes are rarely enforced. However, by criminalizing sexual behaviors between people of the same sex, our legal system uses the existence of these laws to continue other forms of discrimination against homosexuals—such as deeming lesbian mothers or gay fathers unfit to care for their own children. (See also **Criminal Law**; **Sodomy**.) In the year 2000, approximately one-third of the states still have sex statutes that criminalize same-sex sexual behaviors:

- Illegal between persons of the same sex: Arkansas, Kansas, Missouri.
- Illegal for all: Arizona, Florida, Idaho, Louisiana, Maryland, Michigan, Minnesota, Mississippi, North Carolina, Oklahoma, South Carolina, Virginia.
- Illegal with anyone other than spouse: Alabama, Utah.

Laws sometimes specifically target same-sex behaviors, sometimes target specific sexual behaviors regardless of whether committed by homosexual or heterosexual partners, and at other times target all of those who are not married. Typically, until sex statutes are revoked, antidiscrimination provisions at the state or local level are not implemented based on sexual orientation or identity.

Civil Rights Laws

Many cities and local governments have begun to address the civil rights of lesbians, gay men, and transgendered persons. When such ordinances are passed, they state specific areas in which discrimination is not allowed. These laws often cover a number of areas, including public and private employment, union practices, public accommodations, education, credit, and housing. Approximately 37 million Americans (14 percent of the total U.S. population) are afforded protections only by local laws and have no overriding state protections. Taken together, 170 million Americans (61 percent of the population) have no legislative protection against discrimination based on sexual orientation in private employment at the local or state level.

- Public employment: As of 1999, seven states provided protection from discrimination in public employment based on sexual orientation, gender identity, or both through executive order or civil service rule. (Illinois, Iowa, Maryland, New Mexico, New York, Pennsylvania, and Washington. *Note:* Iowa's executive order also included gender identity discrimination.) (See also **Employment**.)
- Private employment: As of 1999, eleven states and the District of Columbia provided protection from discrimination in private employment based on sexual orientation, gender identity, or both. (California, Connecticut, District of Columbia, Hawaii, Massachusetts, Minnesota, Nevada, New Hampshire, New Jersey, Rhode Island, Vermont, and Wisconsin. *Note:* Minnesota included gender identity protection. In *Tanner v. OHSU,* it was determined that discrimination based on sexual orientation in Oregon was prohibited, although there was no specific legislation.) There were also eighty-seven cities and fifteen counties in 1999 that provided similar protections. (See also **Employment**.)
- Union practices: Very few states, counties, or cities have begun to address the issue of sexual orientation within union practices, that is, to make sure that sexual orientation is a characteristic considered during union negotiations (Eriskopp and Silverstein 1998).

- Public accommodations: In only nine states and the District of Columbia are lesbians and gay men guaranteed the right to the use of hotels, restaurants, medical offices, and other places considered places of public accommodations. A few cities have also addressed this important issue. In all other states and locales, discrimination still often occurs without legal recourse.
- Education: There is a wide range of statutes concerning education within each state. A few states have begun to address the issues of lesbian and gay male students, faculty, and staff. (See also **Education**.)
- Credit: Institutions that provide credit and other financial services sometimes concern themselves with the sexual orientation of their clients. A few cities and states have begun to address the issue of keeping this kind of information out of the decision process.
- Housing: Zoning laws and other real estate regulations often allow for discrimination against single cohabiting people, or specifically against lesbians and gay men. A few counties and cities have begun to include sexual orientation discrimination protections for those attempting to rent or buy property.

ANTIMARRIAGE LEGISLATION/AMENDMENTS

In a backlash against the prospect that lesbian and gay male couples might achieve legally sanctioned marriage, thirty-one states enacted legislation to define marriage as being between one man and one woman. (Alabama, Alaska, Arizona, Arkansas, California, Delaware, Florida, Georgia, Hawaii, Idaho, Illinois, Indiana, Iowa, Kansas, Kentucky, Louisiana, Maine, Michigan, Minnesota, Mississippi, Montana, North Carolina, North Dakota, Oklahoma, Pennsylvania, South Carolina, South Dakota, Tennessee, Utah, Virginia, and Washington.) Sometimes the language includes specific prohibitions against same-sex marriage and the recognition of same-sex marriages performed elsewhere. Three states (Alaska, California, and Hawaii) modified their state constitution to prohibit same-sex marriages.

Yet states that have also passed legislation to provide antidiscrimination provisions based on sexual orientation or gender identity have found themselves with conflicting statutes. On the one hand, their statutes prohibit discrimination, yet on the other hand they prohibit the legal recognition of same-sex relationships and families.

Beginning in 1999, Vermont became embroiled over recognizing same-sex couples. The state's supreme court decided that the state constitution required that same-sex couples be provided the same benefits and legal recognition that married opposite-sex couples have. One strategy to comply with this ruling would have allowed lesbians and gay men to marry. Another approach would be to pass legislation that provided all the same rights and responsibilities—but with another name. At this time, the second strategy is the one Vermont's legislature adopted.

HATE CRIME LEGISLATION

Hate-motivated crimes are increasing in the United States. The federal government began collecting data on hate crimes with the enactment of the Hate Crime Statistics Act. Sexual orientation was a category included in this act. Twenty-five states and the District of Columbia have enacted hate crime legislation (or similar legislation) that includes sexual orientation. Sometimes, this legislation requires only report taking (Maryland, Michigan, and Utah). Other states (Arizona, Connecticut, Delaware, District of Columbia, Florida, Illinois, Iowa, Kentucky, Louisiana, Maine, Massachusetts, Nebraska, Nevada, New Hampshire, New Jersey, Oregon, Rhode Island, Washington, and Wisconsin) impose criminal sanctions on hate-motivated crimes in addition to collecting data. A few states (California, Minnesota, Missouri, and Vermont) also include gender identity under their hate crime statutes. Not all local or state law enforcement agencies have begun recording or reporting on hate crimes, particularly those crimes motivated by antigay hate. Thus, the federal report is incomplete and represents only a small number of actual crimes committed each year against lesbians, gay men, and others.

DOMESTIC PARTNERSHIP BENEFITS AND REGISTRIES

These kinds of benefits are provided to the domestic partners of employees of state, city, or county employees. Two categories of benefits have been applied: (1) "soft" benefits are lower in cost and usually include limited bereavement and sick leave, relocation benefits, and parental leave; and (2) "hard" benefits that include general health and dental insurance coverage, life insurance, long-term care, and day care. (See also **Domestic Partnership**.)

The governments of four states (California, Hawaii, New York, and Vermont) provide both hard and soft benefits to their lesbian or gay state employees as part of their domestic partnership benefits programs. Likewise, three states (Delaware, Massachusetts, and Oregon) provide only soft employment benefits to state employees who are gay or lesbian. In the District of Columbia, Congress has effectively blocked domestic partnership benefits by denying funds for the program.

In addition to these states, approximately fourteen counties provided both hard and soft employment benefits, five counties provided soft employment benefits, fifty-four cities provided both hard and soft employment benefits, and ten cities provided only soft employment benefits to gay and lesbian couples.

Only California has passed legislation to provide a domestic partnership registry. Yet domestic registry programs provide only limited rights that do not begin to equal the rights granted upon marriage. There are also four counties and thirty-seven cities that provided similar registries. In most cases, the registries were open to all persons, with the exception of Madison (Wisconsin), Milwaukee (Wisconsin), New Orleans (Louisiana), and Oak Park (Illinois), which applied only to same-sex couples.

ABBREVIATIONS WITHIN THE APPENDIX

Amd.—"Amending" or "amended on."

Amd. Ord.—"Amending or enacting ordinance." Ordinances are contained within city and county codes.

Amd. Stat. or Amd. Act.—"Amended by" or "enacted by" for statutes or acts. Statutes and acts relate to sections within a state code.

Art.—"Article." Like a section or chapter, this refers to part of a city, state, or county code.

Chap.—"Chapter." Refers to a section of a city, county, or state code.

Eff.—"Effective date."

Ord.—"Ordinance." An Ordinance is a type of municipal or local law.

Res.—"Resolution." A resolution has the same meaning as ordinance.

Sec.—"Section." Refers to a specific section within a city, county, or state code.

S.I.L.—"Signed into law."

ALABAMA

Antimarriage legislation: Defined marriage as opposite-sex couples and prohibited same-sex marriages. 1998 Ala. Act 1998–500 ("Alabama Marriage Protection Act").

Hate crimes: Sexual orientation not included in hate crimes statutes.

Sex statutes (sodomy): Criminalized private and consensual sexual behaviors engaged in by opposite-sex and same-sex people; with the exception of those who are married. "Any act of sexual gratification between persons not married to each other, involving the sex organs of one person and the mouth or anus of another. Consent is no defense." Definite term of imprisonment in the county jail or hard labor for the county for not more than one year. Sexual Misconduct, Ala. Code Sec. 13A-6–65.

ALASKA

Antimarriage legislation: Defined marriage as opposite-sex couples and voided same-sex marriages. Alaska Stat. Sec(s). 25.05.011 and 25.05.013;

also with state constitutional amendment (Alaska State Constitution, Art. 1, Sec. 25).

Hate crimes: Sexual orientation not included in hate crime statutes.

Sex statutes (sodomy): Repealed in 1980.

ARIZONA

Antimarriage legislation: Defined marriage as opposite-sex couples and voided same-sex marriages. Ariz. Rev. Stat. Ann. Sec(s). 25–101 and 25–112.

Hate crimes: Actual or perceived sexual orientation of the victim is used as an aggravating factor during sentencing of perpetrators. Data is collected. Ariz. Rev. Stat. Ann. Sec. 13–702.

Sex statutes (sodomy): Criminalized private and consensual sexual behaviors engaged in by opposite- and same-sex people. "Any person who knowingly and without force commits the infamous crime against nature—Class 3 misdemeanor. If with a child under the age of 15—Class 2 misdemeanor." Class 3 misdemeanor requires an imprisonment for thirty days. Crime Against Nature, Ariz. Rev. Stat. Ann. Sec. 13–1411 and Lewd and Lascivious Acts, Sec. 13–1412.

Phoenix

Civil rights laws: Sexual orientation included in Chap. 18 ("Human Relations"), Art. I. (Amd. Ord. No. G-3558, 7/8/92).

Private employment: Applied only to private employers who have contracts with the city: Sec. 18–4 ("Employers doing business with the city").

Public accommodation: Applied only to services provided by the city: Sec. 18–10.02 ("City services").

Pima County

Domestic partnership employment benefits: Board of Supervisors decided to extend benefits to opposite- and same-sex couples. Hard benefits include medical and dental coverage.

Tucson

Civil rights laws: Sexual orientation included in Tucson Code: Chap. 17 ("Human Relations"), Art. III ("Civil Rights"); Chap. 17, Art. VII ("Fair Housing"); and Chap. 10 ("Civil Service-Human Resources"), Art. I. (Amd. Ord. No. 9199, 2/1/99.) Gender identity also included (Amd. Ord. No. 9199, 2/1/99).

Credit: Protections based upon sexual orientation provided only during the financing of real estate transactions. Tucson Code, Sec. 17–52 (f) ("Discrimination in sale or rental housing").

Domestic partnership employment benefits: Benefits afforded to same-sex couples only. Hard benefits include medical and dental coverage (City Wide Policy No. SS/April 28–97–212).

Education: Sexual orientation included in Tucson Code under Sec. 17–12 (a).

Housing: Sexual orientation included under Sec. 17–52 ("Discrimination in sale or rental housing").

Private employment: Sexual orientation included under Sec. 17–12 (b), (d), and (e).

Public accommodation: Sexual orientation included under Sec. 17–12 (a).

Union practices: Sexual orientation included under Sec. 17–12 (c) and (e).

ARKANSAS

Antimarriage legislation: Defined marriage as opposite-sex and prohibited and voided same-sex marriages. Ark. Code Ann. Sec(s). 9–11–109 and 9–11–208.

Hate crimes: No specific hate crime laws. The civil cause of action may be used in hate crime situations, however, it does not include sexual orientation.

Sex statutes (sodomy): Criminalized private and consensual sexual behaviors engaged in by same-sex people only. "A person commits sodomy if the anus, mouth, or vagina [sic] of a person or animal is penetrated by the penis of a person or animal of the same sex." Sentence shall not exceed one year. Ark. Code Ann. Sec. 5–14–122.

CALIFORNIA

Antimarriage legislation: Defined marriage as opposite-sex couples and voided same-sex marriages through passage of Proposition 22, known as Knight Initiative, in 2000.

Civil rights laws: Sexual orientation included in California Government Code: Title 2, Div. 3, Part 2.8 ("Department of Fair Employment and Housing," Amd. Stat. 1999, 1999 Cal. Stat. Chap. 592); and California Education Code, Title 1, Div. 1, Part 1, Chap. 2 ("Education Equity," Amd. Stat. 1999, 1999 Cal. Stat. Chap. 587). Gender identity also included but applies only to discrimination in education (Amd. Stat. 1999, 1999 Cal. Stat. Chap. 587).

Domestic partnership government employment benefits: Hard benefits provided to same-sex couples. Applies to opposite-sex couples over age sixty-two and those who meet other Social Security Act eligibility criteria. See, Calif. Gov. Code Title 2, Div. 5, Part 5, Chap. 1, Art. 9 ("Domestic Partners," Amd. Stat. 1999, 1999 Cal. Stat. Chap. 588).

Domestic partnership registry: Applies to same-sex couples, as well as opposite-sex couples over age sixty-two or who meet other Social Security Act eligibility criteria. Registry facilitates visits to hospitals. See, Calif. Family Code, Div. 2.5 ("Dom. Partner. Regis.") and Calif. Health and Safety Code, Sec. 1261. (Amd. Stat. 1999, 1999 Cal. Stat. Chap. 588.)

Education: Sexual orientation included under Cal. Educ. Code Sec. 220 and Sec. 66270.

Employment: Employment discrimination protections originally included in the California Labor Code (Sec. 1102.1, Amd. Stat. 1992, c. 915). This codified existing law and practice of the Cal. Labor Commission. See *Gay Law Students' Association v. Pacific Telephone and Telegraph Co.*, 24 Cal. 3d 458 (1979).

Hate Crimes: Actual or perceived sexual orientation of victim may be used as aggravating factor in sentencing. Mandatory sentence used along with separate crime and penalty for hate-motivated crimes. Data collected and gender identity also included. Cal. Pen. Code Sec. 422.6.

Housing: Sexual orientation included under Cal. Gov. Code Sec. 12955.

Private employment: Sexual orientation included under Cal. Gov. Code Sec. 12940.

Public employment: Government employees expressly covered. Cal. Gov. Code Sec. 12940.

Sex statutes (sodomy): Repealed in 1976.

Union practices: Sexual orientation included under Cal. Gov. Code Sec. 12940.

Alameda County

Domestic partnership employment benefits: Soft benefits provided to opposite- and same-sex couples. Benefits include bereavement leave.

Berkeley

Civil rights laws: Sexual orientation included in Berkeley Municipal Code: Chap. 13.28 ("Discrimination on the Basis of Sexual Orientation"); and Chap. 13.30 ("Discrimination on the Basis of AIDS and Related Conditions," Amd. Ord. No. 5106-NS, 11/ 9/87).

Credit: Sexual orientation protections apply only to the financing of real estate transactions. Sec. 13.28.040 (2) ("Credit and Insurance"), and Sec. 13.28.050 A (3) ("Unlawful Housing Practices").

Domestic partnership employment benefits: Hard benefits provided to opposite- and same-sex couples, including health and dental insurance, and bereavement and sick leave. Adopted by City Council, 12/4/84.

Domestic partnership registry: Applies to opposite- and same-sex couples. No specific rights listed (adopted by City Council, 6/91).

Education: Sexual orientation included in Municipal Code under Sec.

13.28.070 ("Educational institutions"), and Sec. 13.30.080 ("Educational institutions").

Housing: Sexual orientation included under Sec. 13.28.040 ("Housing and other real estate transactions"), and Sec. 13.30.050 ("Housing").

Private employment: Sexual orientation included under Sec. 13.28.030 ("Employment"), and Sec. 13.30.040 ("Employment").

Public accommodation: Sexual orientation included under Sec. 13.28.050 ("Business establishments"), and Sec. 13.30.060 ("Business establishments").

Public employment: Government employees expressly covered. Sec. 13.28.030 ("Employment"), and Sec. 13.30.040 ("Employment").

Union practices: Sexual orientation included under Sec. 13.28.030 (4) ("Labor Organizations"), and Sec. 13.30.040 A (3) ("Unlawful Employment Practices").

Costa Mesa

Civil rights laws: Sexual orientation included under Costa Mesa Municipal Code. (Amd. Ord. 98–25, 12/7/98).

Public employment: Sexual orientation included under "Appendix to Purchasing," Chap. VI., Sec. 2–228 ("Discrimination").

Daly City

Civil rights laws: Sexual orientation included under Rules and Regulations of the Classified Service, City of Daly City. (Adopted "Memoranda of Understandings" by City Council during 1998/99.)

Domestic partnership employment benefits: Soft benefits provided to opposite- and same-sex couples and include family, medical, and bereavement leave. See Rule I, Sec. I-I ("Definition" of "Immediate Family")—Memoranda of Understandings.

Public employment: Government employees expressly covered. Rule VI ("Affirmative Action").

Hayward

Civil rights laws: Sexual orientation included under Ordinance Prohibiting Discrimination Based on Race . . . Sexual Orientation [etc.]. (Amd. Ord. No. 94–05, 2/11/94.)

Credit: Sexual orientation included under Sec. 5 ("Credit").

Domestic partnership employment benefits: Soft benefits provided to opposite- and same-sex couples and include bereavement leave. City of Hayward Admin. Rule No. 2.61.

Education: Sexual orientation included under Sec. 4 ("Educational Institutions").

Public accommodation: Sexual orientation included under Sec. 3 ("Business Establishments and Public Accommodations").

Long Beach

Civil rights laws: Sexual orientation included under Long Beach Municipal Code: Chap. 5.09 ("Employment Discrimination," Amd. Ord. No. C-6408, 7/28/87), Chap. 8.94 ("AIDS Discrimination," Amd. Ord. No. C-6635, 8/29/89), and "A Resolution . . . Pertaining to Non-Discrimination in Public and Private Employment in the City of Long Beach" (Res. No. C-24380, 6/9/87).

Domestic partnership registry: Registration applies to opposite- and same-sex couples. Helps to facilitate visits to health care facilities and jails. See Chap. 8.95 ("Domestic Partnership Registration," Amd. Ord. No. C-7460, 4/1/97).

Housing: Sexual orientation included under Sec. 8.94.030 ("Housing and other real estate transactions").

Private employment: Sexual orientation included under Sec. 5.09.020 ("Discrimination prohibited"), Sec. 8.94.020 ("Employment practices"), and "A Resolution . . . Pertaining to Non-discrimination in Public and Private Employment in the City of Long Beach."

Public accommodation: Sexual orientation included under Sec. 8.94.040 ("Business Establishments") and apply only to services provided by the city: Sec. 8.94.050 ("City facilities and services").

Public employment: Government employees expressly covered under "A Resolution . . . Pertaining to Non-Discrimination in Public and Private Employment in the City of Long Beach."

Union practices: Sexual orientation included under Sec. 8.94.020 ("Employment practices").

Los Angeles, City of

Civil rights laws: Sexual orientation included under Los Angeles Municipal Code: Chap. IV, Art. 12 ("Discrimination on the Basis of Sexual Orientation," Amd. Ord. No. 152,458, Eff. 7/8/79); Chap. IV ("Public Welfare"), Art. 5.8 ("Prohibition against Discrimination Based on . . . AIDS . . . ," Amd. Ord. No. 160,289, Eff. 8/19/85); and Introduction endnote 10 (p.18).

Credit: Sexual orientation included under Art. 12, Sec. 49.74(a)(2) ("Credit").

Domestic partnership employment benefits: Hard benefits provided to opposite- and same-sex couples and include sick and bereavement leave (Amd. Ord. No. 168238, 9/8/92), and dental and health insurance (Amd. Ord. No. 169373, 2/18/94). See L.A. Admin. Code Div. 4, Chap. 2, Art. 10, Sec. 4.127 and Sec. 4.127.1.

Education: Sexual orientation included under Art. 12, Sec. 49.75 ("Educational Institutions"), and Art. 5.8, Sec. 45.86 ("Educational Institutions").

Housing: Sexual orientation included under Art. 12, Sec. 49.73 ("Housing and Other Real Estate Transactions"), and Art. 5.8, Sec. 45.83 ("Rental Housing").

Private employment: Sexual orientation included under Art. 12, Sec. 49.72 ("Employment"), and Art. 5.8, Sec. 45.82 ("Employment").

Public accommodation: Sexual orientation included under Art. 12, Sec. 49.74 ("Business Establishments"), and Art. 5.8, Sec. 45.84 ("Business Establishments").

Public employment: Sexual orientation included for all employers and all employees under Art. 12, Sec. 49.72 ("Employment"), and Art. 5.8, Sec. 45.82 ("Employment").

Union practices: Sexual orientation included under Art. 12, Sec. 49.72 (4) ("Labor Organizations"), and Art. 5.8, Sec. 45.82 ("Employment").

Los Angeles County

Civil rights laws: Sexual orientation included under Los Angeles County Code: Chap. 2.78, which created the "Commission on Human Relations" to eradicate discrimination; Chap. 13.70 ("Prohibited Discriminatory Practices"); and, Chap. 2.150 ("Persons with AIDS or AIDS-Related Conditions," Amd. Ord. 89–0015, 1989).

Domestic partnership employment benefits: Hard benefits provided to opposite- and same-sex couples and include dental (1995) and medical (January 1, 1996) benefits (Minutes of the Board of Supervisors, 12/19/95).

Domestic partnership registry: Applies to opposite- and same-sex couples. See Title 2 ("Administration"), and Chap. 2.210 ("Domestic Partnership Registry," Amd. Ord. No. 99–0021, 4/6/99).

Education: Sexual orientation included under Sec. 13.70.060 ("Educational institutions").

Housing: Sexual orientation included under Sec. 13.70.040 ("Housing and other real estate transactions").

Private employment: Protections apply only to AIDS (Sec. 13.70.030, "Employment practices").

Public accommodation: Sexual orientation included under Sec. 13.70.050 ("Business establishments").

Union practices: Protections apply only to AIDS (Sec. 13.70.030 (D), "Employment practices").

Marin County

Civil rights laws: Sexual orientation included under Marin County Code.

Domestic partnership employment benefits: Hard benefits provided to opposite- and same-sex couples and include bereavement and sick leave, medical insurance, and pension (Amd. Ord. No. 3140).

Domestic partnership registry: Applies to opposite- and same-sex couples and helps facilitate hospital visitation.

Public employment: Sexual orientation included under Chap. 2.42.020.

Oakland

Civil rights laws: Sexual orientation included under Oakland Municipal Code: Chap. 3 (Amd. Ord. No. 10427, 1/10/84).

Credit: Applied to the financing of real estate transactions only. Sec. 2 (a)(2) ("Real Estate").

Domestic partnership employment benefits: Hard benefits provided to opposite- and same-sex couples and include family sick leave, and dental, vision, and medical insurance. See Admin. Instruction 559, Res. 74174, 73024, 72751 and 72752.

Domestic partnership registry: Applies to opposite- and same-sex couples and helps facilitate hospital and jail visitations. Under certain conditions, domestic partnerships are exempt from Real Estate Transfer Tax.

Housing: Sexual orientation included under Sec. 2 (a)(2) ("Real Estate").

Private employment: Sexual orientation included under Sec. 2(a)(1) ("Employment).

Public accommodation: Sexual orientation included under Sec. 2(a)(3) ("Business Establishments"), (4) ("City Services and Facilities"), and (5) ("City Supported Services and Facilities").

Public employment: All employees and employers covered under Sec. 2(a)(1) ("Employment).

Union practices: Sexual orientation included under Sec. 2(a)(1) ("Employment).

Pasadena

Civil rights laws: Sexual orientation included under City Manual of Personnel Rules, Practices and Procedures, 8/15/92.

Public employment: Sexual orientation included under Sec. 505.

Sacramento

Civil rights laws: Sexual orientation included under Sacramento City Code: Chap. 14.01 ("Discrimination—Sexual Orientation," Amd. Ord. No. 86–042, 4/1/86); and city contractors and some private employers required to provide equivalent "unpaid related person leave" to domestic partner (Chap. 82, "Domestic Partners," Sec.82.07, Amd. Ord. No. 92–062, 11/5/92).

Credit: Sexual orientation included under Sec. 14.01.102 (2) ("Business Establishments").

Domestic partnership employment benefits: Hard benefits provided to opposite- and same-sex couples and include family care leave as specified by "Personnel Policy Instruction."

Domestic partnership registry: Applied to opposite- and same-sex couples and helps facilitate hospital visits, along with housing protection as family members (Chap. 82, Amd. Ord. No. 92–062, 11/5/92).

Education: Sexual orientation included under Sec. 14.01.105 ("Educational Institutions").

Housing: Sexual orientation included under Sec. 14.01.103 ("Real Estate Transactions").

Private employment: Sexual orientation included under Sec. 14.01.101 ("Employment").

Public accommodation: Sexual orientation included under Sec. 14.01.102 ("Business Establishments").

Public employment: All employees and employers covered under Sec. 14.01.101 ("Employment").

Union practices: Sexual orientation included under Sec. 14.01.101 (3) ("Employment").

San Diego

Civil rights laws: Sexual orientation included under San Diego Municipal Code: Chap. 5 ("Public Safety, Morals and Welfare"), and Div. 96 ("Discrimination Based on Sexual Orientation," Amd. Ord. No. 0–17453 N.S., 4/16/90).

Credit: Sexual orientation included under Sec. 52.9605 (A)(2) ("Business Establishments—Credit").

Domestic partnership employment benefits: Hard benefits provided to opposite- and same-sex couples. Health insurance can be purchased at reduced "domestic partnership" rate.

Education: Sexual orientation included under Sec. 52.9607 ("Educational Institutions").

Housing: Sexual orientation included under Sec. 52.9604 ("Housing and Other Real Estate Transactions").

Private employment: Sexual orientation included under Sec. 52.9603 ("Employment").

Public accommodation: Sexual orientation included under Sec. 52.9605 ("Business Establishments"), and limited to services provided by the city (Sec. 52.9606, "City Facilities and Services").

Union practices: Sexual orientation included under Sec. 52.9603 (A)(4) ("Employment—Labor Organizations").

San Francisco

Civil rights laws: Sexual orientation included under San Francisco Police Code (Amd. 1978) and Administrative Code, Chap. 12B and 12C ("Equal Benefits Ordinance") that requires benefits for domestic partners equal to spouses of those employees providing services to the city (Amd. 11/4/96,

Eff. 6/1/97). Gender identity was included (Amd. Ord. No. 433–94, 12/6/94).

Credit: Sexual orientation applies to the financing of real estate transactions only. San Francisco Police Code Art. 33 ("Prohibiting Discrimination Based on . . . Sexual Orientation, Gender Identity"), Sec. 3304 (3) ("Housing").

Domestic partnership employment benefits: Hard benefits provided, including health and dental coverage and retirement and survivorship.

Domestic partnership registry: Registry provided for both opposite- and same-sex couples. In 1999, federal court in *Air Transport Association of America v. City and County of San Francisco* decided that cities could enforce regulations prohibiting discrimination with regard to the provision of hard employment benefits (such as health care and pension benefits) against those companies doing business with the city, unless the city was acting as a "regulator" (as it was in regard to the airline industry because it had control over the use of airports). In those situations, cities could not force hard benefits upon service providers. However, cities could still enforce equivalent soft benefits.

Education: Sexual orientation included under San Francisco Administrative Code Chap. 12A ("Human Rights Commission"), Sec. 12A.2 ("Declaration of Policy," Amd. 1978), and see Board of Education Policy No. P5163, San Francisco Unified School District Board of Education, Res. No. 512–10Sp2, 1/14/96.

Housing: Sexual orientation included under San Francisco Police Code Art. 33 ("Prohibiting Discrimination Based on . . . Sexual Orientation, Gender Identity . . ."), Sec. 3304 ("Housing").

Private employment: Sexual orientation included under San Francisco Police Code Art. 33 ("Prohibiting Discrimination Based on . . . Sexual Orientation, Gender Identity . . ."), Sec. 3303 ("Employment"), and "Equal Benefits Ordinance."

Public accommodation: Sexual orientation included under San Francisco Police Code Art. 33 ("Prohibiting Discrimination Based on . . . Sexual Orientation, Gender Identity . . ."), Sec. 3305 ("Business Establishments and Public Accommodations").

Public employment: All employees and employers covered. See San Francisco Police Code Art. 33 ("Prohibiting Discrimination Based on . . . Sexual Orientation, Gender Identity . . ."), Sec. 3303 ("Employment").

Union practices: Sexual orientation included under San Francisco Police Code Art. 33 ("Prohibiting Discrimination Based on . . . sexual Orientation, Gender Identity . . ."), Sec. 3303 (3) ("Employment").

San Jose

Civil rights laws: Sexual orientation included under Chap. 4.08 ("Nondiscrimination Requirements for Contracts," Amd. Ord. No. 25207, 11/21/96), "Human Rights Commission" general mandate Chap. 2.08 ("Board Bureaus and Com."), Sec. 2.08.3030 (Amd. Ord. No. 23383, 2/20/90).

Private employment: Applied only to private contractors with the city: Sec. 4.08.070 ("Nondiscrimination Requirements for Contracts"), and Sec. 10.48.030 ("Employment"). Also, discrimination based on AIDS in private employment, public employment, public accommodations, union practices, education, and credit was prohibited pursuant to Chap. 10.48 ("Prohibition against Discrimination on AIDS," Amd. Ord. No. 22878, 8/2/88).

Public employment: Sexual orientation included under Affirmative Action Guidelines, Res. No. 58076, 2/5/85.

San Mateo County

Civil rights laws: Sexual orientation included under Affirmative Action Plan, 12/31/92.

Domestic partnership employment benefits: Hard benefits include dental, medical, and vision care insurance, employee assistance program, and bereavement leave (7/1/90).

Public employment: All government employees expressly covered. See Sec. III-A.

Santa Barbara, City of

Civil rights laws: Sexual orientation included under Res. No. 93–134, 11/9/93.

Domestic partnership employment benefits: Hard benefits.

Santa Barbara County

Civil rights laws: Sexual orientation included under County Code of Santa Barbara. Res. No. 82–536 ("Resolution Regarding Discrimination-Free Workplace Policy to the Affirmative Action Program of the County of Santa Barbara," Amd. 10/11/82).

Domestic partnership registry: Registry for both opposite- and same-sex couples. See Chap. 42 ("Domestic Partnership Registration," Amd. Ord. No. 4361, 6/8/99).

Santa Clara County

Civil rights laws: Sexual orientation included under Santa Clara County Board of Supervisors, Policy on Sexual Harassment, 8/20/91 and Equal Opportunity Policy, 12/12/95.

Domestic partnership employment benefits: Although a law was passed, it was repealed 2/24/98 under threat of ballot initiative.

Private employment: Private employer contracts with the city apply.

Public accommodation: Services provided by city only apply.

Public employment: All government employees expressly covered.

Santa Monica

Civil rights laws: Sexual orientation included under Santa Monica Municipal Code: Chap. 9 ("Discrimination on the Basis of Sexual Orientation," Amd. Ord. No. 1317 (CCS), 10/9/84); and Chap. 4.40 ("Discrimination on the Basis of Sexual Orientation or Domestic Partnership," Amd. Ord. No. 1812 (CCS), 9/12/95).

Credit: Sexual orientation included under Chap. 9, Sec. 4904 (a) (2) ("Credit").

Domestic partnership employment benefits: Hard benefits provided to opposite- and same-sex couples and include bereavement and sick leave, and medical support.

Domestic partnership registry: Sexual orientation included under Chap. 4.60 ("Domestic Partnership Registry," Amd. Ord. No. 1821CCS, 10/17/95), and "housing" below.

Education: Sexual orientation included under Chap. 9, Sec. 4906 ("Educational Institutions").

Housing: Sexual orientation included under Chap. 9, Sec. 4903 ("Housing and other real estate transactions"), and Chap. 4.40, Sec. 4.40.040 ("Housing and other real estate transactions").

Private employment: Sexual orientation included under Chap. 9, Sec. 4902 ("Employment").

Public accommodation: Sexual orientation included under Chap. 9, Sec. 4904 ("Business Establishments").

Public Employment: All employees and employers covered. Chap. 9, Sec. 4902 ("Employment").

Union practices: Sexual orientation included under Chap. 9, Sec. 4902 (a) (4) ("Labor Organizations").

West Hollywood

Civil rights laws: Sexual orientation included under West Hollywood Municipal Code: Art. IV ("Public Peace"), Chap. II ("Prohibition on Discrimination"), Part A ("Sexual Orientation and Gender Identity," Amd. Ord. No. 7, November 30, 1984). Gender identity was included (Amd. Ord. No. 98–520, 7/20/98).

Credit: Applied to financing of real estate transactions. Sec. 4202 ("Housing—Prohibited Activity").

Domestic partnership employment benefits: Hard benefits that include sick and bereavement leave, and medical insurance.

Domestic partnership registry: Registry applied to both opposite- and same-sex couples and helps facilitate visits to jails and hospitals.

Housing: Sexual orientation included under Sec. 4202 ("Housing—Prohibited Activity").

Private employment: Private employers who have contracts with the city covered. See Sec. 4204 ("Contractors and Subcontractors for City Public Works, Goods and Services").

Public accommodation: Sexual orientation included under Sec. 4203 ("Public Accommodations—Prohibited Activity").

Union practices: Law applies only to labor organizations that are associated with private employers who have contracts with the city. See Sec. 4204 ("Contractors and Subcontractors for City Public Works, Goods and Services").

COLORADO

Antimarriage legislation: "Marriage Is Between One Man and One Woman" bill passed and signed into law by Governor Bill Owens in June, 2000.

Civil rights laws: Sexual orientation included under Executive Order 90–13–98 (1990) protecting "state employees." However, it expired 1/99.

Hate crimes: Sexual orientation is not included in hate crime statutes.

Sex statutes (sodomy): Repealed in 1972.

Arvada

Civil rights laws: Sexual orientation included under Arvada City Code, Chap. 9.

Private employment: Sexual orientation applies to those who operate community television stations only (Sec. 9–140).

Public accommodation: Sexual orientation is protected with regards to the rates charged by those who operate community television stations (Sec. 9–140).

Boulder, City of

Civil rights laws: Sexual orientation included under Boulder City Code: Title 12, Chap. 1 ("Prohibition of Discrimination in Housing, Employment, and Public Accommodations"), Chap. 2 ("Landlord-Tenant Relations"), and Chap. 3 ("Drug Testing," Amd. Ord. No. 5061, 1987).

Credit: Sexual orientation applies to the financing of real estate transactions only. Sec. 12–1–2 ("Discrimination in Housing Prohibited").

Domestic partnership employment benefits: Hard benefits provided.

Domestic partnership registry: Registry opened to opposite- and same-sex couples.

Housing: Sexual orientation included under Sec. 12–1–2 ("Discrimination in Housing Prohibited").

Private employment: Sexual orientation included under Sec. 12–1–3 ("Discrimination in Employment Practices Prohibited").

Public accommodation: Sexual orientation included under Sec. 12–1–4 ("Discrimination in Public Accommodations Prohibited").

Public employment: All government employers expressly covered: Sec. 12–1–3 ("Discrimination in Employment Practices Prohibited").

Union practices: Sexual orientation included under Sec. 12–1–3 (a) (3) ("Discrimination in Employment Practices Prohibited").

Boulder County

Civil rights laws: Sexual orientation included under Boulder County Policy Manual, adopted by the Board of County Commissioners, 10/92.

Public employment: All government employers expressly covered. See Boulder County, Colorado Personnel Manual, Chap. I ("Statement of General Policy"), definition of "Harassment and/or Discrimination."

Denver

Civil rights laws: Sexual orientation included under Municipal Code, City and County of Denver. See Chap. 28 ("Human Rights"), Art. IV ("Prohibition of Discrimination in Employment, Housing and Commercial Space, Public Accommodations, Educational Institutions and Health and Welfare Services," Amd. Ord. No. 623, 10/15/90).

Credit: Sexual orientation applied to the financing of real estate transactions only. Sec. 28–95 (a)(3) ("Discriminatory practices in real estate transactions").

Domestic partnership employment benefits: Hard benefits provided for same-sex couples only. Benefits included health, dental, and vision care (Chap. 18, Art. VIII, Div. 1, Sec. 18–321).

Domestic partnership registry: Registry opened to opposite- and same-sex couples. No rights specified.

Education: Sexual orientation included under Sec. 28–94 ("Discriminatory practices in educational institutions").

Housing: Sexual orientation included under Sec. 28–95 ("Discriminatory practices in real estate transactions").

Private employment: Sexual orientation included under Sec. 28–93 ("Discriminatory practices in employment").

Public accommodation: Sexual orientation included under Sec. 28–96 ("Discriminatory practices in places of public accommodation").

Public employment: No explicit prohibition, however, Chap. 12, Art. II ("Agency for Human Rights and Community Relations"), Sec. 28–17 ("Powers and duties") includes "sexual orientation" during city discrimination investigations.

Union practices: Sexual orientation included under Sec. 28–93 (a) (3) ("By a labor organization") and (4).

CONNECTICUT

Civil rights laws: Sexual orientation included under Connecticut General

Statutes Annotated: Title 46a ("Human Rights"), Chap. 814c ("Human Rights and Opportunities"); and, Title 10 ("Education and Culture"), Chap. 164 ("Educational Opportunities," Amd. Act 1991, P.A. 91–58).

Credit: Sexual orientation included under Sec. 46a–81f ("Sexual orientation discrimination: Credit practices").

Education: Sexual orientation included under Sec. 10–15c ("Discrimination in public schools prohibited").

Hate crimes: Sexual orientation included under Conn. Gen. Stat. Ann. Sec. 53a–181b. Separate crime and penalty established that allows for enhancement for habitual offenders.

Housing: Sexual orientation included under Sec. 46a–81e ("Sexual orientation discrimination: Housing").

Private employment: Sexual orientation included under Sec. 46a–60 ("Discriminatory employment practices prohibited") and Sec. 46a–81c ("Sexual orientation discrimination: Employment").

Public accommodation: Sexual orientation included under Sec. 46a–81d ("Sexual orientation discrimination: Public accommodations").

Public employment: All government employers expressly covered: Sec. 46a–60 ("Discriminatory employment practices prohibited"), 46a–81c ("Sexual orientation discrimination: Employment"), and Sec. 46a–81h ("Sexual orientation discrimination: Equal employment in state agencies").

Sex statutes (sodomy): Repealed in 1971.

Union practices: Sexual orientation included under Sec. 46a–60 ("Discriminatory employment practices prohibited") and Sec. 46a–81c ("Sexual orientation discrimination: Employment").

Hartford

Civil rights laws: Sexual orientation included under Hartford Municipal Code: Chap. 2, Art. V, Div. 9(B), Sec. 2–286, which established the "Commission on Lesbian, Gay and Bisexual Issues" (Amd. 1977).

Domestic partnership employment benefits: Hard benefits provided for couples through the inclusive definition of "domestic partnership" found in Part II, Chap. 2, Art. III, Sec. 2–63 ("Domestic partnerships; discrimination").

Domestic partnership registry: Registry open to opposite- and same-sex couples. Not limited to residents and no rights specified.

Housing: Sexual orientation included with those who contract with the city (Part II, Chap. 2, Art. VII, Div. 3, "Purchases and Contracts," Sec. 2–558).

Private employment: Sexual orientation included under Chap. 2, Art. V., Div. 9 ("Com. on Workplace Rights"), Sec. 2–290. This section required the study of sexual orientation discrimination. Sexual orientation applies to city contractors (Chap. 2, Art. VII, Div. 3, "Purchases and Contracts," Sec. 2–558).

Public employment: All government employers expressly covered under Chap. 2, Art. VII, Div. 3 ("Purchases and Contracts"), Sec. 2–558.

New Haven

Civil rights laws: Sexual orientation included under New Haven City Code: Chap. 12 1/2, Art. I- V. (Amd. Ord. 1051, amending Sec. 12 1/2–2 ("Findings") to state: "It is further against the public policy of the City . . . to deny equal opportunities on the basis of sexual orientation." Not all sections were changed to include sexual orientation, and, as such, the scope of protection is unclear.

Public employment: All government employers expressly covered. See above.

Stamford

Civil rights laws: Sexual orientation included under Stamford Charter and City Code: Chap. 47 ("Personnel"), Art. VIII ("Discrimination," Amd. Ord. No. 882/91).

Public employment: Sexual orientation included under Sec. 47–23.

DELAWARE

Antimarriage legislation: Del. Code Ann. tit. 13, Sec. 13–101 prohibited and voided same-sex marriage. This legislation also established penalties for those who enter into prohibited marriages.

Domestic partnership employment benefits: Soft benefits provided to opposite- and same-sex couples. Benefits include sick and bereavement leave (Merit Rules, Chap. 1–4, Sec. 6.0460).

Hate crimes: Separate crimes and penalty established due to aggravating factor (Del. Code Ann. Tit. 11, Sec. 1304).

Sex statutes (sodomy): Repealed in 1973.

DISTRICT OF COLUMBIA

Civil rights laws: Sexual orientation included under District of Columbia Code: Title 1 ("Administration"), Chap. 25 ("Human Rights"), Subchapter II ("Prohibited Acts of Discrimination," Amd. 1977).

Credit: Sexual orientation applied to the financing of real estate transactions only: Part C ("Housing and Commercial Space"), Sec. 1–2515 (a) (3) ("Unlawful Discriminatory Practices in Real Estate Transactions").

Domestic partnership employment benefits: The U.S. Congress blocked the implementation of the benefit provisions passed by the City Council by denying funds for that purpose.

Domestic partnership registry: Because no funds were allocated to set up a registry (see above), lesbian and gay couples have resorted to sending in paperwork using registered mail—the receipt becoming proof of registration.

Education: Sexual orientation included under Part E ("Educational Institutions"), Sec. 1–2520 ("Unlawful Discriminatory Practices in Educational Institutions").

Hate crimes: Separate crime and penalty established besides being used as an aggravating factor in sentencing first-degree murder. Crime based on actual or perceived sexual orientation and data is collected (District of Columbia Code, Sec. 22–4001).

Housing: Sexual orientation included under Part C ("Housing and Commercial Space"), Sec. 1–2515 ("Unlawful Discriminatory Practices in Real Estate Transactions").

Private employment: Sexual orientation included under Part B ("Employment"), Sec. 1–2512 ("Unlawful Discriminatory Practices in Employment").

Public accommodation: Sexual orientation included under Part D ("Public Accommodations"), Sec. 1–2519 ("Unlawful Discriminatory Practices in Public Accommodations").

Public employment: All government employers expressly covered: Part B ("Employment"), Sec. 1–2512 ("Unlawful Discriminatory Practices in Employment").

Sex statutes (sodomy): Repealed in 1992.

Union practices: Sexual orientation included under Part B ("Employment"), Sec. 1–2512 (a)(3) ("By a labor organization") and (4) ("By an employer, employment agency, or labor organization").

FLORIDA

Antimarriage legislation: Defined marriage between opposite-sex couples and prohibited same-sex marriage (Fla. Stat. Sec. 741.212).

Hate crimes: Sexual orientation of victim used as aggravating factor in sentencing with mandatory sentences enhanced. Data is also collected (Fla. Stat. Sec. 775.085).

Sex statutes (sodomy): Criminalized private and consensual sexual behaviors engaged in by opposite- and same-sex people. "Whoever commits any unnatural and lascivious act with another person." Imprisonment not exceeding sixty days. Fines not to exceed $500. Unnatural and Lascivious Act, Fla. Stat. Sec. 800.02.

Broward County

Civil rights laws: Sexual orientation included under Broward County Code of Ordinances: Chap. 16 1/2 ("Human Rights Act," Amd. Ord. 95–26, 6/13/95, Eff. 6/27/95).

Domestic partnership employment benefits: Hard benefits provided to opposite- and same-sex couples. These include insurance, and sick, annual, family illness, and bereavement leave (Chap. 16 1/2, Art. VI, "Domestic Partnership Act," Amd. Ord. No. 1999–18, 4/27/99).

Domestic partnership registry: Registry open to opposite- and same-sex couples. Helps facilitate visits to hospitals and jails and designation of health care surrogates (Chap. 16 1/2, Art. VI, "Domestic Partnership Act," Amd. Ord. No. 1999–18, 4/27/99). A preference (in the amount of 1 percent) was to be given to county contractors who extended equivalent benefits to same-sex partners of employees as it did to spouses (Chap. 16 1/2, Art. VI. Sec. 16 1/2–157. Ord. No. 1999–18).

Private employment: Sexual orientation included under Art. I, Sec. 16 1/2–21 ("Discrimination in Employment").

Public accommodation: Sexual orientation included under Art. II, Sec. 16 1/2–22 ("Discrimination in public accommodations").

Public employment: Sexual orientation included under Art. I, Sec. 16 1/2–21 ("Discrimination in Employment").

Union practices: Sexual orientation included under Art. I, Sec. 16 1/2–21 ("Discrimination in Employment").

Coral Springs

Civil rights laws: Sexual orientation included under Coral Springs City Code.

Public accommodation: The provision of cable television services apply (Chap. 20, Article I, Sec. 20–4).

Gainesville

Civil rights laws: Sexual orientation included under Gainesville Code of Ordinances: Chap. 8 ("Discrimination," Amd. 7/98).

Credit: Prohibition of sexual orientation discrimination applies to the financing of real estate transactions only. Art. V, Sec. 8–91 ("Prohibition of discrimination in financing of housing or in residential real estate transactions").

Housing: Sexual orientation included under Art. V, Sec. 8–88 ("Prohibition of discrimination in the sale or rental of housing").

Private employment: Sexual orientation included under Art. III, Sec. 8–48 ("Prohibition of discrimination in employment practices").

Public accommodation: Sexual orientation included under Art. IV, Sec. 8–67 ("Prohibition of discrimination in places of public accommodation; equal access.").

Public employment: Sexual orientation included under Art. III, Sec. 8–48 ("Prohibition of discrimination in employment practices").

Union practices: Sexual orientation included under Art. III, Sec. 8–48 ("Prohibition of discrimination in employment practices").

Miami Beach

Civil rights laws: Sexual orientation included under Miami Beach City Code: Chap. 25A ("City of Miami Beach Human Rights Ordinance," Amd. Ord. No. 92–2824, 3/1/93).

Credit: Sexual orientation applies to the financing of real estate transactions only. Sec. 25A-7 (5) and (7) ("Discrimination in Housing").

Domestic Partnership employment benefits: Soft benefits provided to opposite- and same-sex couples. Benefits include sick leave, family medical insurance, and annual and bereavement leave (Ord. Nos. 98–3125, 98–3126, and 98–3127).

Housing: Sexual orientation included under Sec. 25A-7 ("Discrimination in Housing").

Private employment: Sexual orientation included under Sec. 25A-5 ("Discrimination in Employment").

Public accommodation: Sexual orientation included under Sec. 25A-6 ("Discrimination in Public Accommodations").

Public employment: All government employers expressly covered (25A-5 "Discrimination in Employment").

Union practices: Sexual orientation included under Sec. 25A-5 ("Discrimination in Employment") and Sec. 25A-3 ("Definition" of "person" as including "unions").

Miami-Dade County

Civil rights laws: Sexual orientation included under Code of Metropolitan Miami-Dade County: Chap. 11-A ("Discrimination," Amd. Ord. No. 98–170, 12/1/98).

Credit: Sexual orientation applies to the financing of real estate transactions only. Art. II ("Housing"), Sec. 11A-12 (e) and (f) ("Unlawful housing practices").

Housing: Sexual orientation included under Art. II ("Housing"), Sec. 11A-12 ("Unlawful housing practices").

Private employment: Sexual orientation included under Art. IV ("Employment"), Sec. 11A-26 ("Unlawful employment practices").

Public accommodation: Sexual orientation included under Art. III (Public Accommodations"), Sec. 11A-19 ("Unlawful public accommodations practices").

Public employment: All government employers expressly covered: Art. VI ("Office of Fair Employment Practices"), Sec. 11A-34 ("Declaration of policy").

Union practices: Sexual orientation included under Art. IV ("Employment"), Sec. 11A-26 (3) ("Unlawful employment practices").

Monroe County

Civil rights laws: Sexual orientation included under Monroe County

Code: Art. VI ("Discrimination"), Div. 2 ("Fair Housing," Amd. Ord. No. 22–1986).

Credit: Sexual orientation applies to the financing of real estate transactions only. Sec. 13–115 (9) ("Unlawful practices").

Domestic partnership employment benefits: Hard benefits provided to opposite- and same-sex couples. All employment benefits offered to spouses (Monroe County Policies and Procedures Manual, Sec. 14, Amd. Res. No. 081–1998, 2/11/98).

Housing: Sexual orientation included under Sec. 13–115 ("Unlawful practices").

Okaloosa County

Civil rights laws: Sexual orientation included under Okaloosa County Code.

Housing: Sexual orientation applies to loan application process for low-income housing assistance program. Chap. 11.5 ("Housing"), Art. III ("Affordable Housing"), Sec. 11.5–59 ("SHIP program administration and implementation").

Palm Beach County

Civil rights laws: Sexual orientation included under Palm Beach County Code: Chap. 15 ("Human Rights"), Art. III ("Housing, Places of Public Accommodation," Amd. Ord. No. 90–1, 1/16/90).

Credit: Sexual orientation applies to the financing of real estate transactions only. Sec. 15–59 ("Discrimination in the financing of housing").

Housing: Sexual orientation included under Sec. 15–58 ("Discriminatory housing practices"), and Chap. 14 ("Housing Code") Art. V, Sec. 14–247 ("Local Housing Assistance Program").

Public accommodation: Sexual orientation included under Sec. 15–57 ("Unlawful discriminatory practices in public accommodations"), and to the operation of television cable service: Chap. 8 ("Cable Television") Sec. 8.15.

Santa Rosa County

Civil rights laws: Sexual orientation included under County Code of Santa Rosa: Chap. 2 ("Administration"), Art. IV ("Boards, Commissions, Authorities, Etc."), Div. 5 ("Affordable Housing").

Housing: Applicable to the loan application process for local low-income housing program. Sec. 2–139 ("SHIP program administration and implementation").

Tampa

Civil rights laws: Sexual orientation included under City Code of Tampa: Chap. 12 (Amd. Ord. 92–147, 9/10/92).

Housing: Sexual orientation included under Art. IV ("Discrimination in Housing").

Private employment: Sexual orientation included under Art. II ("Employment Discrimination").

Public accommodation: Sexual orientation included under Art. III ("Discrimination in Public Accommodations").

Public employment: Sexual orientation included under Art. II ("Employment Discrimination").

Union practices: Sexual orientation included under Art. II ("Employment Discrimination").

GEORGIA

Antimarriage legislation: Prohibits the performance or recognition of same-sex marriages. It invalidates same-sex marriages and declares them to be against public policy. Ga. Code Ann. Sec. 19–3–3.1 and 19–3–30.

Sex statutes (sodomy): Invalidated by *Powell v. Georgia,* 510 S.E.2d 18 (Ga. 1998).

Atlanta

Civil rights laws: Sexual orientation included under Atlanta Code: Chap. 94 ("Human Relations"), Art. III ("Discrimination Generally"), and Chap. 114 (Amd. 3/3/86).

Domestic partnership employment benefits: Hard benefits provided to opposite- and same-sex couples. Benefits include sick, funeral, and annual leave, and health and dental insurance (Eff. 1/1/97). See Atlanta Code, Sec. 2–858 (Amd. Ord. 96–0–1018, 9/96).

Domestic partnership registry: Registry opened to opposite- and same-sex couples and helps facilitate visits to jails and prisons. Chap. 94 ("Human Relations"), Art. V ("Domestic Partnerships").

Hate crimes: Police are to collect data on bias-motivated crimes, including those based on sexual orientation (Chap. 98, Article II, Sec. 98–39).

Public accommodation: Sexual orientation included under Sec. 94–68 ("Unlawful Discrimination").

Public employment: Sexual orientation included under Sec. 114–51.

De Kalb County

Civil rights laws: Sexual orientation included under De Kalb Code, 1976 (Amd. Ord. No. 91–03, 2/26/91).

Public employment: Complaints may be filed with the chief executive claiming sexual orientation discrimination during application for employment with the county (Sec. 2–3073).

Fulton County

Civil rights laws: Sexual orientation included under Equal Employment Opportunity Policy, 8/19/92.

Public employment: Sexual orientation specifically denied under 92-RC-390.

HAWAII

Antimarriage constitutional amendment: Voters of Hawaii passed a constitutional amendment that permitted the legislature to limit marriage to opposite-sex couples, but did not require them to do so (Hawaii State Constitution, Art. 1, Sec. 23).

Civil rights laws: Sexual orientation included under Hawaii Revised Statutes: Chap. 378 ("Employment Practices," Amd. 3/21/91).

Domestic partnership employment benefits: Hard benefits provided to same-sex couples only. Gay and lesbian families are recognized through Reciprocal Beneficiaries Law, House Bill 118 that afforded same-sex couples a broad package of rights and benefits (7/97).

Hate crimes: No such law based on any characteristic.

Private employment: Sexual orientation included under Sec. 378–2 ("Discriminatory practices made unlawful; offenses defined").

Public employment: Sexual orientation included under Sec. 378–2 ("Discriminatory practices made unlawful; offenses defined").

Sex statutes (sodomy): Repealed in 1973.

Union practices: Sexual orientation included under Sec. 378–2 ("Discriminatory practices made unlawful; offenses defined").

Honolulu

Civil rights laws: Sexual orientation included under City and County Code of Honolulu.

IDAHO

Antimarriage legislation: Voids same-sex marriages and declares them to be against public policy (Idaho Code Sec. 32–209).

Hate crimes: Sexual orientation is not included in hate crime statutes.

Sex statutes (sodomy): Criminalizes private and consensual sexual behaviors engaged in by opposite- and same-sex people. "Crime Against Nature." Imprisonment five years to life (Idaho Code Sec. 18–6605).

ILLINOIS

Antimarriage legislation: Prohibits and voids same-sex marriages. Declares same-sex marriages to be against public policy (750 Ill. Comp. Stat. 5/212).

Civil rights laws: Sexual orientation included under Administrative

Order No. 2 ("Directive to all Directors and Agency Heads Regarding Prohibition of Discrimination"), 1996. The Illinois Department of Human Rights must also track discrimination complaints based on sexual orientation.

Hate crimes: Separate crime and penalty established for bias crime committed on actual or perceived sexual orientation of victim. Data collection required (720 Ill. Comp. Stat. 5/12–7.1).

Public employment: All government employers expressly covered (Administrative Order No. 2) clarifying that Ill. Code, Sec. 302.790 ("Personnel Rules, Prohibition of Discrimination") includes "sexual orientation").

Sex statutes (sodomy): Repealed in 1962.

Chicago

Civil rights laws: Sexual orientation included under Chicago City Code: Chicago Human Rights Ordinance and Chicago Fair Housing Ordinance (Amd. 1988).

Credit: Sexual orientation included under Sec. 2–160–060 (Unlawful discriminatory practices—Credit transactions).

Domestic partnership employment benefits: Hard benefits provided to same-sex couples. However, attempts have been made to block this extension of health and other benefits to the same-sex domestic partners of municipal employees.

Housing: Sexual orientation included under Sec. 5–08–010 ("Declaration of city policy").

Private employment: Sexual orientation included under Sec. 2–160–030 ("Unlawful discriminatory practices—Employment").

Public accommodation: Sexual orientation included under Sec. 2–160–070 ("Unlawful discriminatory practices—Public accommodations").

Public employment: All employers and employees covered. Sec. 2–160–030 ("Unlawful discriminatory practices—Employment").

Cook County

Civil rights laws: Sexual orientation included under "Cook County Human Rights Ordinance" (Amd. Ord. No. 93–0–13, 3/16/93).

Credit: Sexual orientation included under Part IV ("Credit Transactions").

Domestic partnership employment benefits: Hard benefits provided to same-sex couples only. Benefits include medical, vision, and dental insurance, and leave ("Cook County Employee Domestic Partnership Benefits Resolution," 4/6/99).

Housing: Sexual orientation included under Part VI ("Housing").

Private employment: Sexual orientation included under Part III ("Employment").

Public accommodation: Sexual orientation included under Part V ("Public Accommodations"). Also, applicable to services provided by the county. Part VII ("County Facilities, Services, and Programs").

Public employment: Unknown and untested.

Union practices: Sexual orientation included under Part III (B) (3) ("Labor Organizations").

INDIANA

Antimarriage legislation: Defined marriage as opposite-sex only and voided same-sex marriages (Ind. Code Sec. 31–11–1–1).

Hate crimes: No statutes based on any characteristics.

Sex statutes (sodomy): Repealed in 1977.

Indianapolis

Civil rights laws: Sexual orientation included under Indianapolis City Code, Title 1, Chap. 251, Art. I., Div. 3, Sec. 251–131 ("Citizens police complaint office"). These sections provide an open complaints process without regard to "sexual orientation."

IOWA

Antimarriage legislation: Defined marriage as opposite-sex only and voided same-sex marriages (1998 Iowa Acts 1099 Amd. Iowa Code Sec. 595.2 and 595.20).

Civil rights laws: Sexual orientation included under Executive Order No. 7, 9/14/99. Gender identity also included under Executive Order No. 7, 9/14/99.

Hate crimes: Separate crime and penalty established for bias crime committed on actual or perceived sexual orientation of victim. Data collection required.

Public employment: All government employers expressly covered.

Sex statutes (sodomy): Repealed in 1978.

KANSAS

Antimarriage Legislation: Defined marriage as opposite-sex only, voided same-sex marriages, and declared that same-sex marriages are against public policy (Kan. Stat. Ann. Sec. 23–101 and 23–115).

Hate crimes: No statutes based on any characteristics.

Sex statutes (sodomy): Criminalizes private and consensual sexual behaviors engaged in by same-sex people only. "Sodomy is oral or anal copulation between persons who are not husband and wife or consenting adult members of the opposite sex, or between a person and an animal." Imprisonment not to exceed six months or a fine not exceeding $1,000 (Kan. Stat. Ann. Sec. 21–3505).

Topeka

Civil rights laws: Sexual orientation included under Topeka City Code.

Public accommodation: Sexual orientation applied to the provision of cable television services only. App. B ("Franchises"), Art. VI. ("TCI Cablevision of Kansas, Inc."), Exh. 1 ("City of Topeka Consumer Protection Policies and Standards"), Sec. 11.1 ("Non-discrimination").

Wichita

Hate crimes: Misdemeanor offense for bias-motivated crimes, including sexual orientation. Code of the City of Wichita, Chap. 5.01 ("Ethnic Intimidation or Bias Crimes," Amd. Ord. No. 41–937 and Ord. No. 41–204).

KENTUCKY

Antimarriage legislation: Voided same-sex marriages and declared them against public policy (Ky. Rev. Stat. Sec(s). 402.040 and 402.045).

Hate crimes: Aggravation by bias may be considered in probation and parole decisions (Ky. Rev. Stat. Sec. 532.031).

Sex statutes (sodomy): Invalidated by the Kentucky Supreme Court in *Commonwealth v. Wasson,* 842 S.W.2d 487 (Ky. 1992).

Jefferson County

Civil rights laws: Sexual orientation included under Jefferson County Code: Chap. 92. (Amd. Ord. No. 36, 10/12/99). Gender identity also included (Amd. Ord. No. 36, 10/12/99).

Credit: Sexual orientation applied to the financing of real estate transactions only. Sec. 92.03 (B) ("Unlawful Practices in Connection with Housing").

Housing: Sexual orientation included under Sec. 92.03 ("Unlawful Practices in Connection with Housing").

Private employment: Sexual orientation included under Sec. 92.06 ("Unlawful Practices in Connection with Employment").

Public accommodation: Sexual orientation included under Sec. 92.05 ("Unlawful Practices in Connection with Public Accommodations").

Public employment: All government employers expressly covered. Sec. 92.06 ("Unlawful Practices in Connection with Employment").

Union practices: Sexual orientation included under Sec. 92.06 ("Unlawful Practices in Connection with Employment").

Lexington-Fayette

Civil rights laws: Sexual orientation included under Lexington-Fayette Urban County Code: Sec. 2–33. (Amd. Ord. No. 202D, 7/8/99). Gender identity also included (Amd. Ord. No. 202D, 7/8/99).

Louisville

Civil rights laws: Sexual orientation included under City of Louisville Code of Ordinances: Chap. 98 (Amd. Ord. No. 9, 1/26/99). Gender identity also included (Amd. Ord. No. 9, 1/26/99).

Private employment: Sexual orientation included under Sec. 98.17 ("Unlawful Practices").

Public employment: All government employers expressly covered under Sec. 98.17 ("Unlawful Practices").

Union practices: Sexual orientation included under Sec. 98.17 ("Unlawful Practices").

LOUISIANA

Antimarriage legislation: Same-sex marriages have been prohibited since 1803. New legislation declared them to be against public policy and prohibited their recognition (La. Rev. Stat. Ann. Art(s). 89 and 3520).

Hate crimes: Separate crime and penalty established for bias crime committed on actual or perceived sexual orientation of victim. Data collection required. Enforcement discretionary (La. Rev. Stat. Ann. Sec. 14.107.2).

Sex statutes (sodomy): Criminalized private and consensual sexual behaviors engaged in by opposite-sex and same-sex people. "The unnatural carnal copulation between a human being with another person of the same or opposite sex or with an animal." Imprisonment for not more than five years and fine not to exceed $1,000. Crime Against Nature, La. Rev. Stat. Ann. Sec. 14.89.

New Orleans

Civil rights laws: Gender identity also included (Amd. Ord. 18794, 7/1/98).

Domestic partnership employment benefits: Hard benefits provided to same-sex couples only. Benefits include health insurance and family medical and bereavement leave. Rules of the Civil Service Commission, Rule I, Item 34 ("Definition" of "Immediate Family"), and Rule VIII, Sec. 10 ("Family Medical Leave"). Established by Mayoral Executive Order MHM 97–005, 5/17/97.

Domestic partnership registry: Registry for same-sex couples only (City Code, Chap. 86, Art. V).

Oachita Parish

Civil rights laws: Sexual orientation included under Oachita Parish Code: Chap. 1 ("Administration"), Art. II ("Personnel Policies"), Div. 1 ("Generally").

Public employment: Sexual orientation included under Sec. 1–49. "Sexual preference" included in sexual harassment policy.

MAINE

Antimarriage legislation: Voided same-sex marriages and prohibits the state from enforcing marriage statutes for the benefit of same-sex marriages. Me. Rev. Stat. Ann. tit. 19 Sec(s). 34 and 93; tit. 19-A Sec. 650 and Sec. 701(1-A) and Sec. 701(5).

Hate crimes: Separate crime and penalty established for bias crime committed on actual or perceived sexual orientation of victim. Data collection required (Me. Rev. Stat. Ann. tit. 17 Sec. 2931).

Sex statutes (sodomy): Repealed 1976.

MARYLAND

Civil rights laws: Sexual orientation included under Executive Order 01.01.1995.19 (Eff. 7/17/95).

Hate crimes: Only data collected on sexual orientation.

Public employment: All government employers expressly covered.

Sex statutes (sodomy): Criminalized private and consensual sexual behaviors engaged in by opposite-sex and same-sex people. "A person who performs or submits to any sexual act involving the placing of the sexual organs into his or her mouth." Fine not more than $1,000 or imprisonment for a period not exceeding ten years (or both). There is confusion as to whether or not these sex statutes were invalidated by *Williams v. Glendening*, 1998.

Baltimore

Civil rights laws: Sexual orientation included under Baltimore City Code: Art. 4 ("Community Relations," Amd. Ord. No. 79, 6/3/88).

Credit: Sexual orientation applied to the financing of real estate transactions only. Sec. 13A(3) ("Unlawful financing practices").

Domestic partnership employment benefits: Hard benefits provided for same-sex couples only. Benefits include health insurance, prescription drug and vision/optical coverage, bereavement and family leave (Administrative Policy Amendment A.M. 204–23, 203–2 and 204–8, adopted by Board of Estimates, City Government, 12/15/93).

Education: Sexual orientation included under Sec. 12 ("Same; educational institutions").

Housing: Sexual orientation included under Sec. 13A ("Unlawful housing practices; exceptions").

Private employment: Sexual orientation included under Sec. 10 ("Unlawful employment practices").

Public accommodation: Sexual orientation included under Sec. 11 ("Unlawful practices; place of public accommodation, etc."). Also, applicable to city health and welfare agencies. Sec. 13 ("Same; health and welfare agencies").

Public employment: All government employers expressly covered. Sec. 10 ("Unlawful employment practices").

Union practices: Sexual orientation included under Sec. 10 ("Unlawful employment practices").

Howard County

Civil rights laws: Sexual orientation included under Howard County Charter: Title 12 ("Health and Social Services"), Subtitle 2 ("Human Rights," Amd. Council Bill No. 2, 1983).

Credit: Sexual orientation included under Sec. 12.211 ("Unlawful financing practices").

Housing: Sexual orientation included under Sec. 12.207 ("Unlawful housing practices").

Private employment: Sexual orientation included under Sec. 12.208 ("Unlawful employment practices").

Public accommodation: Sexual orientation included under Sec. 12.210 ("Unlawful public accommodations practices").

Public employment: Sexual orientation included under Sec. 12.200 ("Equal Opportunity Employment Policy").

Union practices: Sexual orientation included under Sec. 12.208 ("Unlawful employment practices").

Montgomery County

Civil rights laws: Sexual orientation included under Montgomery County Code: Chap. 27 ("Human Relations and Civil Liberties," Amd. 9/14/84).

Credit: Sexual orientation applied to the financing of real estate transactions only. Div. 2, Sec. 27–12 (b) ("Unlawful practices").

Domestic partnership employment benefits: Hard benefits provided to same-sex couples only. Benefits include medical coverage.

Housing: Sexual orientation included under Div. 2 ("Discrimination in Real Estate").

Private employment: Sexual orientation included under Div. 3 ("Discrimination in Employment").

Public accommodation: Sexual orientation included under Div. 1 ("Discrimination in Places of Public Accommodation").

Public employment: All government employers expressly covered under Div. 3 ("Discrimination in Employment").

Union practices: Sexual orientation included under Div. 3, Sec. 27–19 (3) ("Unlawful employment practices. . . . For a labor organization").

Prince George's County

Civil rights laws: Sexual orientation included under Prince George's

County Code: Subtitle 2 ("Administration"), Div. 12 ("Human Relations Commission"), and "Procurement Regulations" (Amd. Bill No. CB-23–1991, 6/14/91).

Credit: Sexual orientation applied to the financing of real estate transactions only. Subdivision 5 ("Prohibited Acts in Housing and Residential Real Estate"), Sec. 2–211.01 ("Financing").

Education: Confusing statutes. See Subdivision 1(b) ("General Provisions").

Housing: Sexual orientation included under Subdivision 5 ("Prohibited Acts in Housing and Residential Real Estate"), and Subdivision 9 ("Prohibited Acts in Commercial Real Estate").

Private employment: Sexual orientation included under Subdivision 7 ("Prohibited Acts in Employment"). Also applied to private employers who have contracts with the city ("Procurement Regulations" Sec. 10A-122).

Public accommodation: Sexual orientation included under Subdivision 6 ("Prohibited Acts in Public Accommodations").

Public employment: All government employers expressly covered. See, Subdivision 7 ("Prohibited Acts in Employment").

Union practices: Sexual orientation included under Subdivision 7 ("Prohibited Acts in Employment"), and Sec. 2–224 ("Discrimination by labor unions prohibited").

MASSACHUSETTS

Civil rights laws: Sexual orientation included under Massachusetts General Laws Annotated: Chap. 151B ("Unlawful Discrimination Because of Race, Color . . . or Sex"), Chap. 272 ("Crimes Against Chastity . . . and Good Order," Amd. Stat. 1989, St.1989, c. 516), Chap. 76 ("School Attendance"), and Chap. 71 ("Public Schools/Charter Schools," Amd. Stat. 1993, St.1993, c. 282).

Credit: Sexual orientation included under Chap. 151B, Sec. 4 (14).

Domestic partnership employment benefits: Soft benefits limited to a small number of high-ranking gubernatorial appointees and include opposite- and same-sex couples. Benefits include sick and bereavement leave. Helps to facilitate visitation rights in state prisons and hospitals. Enacted through Executive Order.

Education: Sexual orientation included under Chap. 76, Sec. 5 ("Place of attendance; discrimination"). Regarding nonresident students, see Chap. 76, Sec. 12B (j). Charter schools covered by Chap. 71, Sec. 89 (f).

Hate crimes: Separate crime and penalty established for bias crime committed on actual or perceived sexual orientation of victim. Data collection required (Mass. Gen. Laws Ann. Sec. 265.39).

Housing: Sexual orientation included under Chap. 151B, Sec. 4 (6).

Private employment: Sexual orientation included under Chap. 151B, Sec. 4 (1).

Public accommodation: Sexual orientation included under Chap. 272, Sec. 98 ("Discrimination in admission to, or treatment in, place of public accommodation; punishment; forfeiture; civil right).

Public employment: All government employers expressly covered (Chap. 151B, Sec. 4 (1)).

Sex statutes (sodomy): Repealed 1999.

Union practices: Sexual orientation included under Chap. 151B, Sec. 4 (2).

Boston

Civil rights laws: Sexual orientation included under Boston City Code: Chap. 12–9 ("Human Rights," Amd. 7/84).

Credit: Sexual orientation included under Sec. 12–9.5 ("Discriminatory Practices Regarding Credit Transaction, Bonding and Insurance").

Domestic partnership employment benefits: By Executive Order of Mayor Thomas Menino, benefits were extended to both opposite- and same-sex couples. However, this was struck down by the state supreme court (7/9/99).

Domestic partnership registry: Registry opened to opposite- and same-sex couples. Facilitates visits to health care facilities, juvenile correction centers, jails, prisons, schools, and day care centers Chap. 12–9A ("Protection of Families," Amd. Ord. No. 1993 c. 12).

Education: Sexual orientation included under Sec. 12–9.6 ("Discriminatory Practices Regarding Education").

Private employment: Sexual orientation included under Sec. 12–9.3 ("Discriminatory Practices Regarding Employment").

Public accommodation: Sexual orientation included under Sec. 12–9.7 ("Discriminatory Practices Regarding Public Accommodations and Services").

Public employment: All government employers expressly covered. Sec. 12–9.3 ("Discriminatory Practices Regarding Employment").

Union practices: Sexual orientation included under Sec. 12–9.4 ("Discriminatory Practices Regarding Labor Organizations").

Cambridge

Civil rights laws: Sexual orientation included under Cambridge Municipal Code: Chap. 2.76 ("Human Rights Commission," Amd. Ord. No. 1016, 9/24/84). Gender identity also included (Amd. Ord. No. 1182, 2/24/97).

Credit: Sexual orientation included under Sec. 2.76.120 I. ("Acts deemed lawful and unlawful—Exemptions").

Domestic partnership employment benefits: Hard benefits provided to opposite- and same-sex couples. Benefits include health insurance, and bereavement, sick, and parental leave. See Chap. 2.119 ("Domestic Partnerships," Amd. Ord. No. 1144 (part), 1992).

Domestic partnership registry: Registry open to opposite- and same-sex couples. Facilitates hospital and jail visitation and access to school records. See Chap. 2.119 ("Domestic Partnerships," Amd. Ord. No. 1144 [part], 1992).

Education: Sexual orientation included under Sec. 2.76.120 A. and L. ("Acts deemed lawful and unlawful—Exemptions").

Housing: Sexual orientation included under Sec. 2.76.120 H. ("Acts deemed lawful and unlawful—Exemptions").

Private employment: Sexual orientation included under Sec. 2.76.120 D. ("Acts deemed lawful and unlawful—Exemptions").

Public accommodation: Sexual orientation included under Sec. 2.76.120 M. ("Acts deemed lawful and unlawful—Exemptions").

Public employment: All government employers expressly covered. Sec. 2.76.120 A. ("Acts deemed lawful and unlawful—Exemptions").

Union practices: Sexual orientation included under Sec. 2.76.120 F. ("Acts deemed lawful and unlawful—Exemptions").

Worcester

Civil rights laws: Sexual orientation included under Worcester Code: Chap. 2, Art. 22 (Amd. 11/12/96).

MICHIGAN

Antimarriage legislation: Defined marriage as composed of opposite-sex couples, prohibited same-sex marriages and, further, declared same-sex marriages invalid (Chap. Comp. Laws Sec(s). 551.1–551.4, 551.271, and 551.272).

Civil rights laws: Sexual orientation included under Michigan Compiled Laws: Chap. 333 ("Health," Amd. Act 1988, P.A. 88 of 1988, Eff. 5/13/88).

Hate crimes: Only data collected on sexual orientation.

Public accommodation: Applies only to health care facilities: Sec. 333.21761 and Sec. 333.20201.

Sex statutes (sodomy): Criminalized private and consensual sexual behaviors engaged in by opposite-sex and same-sex people. "Any person who commits the abominable and detestable crime against nature either with mankind or with any animal." Imprisonment of not less than one day and the maximum of life (Mi. Chap. Comp. Laws Ann. Sec. 750.158). In *Michigan Organization for Human Rights v. Kelley,* the sodomy law was deemed unconstitutional. However, it is unclear if this will remain unconstitutional in face of efforts to resuscitate the sodomy statute.

Ann Arbor

Civil rights laws: Sexual orientation included under Code of the City of Ann Arbor: Title IX, Chap. 112 ("Non-Discrimination," Amd. Ord. No. 4–78, 3/13/78). HIV status is also a protected class. Gender identity also included (Amd. Ord. No. 10–99, 3/2/99).

Credit: Sexual orientation applied to the financing of real estate transactions only. Sec. 9:152 ("Discriminatory Housing Practices").

Domestic partnership employment benefits: Hard benefits provided to same-sex couples only. Benefits included health, dental, vision, and life insurance, and child care reimbursement assistance, besides sick and funeral leave (Amd. Res. R-397–8–92, 8/17/92).

Domestic partnership registry: Registry open to opposite- and same-sex couples. Not limited to residents and no rights specified. Chap. 110 ("Domestic Partnerships," Amd. Ord. No. 62–91, 1. . ..../91).

Education: Sexual orientation included under Sec. 9:153 ("Discriminatory Public Accommodation Practices"), and Sec. 9:151 (15) ("Definition" of "Place of Public Accommodation").

Housing: Sexual orientation included under Sec. 9:152 ("Discriminatory Housing Practices").

Private employment: Sexual orientation included under Sec. 9:154 ("Discriminatory Employment Practices").

Public accommodation: Sexual orientation included under Sec. 9:153 ("Discriminatory Public Accommodation Practices").

Public employment: Any employer or all employers covered. Sec. 9:154 ("Discriminatory Employment Practices").

Union practices: Sexual orientation included under Sec. 9:154 (2) ("Discriminatory Employment Practices").

Detroit

Civil rights laws: Sexual orientation included under Detroit City Code: Chap. 27 ("Human Rights"), and Chap. 27, Art. VII ("Discrimination on the Basis of AIDS and Conditions Related to AIDS," Amd. Ord. No. 330-H, 7/16/79).

Credit: Sexual orientation included under Sec. 27–4–9 ("Unlawful loan practices").

Domestic partnership employment benefits: Hard benefits provided.

Education: Sexual orientation included under Art. V ("Educational Institution Practices"), and Art. VII, Sec. 27–7–6 ("Educational Institutions").

Housing: Sexual orientation included under Art. IV ("Real Estate, Insurance and Loan Practices"), and Art. VII, Sec. 27–7–4 ("Housing").

Private employment: Sexual orientation included under Art. III ("Employment Practices"), and Art. VII, Sec. 27–7–3 ("Employment").

Public accommodation: Sexual orientation included under Art. VI

("Public Accommodation Practices"), and Art. VII, Sec. 27–7–5 ("Business establishments").

Public employment: All government employers expressly covered. See Art. III ("Employment Practices"), and Art. VII, Sec. 27–7–3 ("Employment").

Union practices: Sexual orientation included under Art. III ("Employment Practices"), Sec. 27–3–1 (4), (5), and (6) ("Unlawful employment practices"), and Art. VII, Sec. 27–7–3 (4) ("Employment").

Grand Rapids

Civil rights laws: Sexual orientation included under Grand Rapids City Code: Chap. 8, Art. 3 ("Community Relations Commission"), Sec. 1.347 ("Civil Rights Defined," Amd. Ord. 94–18, 5/10/94). Gender identity also included (Amd. Ord. 94–18, 5/10/94).

Wayne County

Civil rights laws: Sexual orientation included under Wayne County Code.

Domestic partnership employment benefits: Hard benefits provided.

Private employment: Applied only to private employers who have contracts with the city. See Part II, Chap. 125 ("Equal Contracting Opportunity"), Sec. 125–4 ("Antidiscrimination policies").

MINNESOTA

Antimarriage legislation: Defined marriage to be opposite-sex only. Same-sex marriages were prohibited and voided (Minn. Stat. Sec(s). 517.01, 517.03, 517.08(1a), and 517.20).

Civil rights laws: Sexual orientation included under Minnesota Statutes Annotated: Chap. 363 ("Department of Human Rights"), Sec. 363.03 ("Unfair discriminatory practices," Amd. Stat. 1993, Laws 1993, c. 22). Gender identity also included (Amd. Stat. 1993, Laws 1993, c. 22).

Credit: Sexual orientation included under Subdivision 8 ("Credit; discrimination").

Education: Sexual orientation included under Subdivision 5 ("Educational institution").

Hate crimes: Separate crime and penalty established for bias crime committed on actual or perceived sexual orientation of victim. Data collection required. Gender identity is included. (Minn. Stat. Sec. 609.2231).

Housing: Sexual orientation included under Subdivision 2 ("Real property").

Private employment: Sexual orientation included under Subdivision 1 ("Employment").

Public accommodation: Sexual orientation included under Subdivision 3 ("Public accommodations").

Public employment: All government employers expressly covered. See Subdivision 1 ("Employment").

Sex statutes (sodomy): Criminalized private and consensual sexual behaviors engaged in by opposite-sex and same-sex people. "'Sodomy' means carnally knowing any person by the anus or by or with the mouth." Imprisonment not to exceed one year or a fine of not more than $1,000 (Minn. Stat. Ann. Sec. 609.293).

Union practices: Sexual orientation included under Subdivision 1 ("Employment").

Hennepin County

Civil rights laws: Sexual orientation included under Diversity and Nondiscrimination Policy (Amd. Res. No. 96–2–60R1, 2/15/96).

Domestic partnership employment benefits: Soft benefits provided to opposite-sex and same-sex couples.

Public employment: All government employers expressly covered.

Minneapolis

Civil rights laws: Sexual orientation included under City of Minneapolis' Code of Ordinances: Chap. 139 ("In General," Amd. Ord. No 99–68, 3/29/74). Gender identity also included (Amd. Ord. No 99–68, 3/29/74).

Credit: Sexual orientation included under Sec. 139.40 (h) ("Discrimination in lending").

Domestic partnership employment benefits: Court invalidated statutes.

Domestic partnership registry: Court invalidated statutes.

Education: Sexual orientation included under Sec. 139.40 (k) ("Discrimination in educational institutions").

Housing: Sexual orientation included under Sec. 139.40 (e) ("Discrimination in real estate").

Private employment: Sexual orientation included under Sec. 139.40 (b) ("Discrimination in employment"), and only applied to private employers who have contracts with the city. Sec. 139.50 ("Provisions required in contracts with city").

Public accommodation: Sexual orientation included under Sec. 139.40 (i) ("Discrimination in public accommodations").

Public employment: All government employers expressly covered. Sec. 139.40 (b) ("Discrimination in employment").

Union practices: Sexual orientation included under Sec. 139.40 (a) ("Discrimination by a labor organization").

St. Paul

Civil rights laws: Sexual orientation included under St. Paul Legislative Code: Chap. 183 ("Human Rights," Amd. Ord. No. 17744, 6/26/90). Gender identity also included (Amd. Ord. No. 17744, 6/26/90).

Credit: Sexual orientation included under Sec. 183.11 ("Credit discrimination").

Domestic partnership employment benefits: Unknown.

Education: Sexual orientation included under Sec. 183.05 ("Prohibited acts in education").

Housing: Sexual orientation included under Sec. 183.06 ("Prohibited acts in real property").

Private employment: Sexual orientation included under Sec. 183.03 ("Prohibited acts in employment").

Public accommodation: Sexual orientation included under Sec. 183.07 ("Prohibited acts in public accommodations").

Public employment: All government employers expressly covered. Sec. 183.03 ("Prohibited acts in employment").

Union practices: Sexual orientation included under Sec. 183.03 ("Prohibited acts in employment").

MISSISSIPPI

Antimarriage legislation: Prohibited same-sex marriages and declared them invalid, null, and void (Miss. Code Ann. Sec. 93–1–1).

Hate crimes: No statutes based on any characteristic.

Sex statutes (sodomy): Criminalized private and consensual sexual behaviors engaged in by opposite-sex and same-sex people. "Convicted of the detestable and abominable crime against nature committed with mankind or with a beast." Imprisonment not to exceed ten years (Miss. Code Ann. Sec. 97–29–59).

MISSOURI

Hate crimes: Crimes motivated by bias against sexual orientation and gender identity. Sentence enhancement is discretionary (Mo. Stat. Ann. Sec. 557.035).

Sex statutes (sodomy): Criminalized private and consensual sexual behaviors engaged in by same-sex people. "Sexual misconduct between same sex." Imprisonment not to exceed one year or fine of $1000 (Mo. Stat. Ann. Sec. 566.090).

Joplin

Civil rights laws: Sexual orientation included under City Code of Joplin (Amd. Ord. No. 98–160, 1998).

Public accommodation: Statutes apply to taxi operators refusing service to an orderly passenger because of his or her sexual orientation. Part II, Chapter 126 ("Vehicles for Hire") Art. I Sec. 126–12.

Kansas City

Civil rights laws: Sexual orientation included under Kansas City Code: Chap. 38 ("Human Relations"), Art. III ("Discriminatory Practices," Amd. Ord. No. 930612, 6/3/93).

Credit: Applied only to the financing of commercial real estate transactions. Sec. 38–134 ("Discrimination in commercial real estate loans").

Housing: Sexual orientation included under Sec. 38–133 ("Housing").

Private employment: Sexual orientation included under Sec. 38–132 ("Employment").

Public accommodation: Sexual orientation included under Sec. 38–137 ("Discriminatory accommodation practices").

Union practices: Sexual orientation included under Sec. 38–132 ("Employment").

St. Louis

Civil rights laws: Sexual orientation included under Board Bill No. 124, Sec. 9 ("Prohibited Discriminatory Practices," Amd. Ord. No. 62710, 10/6/92).

Credit: Sexual orientation applied to the financing of real estate transactions only. Sec. 9 (C)(1)(b) ("Discrimination in Provision of Housing or Realty").

Domestic partnership registry: Registry opened to opposite- and same-sex couples. Helps facilitate visitation to medical facilities and jails. Board Bill No. 10, Ord. No. 64401, 7/1/98.

Housing: Sexual orientation included under Sec. 9 (C) ("Discrimination in Provision of Housing or Realty").

Private employment: Sexual orientation included under Sec. 9 (B) ("Discrimination in Employment").

Public accommodation: Sexual orientation included under Sec. 9 (D) ("Discrimination in Public Accommodations").

Public employment: Any employer or all employers covered. Sec. 9 (B) ("Discrimination in Employment").

Union practices: Sexual orientation included under Sec. 9 (B)(2) and (4) ("Discrimination in Employment").

MONTANA

Antimarriage legislation: Same-sex marriages prohibited and mechanisms enacted to declare such marriages invalid (Mont. Code Ann. Sec(s). 40–1–401 and 40–1–402).

Hate crimes: Sexual orientation is not included in hate crimes statutes.

Sex statutes (sodomy): Invalidated by state supreme court decision in *Gryczan v. Montana,* 942 P.2d 112 (Mont. 1997).

NEBRASKA

Antimarriage: Ballot initiative limiting marriage to one woman and one man passed at the polls in November, 2000.

Hate crimes: Mandatory sentence enhancement for bias crimes based on sexual orientation. Data collection required. Neb. Rev. Stat. Sec 28.110–28.114.

Sex statutes (sodomy): Repealed in 1978.

NEVADA

Civil rights laws: Sexual orientation included under Nevada Revised Statutes: Title 23 ("Public Officers and Employees"), Chap. 281 ("General Provisions"); Title 28, Chap. 338 ("Public Works Projects"); Title 53 ("Labor and Indus. Rel."), Chap. 610 ("Apprenticeships"); and Title 53, Chap. 613 ("Employment Practices," Amd. Stat. 1999, 1999 Nev. Stat. Chap. 410, Eff. 10/1/99).

Hate crimes: Separate crime and penalty established besides being used as an aggravating factor in sentencing first-degree murder. Bias toward actual or perceived sexual orientation of victim relevant. Data collection required. Nev. Rev. Stat. Sec. 193.175.

Private employment: Sexual orientation included under Sec. 613.330, Sec. 610.150 (10) (apprentices), and Sec. 338.125 (public contractors).

Public employment: All government employers expressly covered. Sec(s). 281.370, 613.330, and 610.150 (10) (apprentices).

Sex statutes (sodomy): Repealed in 1993.

Union practices: Sexual orientation included under Sec. 613.330.

NEW HAMPSHIRE

Civil rights laws: Sexual orientation included under New Hampshire Revised Statutes Annotated: Title 31 ("Trade and Commerce"), Chap. 354-A ("Law Against Discrimination," Amd. Stat. 1997, c. 108, Eff. 1/1/98).

Hate crimes: Discretionary sentence enhancement for bias crimes based on sexual orientation of victim (N.H. Rev. Stat. Ann. Sec. 651:6).

Housing: Sexual orientation included under Sec. 354-A:8 ("Equal Housing Opportunity without Discrimination a Civil Right") and Sec. 354-A:10 ("Unlawful Discriminatory Practices").

Private employment: Sexual orientation included under Sec. 354-A:6 ("Opportunity for Employment without Discrimination a Civil Right") and Sec. 354-A:7 ("Unlawful Discriminatory Practices").

Public accommodation: Sexual orientation included under Sec. 354-A:16 ("Equal Access to Public Accommodations a Civil Right") and

Sec. 354-A:17 ("Unlawful Discriminatory Practices in Public Accommodations").

Public employment: All government employers expressly covered. Sec. 354-A:6 ("Opportunity for Employment without Discrimination a Civil Right") and Sec. 354-A:7 ("Unlawful Discriminatory Practices").

Sex statutes (sodomy): Repealed in 1975.

Union practices: Sexual orientation included under Sec. 354-A:6 ("Opportunity for Employment without Discrimination a Civil Right") and Sec. 354-A:7 ("Unlawful Discriminatory Practices").

NEW JERSEY

Civil rights laws: Sexual orientation included under New Jersey Statutes Annotated: Title 10 ("Civil Rights"), Chap. 5 ("Law Against Discrimination," Amd. Stat. 1991, L.1991, c. 519).

Credit: Sexual orientation included under Sec. 10:5–12 (i) ("Unlawful employment practice or unlawful discrimination").

Education: Sexual orientation included under Sec. 10:5–12 (f) ("Unlawful employment practice or unlawful discrimination").

Hate crimes: Separate crime and penalty established along with mandatory sentence enhancement. Data collection required. N.J. Stat. Ann. Sec. 2C:12–1, 2C:34–4, 2C:44–3.

Housing: Sexual orientation included under Sec. 10:5–12 (g) ("Unlawful employment practice or unlawful discrimination").

Private employment: Sexual orientation included under Sec. 10:5–12 (a) and (c) ("Unlawful employment practice or unlawful discrimination").

Public accommodation: Sexual orientation included under Sec. 10:5–12 (f) ("Unlawful employment practice or unlawful discrimination").

Public employment: All government employers expressly covered. Sec. 10:5–12 (a) and (c) ("Unlawful employment practice or unlawful discrimination").

Sex statutes (sodomy): Repealed in 1979.

Union practices: Sexual orientation included under Sec. 10:5–12 (b) ("Unlawful employment practice or unlawful discrimination").

Gloucester County

Domestic partnership employment benefits: Soft benefits.

NEW MEXICO

Civil rights laws: Sexual orientation included under Executive Order 85–15, 4/1/85.

Hate crimes: No statutes based on any characteristics.

Sex statutes (sodomy): Repealed in 1975.

Albuquerque

Civil rights laws: Sexual orientation included under Mayoral Executive Order (Amd. 3/30/94).

NEW YORK

Civil rights laws: Sexual orientation included under Executive Order No. 28, 11/18/83 and Executive Order No. 33, 4/9/96.

Domestic partnership employment benefits: Hard benefits provided for most New York state public employees.

Hate crimes: Sexual orientation is not included in hate crime statutes.

Sex statutes (sodomy): Invalidated by state supreme court decision in *People v. Onofre*, 415 N.E.2d 936 (N.Y. 1980).

Albany, City of

Civil rights laws: Sexual orientation included under Albany City Code: Chap. 1, Art. XI (Amd. Ord. No. 97.112.92, 12/792).

Albany County

Civil rights laws: Sexual orientation included under Local Law No. 1 (Amd. 6/96).

Buffalo

Civil rights laws: Sexual orientation included under City Code: Sec. 35–12 ("Equal employment opportunity," Amd. Ord. 1983).

Public accommodation: Applies only to city services. Sec. 35–12 (B).

Public employment: Sexual orientation included under Sec. 35–12 (A).

New York

Civil rights laws: Sexual orientation included under Administrative Code: Title 8 ("Civil Rights Amendment," Amd. 1993).

Domestic partnership employment benefits: Hard benefits to opposite- and same-sex couples.

Domestic partnership registry: Registry opened to opposite- and same-sex couples. Helps facilitate visits to jails and hospitals. Under certain conditions, registered couples are exempt from real estate transfer taxes.

Rochester

Civil rights laws: Sexual orientation included under Res. 94–12 ("Resolution Prohibiting Discrimination," Amd. Res. No. 83–58, 12/27/83).

Domestic partnership registry: Registry open to opposite- and same-sex couples. Not limited to residents and no rights specified.

Private employment: Applies only to private employers who have contracts with the city. Res. 94–12, Sec. 3.

Public accommodation: Applies only to services provided by the city. Res. 94–12, Sec. 1; and Res. 94–12, Sec. 3.

Public employment: All government employers expressly covered. Res. 94–12, Sec. 2.

Suffolk County

Civil rights laws: Sexual orientation included under Suffolk County Code: Sec. 89–1 (Amd. Local Law No. 5–3/1/88).

Syracuse

Civil rights laws: Sexual orientation included under Local Law No. 17 ("A Local Law of the City of Syracuse establishing a Fair Practices Law"), and Art. IV ("Unlawful Discriminatory Practices," Amd. 10/1/90).

Education: Sexual orientation applied to "Education corporation(s) or association(s)." See Sec. 4 ("Unlawful discriminatory practices, public accommodation").

Housing: Sexual orientation included under Sec. 5–9 ("Unlawful discriminatory practices, housing accommodation and commercial space").

Private employment: Sexual orientation included under Sec. 1 and 2 ("Unlawful discriminatory practices, employment").

Public accommodation: Sexual orientation included under Sec. 3 ("Unlawful discriminatory practices, public accommodation").

Public employment: All government employers and employees expressly covered. Sec(s). 1 and 2 ("Unlawful discriminatory practices, employment").

Union practices: Sexual orientation included under Sec(s). 1 and 2 ("Unlawful discriminatory practices, employment").

Tompkins County

Civil rights laws: Sexual orientation included under Local Law No. 6–1991 ("Fair Practice"), 12/2/91.

Credit: Sexual orientation included under Sec. V ("Declaration of Rights"), 2 (d) ("Credit").

Education: Sexual orientation included under Sec. V ("Declaration of Rights"), 2 (e) ("Education").

Housing: Sexual orientation included under Sec. V ("Declaration of Rights"), 2 (c) ("Housing Accommodations").

Private employment: Sexual orientation included under Sec. V ("Declaration of Rights"), 2 (a) ("Employment").

Public accommodation: Sexual orientation included under Sec. V ("Declaration of Rights"), 2 (b) ("Public Accommodation").

Public employment: All government employers and employees expressly covered. Sec. V ("Declaration of Rights"), 2 (a) ("Employment").

Union practices: Sexual orientation included under Sec. V ("Declaration of Rights"), 2 (a) (3) ("Employment").

Watertown

Civil rights laws: Sexual orientation included under "Resolution Establishing Equal Employment Affirmative Action Plan for the City of Watertown," 5/2/88.

Public employment: All government employers expressly covered.

NORTH CAROLINA

Antimarriage legislation: Established that same-sex marriages are invalid. N.C. Gen. Stat. Sec. 51–1.2 and 51–2.

Hate crimes: Sexual orientation not included in hate crime statutes.

Sex statutes (sodomy): Criminalized private and consensual sexual behaviors engaged in by opposite-sex and same-sex people. "Commits the crime of buggery whether with mankind or with beast." Imprisonment for five years or shall pay a fine of not less than $500, or both. N.C. Gen. Stat. Sec. 14–177.

Chapel Hill

Civil rights laws: Sexual orientation included under Chapel Hill City Code: Art. IV (Amd. 9/75).

Domestic partnership employment benefits: Hard benefits provided, family and sick leave (Eff. 4/95), and health benefits (Eff. 5/95).

Domestic partnership registry: Registry opened to opposite- and same-sex couples. Not limited to residents and no rights specified.

Durham

Civil rights laws: Sexual orientation included under Personnel Policy Memorandum No. PER-203, R-2 ("Equal Employment Opportunity"), 9/22/89.

Public employment: All government employers expressly covered.

Raleigh

Civil rights laws: Sexual orientation included under Ord. No. (1969)–889 (Amd. Ord. No. (1988)–106, 1/5/88).

Private employment: Applied only to those private employers that have contracts with the city (Sec. 3).

Public accommodation: Applied only to the provision of city services (Sec. 4).

Public employment: All government employers expressly covered. Sec. 4.

NORTH DAKOTA

Antimarriage legislation: Defined marriage as opposite-sex couples only and declared same-sex marriages invalid. (N.D. Cent. Code Sec(s). 14–03–01 and 14–03–08.)

Hate crimes: Sexual orientation not included in hate crime statutes.

Sex statutes (sodomy): Repealed in 1973.

OHIO

Civil rights laws: 1999 executive order prohibiting discrimination in state civil service, unlike its predecessor, omitted explicit protection from discrimination based on sexual orientation.

Hate crimes: Sexual orientation not included in hate crime statutes.

Sex statutes (sodomy): Repealed in 1974.

Cleveland

Civil rights laws: Sexual orientation included under Cleveland City Code (Amd. Ord. No. 77–94, 1/10/94) and (Amd. Ord. No. 272–96, 2/12/96).

Housing: Sexual orientation included under Sec. 665.02 ("Unlawful Discriminatory Housing Practices").

Private employment: Applies only to private employers that have contracts with the city. Sec. 187.04 ("Employment; Nondiscrimination; Goals of Contractors") and Sec. 187.11 ("Equal Opportunity Clause").

Public accommodation: Sexual orientation included under Sec. 667.01 ("Discrimination in Public Accommodations").

Public employment: All employers and employees covered. Sec. 667.05 ("Unlawful Discrimination in Employment").

Union practices: Sexual orientation protections limited to city employee unions. Sec. 667.05 ("Unlawful Discrimination in Employment").

Columbus

Civil rights laws: Sexual orientation included under Title 23 ("General Offenses Code"), Chap. 23.31 ("Discriminatory Practices; Civil Rights; Disclosure," Amd. 1984).

Credit: Sexual orientation applied to the financing of real estate transactions only (Sec. 23.31.02 (3) ("Fair housing").

Housing: Sexual orientation included under Sec. 23.31.02 ("Fair housing").

Private employment: Sexual orientation included under Sec. 23.31.03 ("Unlawful employment practices").

Public accommodation: Sexual orientation included under Sec. 23.31.04 ("Unlawful public accommodations").

Public employment: All government employers expressly covered. Sec. 23.31.03 ("Unlawful employment practices").

Union practices: Sexual orientation included under Sec. 23.31.03 ("Unlawful employment practices").

Cuyahoga County

Civil rights laws: Sexual orientation included under Affirmative Action Plan (Amd. 8/8/86).

Public employment: All government employers expressly covered.

Toledo

Civil rights laws: Sexual orientation included under Toledo Municipal Code: Chap. 554 (Amd. Ord. No. 1183–98, 12/8/98). Gender identity also included (Amd. Ord. No. 1183–98, 12/8/98).

Credit: Sexual orientation applied to the financing of real estate transactions only. Sec. 554.03 (d) ("Prohibited real estate discrimination").

Housing: Sexual orientation included under Sec. 554.03 ("Prohibited real estate discrimination").

Private employment: Sexual orientation included under Sec. 554.02 ("Prohibited employment discrimination; exemptions").

Public accommodation: Sexual orientation included under Sec. 554 ("Business establishments") and ("Places of Public Accommodation").

Public employment: All employers and all employees covered. Sec. 554.02 ("Prohibited employment discrimination; exemptions").

Union practices: Sexual orientation included under Sec. 554.02 ("Prohibited employment discrimination; exemptions").

OKLAHOMA

Antimarriage legislation: Defined marriage as opposite-sex only and declared same-sex marriages invalid. Okla. Stat. tit. 43 Sec. 3 and 3.1.

Hate crimes: Sexual orientation is not included in hate crime statutes.

Sex statutes (sodomy): Criminalized private and consensual sexual behaviors engaged in by same-sex people. "Commits the detestable and abominable crime against nature with mankind or with a beast." Imprisonment in the penitentiary for not more than ten years. Okla. Stat. tit. 21 Sec. 886.

OREGON

Civil rights laws: Although there is no legislation on this issue, an Oregon state court of appeals ruled in *Tanner v. OHSU*, 971 P.2d 435 (Or. Ct. App. 1988), that employment discrimination based on sexual orientation was prohibited, and, further, that domestic partners of employees must be extended equivalent benefits as those given to married spouses.

Domestic partnership employment benefits: Soft benefits provided to opposite- and same-sex couples as the result of collective bargaining agreement. Benefits include bereavement leave.

Hate crimes: Separate crime and penalty established for bias crime committed on actual or perceived sexual orientation of victim. Data collection required. Or. Rev. Stat. Sec 166.155, 166.165.

Sex statutes (sodomy): Repealed in 1972.

Benton County

Civil rights laws: Sexual orientation included under Ord. No. 98–0139, 14/8/98. Gender identity also included (Ord. No. 98–0139, 14/8/98).

Housing: Sexual orientation included under Sec. 6 (2) ("Discrimination in selling, renting, or leasing real property prohibited").

Private employment: Sexual orientation included under Sec. 5 (2) ("Discrimination in Employment Prohibited").

Public accommodation: Sexual orientation included under Sec. 7 (2) ("Discrimination in Places of Public Accommodation Prohibited).

Public employment: All employers and employees covered. Sec. 5 (2) ("Discrimination in Employment Prohibited").

Eugene

Civil rights laws: Sexual orientation included under Eugene Code: Secs. 4.615–4.655 (Amd. Ord. No. 19970, 7/11/94).

Domestic partnership employment benefits: Hard benefits available to nonunionized employees only.

Housing: Sexual orientation included under Sec. 4.630 ("Human Rights—Housing Practices").

Private employment: Sexual orientation included under Sec. 4.620 ("Human Rights—Employment Practices").

Public accommodation: Sexual orientation included under Sec. 4.635 ("Human Rights—Public Accommodations Practices").

Public employment: All government employers expressly covered. Sec. 4.620 ("Human Rights—Employment Practices").

Union practices: Sexual orientation included under Sec. 4.620 (1) (g) ("Human Rights—Employment Practices").

Gresham

Domestic partnership employment benefits: Hard benefits provided to same-sex couples only. Benefits include medical and dental insurance.

Portland

Civil rights laws: Sexual orientation included under Portland City Code: Chap. 23.01 ("Civil Rights," Amd. Ord. No. 164709, 10/3/91), Title 4 ("Portland City Personnel System"), and Res. No. 31510, 12/74. Gender identity also included (Res. No. 1851, 12/23/98 made "gender identity" a protected class in regard only to city employment).

Domestic partnership employment benefits: Hard benefits.

Housing: Sexual orientation included under Sec. 23.01.060 (B) ("Discrimination in Selling, Renting, or Leasing Real Property Prohibited").

Private employment: Sexual orientation included under Sec. 23.01.050 (B) ("Discrimination in Employment Prohibited").

Public accommodation: Sexual orientation included under Sec. 23.01.070 (B) ("Discrimination in Places of Public Accommodation Prohibited").

Public employment: All government employers expressly covered. Sec. 23.01.050 (B) ("Discrimination in Employment Prohibited"), Title 4 ("Portland City Personnel System"), and Res. No. 1851.

PENNSYLVANIA

Antimarriage legislation: Declared same-sex marriages against public policy and void. 23 Pa. Cons. Stat. Ann. Sec. 1704.

Civil rights laws: Sexual orientation included under Executive Order No. 1996–9 ("Equal Employment Opportunity"), 12/20/96. AIDS or HIV status is also protected class as included in Executive Order No. 1988–1.

Hate crimes: Sexual orientation is not included in hate crime statutes.

Public employment: All government employers expressly covered. Sec. 1 ("Prohibition of discrimination and affirmation of equal opportunity").

Sex statutes (sodomy): Invalidated by *Commonwealth v. Bonadio,* 415 A.2d 47 (Pa. 1980).

Philadelphia

Civil rights laws: Sexual orientation included under Philadelphia Code: Chap. 9–1100 ("Fair Practices," Amd. 1982).

Credit: Sexual orientation included under Sec. 9–1105 ("Unlawful Public Accommodations Practice") and Sec. 9–1102 ("Definition of 'Public Accommodation' includes financial institutions").

Domestic partnership employment benefits: By executive order, hard benefits provided to employees who also enjoy housing tax breaks previously given only to married couples (5/7/98).

Education: Sexual orientation included under Sec. 9–1105 ("Unlawful Public Accommodations Practice") and Sec. 9–1102 ("Definition of 'Public Accommodation' includes primary and secondary schools, high school . . . colleges and universities").

Housing: Sexual orientation included under Sec. 9–1104 ("Unlawful Housing Practices").

Private employment: Sexual orientation included under Sec. 9–1103 ("Unlawful Employment Practices").

Public accommodation: Sexual orientation included under Sec. 9–1105 ("Unlawful Public Accommodations Practice").

Public employment: All government employers expressly covered. Sec. 9–1103 ("Unlawful Employment Practices").

Union practices: Sexual orientation included under Sec. 9–1103 ("Unlawful Employment Practices").

Pittsburgh

Civil rights laws: Sexual orientation included under Pittsburgh City Code: Chap. 651 ("Findings and Policy") and Chap. 659 ("Unlawful Practices," Amd. 4/3/90). Gender identity also included (Amd. Ord. 1–1997, Eff. 2/7/97).

Housing: Sexual orientation included under Sec. 659.03 ("Unlawful Housing Practices").

Private employment: Sexual orientation included under Sec. 659.02 ("Unlawful Employment Practices").

Public accommodation: Sexual orientation included under Sec. 659.04 ("Unlawful Public Accommodations Practices").

Public employment: All government employers expressly covered. Sec. 659.02 ("Unlawful Employment Practices").

Union practices: Sexual orientation included under Sec. 659.02 ("Unlawful Employment Practices").

RHODE ISLAND

Civil rights laws: Sexual orientation included under General Laws of Rhode Island: Chap. 28–5 ("Fair Employment Practices"); Chap. 28–5.1 ("Equal Opportunity and Affirmative Action"); Chap. 34–37 ("Rhode Island Fair Housing Practices Act"); and, Chap. 11–24 ("Hotels And Public Places," Amd. Stat. 1995, P.L. 1995, Chap. 32, Eff. 5/22/95).

Credit: Sexual orientation included under Sec. 34–37–4.3 ("Discrimination in granting credit or loans prohibited").

Education: Sexual orientation included under Sec. 28–5.1–8 ("Education, training, and apprenticeship programs").

Hate crimes: Based upon the actual or perceived sexual orientation of victim. Enhanced mandatory sentences (R.I. Gen. Laws Sec. 12–19–38).

Housing: Sexual orientation included under Sec. 34–37–2 ("Rights to equal housing opportunities—Civil rights") and Sec. 34–37–4 ("Unlawful housing practices").

Private employment: Sexual orientation included under Sec. 28–5–5 ("Right to equal employment opportunities") and Sec. 28–5–7 ("Unlawful employment practices").

Public accommodation: Sexual orientation included under Sec. 11–24–2 ("Discriminatory practices prohibited") and Sec. 11–24–2.2 ("Discrimination based on sexual orientation").

Public employment: All government employers expressly covered.

Sec. 28–5–5 ("Right to equal employment opportunities") and Sec. 28–5–7 ("Unlawful employment practices").

Sex statutes (sodomy): Repealed in 1998.

Union practices: Sexual orientation included under Sec. 28–5–5 ("Right to equal employment opportunities") and Sec. 28–5–7 ("Unlawful employment practices").

Providence

Civil rights laws: Sexual orientation included under 95-H 6678, Sub. A (Amd. 5/22/95).

SOUTH CAROLINA

Antimarriage legislation: Prohibited same-sex marriages and declared them void. S.C. Code Ann. Sec. 20–1–10 and 20–1–15.

Hate crimes: No statutes based on any characteristic.

Sex statutes (sodomy): Criminalized private and consensual sexual behaviors engaged in by opposite-sex and same-sex people. "Commits the abominable crime of buggery, whether with mankind or with beast." Imprisonment for five years or pay a fine of not less than $500 or both. S.C. Code Ann. Sec. 16–15–120.

Columbia

Civil rights laws: Sexual orientation included under Personnel Handbook (Amd. 6/15/93).

SOUTH DAKOTA

Antimarriage legislation: Defined marriage as opposite-sex only and declared same-sex marriages invalid. S.D. Codified Laws Sec. 25–1–1 and Sec. 25–1–38.

Hate crimes: Sexual orientation not included in hate crime statutes.

Sex statutes (sodomy): Repealed in 1977.

Minnehaha County

Civil rights laws: Sexual orientation included under Minnehaha County Manual: Chap. 3 ("Minnehaha County Employment Handbook," Amd. 1979).

Public employment: All government employers expressly covered. Sec. A-1 ("Affirmative Action-Statement of Equal Opportunity Employment in Minnehaha County").

TENNESSEE

Antimarriage legislation: Defined marriage as opposite-sex only, prohibited same-sex marriages, and invalidated same-sex marriages. (Tenn. Code Ann. Sec(s). 36–3–103, 36–3–111, 36–3–113, and 36–3–306).

Hate crimes: No specific groups identified in hate crime statutes.

Sex statutes (sodomy): Invalidated by state appellate court in *Campbell v. Sundquist,* 926 S.W.2d 250 (Tenn. Ct. App. 1996).

TEXAS

Hate crimes: No specific groups identified in hate crime statutes.

Sex statutes (sodomy): Repealed in 1999.

Austin

Civil rights laws: Sexual orientation included under Austin City Code Book: Title VII ("Human Resources and Civil Rights"), Chap. 7.1 to 7.4. "Employment" protection—(Amd. Ord. No. 750710-A, 7/10/75), "Housing" protection—(Amd. Ord. 820218-D, 2/18/82); and, Title VII, Chap. 7.5 ("Discrimination against Persons with AIDS," Amd. Ord. 861211-V, 1981).

Housing: Sexual orientation included under Chap. 7.1.

Private employment: Sexual orientation included under Chap. 7.3 and 7.4.

Public accommodation: Sexual orientation included under Chap. 7.2.

Public employment: All government employers expressly covered. Chap. 7.3.

Union practices: Sexual orientation included under Chap. 7.3.

Dallas

Civil rights laws: Sexual orientation included under Dallas City Code (Amd. Ord. 22318, 1/95).

Public employment: Sexual orientation included under Chap. 34, Art. V, Sec. 34–35.

Travis County

Domestic partnership employment benefits: Soft benefits provided that include family sick leave.

UTAH

Antimarriage legislation: Prohibited and voided same-sex marriages. Utah Code Ann. Sec. 30–1–2 (5) and 30–1–4.

Hate crimes: Data only collected on sexual orientation hate crimes.

Sex statutes (sodomy): Criminalize private and consensual sexual behaviors engaged in by anyone who is not married. This includes opposite-sex and same-sex people. "Sodomy is any sexual act with a person over 14 years of age involving the genitals of one person and the mouth or anus of another person, regardless of the sex of either participant." Imprisonment not to exceed six months. Utah Code Sec. 76–5–403.

Salt Lake City

Civil rights laws: Sexual orientation included under Salt Lake City Code: Chap. 2.53. (Amd. Ord. No. 87, 11/17/98). An earlier version of this statute contained the phrase "sexual orientation." It was removed in this version.

Public employment: All government employers expressly covered. Sec. 2.53.030 (B) (2) ("Prohibited in employment decisions and practices"). This section stated that: "(a) the status of having a lifestyle which is irrelevant to successful job performance; and (b) the status of being in or outside of an adult interpersonal relationship or a family relationship" are not "job related criteria" and shall not be considered.

Salt Lake County

Civil rights laws: Sexual orientation included under Salt Lake County Code: Title 2 ("Administration and Personnel), Chap. 2.80 ("Personnel Management," Amd. Ord. No. 1212, 9/30/92).

Public employment: All government employers expressly covered. Sec. 2.80.140 ("Discrimination Prohibited").

VERMONT

Civil rights laws: Sexual orientation included under Vermont Statutes Annotated: Title 21, Chap. 5 ("Employment Practices"); Title 9, Chap. 139 (Discrimination; Public Accommodation; Rental and Sale of Real Estate"); Title 8, Chap. 57 ("Investments and Loans"); and Title 16, Chap. 1 ("Administration Generally"). Amd. Act 1991, No. 135 Adj. Sess. "Human Rights Law."

Civil union: Vermont created a legal category (Vt. St., Title 15, Chp. 23) known as "civil union" that confers upon same-sex couples all the rights and responsibilities afforded marriage.

Credit: Sexual orientation included under Title 8, Chap. 57, Sec. 1211(a) and Sec. 1302(2).

Domestic partnership employment benefits: Hard benefits provided to opposite- and same-sex couples, including medical and dental coverage.

Education: Harassment based on sexual orientation prohibited. Title, 16, Chap. 1, Sec. 11(a)(26) ("Classifications and definitions").

Hate crimes: Separate crime and penalty established, along with mandatory sentence enhancement for bias crimes based on actual or perceived sexual orientation of victim. Data collection required. Gender identity is included. Vt. Stat. Ann Sec. 1454–1457.

Housing: Sexual orientation included under Title 9, Chap. 139, Sec. 4503 ("Unfair housing practices").

Private employment: Sexual orientation included under Title 21, Chap. 5, Sec. 495 ("Unlawful employment practice").

Public accommodation: Sexual orientation included under Title 9, Chap. 139, Sec. 4502 ("Public accommodations").

Public employment: All government employers expressly covered. See Title 21, Chap. 5, Sec. 495 ("Unlawful employment practice").

Sex statutes (sodomy): Repealed in 1977.

Union practices: Sexual orientation included under Title 21, Chap. 5, Sec. 495 ("Unlawful employment practice").

VIRGINIA

Antimarriage legislation: Prohibited and voided same-sex marriages. Va. Code Ann. Sec. 20–45.2.

Hate crimes: Sexual orientation is not included in hate crime statutes.

Sex statutes (sodomy): Criminalized private and consensual sexual behaviors engaged in by opposite-sex and same-sex people. "Carnally know in any manner any brute animal or carnally know any male or female person by the anus or by mouth." Imprisonment of not less than one year nor more than five years and a fine of not more than $1,000 (Va. Code Sec. 18.2–361).

Alexandria

Civil rights laws: Sexual orientation included under Code of the City of Alexandria: Title 12 ("Education, Social Services and Welfare"), Chap. 4 ("Human Rights," Amd. Ord. No. 3328, 10/15/88).

Credit: Sexual orientation included under Sec. 12–4–9 ("Credit").

Education: Sexual orientation included under Sec. 12–4–10 ("Education").

Housing: Sexual orientation included under Sec. 12–4–4 ("Unlawful housing practices").

Private employment: Sexual orientation included under Sec. 12–4–5 ("Unlawful employment practices"), and Sec. 12–4–6 ("City Contracts").

Public accommodation: Sexual orientation included under Sec. 12–4–8 ("Public accommodations"), and Sec. 12–4–7 ("Health and social service practices").

Public employment: All employers and employees covered. Sec. 12–4–5 ("Unlawful employment practices").

Union practices: Sexual orientation included under Sec. 12–4–5 ("Unlawful employment practices").

Arlington County

Civil rights laws: Sexual orientation included under Arlington County Code: Chap. 31 ("Human Rights Law," Amd. 11/14/92).

Credit: Sexual orientation included under Sec. 31–3 (d) ("Prohibited acts—Credit").

Education: Sexual orientation included under Sec. 31–3 (e) ("Prohibited acts—Education").

Housing: Sexual orientation included under Sec. 31–3 (a) ("Prohibited acts—Housing").

Private employment: Sexual orientation included under Sec. 31–3 (b) ("Prohibited acts—Employment").

Public accommodation: Sexual orientation included under Sec. 31–3 (c) ("Prohibited acts—Public accommodations").

Union practices: Sexual orientation included under Sec. 31–3 (b) (3)–(5) ("Prohibited acts—Employment").

Virginia Beach

Civil rights laws: Sexual orientation included under Policy 6.06 ("Equal Employment Opportunity," Amd. 4/95).

Public employment: All government employers expressly covered.

WASHINGTON

Antimarriage legislation: Defined marriage as opposite-sex only, and prohibited and voided same-sex marriages. Rev. Code Wash. Sec. 26.04.010 and 26.04.020.

Civil rights laws: Sexual orientation included under Executive Order No. 85–09 ("Prohibiting Discrimination and Establishing Affirmative Action Policy and Rescinding Executive Order 84–10," 12/24/85).

Hate crimes: Separate crime and penalty established based on actual or perceived sexual orientation of victim. Data collection required. Wash. Rev. Code Sec. 9A.36.078–9A.36.080.

Public employment: All government employers expressly covered.

Sex statutes (sodomy): Repealed in 1976.

Clark County

Civil rights laws: Sexual orientation included under Equal Employment Opportunity Policy (Amd. 10/95).

Public employment: Government employer is expressly covered. Sec. A (2).

King County

Civil rights laws: Sexual orientation included under King County Code: Chap. 12.18 ("Fair Employment Practices," Amd. Ord. No. 7430, 1985), Chap. 12.20 ("Open Housing"), and Chap. 12.22 ("Discrimination in Places of Public Accommodations," Amd. Ord. No. 8625, 1988).

Domestic partnership employment benefits: Hard benefits provided, including medical coverage.

Housing: Sexual orientation included under Sec. 12.20.040 ("Unfair housing practices—Designated").

Private employment: Sexual orientation included under Sec. 12.18.030 ("Unfair employment practices prohibited").

Public accommodation: Sexual orientation included under Sec. 12.22.030 ("Discrimination in places of public accommodation").

Public employment: All government employers expressly covered. Sec. 12.18.030 ("Unfair employment practices prohibited").

Union practices: Sexual orientation included under Sec. 12.18.030 ("Unfair employment practices prohibited").

Seattle

Civil rights laws: Sexual orientation included under Seattle Municipal Code: Chap. 14.04 ("Fair Employment Practices") and Chap. 14.08 ("Unfair Housing Practices," Amd. Ord. No. 109116, 1980). Gender identity also included. "Sexual orientation" includes "transsexuality or transvestitism" (Amd. Ord. No. 112903, 1986). "Gender identity" obtained a separately listed protected class (Amd. Ord. 119628, 8/30/99).

Credit: Sexual orientation applied to the financing of real estate transactions only. Sec. 14.08.060 ("Discrimination in real estate-related transactions."

Domestic partnership employment benefits: Hard benefits provided to opposite- and same-sex couples. Benefits include sick and bereavement leave (8/89) and health and dental coverage (5/1/90).

Domestic partnership registry: Registry open to opposite- and same-sex couples. Not limited to residents and no rights specified.

Housing: Sexual orientation included under Sec. 14.08.040 ("Unfair Practices-Generally").

Private employment: Sexual orientation included under Subchapter II, Sec. 14.04.040 ("Unfair employment practices designated").

Public employment: All government employers expressly covered. Subchapter II, Sec. 14.04.040 ("Unfair employment practices designated").

Union practices: Sexual orientation included under Subchapter II, Sec. 14.04.040 ("Unfair employment practices designated").

Spokane

Civil rights laws: Sexual orientation included under Spokane Municipal Code: Title 1, Chap. 1.06 ("Law Against Discrimination," Amd. Ord. No. C-32232, 1/25/99).

Housing: Sexual orientation included under Sec. 1.06.090 (A) ("Non-Discrimination—Housing Practices").

Private employment: Sexual orientation included under Sec. 1.06.080 ("Nondiscrimination in Employment Practices").

Public accommodation: Sexual orientation included under Sec. 1.06.090 (B) ("Non-Discrimination—Public Accommodation Practices").

Public employment: All government employers expressly covered. Sec. 1.06.080 ("Nondiscrimination in Employment Practices").

Union practices: Sexual orientation included under Sec. 1.06.080 (B) and (D) ("Nondiscrimination in Employment Practices").

Thurston County

Civil rights laws: Sexual orientation included under Thurston County Policy ("Equal Opportunity," Amd. 1987).

Public employment: All government employers expressly covered.

Vancouver

Civil rights laws: Sexual orientation included under Vancouver Municipal Code (Amd. Ord. No. 3084, 10/4/93).

Domestic partnership employment benefits: Hard benefits provided to opposite- and same-sex couples. Benefits include medical, dental, and vision insurance, and family, sick, and bereavement leave.

Public employment: All government employers expressly covered. Chap. 2.69.

WEST VIRGINIA

Hate crimes: Sexual orientation is not included in hate crime statutes.

Sex statutes (sodomy): Repealed in 1976.

WISCONSIN

Civil rights laws: Sexual orientation included under Wisconsin Statutes Annotated: Chap. 111 ("Employment Relations"); Chap. 106 ("Apprentice and Employment Programs"); Chap. 118 ("General School Operations"); Chap. 38 ("Technical College System"); Chap. 36 ("University of Wisconsin System"); and Chap. 224 ("Bankers"). Amd. Act 1981, Chap. 112, Laws of 1981, Eff. 3/3/82.

Credit: Sexual orientation included under Sec. 224.77 (1) (o) ("Prohibited Conduct").

Education: Applies to "public schools": Sexual orientation included under Sec. 118.13, Sec. 118.40 (4) (2), Sec. 38.23, and Sec. 36.12.

Hate crimes: Established separate crime and penalty for bias crimes committed upon belief or perception of sexual orientation of victim. Some enhancement of sentencing. Wis. Stat. Sec 939.654.

Housing: Sexual orientation included under Sec. 106.04 (2) ("Discrimination Prohibited").

Private employment: Sexual orientation included under Sec. 111.321 ("Prohibited bases of discrimination").

Public accommodation: Sexual orientation included under Sec. 106.04 (9) ("Public place of accommodation or amusement").

Public employment: All government employers expressly covered. Sec. 111.321 ("Prohibited bases of discrimination") and Sec. 111.70 ("Municipal Employment").

Sex statutes (sodomy): Repealed in 1983.

Union practices: Sexual orientation included under Sec. 111.075.

Dane County

Civil rights laws: Sexual orientation included under Dane County Code of Ordinances: Chap. 74 (Amd. 1986–1987).

Domestic partnership employment benefits: Soft benefits that include bereavement leave.

Madison

Civil rights laws: Sexual orientation included under Madison City Code: Chap. 3.23 ("Equal Opportunities Ordinance," Amd. 1978).

Credit: Sexual orientation included under Sec. 3.23 (3) ("Credit").

Domestic partnership employment benefits: Hard benefits provided to opposite- and same-sex couples. Benefits include sick and bereavement leave (1988), and medical coverage (Eff. 1/1/2000). Amd. Res. No. 56617, 9/16/99.

Domestic partnership registry: Registry open to opposite- and same-sex couples. Not limited to residents.

Housing: Sexual orientation included under Sec. 3.23 (4) ("Housing").

Private employment: Sexual orientation included under Sec. 3.23 (8) ("Employment Practices").

Public accommodation: Sexual orientation included under Sec. 3.23 (5) ("Public Place of Accommodation or Amusement").

Public employment: All government employers expressly covered. Sec. 3.23 (8) ("Employment Practices").

Union practices: Sexual orientation included under Sec. 3.23 (8)(d) ("Employment Practices").

Milwaukee

Civil rights laws: Sexual orientation included under Milwaukee City Code: Chap. 109 ("Housing and Employment Discrimination," Amd. Ord. No. 892540, 10/16/90, Eff. 1/2/91).

Credit: Sexual orientation applied to the financing of real estate transactions only. Sec. 109–5 ("Housing Discrimination Prohibited").

Domestic partnership registry: Registry applies to same-sex couples only. No rights specified. Chap. 111 ("Domestic Partnership," Amd. Ord. No. 990224, 7/13/99).

Housing: Sexual orientation included under Sec. 109–5 ("Housing Discrimination Prohibited").

Private employment: Sexual orientation included under Sec. 109–9 ("Employment Discrimination Prohibited").

Union practices: Sexual orientation included under Sec. 109–9 ("Employment Discrimination Prohibited").

WYOMING

Hate crimes: No statutes based on any characteristics.

Sex statutes (sodomy): Repealed in 1977.

Appendix B: Resources

ADVOCACY ORGANIZATIONS

There are three major organizations in the United States that are involved in promoting equal rights for lesbians and gay men. Both have extensive libraries and produce annual reports, many of which are available on the Internet.

Human Rights Campaign
919 18th Street, NW, Suite 800
Washington, DC 20006
Phone: (202) 628-4160
Fax: (202) 347-5323
Website: www.hrcusa.org

Lambda Legal Defense and Education Fund
120 Wall Street, Suite 1500
New York, NY 10005
Phone: (212) 809-8585
Website: www.digitopia.com/lambda/lambda.html

National Gay and Lesbian Task Force (NGLTF)
1700 Kalorama Road, NW
Washington, DC 20009-2624
Phone: (202) 332-6483
Website: www.ngltf.org

For this book, the following publications from the NGLTF were used: *Legislating Equality: A Review of Laws Affecting Gay, Lesbian, Bisexual, and Transgendered People in the United States* (1999); *Calculated Compassion: How the Ex-Gay Movement Serves the Right's Attack on Democracy* (1998); and, *The Domestic Partnership Organizing Manual for Employee Benefits* (1999).

Other sources on lesbian and gay legal information are available online:

Law Enforcement Gays and Lesbians International (LEGAL)
Website: Members.aol.com/legalint/index.html

Law and Sexuality: A Review of Lesbian, Gay, Bisexual, and Transgender Legal Issues
Tulane Law School
6329 Freret Street
New Orleans, LA 70118
Phone: (504) 865-5835
Fax: (504) 862-6748
Website: www.law.tulane.edu/journals/l&s/contact.htm

Lesbian and Gay Law Association of Greater New York, Inc.
799 Broadway, Suite 340
New York, NY 10003
Phone: (212) 353-9118
Fax: (212) 353-2970
E-mail: le-gal@interport.net

National Center for Lesbian Rights
870 Market Street, Suite 570
San Francisco, CA 94102
Phone: (415) 392-6257
Fax: (415) 392-8442
E-mail: info@nclrights.org
Website: www.nclrights.org

***National Journal of Sexual Orientation Law* (online-journal)**
E-mail: gaylaw@email.unc.edu
Website: sunsite.unc.edu/gaylaw

National Lesbian and Gay Law Association
P.O. Box 180417
Boston, MA 02118
Phone: (508) 982-8290
E-mail: nlgla@aol.com
Website: www.nlgla.org

Queer Law
Gives daily update of court decisions, lawsuit filings, and articles on lesbian

and gay issues and the law. Hosted by Queer Resources Directory (QRD), and maintained by Dr. Ron Buckmire, Occidental College, California. Email: queerlaw@abacus.oxy.edu.

BOOKS AND JOURNALS

Blumenfeld, W. J., and D. Raymond. ***Looking at Gay and Lesbian Life,*** Rev. ed. Boston, MA: Beacon Press, 1993.

This book was the first comprehensive overview of lesbian and gay research, history, law, health, and culture. It could be used as the core text for introductory courses on homosexuality. It reads easily and is well documented.

Comstock, G. D. ***Violence against Lesbians and Gay Men.*** New York: Columbia University Press, 1991.

This is an excellent book reviewing the research on antigay violence. It provides a historical overview, empirical data on victims and perpetrators, and an understanding of the patriarchal underpinnings of antigay violence. It also analyzes the connection between conservative religious beliefs and antigay violence. It is well written and documented for college readers. For complementary materials, see the works of Gregory Herek.

Eskridge, W. N., Jr. ***Gaylaw: Challenging the Apartheid of the Closet.*** Cambridge, MA: Harvard University Press, 1999.

This is an impressive historical review of the politics and changes in U.S. law that constructed the modern gay closet. This is written for law and college students. At the end of the book, Eskridge discusses many of the paradoxes surrounding sex, consent, and the law, and their future implications. The unique appendix traces the changes in sex statutes from the 1600s to the present. The appendix alone is worth the price of the book. In many ways, this is an update of the well-written book, *Intimate Matters: A History of Sexuality in America,* by John D'Emilio and Estelle B. Freedman, New York: Harper & Row, 1988.

Gay Almanac, The. Complied by the National Museum and Archive of Lesbian and Gay History. New York: Berkley Books, 1996.

This is a wonderful resource on the gay community, its history, famous people, quotes, glossary, statistics, and other topics. It contains a comprehensive list of lesbian and gay community centers and a national directory of lesbian and gay organizations.

Gonsiorek, J. C., and J. D. Weinrich, eds. ***Homosexuality: Research Implications for Public Policy.*** Newbury Park, CA: Sage, 1991.

Although other books have reviewed the research into homosexuality, the selected articles in this book are viewed with respect to the impact such research has on government and organizational policies. Topics include the origins of human sexuality, the medicalization and "deviancy" of homosexuality, cross-cultural analysis, a review of law, reparative therapy, lesbian and gay relationships, and families. This is well written and aimed for college-level readers.

Greenberg, J. A. **"Defining Male and Female: Intersexuality and the Collision between Law and Biology."** *Arizona Law Review* 41(Summer 1999): 265.

This is what is termed the "mother" of all articles, that is, it reviews all previous articles and research on the subject of intersex. It contains medical definitions and the impact on sex statutes, legal identity, and documents. It is very important for its legal analysis and the impact on law defining gender, sex, and sexual orientation.

Harbeck, K. M., ed. ***Coming Out of the Classroom Closet: Gay and Lesbian Students, Teachers, and Curricula.*** New York: Harrington Park Press, 1992.

This was the first book aimed at educational issues. It contains research articles on the attitudes and beliefs of educational professionals, a legal review of cases and statutes as they apply to students and staff, suggestions on curriculum development, and a number of personal experiences. Everyone interested in the school setting should read this book.

Harvard Law Review editors. ***Sexual Orientation and the Law.*** Cambridge, MA: Harvard University Press, 1990.

Written as a guide for legal professionals, this book presents topics such as criminal justice, employment, education, same-sex couples, family, immigration, and others with a concise explanation of the law and some of the controversy. It does not contain academic research on homosexuality. It is outdated, but still useful.

Hunter, N. D., S. E. Michaelson, and T. B. Stoddard. ***The Rights of Lesbians and Gay Men: The Basic ACLU Guide to a Gay Person's Rights.*** 3d ed. Carbondale and Edwardsville, IL: Southern Illinois University Press, 1992.

This very small handbook is a concise summary of the laws and court cases relating to lesbians and gay men in the United States. It desperately needs to be updated, yet it is still usable to guide researchers in their own work. It is written for both the lay reader and legal professional.

Keen, Lisa, and Suzanne B. Goldberg. ***Strangers to the Law: Gay People on Trial.*** Ann Arbor, MI: University of Michigan Press, 1999.

This book traces the development of Colorado's Amendment 2 and its ultimate defeat by the U.S. Supreme Court in 1996 in *Romer v. Evans.* Written by Suzanne Goldberg, lawyer for the Lambda Legal Defense and Education Fund, and Lisa Keen, editor for the *Washington Blade,* the book is a captivating glimpse of the struggles Colorado experienced with the attempt to block antidiscrimination laws for lesbians and gay men. This is well written and appropriate for high school and college students. It contains much of the Supreme Court dialogue, and the complete written decision.

Marotta, T. ***The Politics of Homosexuality.*** Boston: Houghton Mifflin Company, 1981.

Although this is a very old book, it has one of the best historical accounts of the founding of the modern gay civil rights movement. It reviews the founding of the Mattachine Society and subsequent activists groups such as the Gay Liberation Front, the Gay Activists Alliance, the Radicalesbians, the Daughters of Bilitis, and others. More than anything, this book shows how a handful of activists was able to make significant strides toward gaining equal rights. These achievements were not made through intimidation, but rather through educating the heterosexual establishment about gay and lesbian issues and concerns. This is a "must have" book for any student of gay history.

Mohr, R. D. ***Gay/Justice—A Study of Ethics, Society, and Law.*** New York: Columbia University Press, 1988.

Written for the legal professional, this book engages in deep legal analysis of a number of issues including discrimination, sodomy, privacy, gay rights, and AIDS. It is perfect for class debates about gay legal issues. Although the laws regarding homosexuality have changed considerably since the publication of this book, it contains many of the classic arguments on freedom and social responsibility.

Richards, D. A. J. ***Women, Gays, and the Constitution: The Grounds for Feminism and Gay Rights in Culture and Law.*** Chicago: University of Chicago Press, 1998.

Written for the legal analyst and college student, this book makes the argument that sex statutes are examples of what Richards calls "moral slavery." He achieves this end by tracing the writings of early first-wave feminists and their analysis of slavery. Ultimately, Richards provides arguments as to why sexual orientation should be made a suspect class, gay marriages should be made legal, and other topics. It is perfect for the college law class.

Robson, R. ***Gay Men, Lesbians, and the Law.*** New York: Chelsea House Publishers, 1997.

This thin book is probably the best-written book for the lay reader or high school student. It reviews in nontechnical terms sex statutes, discrimination, education, families, criminal justice, health concerns, and the legal profession. It was mainly written to present the current legal status of gay men, lesbians, and the law. Its brevity limits the depth of the topics discussed.

Stewart, C. ***Sexually Stigmatized Communities—Reducing Heterosexism and Homophobia: An Awareness Training Manual.*** Thousand Oaks, CA: Sage, 1999.

This is a very large training manual for developing and delivering educational programs to reduce heterosexism and homophobia. Chapter 3 contains over 100 topic papers concisely presenting what is known about homosexuality. It could be used for a high school or college-level course on homosexuality. It summarizes the legal status of homosexuality.

Strasser, M. ***Legally Wed: Same-sex Marriage and the Constitution.*** Ithaca, NY: Cornell University Press, 1997.

This book focuses in on the controversy over same-sex marriage. It is written for the college-level reader. It contains a detailed discussion of the legal aspects of marriage, full faith and credit, the federal Defense of Marriage Act, and the impact same-sex marriage would have on child custody and adoptions. It is easy to read and not overburdened with references.

Walworth, J. ***Transsexual Works: An Employer's Guide.*** Westchester, CA: Center for Gender Sanity, 1998.

This is an excellent resource on the issue of transsexual workers. It gives many practical suggestions and some review of the law. Every business should have a copy of this book.

Williams, W. ***The Spirit and the Flesh: Sexual Diversity in American Indian Culture.*** Boston, MA: Beacon Press, 1992.

Although there are numerous books that look at other cultures with respect to homosexuality, *The Spirit and the Flesh* is probably the best. Written for the high school or college-level reader, it reads easily yet is authoritative. It is important for persons studying homosexuality to read a book such as this to gain a better understanding of the greater diversity in human sexuality than the simple binary heterosexual-homosexual paradigm.

The following journals also contain useful articles about gay, lesbian, bisexual, and transgender issues:

The Georgetown Journal of Gender and the Law
600 New Jersey Ave., N.W.
Washington, DC 20001
Phone:(202) 662-9460
Fax: (202) 662-9492 (f)
E-mail: gjgl@law.georgetown.edu

Journal of Homosexuality
Haworth Press
10 Alice St.
Binghamton, NY 13904-1580
Phone: (800) HAWORTH or (607) 722-5857
E-mail: getinfo@haworthpressinc.com

Law and Sexuality: A Review of Lesbian, Gay, Bisexual, and Transgender Legal Issues
Tulane University School of Law
John Giffen Weinmann Hall
6329 Freret St.
New Orleans, LA 70118
Phone: (504) 865-5835
www.law.tulane.edu/journals.htm

FEDERAL AND STATE AGENCIES FOR FILING DISCRIMINATION COMPLAINTS

Here are federal and state agencies with which discrimination complaints may be filed. The Equal Employment Opportunity Commission (EEOC) covers discrimination based upon race, color, religion, sex, national origin, age, and disabilities. Although the EEOC does not cover sexual orientation, often times other forms of discrimination accompany antigay and antilesbian discrimination and should also be filed. Even though the EEOC is not the appropriate agency with which to file discrimination claims based solely on sexual orientation, some state laws require the complainant to file with a federal agency at the same time. Thus, one is advised to file with the EEOC.

Protections afforded lesbians, gays, bisexuals and transgenders are a patchwork quilt of state and local legislation. Below is a list of human rights commissions for each state. These are good starting points for locating the appropriate agency with which to file discrimination complaints. Also, your local lesbian and gay community center or college lesbian, gay, bisexual, transgender resource centers (LGBT resource center) are places to contact for discovering the appropriate agency and procedures by which to file discrimination complaints.

The U.S. Equal Employment Opportunity Commission
1801 L Street, NW
Washington, DC 20507
Phone: (202) 663-4900
TDD: (202) 663-4494
To be connected automatically with the nearest EEOC field office, call:
Phone: (800) 669-4000
TDD: (800) 669-6820

Alabama
Birmingham District Office
1900 3rd Avenue North, Suite 101
Birmingham, AL 35203-2397
Phone: (205) 731-1359
TDD: (205) 731-0175

Arizona
Phoenix District Office
3300 N. Central Avenue
Phoenix, AZ 85012-1848
Phone: (602) 640-5000
TDD: (602) 640-5072

Arkansas
Little Rock Area Office
425 West Capitol Avenue, Suite 625
Little Rock, AR 72201
Phone: (501) 324-5060
TDD: (501) 324-5481

California
Fresno Local Office
1265 West Shaw Avenue, Suite 103
Fresno, CA 93711
Phone: (209) 487-5793

TDD: (209) 487-5837
Los Angeles District Office
255 E. Temple, 4th Floor
Los Angeles, CA 90012
Phone: (213) 894-1000
TDD: (213) 894-1121
Oakland Local Office
1301 Clay Street, Suite 1170-N
Oakland, CA 94612-5217
Phone: (510) 637-3230
TDD: (510) 637-3234
San Diego Area Office
401 B Street, Suite 1550
San Diego, CA 92101
Phone: (619) 557-7235
TDD: (619) 557-7232
San Francisco District Office
901 Market Street, Suite 500
San Francisco, CA 94103
Phone: (415) 356-5100
TDD: (415) 356-5098
San Jose Local Office
96 North 3rd Street, Suite 200
San Jose, CA 95112
Phone: (408) 291-7352
TDD: (408) 291-7374

Colorado
Denver District Office
303 E. 17th Avenue, Suite 510
Denver, CO 80203
Phone: (303) 866-1300
TDD: (303) 866-1950

District of Columbia
Washington Field Office
1400 L Street, NW, Suite 200
Washington, DC 20005
Phone: (202) 275-7377
TDD: (202) 275-7518

Florida

Miami District Office
2 South Biscayne Boulevard, Suite 2700
Miami, FL 33131
Phone: (305) 536-4491
TDD: (305) 536-5721

Tampa Area Office
501 East Polk Street, 10th Floor
Tampa, FL 33602
Phone: (813) 228-2310
TDD: (813) 228-2003

Georgia

Atlanta District Office
100 Alabama Street, Suite 4R30
Atlanta, GA 30303
Phone: (404) 562-6800
TDD: (404) 562-6801

Savannah Local Office
410 Mall Boulevard, Suite G
Savannah, GA 31406-4821
Phone: (912) 652-4234
TDD: (912) 652-4439

Hawaii

Honolulu Local Office
300 Ala Moana Boulevard, Room 7123-A
P.O. Box 50082
Honolulu, HI 96850-0051
Phone: (808) 541-3120
TDD: (808) 541-3131

Illinois

Chicago District Office
500 West Madison Street, Suite 2800
Chicago, IL 60661
Phone: (312) 353-2713
TDD: (312) 353-2421

Indiana

Indianapolis District Office
101 W. Ohio Street, Suite 1900
Indianapolis, IN 46204-4203

Phone: (317) 226-7212
TDD: (317) 226-5162

Kansas
Kansas City Area Office
400 State Avenue, Suite 905
Kansas City, KS 66101
Phone: (913) 551-5655
TDD: (913) 551-5657

Kentucky
Louisville Area Office
600 Dr. Martin Luther King Jr. Place, Suite 268
Louisville, KY 40202
Phone: (502) 582-6082
TDD: (502) 582-6285

Louisiana
New Orleans District Office
701 Loyola Avenue, Suite 600
New Orleans, LA 70113-9936
Phone: (504) 589-2329
TDD: (504) 589-2958

Maryland
Baltimore District Office
10 South Howard Street, 3rd Floor
Baltimore, MD 21201
Phone: (410) 962-3932
TDD: (410) 962-6065

Massachusetts
Boston Area Office
1 Congress Street, 10th Floor, Room 1001
Boston, MA 02114
Phone: (617) 565-3200
TDD: (617) 565-3204

Michigan
Detroit District Office
477 Michigan Avenue, Room 865
Detroit, MI 48226-9704
Phone: (313) 226-7636
TDD: (313) 226-7599

Minnesota
Minneapolis Area Office
330 South Second Avenue, Suite 430
Minneapolis, MN 55401-2224
Phone: (612) 335-4040
TDD: (612) 335-4045

Mississippi
Jackson Area Office
207 West Amite Street
Jackson, MS 39201
Phone: (601) 965-4537
TDD: (601) 965-4915

Missouri
St. Louis District Office
122 Spruce Street, Room 8.100
St. Louis, MO 63103
Phone: (314) 539-7800
TDD: (314) 539-7803

New Jersey
Newark Area Office
1 Newark Center, 21st Floor
Newark, NJ 07102-5233
Phone: (201) 645-6383
TDD: (201) 645-3004

New Mexico
Albuquerque District Office
505 Marquette Street, NW, Suite 900
Albuquerque, NM 87102
Phone: (505) 248-5201
TDD: (505) 248-5240

New York
Buffalo Local Office
6 Fountain Plaza, Suite 350
Buffalo, NY 14202
Phone: (716) 846-4441
TDD: (716) 846-5923
New York District Office
7 World Trade Center, 18th Floor

New York, NY 10048-0948
Phone: (212) 748-8500
TDD: (212) 748-8399

North Carolina
Charlotte District Office
129 West Trade Street, Suite 400
Charlotte, NC 28202
Phone: (704) 344-6682
TDD: (704) 344-6684
Greensboro Local Office
801 Summit Avenue
Greensboro, NC 27405-7813
Phone: (910) 333-5174
TDD: (910) 333-5542
Raleigh Area Office
1309 Annapolis Drive
Raleigh, NC 27608-2129
Phone: (919) 856-4064
TDD: (919) 856-4296

Ohio
Cincinnati Area Office
525 Vine Street, Suite 810
Cincinnati, OH 45202-3122
Phone: (513) 684-2851
TDD: (513) 684-2074
Cleveland District Office
1660 West Second Street, Suite 850
Cleveland, OH 44113-1454
Phone: (216) 522-2001
TDD: (216) 522-8441

Oklahoma
Oklahoma Area Office
210 Park Avenue
Oklahoma City, OK 73102
Phone: (405) 231-4911
TDD: (405) 231-5745

Pennsylvania
Philadelphia District Office
21 South 5th Street, 4th Floor

Philadelphia, PA 19106
Phone: (215) 451-5800
TDD: (215) 451-5814
Pittsburgh Area Office
001 Liberty Avenue, Suite 300
Pittsburgh, PA 15222-4187
Phone: (412) 644-3444
TDD: (412) 644-2720

South Carolina
Greenville Local Office
15 South Main Street, Suite 530
Greenville, SC 29601
Phone: (803) 241-4400
TDD: (803) 241-4403

Tennessee
Memphis District Office
1407 Union Avenue, Suite 521
Memphis, TN 38104
Phone: (901) 544-0115
TDD: (901) 544-0112
Nashville Area Office
50 Vantage Way, Suite 202
Nashville, TN 37228
Phone: (615) 736-5820
TDD: (615) 736-5870

Texas
Dallas District Office
207 S. Houston Street, 3rd Floor
Dallas, TX 75202-4726
Phone: (214) 655-3355
TDD: (214) 655-3363
El Paso Area Office
4171 N. Mesa Street, Building C, Suite 100
El Paso, TX 79902
Phone: (915) 534-6550
TDD: (915) 534-6545
Houston District Office
1919 Smith Street, 7th Floor
Houston, TX 77002
Phone: (713) 209-3320

TDD: (713) 209-3367
San Antonio District Office
5410 Fredericksburg Road, Suite 200
San Antonio, TX 78229-3555
Phone: (210) 229-4810
TDD: (210) 229-4858

Virginia
Norfolk Area Office
101 West Main Street, Suite 4300
Norfolk, VA 23510
Phone: (804) 441-3470
TDD: (804) 441-3578
Richmond Area Office
3600 West Broad Street, Room 229
Richmond, VA 23230
Phone: (804) 278-4651
TDD: (804) 278-4654

Washington
Seattle District Office
909 First Avenue, Suite 400
Seattle, WA 98104-1061
Phone: (206) 220-6883
TDD: (206) 220-6882

Wisconsin
Milwaukee District Office
310 West Wisconsin Avenue, Suite 800
Milwaukee, WI 53203-2292
Phone: (414) 297-1111
TDD: (414) 297-1115

STATE HUMAN RIGHTS COMMISSION OFFICES

Please call and confirm any of these addresses before you mail correspondence. The frequency with which these offices change contact information makes it impossible to keep this list up to date.

Alabama
Civil Rights and EEO Office
649 Monroe Street
Montgomery, AL 36131
Phone: (334) 242-8496

Alaska
Human Rights Commission
800 A Street, Suite 202
Anchorage, AK 99501-3628
Phone: (907) 276-7474

Arizona
Civil Rights Division
1275 W. Washington
Phoenix, AZ 85007
Phone: (602) 542-5263

California
Fair Employment and Housing Commission
1390 Market Street, Room 410
San Francisco, CA 94102-5377
Phone: (415) 557-2325

Colorado
Civil Rights Division
1560 Broadway, Suite 1050
Denver, CO 80202
Phone: (303) 894-2997

Connecticut
Human Rights and Opportunities Commission
90 Washington Street
Hartford, CT 06106
Phone: (203) 566-3350

Delaware
Human Relations Division
820 N. French Street
Wilmington, DE 19801
Phone: (302) 577-3485

District of Columbia
Human Rights Commission
51 N Street, NE, 6th Floor
Washington, DC 20002
Phone: (202) 724-0656

Florida
Civil Rights Division
2012 Capitol Circle, SE
Tallahassee, FL 32399-2152
Phone: (904) 488-5905

Georgia
Fair Employment Practices Office
156 Trinity Avenue, SW, Room 208
Atlanta, GA 30303
Phone: (404) 656-1736

Hawaii
Labor and Industrial Relations Department
830 Punchbowl Street
Honolulu, HI 96813
Phone: (808) 548-4533

Idaho
Human Rights Commission
P.O. Box 83720
Boise, ID 83720-0040
Phone: (208) 334-2873

Illinois
Human Rights Department
100 W. Randolph Street, Suite 10-100
Chicago, IL 60601
Phone: (312) 814-6245

Indiana
Civil Rights Commission
100 N. Senate Ave, Room N-103
Indianapolis, IN 46204
Phone: (317) 232-2600

Iowa
Human Rights Department
Lucas State Office Building
Phone: (515) 281-7300

Kansas
Civil Rights Commission
900 Jackson Street, SW, Suite 851-S
Topeka, KS 66612-1252
Phone: (913) 296-3206

Kentucky
Human Rights Commission
332 W Broadway, 7th Floor
Louisville, KY 40202
Phone: (502) 595-4024

Louisiana
Civil Rights
P.O. Box 3776
Baton Rouge, LA 70821
Phone: (504) 342-2700

Maine
Human Rights Commission
State House, Station 51
Augusta, ME 04333
Phone: (207) 624-6050

Maryland
Human Relations Commission
6 Saint Paul Street, 9th Floor
Baltimore, MD 21202
Phone: (410) 767-8600

Massachusetts
Commission Against Discrimination
One Ashburton Place, Room 601
Boston, MA 02108
Phone: (617) 727-3990

Michigan
Civil Rights Department
201 N. Washington Square
Lansing, MI 48913
Phone: (517) 335-3165

Minnesota
Human Rights Department
7th Place and Minnesota Street, Suite 500
St. Paul, MN 55101
Phone: (612) 296-5665

Mississippi
Appeals Board
301 N. Lamar Street, Room 100
Jackson, MS 39201
Phone: (601) 359-1406

Missouri
Human Rights Commission
3315 W. Truman Blvd
Jefferson City, MO 65102-1129
Phone: (573) 751-3325

Montana
Human Rights Division
P.O. Box 1728
Helena, MT 59624
Phone: (406) 444-3870

Nebraska
Equal Opportunity Commission
P.O. Box 94934
Lincoln, NE 68509
Phone: (402) 471-2024

Nevada
Equal Rights Commission
1515 E. Tropicana Avenue, Suite 590
Las Vegas, NV 89158
Phone: (702) 486-7161

New Hampshire
Human Rights Commission
163 Louden Road
Concord, NH 03301
Phone: (603) 271-2767

New Jersey
Civil Rights Division
383 W. State Street, Room CN089
Trenton, NJ 08625
Phone: (609) 984-3100

New Mexico
Human Rights Division
1596 Pacheco Street
Santa Fe, NM 87502
Phone: (505) 827-6823

New York
Human Rights Division
55 W. 125th Street
New York, NY 10027
Phone: (212) 870-8790

North Carolina
Human Relations Commission
217 W. Jones Street
Raleigh, NC 27603
Phone: (919) 733-7996

North Dakota
Equal Employment Opportunity Commission
600 E. Boulevard Avenue
Bismarck, ND 58505
Phone: (701) 328-2660

Ohio
Civil Rights Commission
220 Parsons Ave
Columbus, OH 43215
Phone: (614) 466-2785

Oklahoma
Human Rights Commission
2101 N. Lincoln Boulevard, Room 480
Oklahoma City, OK 73105
Phone: (405) 521-3441

Oregon
Civil Rights Division
800 Oregon Street, NE, #32, Suite 1045
Portland, OR 97232
Phone: (503) 731-4873

Pennsylvania
Human Relations Commission
P.O. Box 3145
Harrisburg, PA 17105
Phone: (717) 787-4410

Rhode Island
Human Rights Commission
10 Abbott Park Place
Providence, RI 02903
Phone: (401) 277-2661

South Carolina
Human Affairs Commission
P.O. Box 4490
Columbia, SC 29240
Phone: (803) 253-6336

South Dakota
Human Rights Division
910 E. Sioux, State Capitol
Pierre, SD 57501
Phone: (605) 773-4493

Tennessee
Human Rights Commission
400 Cornerstone Square Building
Nashville, TN 37243
Phone: (615) 741-4940

Texas
Human Rights Commission
8100 Cameron Road, Building B, Suite 525
Austin, TX 78754
Phone: (512) 837-8534

Utah
Labor Division and Antidiscrimination Division
160 E. 300 South, 3rd Floor
Salt Lake City, UT 84114
Phone: (801) 530-6921

Vermont
Public Protection Division
109 State Street
Montpelier, VT 05602
Phone: (802) 828-3171

Virginia
Human Rights Council
P.O. Box 717
Richmond, VA 23206
Phone: (804) 225-2292

Washington
Human Rights Commission
711 S. Capitol Way, Suite 402
Olympia, WA 98504
Phone: (360) 753-6770

West Virginia
Human Rights Commission
1321 Plaza East, Room 104–106
Charleston, WV 25301-1400
Phone: (304) 558-2616

Wisconsin
Equal Rights Division
P.O. Box 8928
Madison, WI 53708
Phone: (608) 266-0945

Wyoming
Labor Standards and Fair Employment Division
Herschler Building, 2nd Floor East
Cheyenne, WY 82002
Phone: (307) 777-6381

Table of Cases

Able v. United States, 88 F.3d 1280 (2nd Cir. 1996)
ACLU v. Reno I, 117 S. Ct. 2329 (1997)
ACLU v. Reno II, 31 F. Supp. 2d 473 (E.D. Pa. 1999)
Adam v. Gay, 19 Vt. 358 (1847)
Air Transport Association of America v. City and County of San Francisco, 27 West. St. U. L. Rev. 323 (1999–2000)
Albright v. Commonwealth ex rel. Fetters, 421 A.2d 157 (Pa. 1980)
Alison D. v. Virginia M., 572 N.E.2d 27 (N.Y. 1991)
Allstate Insurance Co. v. Hague, 449 U.S. 302 (1981)
Altman v. Minnesota Department of Corrections, 1999 U.S. Dist. LEXIS 14897 (D. Minn. 1999)
Ancafora v. Board of Education, 491 F.2d 498 (4th Cir. 1974)
Anonymous v. Mellon, 398 N.Y.S.2d 99 (N.Y. Sup. Ct. 1977)
Appeal of Ritchie, 155 Neb. 824, 828, 53 N.W.2d 753, 755 (1952)
Avis Rent-A-Car System, Inc. v. Aguilar, 980 P.2d 846 (Cal. 1999)
B. v. B., 355 N.Y.S.2d 712 (N.Y. Sup. Ct. 1974)
Baehr v. Lewin, 852 P.2d 44 (Haw.), *reh'g granted in part,* 875 P.2d 225 (Haw. 1993)
Baker v. Nelson, 191 N.W.2d 185 (Minn. 1971)
Baker v. Vermont, 744 A.2d 864 (Vt. 1999)
Baluyut v. Superior Court, 12 Cal.4th 826 (1996)
Bennett v. State, 677 S.W.2d 121 (Tex. Crim. App. 1984)
Ben-Shalom v. Marsh, 881 F.2d 454, 464 (7th Cir. 1989)
Berrill v. Houde, Connecticut, 1997 Conn. Super. LEXIS 1272. May 13, 1997. Unreported.
Bethel School District No. 403 v. Fraser, 478 U.S. 675 (1986)
Bezio v. Patenaude, 410 N.E.2d 1207 (Mass. 1980)
Big Brothers, Inc. v. Minneapolis Commission on Civil Rights, 284 N.W.2d 823 (Minn. 1979)
Board of Education of Westside Community School v. Mergens, 496 U.S. 226 (1990)
Board of Education v. Pico, 457 U.S. 853 (1982)
Board of Regents v. Southworth, 120 S.Ct. 1346 (2000)
Bottoms v. Bottoms, 444 S.E.2d 276, (Va. Ct. App. 1994), *rev'd,* 457 S.E.2d 102 (Va. 1995)
Bowen v. Gilliard, 483 U.S. 587 (1987)
Bowers v. Hardwick, 478 U.S. 186 (1986)
Boy Scouts of America v. Dale, 120 S.Ct. 2446 (2000)
Bradley v. Pizzaco of Nebraska, 939 F.2d 610 (8th cir. 1991)

Bragdon v. Abbott, 912 F.Supp. 580 (1998)
Braschi v. Stahl Associates Co., 543 N.E.2d 49 (N.Y. 1989)
Brown v. Board of Education, 347 U.S. 483 (1954)
Buckley v. Valeo, 424 U.S. 1 (1976)
Bulloch v. United States, 487 F. Supp. 1078 (D.N.M. 1980)
Burlington Industries, Inc. v. Ellerth, 118 S.Ct. 2257 (1998)
Cammermeyer v. Aspin, 850 F. Supp. 910, 918 (W.D. Wash. 1994)
Campbell v. Sundquist, 926 S.W.2d 250 (Tenn. Ct. App. 1996)
Carroll v. Talman Federal Savings & Loan Association, 604 F.3d 1028 (7th Cir. 1979), *cert. denied*, 445 U.S. 929 (1980)
Ceniceros v. Board of Trustees of the San Diego Unified School District, 66 F.3d 1535 (9th Cir. 1995)
Chaffin v. Frye, 119 Cal. Rptr. 22 (1975)
Chaplinsky v. New Hampshire, 315 U.S. 568 (1942)
Childers v. Dallas Police Department, 513 F. Supp. 134 (N.D. Tex. 1981)
City of Ladue v. Horn, 720 S.W.2d 745 (Mo. Ct. App. 1986)
Cleburne v. Cleburne Living Center, Inc., 473 U.S. 433, 448 (1985)
Commonwealth v. Bonadio, 415 A.2d 47 (Pa. 1980)
Commonwealth v. Carr, 398 Pa. Super. 306, 580 2d. 1362 5–88 (1990)
Commonwealth v. Clary, 447 N.E.2d 1217 (Mass. 1983)
Commonwealth v. Goodman, 676 A.2d 234 (Pa. 1966)
Commonwealth v. Wasson, 842 S.W.2d 487 (Ky. 1992)
Connell v. Francisco, 898 P.2d 831 (Wash. 1995)
Constant A. v. Paul C.A., 496 A.2d 1 (Pa. Super. Ct. 1985)
Corbett v. Corbett, 2 All E.R. 33 (1970)
Dailey v. Dailey, 635 S.W.2d 391 (Tenn. Ct. App. 1981)
Davis v. Monroe County Board of Education, 526 U.S. 629 (1999)
DeSantis v. Pacific Telephone and Telegraph Co., 608 F.2d 327 (9th Cir. 1979)
Dillon v. Legg, 441 P.2d 912 (Cal. 1968)
Dobre v. Amtrak, 850 F. Supp. 284 (E.D. Pa. 1993)
Doby v. Carroll, 274 Ala. 273, 276, 147 So.2d 803, 805 (1962)
Doe v. Brockton School Committee, No. 2000-J-638 (Mass. App. Ct. 2000)
Doe v. Mutual of Omaha Insurance Co., 179 F.3d 557 (7th Cir. 1999)
Doe v. Virginia, 403 F. Supp. 1199 (E.D. Va 1975), *aff'd mem.*, 425 U.S. 901 (1976)
Downs v. Los Angeles Unified School District, D.C. No. CV-98–09876-SVW, No. 99–56797 (9th Cir. Ct. 2000)
East 53rd Street Associates v. Mann, 121 A.D.2d 289, 503 N.Y.S.2d 752 (1986)
East High Gay/Straight Alliance v. Board of Education, 81 F.Supp. 2d 1166 (1999)
Eisenstadt v. Baird, 405 U.S. 438 (1972)
Elden v. Sheldon, 758 P.2d 582 (Cal. 1988)
Ennis v. National Association of Business & Education Radio, Inc., 53 F.3d 55 (4th Cir. 1995)
Evans v. Romer, 882 P.2d 1335 (Colo. 1994) (Evans II)
Faragher v. City of Boca Raton, 118 S.Ct.2275 (1998)
Farmer v. Brennan, 511 U.S. 825 (1994)
Frances B. v. Mark B., 355 N.Y.S.2d 712 (N.Y. Sup. Ct. 1974)
Fricke v. Lynch, 491 F. Supp. 381 (D.R.I. 1980)
Frontiero v. Richardson, 411 U.S. 677 (1973)

G.A. v. D.A., 745 S.W.2d 726 (Mo. Ct. App. 1987)
Gay Activists Alliance v. Lomenzo, 329 N.Y.S. 2d 181 (N.Y. App. Div. 1972), *aff'd*, 31 N.Y.2d 965 (1973)
Gay Law Students' Association v. Pacific Telephone and Telegraph Co., 595 P.2d 592 (Cal. 1979)
Gay Rights Coalition of Georgetown University Law Center v. Georgetown University, 536 A.2d 1 (D.C. App. 1987)
Gaylord v. Tacoma School District No. 10, 559 P. 2d 1340 (Wash. 1977), *cert. denied*, 434 U.S. 879 (1977)
Gay Students Organization v. Bonner, 367 F. Supp. 1088 (D.N.H.), *aff'd*, 509 F.2d 652 (1st Cir. 1974)
Gerald & Margaret D. v. Peggy R., No. C-9104, Petition No. 9–12–143-CV (Del. Fam. Ct. Nov. 17, 1980) (LEXIS, States library, Del. file)
Gilvin v. State, 418 So. 2d 996 (Fla. 1982)
Godkin v. San Leandro School District, (U.S. Dist. Ct., Calif., Walker, J., Oct. 1999)
Griswold v. Connecticut, 381 U.S. 479 (1965)
Gryczan v. Montana, 942 P.2d 112 (Mont. 1997)
Hartin v. Director of Bureau of Records, 347 N.Y.S.2d 515 (N.Y. Sup. Ct. 1973)
Hartogs v. Employers Mutual Liability Co., 89 Misc.2d 486 (N.Y. 1977)
Hatheway v. Gannett Satellite Information Network, Inc., 459 N.W.2d 873 (Wis. Ct. App. 1990)
Hazelwood School District v. Kuhlmeier, 484 U.S. 260 (1988)
Healy v. James, 408 U.S. 169 (1971)
High Tech Gays v. Defense Industry Security Clearance Office, 668 F. Supp. 1361 (N.D. Cal. 1987), *rev'd*, 909 F.2d 375 (9th Cir. 1990)
Hinman v. Department of Personnel Administration, 213 Cal. Rptr. 410 (Cal. Ct. App. 1985)
Hoepfl v. Barlow, 906 F. Supp. 317 (E.D. Va. 1995)
Holloway v. Arthur Anderson, 566 F.2d 659 (9th Cir. 1977)
Holman v. State of Indiana, 211 F.3d 399 (7th Cir. 2000), cert. denied
Holmes v. California Army National Guard, 920 F. Supp. 1510 (N.D. Cal. 1996)
Holmes/Watson v. California Army National Guard, 124 F.3d 1126 (1997)
Hosford v. School Committee of Sandwich, 421 Mass. 708 (1996)
Hunter v. Erickson, 393 U.S. 385 (1969)
Hurley v. Irish-American Gay, Lesbian, and Bisexual Group of Boston, 115 S.Ct. 2338 (1995)
In re Adoption of Robert Paul P., 63 N.Y.2d 233, 236, 471, N.E.2d 424, 425, 481 N.Y.S.2d 652, 653 (1984)
In re Breisch, 434 A.2d 815 (Pa. Super. Ct. 1981)
In re Eck, 584 A.2d 859 (N.J. Super. Ct. App. Div. 1991)
In re Grimes, 609 A.2d 158 (Pa. 1992)
In re Holt, 102 Idaho 44, 625 P.2d 398 (1981)
In re J.S. & C., 129 A.2d 90 (N.J. Super. 1974), *aff'd* 142 N.J. Super. 499, *aff'd* 362 A.2d 254 (1976)
In re Jane B., 85 Misc. 2d 515, 528, 380 (N.Y.S. 2d 848, 860, 1976)
In re Kaufmann's Will, 247 N.Y.S.2d 664 (N.Y. App. Div. 1964), *aff'd*, 205 N.E.2d 864 (N.Y. 1965)
In re Marriage of Birdsall, 197 Cal. App. 3d at 1024, 1028, 243 Cal. Rptr. at 287, 289 (1988)

In re McIntyre, 715 A.2d 400, 401 (Pa. 1998)
In re Toboso-Alfonso, 13 Immigr. Rep. (MB B1–29) (B.I.A. 1990)
Irish v. Irish, 300 N.W.2d 739 (Mich. Ct. App. 1980)
J. L. P.(H.) v. D.J.P., 643 S.W.2d 685 (Mo. App. 1982)
Jaffee v. Redmond, No. 95–266 (1996, June 13)
Jones v. Hallahan, 501 S.W.2d 588 (Ky. Ct. App. 1973)
Keyishian v. Board of Regents, 385 U.S. 589 (1967)
Kramarsky v. Stahl Management, 401 N.Y.S.2d 943 (N.Y. Sup. Ct. 1977)
Loving v. Virginia, 388 U.S. 1 (1967)
Magnolia Petroleum Co. v. White, 320 U.S. 430 (1943)
Marriage of Cabalquinto, 669 P.2d 886 (Wash. 1983)
Marvin v. Marvin, 557 P.2d 106 (Cal. 1976)
Massachusetts Board of Retirement v. Murgia, 427 U.S. 307 (1976)
Max v. McLynn, 88 N.Y. 358 (1882)
McWilliams v. Fairfax County Board of Supervisors, 72 F.3d 1191 (1st Cir. 1996)
Meinhold v. United States Dep't of Defense, 34 F.3d 1469, 1477 (9th Cir. 1994)
Meritor Savings Bank v. Vinson, 477 U.S. 57 (1986)
Michigan Organization for Human Rights v. Kelly, No. 88–81 5820CZ (MI. Chap. Cir. Ct. July 9, 1990)
Miller v. California, 413 U.S. 15 (1973)
Moore v. City of East Cleveland, 431 U.S. (1977)
Morrison v. State Board of Education, 461 P.2d 375 (Cal. 1969)
Moskowitz v. Moskowitz, 385 A.2d 120 (N.H. 1978)
Nabozny v. Podlesny, 92 F.3d 446 (7th Cir. 1996)
National Gay Task Force v. Board of Education, 729 F.2d 1270 (10th Cir. 1984), *aff'd,* 470 U.S. 903 (1985)
Neville v. State, 430 A.2d 570 (Md. 1981)
N.K.M. v. L.E.M., 606 S.W.2d 179 (Mo. Ct. App. 1980)
Norton v. Macy, 417 F.2d 1161 (D.C. Cir. 1969)
Olivieri v. Ward, 801 F.2d 602 (2d Cir. 1986)
Oncale v. Sundowner Offshore Services, Inc., 523 U.S. 75 (1998)
One, Inc. v. Olesen, 355 U.S. 371 (1958)
Padula v. Webster, 822 F.2d 97 (D.C. Cir. 1987)
Parisie v. Greer, 705 F.2d 882 (7th Cir.) (per curiam), *cert. denied,* 464 U.S. 950 (1983)
Payne v. Western Atlantic Railroad, 81 Tenn. 507 (1884), *rev'd on other grounds sub nom. Hutton v. Watters,* 179 S.W. 134 (1915)
People of Illinois v. Rokicki, 718 N.E.2d 333 (Ill. App., 2nd Dist., Sept. 28, 1999)
People v. Berck, 300 N.E.2d 411 (N.Y. 1973)
People v. Brown, 212 N.W.2d 55 (Mich. Ct. App. 1973)
People v. Onofre, 415 N.E.2d 936 (N.Y. 1980)
Pickering v. Board of Education, 391 U.S. 563 (1969)
Pope v. East Brunswick Board of Education, 12 F.3d 1244 (3d Cir. 1993)
Powell v. Georgia, 510 S.E.2d 18 (Ga. 1998)
Price Waterhouse v. Hopkins, 490 U.S. 228 (1989)
Pruitt v. Cheny, 963 F.2d 1160 (9th Cir. 1991)
Regents of the University of California v. Bakke, 438 U.S. 265 (1978)
Reynolds v. United States, 98 U.S. 244 (1879)
Richenberg v. Perry, 97 F.3d 256 (8th Cir. 1996)

Roberts v. Roberts, 212 S.E.2d 410 (N.C. Ct. App. 1975)
Roberts v. Roberts, 489 N.E.2d 1067 (Ohio Ct. App. 1985)
Roberts v. United States Jaycees, 468 U.S. 609 (1984)
Rochin v. California, 342 U.S. 165 (1952)
Roe v. Roe, 324 S.E.2d 691 (Va. 1985)
Romer v. Evans, 116 S.Ct. 1620 (1996)
Rosa v. Park West Bank & Trust Co., 2000 WL 726228 (Jun. 8)
Rose v. Locke, 423 U.S. 48 (1975)
Rose v. Rose, 481 U.S. 619 (1987)
Rowland v. Mad River Local School District, 470 U.S. 1009 (1985)
Roy v. Hartogs, 381 N.Y.S.2d, 587 (N.Y. App. Ct. 1976)
Rubano v. DiCenzo, No. 97–604-A (RI Sup. Ct., 9/25/2000)
S. v. S. (otherwise W.), 3 All E.R. 55 (1962)
Santosky v. Kramer, 455 U.S. 745 (1982)
School Board of Nassau County v. Arline, 480 U.S. 273 (1987)
Schwenk v. Hartford, 9735870, U.S. 9th Circuit Court of Appeals (2000, March 11)
Shelton v. Tucker, 364 U.S. 479 (1960)
Sherrer v. Sherrer, 334 U.S. 343 (1948)
Shuttleworth v. City of Birmingham, 394 U.S. 147 (1969)
Singer v. Hara, 522, P.2d 1187 (Wash. Ct. App. 1974)
Singer v. U.S. Civil Service Commission, 530 F.2d 247 (9th Cir. 1976), *vacated and remanded,* 429 U.S. 1034 (1977)
Smith v. Liberty Mutual Insurance Co., 569 F.2d 325 (5th Cir. 1978)
Solmitz v. Maine School Administrative District No. 59, 495 A.2d 812 (Me. 1985)
Stanley v. Georgia, 394 U.S. 557 (1969)
State v. Viggiani, 431 N.Y.S.2d 979 (N.Y. Crim. Ct. 1980)
State v. Walsh, 713 S.W.2d 508 (Mo. 1986) (en banc)
Steffan v. Perry, 41 F.3d 677, 694–95 (D.C. Cir. 1994) (en banc)
Sterling v. Borough of Minersville, 2000 WL 1664909 (Nov. 6)
Tanner v. OHSU, 971 P.2d 435 (Or. Ct. App. 1988)
Terminiello v. Chicago, 337 U.S. 1 (1949)
Thomasson v. Perry, 80 F.3d 915 (4th Cir.) (en banc)
Tinker v. Des Moines Independent Community School District, 393 U.S. 503 (1969)
Transcript of reconsideration hearing, p. 22, ln. 11–16. *In Meinhold v. United States Dep't of Defense,* 34 F.3d 1469, 1477 (9th Cir. 1994), p. 8.
Turner v. Safley, 482 U.S. 78 (1987)
Ulane v. Eastern Airlines, 581 F. Supp. 821 (N.D. Ill. 1983)
United States v. Carolene Products Co., 304 U.S. 144 (1938)
United States v. Guest, 383 U.S. 747 (1966)
Van Ootegehm v. Gray, 628 F.2d 488 (5th Cir. 1980), *aff'd en banc,* 654 F.2d 304 (1981), *cert. denied,* 455 U.S.909 (1982)
Watkins v. United States Army, 875 R.2d 699 (9th Cir. 1989) (en banc), cert. denied, 498 U.S. 957 (1990)
Watson v. Perry, 918 F. Supp. 1403 (W.D. Wash. 1996)
Weaver v. Nebo School District, et al., No. 2:97-CV-819J (D. Utah 1998)
Whorton v. Dillingham, 248 Cal. Rptr. 405 (Ct. App. 1988)
Williams v. Glendening (Md. Cir. Ct., Baltimore City, Oct. 15, 1998)

Williams v. Pryor, 2000 WL 1513756 (Oct. 12)
Wood v. C.G. Studios Inc., 660 F. Supp. 176 (E.D. Pa. 1987)
Wrightson v. Pizza Hut, 99 F.3d 138 (4th Cir. 1996)
Yost v. Board of Regents, not reported in F. Supp., 1993 WL 524757 (D. Md. 1993)
Zablock v. Redhail, 434 U.S. 374 (1978)

Table of Statutes

Executive and Congressional Orders

Americans with Disabilities Act of 1990 (ADA), 42 U.S.C. 12101

Child Online Protection Act (COPA), Title XIV, 47 U.S.C. 231

Civil Service Reform Act of 1978, 5 U.S.C. 71, § 2302(b)(10)

Communications Decency Amendment (CDA), amending § 223 of the Obscene or Harassing Use of Telecommunications Facilities under the Communications Act of 1934, 47 U.S.C. 223. (Struck down by the Supreme Court in *ACLU v. Reno I*, 117 S. Ct. 2329 (1997)

"Don't Ask, Don't Tell, Don't Pursue" Policy. Informal name for 37 U.S.C. 546, 1993

Equal Access Act, 20 U.S.C. §§ 4071–4074

Executive Order No. 13140 signed on October 6, 1999, that amended the *Manual for Courts-Martial* to include sexual orientation in hate crime reporting and prosecution. Accessed on the web at www.pub.whitehouse.gov/uri-res/I2R?urn:pdi://oma.eop.gov.us/1999/10/7/11.text.2

Federal Employment Non-Discrimination Act. (1998, May 28). Executive Order 13087 that amends Section 1 of Executive Order 11478 (1969). Accessed on the web at www.pub.whitehouse.gov/uri-res/I2R?urn:pdi://oma.eop.gov.us/1998/6/1/8.text.2

Hate Crime Statistics Act, 28 U.S.C. 534, 1990

Presumption of Homosexual Conduct, 37 U.S.C § 654(b)(2)

The Public Health and Welfare Act, 42 U.S.C. §§ 1437, Chapter 8 Low-Income Housing, 42 U.S.C. § 1437b(3)

State Statutes

Child Adoption: Notification of Adoption Proceedings, Ga. Code Ann. § 19-8-12 (1982)

Child Adoption: Surrender of Parental Rights , Ga. Code Ann. § 19-8-11 (1982)

Discrimination in Selling, Renting, or Leasing Rental Property Prohibited, Or. Rev. Stat. § 659.033 (1996).

N.Y. Exec. Law Chp. 44, Art. 11, § 296 (1988).

Obscenity, Ala. Code § 13A-200.1

Unfair Housing Practices Prohibited Act, Colo. Rev. Stat. § 24-34-502 (1989).

References

Adam, B. 1978. *The Survival of Domination: Inferiorization in Everyday Life*. New York: Elsevier.

Adams, H. E., L. W. Wright, and B. A. Lohr. 1996. "Is Homophobia Associated with Homosexual Arousal?" *Journal of Abnormal Psychology* 105(3): 440–445.

Allport, G. 1954. *The Nature of Prejudice*. Reading, MA: Addison-Wesley.

Andrisani, P. J., and M. B. Shapiro. 1978. "Women's Attitudes toward Their Jobs: Some Longitudinal Data on a National Sample." *Personnel Psychology* 31: 15–34.

"Appeals Court Overturns Awarding of Estate to Gay Partner." (17 February 2000). Associated Press website: www.wire.ap.org/APnews.

"Artificial Insemination: A New Wave." 1977. *British Journal of Sexual Medicine* 27(2) (February): 206.

Bagnall, R. G. 1984. "Burdens on Gay Litigants and Bias in the Court System: Homosexual Panic, Child Custody, and Anonymous Parties." *Harvard Civil Rights-Civil Liberties Law Review* 19: 498–515.

Bailey, J. M., D. Bobrow, M. Wolfe, and S. Mikach. 1995. "Sexual Orientation of Adult Sons of Gay Fathers." *Developmental Psychology* 31: 124–129.

Bard, M., and D. Sangrey. 1979. *The Crime Victim's Book*. New York: Basic Books.

Bayer, R. 1981. *Homosexuality and American Psychiatry*. New York: Basic Books.

Becker, L. 1995. "Recognition of Domestic Partnerships by Governmental Entities and Private Employers." *National Journal of Sexual Orientation Law* 1(1): 91–104.

Bedrick, B. R. 1997. "Report on The Defense of Marriage Act." Government Accounting Office website: www.gao.gov (31 January 1997).

Bem, S. 1974. "The Measurement of Psychological Androgyny." *Journal of Consulting and Clinical Psychology* 42: 155–162.

Berlet, C. 1998. "Who Is Mediating the Storm? Right-Wing Alternative Information Networks." In *Media, Culture, and the Religious Right*, edited by L. Kintz and J. Lesage. Minneapolis, MN: University of Minnesota Press.

Berube, A. 1990. *Coming Out Under Fire: The History of Gay Men and Women in WWII*. New York: Plume.

Bidwell, R.J. 1992. "Adolescent Issues." In *Project 10 Handbook*. Los Angeles: Friends of Project 10.

Birk, L. 1980. "The Myth of Classical Homosexuality: Views of a Behavioral Psychotherapist." In *Homosexual Behavior: A Modern Reappraisal*, edited by J. Marmor. New York: Basic Books.

Black's Law Dictionary. 1990. 6th ed.

Blumenfeld, W. J., and D. Raymond, eds. 1993. *Looking at Gay and Lesbian Life*. Rev. ed. Boston: Beacon Press.

Bolin, A. 1988. *In Search of Eve: Transsexual Rites of Passage*. New York: Bergin & Garvey.

Bonauto, M. 2000. "Vermont House Gives Final Approval to Civil Union Bill." Gay and Lesbian Advocates and Defenders (GLAD) website: www.glad.org. Accessed 25 April 2000.

Boswell, J. 1980. *Christianity, Social Tolerance, and Homosexuality: Gay People in Western Europe from the Beginning of the Christian Era to the Fourteenth Century*. Chicago: University of Chicago Press.

Bozett, F. W. 1993. "Gay Fathers: A Review of the Literature." In *Psychological Perspectives on Lesbian and Gay Male Experiences*, edited by L. D. Garnets and D. C. Kimmel. New York: Columbia University Press.

Bracton, H. 1968. *On the Laws and Customs of England*. Translated with revisions and notes, by Samuel E. Thorne. Cambridge: Published in association with the Selden Society, the Belknap Press of Harvard University Press.

"Brockton Court Rules in Favor of Transgender Student." (12 October 2000). Associated Press website: www.wire.ap.org/APnews.

"Brother Admits Shooting Gays." (7 November 1999). Associated Press website: www.wire.ap.org/APnews.

Bruce, T. M. 1996. "Doing the Nasty: An Argument for Bringing Same-Sex Erotic Conduct Back into the Courtroom." *Cornell Law Review* 81:1135–1151. Citing, "Senators loudly debate gay ban." *New York Times* (8 May 1993): A9.

"Buchanan Calls AIDS 'Retribution.'" 1992. *San Francisco Chronical* (28 February 1992): A1.

Buchanan, P. 1988. *Right from the Beginning*. Boston: Little, Brown.

Buie, J. 1990. "'Heterosexual Ethic' Mentality Is Decried." *American Psychological Association Monitor* 21(3): 20–21.

Burr, C. 1996. *A Separate Creation: The Search for the Biological Origins of Sexual Orientation*. New York: Hyperion.

Cabaj, R. P., and T. S. Stein. 1996. *Textbook of Homosexuality and Mental Health*. Washington, DC: American Psychiatrist Press.

Cain, R. 1990. "Stigma Management and Gay Identity Development." *Social Work* 36(1): 67–73.

Califia, P. 1983. "Justifiable Homicide?" *The Advocate*, 12 May, 12.

Call, Hall. 1956. Letter to Dwight Huggins, Sam Morford, Tony Segura, et al., 30 August. Reported in T. Marotta, *The Politics of Homosexuality*, p. 15. Boston: Houghton Mifflin.

Capers, B. 1991. "Sex(ual Orientation) and Title VII." *Columbia Law Review* 91(5): 1158–1187.

Carter, K. 1997. "Group Monitors Pervasiveness of Comments: Gay Slurs Abound, Students Say." *Des Moines Register* (7 March 1997): B3.

"Case Dismissed." 2000. *Frontiers* 18(22): 32.

Cass, V. 1979. "Homosexual Identity Formation: A Theoretical Model." *Journal of Homosexuality* 4(3): 219–235.

Center for Lesbian and Gay Civil Rights. "Gay Group Demands City Withdrawal of Support for Boy Scouts." 2000. Press release, 28 June. Available at www.center4civilrights.org.

Chiang, H. 2000. "Ruling Protects Gay Juror Rights." *San Francisco Chronicle* (3 February 2000): A1.

Chuang, H. T., and D. Addington. 1988. "Homosexual Panic: A Review of Its Concept." *Canadian Journal of Psychiatry* 33(7): 613–617.

Civil Service Bulletin. 1973. (21 December). Quoted in *Aston v. Civiletti*, 613 F.2d 923, 927 (D.C. Cir. 1979).

Clark, H. 1988. *The Law of Domestic Relations in the United States*. 2d ed. St. Paul, MN: West Publishing Co.

Clark, J. P., and L. L. Tifft. 1966. "Polygraph and Interview Validation of Self-Reported Deviant Behavior." *American Sociological Review* 31(4): 516–23.

Coke, E. 1812. *The First Part of the Institutes of the Laws of England*. Institutes 8.a.

Coleman, E. 1981–1982. "Developmental Stages of the Coming Out Process." *Journal of Homosexuality* 7(2/3): 31–44.

Comstock, G. D. 1991. *Violence Against Lesbians and Gay Men*. New York: Columbia University Press.

Corn, D. 1995. "Buchanan Rages on a Potent Trinity—God, Country and Me." *The Nation* (26 June 1995): 915.

Crosby, R. 1982. *Relative Deprivation and Working Women*. New York: Oxford University Press.

"Custody Denials to Parents in Same-Sex Relationships: An Equal Protection Analysis." 1989. *Harvard Law Review* 102(3): 617.

Dean, H. 2000. State of the State Address. 5 January, at Montpelier, Vermont. Vermont governor's website: www.state.vt.us/governor/0002.htm.

D'Emilio, J. 1983. *Sexual Politics, Sexual Communities: The Making of a Homosexual Minority in the United States, 1940–1970*. Chicago: University of Chicago Press.

D'Emilio, J., and E. B. Freedman. 1988. *Intimate Matters: A History of Sexuality in America*. New York: Harper & Row.

"Denver Public School Escapes Legal Battle with Teacher." 2001. Colorado Legal Initiative Project website: www.clipcolorado.net.

Devor, H. 1997. *FTM: Female-to-Male Transsexuals in Society*. Bloomington, IN: Indiana University Press.

Diagnostic and Statistical Manual of Mental Disorders. 1994. 4th ed. Washington, DC: American Psychiatric Association.

Diamond, M. 1993. "Homosexuality and Bisexuality in Different Populations." *Archives of Sexual Behavior* 22(4): 291–310.

———. 1997. "Sexual Identity and Sexual Orientation in Children with Traumatized or Ambiguous Genitalia." *Journal of Sex Research* 199: 34.

Dicks, G. H., and A. T. Childers. 1934. "The Social Transformation of a Boy Who Had Lived His First Fourteen Years as a Girl: A Case History." *American Journal of Orthopsychiatry* 4(4): 508–517.

———. 1944. "The Social Transformation of a Boy Who Had Lived His First Fourteen Years as a Girl II: Fourteen Years Later." *American Journal of Orthopsychiatry* 14(3): 448–452.

"Does a Gay Pass Justify a Murder?" 1983. *Montrose* (Texas) *Voice* (1 April 1983): 14.

"Does Boy Scouts' Policy on Homosexuals Preclude Tax-Exempt Status?" 2000. *Tax Analysts' Tax Notes Today* (11 December 2000).

Donovan, J. M. 1998. "An Ethical Argument to Restrict Domestic Partnerships to Same-Sex Couples." *Law and Sexuality* 8: 649–670.

"*Donovan v. County of Los Angeles and State Compensation Insurance Fund*: California's Recognition of Homosexuals' Dependency Status in Actions for Workers' Compensation Death Benefits." 1986. *Journal of Contemporary Law* 12(151): 159–160.

Dreger, A. D. 1998. "When Medicine Goes Too Far in the Pursuit of Normality.

One Person's Abnormality Is Another Person's Life." *New York Times* (28 July 1998): B10.

"Dressed Down." 2000. *Frontiers* 18(23): 30.

Dudley, W., ed. 1993. *Homosexuality: Opposing Viewpoints*. San Diego, CA: Greenhaven Press.

Dyer, K. 1990. *Gays in Uniform: The Pentagon Secret Report*. Boston: Alyson Press.

Duffy, S. P. 2000. "Outing Gay Men." *The Legal Intelligencer.* Available at www.law.com. Accessed 7 November 2000.

"Dying in Silence." 2000. *Frontiers* 18(21): 33.

Dynes, W. 1985. "Homolexis: A Historical and Cultural Lexicon of Homosexuality." *Gai Saber Monographs* 4. New York: The Scholarship Committee of the Gay Academic Union.

Egelko, B. 1999. "Court to Reconsider Ruling on Religious Landlords." (19 October 1999). Associated Press website: www.wire.ap.org/APnews.

Eitzen, D. S. 1980. *Social Problems*. Boston: Allyn & Bacon.

Ellis, A. L., and E. D. B. Riggle. 1995. "The Relation of Job Satisfaction and Degree of Openness about One's Sexual Orientation for Lesbians and Gay Men." *Journal of Homosexuality* 30(2): 75–85.

Equal Employment Opportunity Commission. 1999. *EEOC Enforcement Guidance: Vicarious Employer Liability for Unlawful Harassment by Supervisors*. Washington, DC: Government Printing Office.

Erikson Education Foundation. 2000. *Information and Guidelines for Transsexuals*. Erikson Education Foundation (now renamed Renaissance Transgender Association) website: www.ren.org.

Eriskopp, A., and S. Silverstein. 1998. *Straight Jobs, Gay Lives: Gay and Lesbian Professionals, the Harvard Business School, and the American Workplace*. New York: Simon & Schuster.

Ersine, N. 1933. *Dictionary of Underworld and Prison Slang*. Upland, IN: Freese.

Falk, P. 1993. "Lesbian Mothers: Psychosocial Assumptions in Family Law." In *Psychological Perspectives on Lesbian and Gay Male Experiences*, edited by L. D. Garnets and D. C. Kimmel. New York: Columbia University Press.

Fausto-Sterling, A. 1993. "How Many Sexes Are There? Intersexuality Is a Biological Condition, Not a Disease, and Medical Policy toward It Should Be Reevaluated." *New York Times* (12 March 1993): A15.

"First Circuit Gives Cross-Dresser a Day in Federal Court." 2000. *Lesbian/Gay Law Notes* (July/August 2000).

"First Sentences Handed Down under Law Boosting Penalties for Crimes against Transgendered." 1999. *Frontiers* 18(11): 23.

Flaks, D. K., I. Ficher, F. Masterpasqua, and G. Joseph. 1995. "Lesbians Choosing Motherhood: A Comparative Study of Lesbian and Heterosexual Parents and Their Children." *Developmental Psychology* 31: 105–114.

Flugel, J. C. 1971. *The Psychology of Clothes*. London: Woolf.

Freiberg, P. 2000. "Utah Approves Gay Adoption Ban." *Washington Blade* 31(9): 12.

Friedman, R. C., and J. I. Downey. 1994. "Homosexuality." *New England Journal of Medicine* 331(14): 923–930.

Garnets, L. D., G. M. Herek, and B. Levy. 1993. "Violence and Victimization of Lesbians and Gay Men: Mental Health Consequences." In *Psychological Perspectives on Lesbian and Gay Male Experiences*, edited by L. D. Garnets and D. C. Kimmel. New York: Columbia University Press.

Gay Almanac, The. 1996. Complied by the National Museum and Archive of Lesbian and Gay History. New York: Berkley Books.

Gay and Lesbian Advocates and Defenders. 2000. "Massachusetts Court Orders State to Provide Health Care to Transsexual Woman." Gay and Lesbian Advocates and Defenders press release on website: www.glad.org. Accessed 4 May 2000.

"Gay Refugees Tell of Torture, Oppression in Cuba." 1980. *The Advocate* (27 November 1980): 15.

"Gays Say Murderer Set Free." 1986. *Kalamazoo News* (14–20 February 1986): 1.

Ghabrial, F., and S. M. Girgis. 1962. "Reorientation of Sex: Report of Two Cases." *International Journal of Fertility* 249 (July–September): 7.

Giger, B. 1991. "Is 10 Percent Too High?" *Frontiers* 10(4): 43.

Goldstein, J., A. Freud, and A. Solnit. 1973. *Beyond the Best Interests of the Child*. New York: Free Press.

Goleman, D. 1990. "Studies Discover Clues to the Roots of Homophobia." *New York Times*, (10 July 1990). Available at youth.org/loco/PERSONProject/Resources/ResearchStudies/homophobia.html.

Golombok, S., A. Spence, and M. Rutter. 1983. "Children in Lesbian and Single-Parent Households: Psychosexual and Psychiatric Appraisal." *Journal of Child Psychology and Psychiatry* 24: 551–572.

Gonsiorek, J. C., and M. Shernoff. 1991. "AIDS Prevention and Public Policy: The Experience of Gay Males." In *Homosexuality: Research Implications for Public Policy*, edited by J. C. Gonsiorek and J. D. Weinrich. Newbury Park, CA: Sage.

Goodman, B. 1977. *The Lesbian: A Celebration of Difference*. East Haven, CT: Out & Out Books.

Gostin, L. 1988. "Forum on Surrogate Motherhood." *Law, Medicine and Health Care* 16(1–2): 5–6.

Graham, B. 1997. "Military Reviews Allegations of Harassment against Gays." *Washington Post* (14 May 1997): A01.

Green, R. 1978. "Sexual Identity of 37 Children Raised by Homosexual or Transsexual Parents." *American Journal of Psychiatry* 135(6): 692–697.

Green, R., J. B. Mandel, M. E. Hotvedt, J. Gray, and L. Smith. 1986. "Lesbian Mothers and Their Children: A Comparison with Solo Parent Heterosexual Mothers and Their Children." *Archives of Sexual Behavior* 15(2): 167–184.

Greenberg, J. A. 1999. "Defining Male and Female: Intersexuality and the Collision between Law and Biology." *Arizona Law Review* 41(2): 265–328.

Greif, M. 1989. *The Gay Book of Days*. New York: Lyle Stuart.

Groth, A. N., and H. J. Birnbaum. 1978. "Adult Sexual Orientation and Attraction to Underage Persons." *Archives of Sexual Behavior* 7(3): 175–181.

Hackworth, D. 1993. "The Military Should Not Accept Homosexuals." In *Homosexuality: Opposing Viewpoints*, edited by W. Dudley. San Diego, CA: Greenhaven Press.

Haldeman, D. C. 1991. "Sexual Orientation Conversion Therapy for Gay Men and Lesbians: A Scientific Examination." In *Homosexuality: Research Implications for Public Policy*, edited by J. C. Gonsiorek and J. D. Weinrich. Newbury Park, CA: Sage.

Halsall, P. 1994. *Queers in History*. Available at www.dezines.com/rainbow/queers.htm.

Hammer, S. L. 1982. "Adolescence." In *Practice of Pediatrics*, edited by V. C. Kelley. Philadelphia: Harper & Row.

Hanna, J. 1999. "Court Rules Homosexual Slurs Were Hate Crime." *Chicago Tribune* (4 October 1999): 3.

Hanscombe, G., and J. Forster. 1982. *Rocking the Cradle—Lesbian Mothers: A Challenge in Family Living*. Boston: Alyson Publications.

Harris, D. R. 1989. "Non-Nuclear Proliferation." *Utne Reader* 32 (March–April): 22–23.

Harris, L. 1988. Reprint. "The Lynn Harris Story." *Social Issues Resources Series* 3(19) [cover story]. Originally appeared in *Los Angeles Herald Examiner* (28 November 1988): B1.

Harvard Law Review staff. 1990. *Sexual Orientation and the Law*. Cambridge, MA: Harvard University Press.

Henry, W., III. 1990. "The Lesbians Next Door." *Time*, special fall issue, 78.

Herek, G. M. 1991. "Myths about Sexual Orientation: A Lawyers' Guide to Social Science Research." *Law and Sexuality* 1: 133–172.

Hodges, A., and D. Hutter. 1979. *With Downcast Gays: Aspects of Homosexual Self-Oppression*. Rev. ed. Toronto: Pink Triangle Press.

Hoeffer, B. 1981. "Children's Acquisition of Sex-Role Behavior in Lesbian-Mother Families." *American Journal of Orthopsychiatry* 51: 536–544.

Hooker, E. 1963. "The Adjustment of the Male Overt Homosexual." In *The Problem of Homosexuality*, edited by H. M. Ruitenbeed. New York: Dutton.

Horn, B. P. 1997. "Is There a Cure for America's Gambling Addiction?" *USA Today Magazine* 125(2624): 34.

Hudson, W., and W. Ricketts. 1980. "A Strategy for the Measurement of Homophobia." *Journal of Homosexuality* 5(4): 357–372.

Huggins, S. L. 1989. "A Comparative Study of Self-Esteem of Adolescent Children of Divorced Mothers and Divorced Heterosexual Mothers." In *Homosexuality and the Family*, edited by F. W. Bozett. New York: Hawthorn.

Humphreys, L. 1970. *Tearoom Trade*. Chicago: Aldine.

Hunter, N. D. 1991. "Marriage, Law, and Gender: A Feminist Inquiry." *Journal of Law and Sexuality* 1: 19.

Hunter, N. D., S. E. Michaelson, and T. B. Stoddard. 1992. *The Rights of Lesbians and Gay Men: The Basic ACLU Guide to a Gay Person's Rights*. 3d ed. Carbondale and Edwardsville, IL: Southern Illinois University Press.

"I'm Just Ashamed." 2000. *Frontiers* 18(22): 36.

International Gay and Lesbian Human Rights Commission. 2000. "Alleged Transvestites Sentenced to Brutal Flogging: IGLHRC Condemns Court Ruling in Saudi Arabia." Press release on International Gay and Lesbian Human Rights Commission website: www.IGLHRC.org/news/press/pr_000420.htm. Accessed 20 April 2000.

Janus, S. S., and C. L. Janus. 1993. *The Janus Report on Sexual Behavior*. New York: John Wiley & Sons.

Jenny, C., T. Roesler, and K. Poyer. 1994. "Are Children at Risk for Sexual Abuse by Homosexuals?" *Pediatrics* 94(1): 41–44.

"Judge Nixes Book-Removal Resolution." (20 September 2000). Associated Press website: www.wire.ap.org/APnews.

"Judge Refuses to Block Lexington Program on 'Respecting Differences.'" (12 October 2000). Associated Press website: www.wire.ap.org/APnews.

Kane, R. 1999. "An Incomplete History of Gay and Lesbian OC." *Orange County Weekly* (13–19 August 1999) website: www.ocweekley.com/ink/99/49/news-kane.shtml.

Katz, J. 1976. *Gay American History: Lesbians and Gay Men in the U.S.A.* New York: Thomas Y. Crowell.

Keen, L., and S. B. Goldberg. 1999. *Strangers to the Law: Gay People on Trial.* Ann Arbor, MI: University of Michigan Press.

Kennedy, Edward. 1989. "Senator Kennedy of Massachusetts speech," *Cong. Rec.*, 7 September, vol. 135, S10789 (daily ed.).

Kessler, S. J. 1990. "The Medical Construction of Gender: Case Management of Intersexed Infants." *Signs* 16(1): 3.

Khan, S. 1998. *Calculated Compassion: How the Ex-Gay Movement Serves the Right's Attack on Democracy.* Washington, DC: Political Research Associates, the Policy Institute of the National Gay and Lesbian Task Force, and Equal Partners in Faith.

Kinsey, A. C., W. B. Pomeroy, and C. E. Martin. 1948. *Sexual Behavior in the Human Male.* Philadelphia: W. B. Saunders Co.

Kinsey, A. C., W. B. Pomeroy, C. E. Martin, and R. H. Gebhard. 1953. *Sexual Behavior in the Human Female.* Philadelphia: W. B. Saunders Co.

Kirkpatrick, M. 1987. "Clinical Implications of Lesbian Mother Studies." *Journal of Homosexuality* 14(1–2): 201–211.

Kirkpatrick, M., A. Smith, and R. Roy. 1981. "Lesbian Mothers and Their Children: A Comparative Study." *American Journal of Orthopsychiatry* 51: 545–551.

Kohn, S. 1999. *NGLTF Domestic Partnership Organizing Manual for Employee Benefits.* Washington, DC: National Gay and Lesbian Task Force.

Konigsberg, E. 1993. "The Military Should Accept Homosexuals." In *Homosexuality: Opposing Viewpoints*, edited by W. Dudley. San Diego, CA: Greenhaven Press.

Kooden, J. D., S. F. Morin, D. F. Riddle, M. Rogers, B. E. Sang, and F. Strassburger. 1979. *Removing the Stigma: Final Report, Task Force on the Status of Lesbian and Gay Male Psychologists.* Washington, DC: The American Psychological Association.

Kweskin, S. L., and A. S. Cook. 1982. "Heterosexual and Homosexual Mothers' Self-Described Sex-Role Behavior and Ideal Sex-Role Behavior in Children." *Sex Roles* 8: 967–975.

Lambda Legal Defense and Education Fund. 1999. "Gay/Straight Alliance's Lawsuit to Proceed Against Salt Lake School Board." Press release on Lambda Legal Defense and Education Fund website: www.lldef.org/cgi-bin/pages/documents/record?record=485. Accessed 8 October 1999.

———. 2000. "Lambda Back in Court for Lapd Lewd Conduct Arrest Records." 2000. Press release on Lambda Legal Defense and Education Fund website: www.lldef.org/cgi-bin/pages/documents/record?record=555. Accessed 20 January 2000.

Laumann, E. O., J. H. Gagnon, R. T. Michael, and S. Michaels. 1994. *The Social Organization of Sexuality: Sexual Practices in the United States.* Chicago: University of Chicago Press.

Laver, J. 1969. *Modesty in Dress.* Boston: Houghton Mifflin.

Lawson, R. 1987. "Scandal in the Adventist-Funded Program to 'Heal' Homosexuals: Failure, Sexual Exploitation, Official Silence, and Attempts to Rehabilitate the Exploiter and His Methods." Paper presented at the meeting of the American Sociological Association, Chicago, Palmer House, 17–21 August 1987.

Leland, J. 1995. "Bisexuality Is the Wild Card of Our Erotic Life." *Newsweek* (17 July 1995): 44–50.

Levi-Strauss, C. 1977. *Tristes Tropiques*. New York: Atheneum.

Lewin, T. 1988. "Gay Groups Suggest Marines Selectively Prosecute Women." *New York Times* (4 September 1988): 1.

Los Angeles County Commission on Human Relations. 1988. *Hate Crime in Los Angeles County*. Los Angeles: Los Angeles County Commission on Human Relations.

Maccoby, E. E., and C. N. Jacklin. 1974. *The Psychology of Sex Differences*. Palo Alto, CA: Stanford University Press.

Malyon, A. K. 1981. "The Homosexual Adolescent: Developmental Issues and Social Bias." *Child Welfare* 60: 321–330.

"Man Loses Sex Harassment Case against Man." 2000. Washington Blade (8 September 2000): Legal Briefs.

Mandel, J., and M. Hotvedt. 1980. "Lesbians as Parents." *Husarts and Praktijk* 4: 31–34.

Marcus, R. 1990. "Powell Regrets Backing Sodomy Law." *Washington Post* (26 October 1990): A3.

Marotta, T. 1981. *The Politics of Homosexuality*. Boston: Houghton Mifflin.

Martin, A. D. 1982. "Learning to Hide: The Socialization of the Gay Adolescent." In *Adolescent Psychiatry*, vol. 10, edited by S. C. Feinstein. Chicago: University of Chicago Press.

McConaghy, N. 1981. "Controlled Comparison of Aversive Therapy and Covert Sensitization in Compulsive Homosexuality." *Behavior Research and Therapy* 19(5): 425–434.

McDermott, T. 2000. "All Smiles after Kiss Commotion." *Los Angeles Times* (24 August 2000): A2.

Michael, R. T., J. H. Gagnon, E. O. Laumann, and G. Kolata. 1995. *Sex in America: A Definitive Survey*. New York: Little, Brown.

Miller, B. 1979. "Gay Fathers and Their Children." *The Family Coordinator* (October): 545–552.

Mills, J. S. 1885. *On Liberty*. New York: Holt.

Mirken, B. 1993. "School Programs Should Stress Acceptance of Homosexuality." In *Homosexuality: Opposing Viewpoints*, edited by W. Dudley. San Diego, CA: Greenhaven Press.

Mohr, R. D. 1988. *Gay Justice—A Study of Ethics, Society, and Law*. New York: Columbia University Press.

Money, J., and A. A. Ehrhardt. 1972. *Man and Woman, Boy and Girl: Differentiation and Dimorphism of Gender Identity from Conception to Maturity*. Baltimore, MD: Johns Hopkins Press.

Mookas, I. 1998. "Faultlines: Homophobic Innovation in Gay Rights/Special Rights." In *Culture, Media, and the Religious Right*, edited by L. Kintz and J. Lesage. Minneapolis: University of Minnesota Press.

Moore, R. 1989. "Justice Is Not Blind for Gays." *San Diego Union* (10 January 1989): B7.

Morganthaus, T. 1997. "Baptists vs. Mickey: Why the Boycott against Disney Faces Steep Odds." *Newsweek* (30 June 1997): 51.

"Nadler Fights Homophobic Immigration Law." 2000. *Fab* (3 March 2000): 17.

National Gay and Lesbian Task Force. 1989. *Antigay and Lesbian Victimization*. Washington, DC: National Gay and Lesbian Task Force.

———. 2000. "Nondiscrimination Laws Now Cover 100 Million Americans, New Report Finds." Press release on National Gay and Lesbian Task Force website: www.ngltf.org/press/010300.html. Accessed 3 January 2000.

Nava, M., and R. Dawidoff. 1994. *Created Equal: Why Gay Rights Matter to America.* New York: St. Martin's Press.

Neisen, J. 1990. "Heterosexism or Homophobia?" *Out/Look* 3(2): 36.

New York City Gay and Lesbian Anti-Violence Project. 1996. *Anti-Lesbian, Gay, Bisexual, and Transgendered Violence in 1996.* New York: New York City Gay and Lesbian Anti-Violence Project.

Newswatch Briefs. 1990. *Gay Chicago Magazine* (22 February), 43.

Newton, D. E. 1978. "Homosexual Behavior and Child Molestation: A Review of the Evidence." *Adolescence* 13: 29–43.

Oliver, C. 1989. "Georgia on My Mind." *Reason* 21(5): 14.

Pagelow, M. D. 1980. "Heterosexual and Lesbian Single Mothers: A Comparison of Problems, Coping, and Solutions." *Journal of Homosexuality* 5(3): 189–204.

"Panel to Examine Remarks by Judge on Homosexuals." 1988. *New York Times* (21 December 1988): A16.

Parmet, W. E., and D. J. Jackson. 1997. "No Longer Disabled: The Legal Impact of the New Social Construction of HIV." *American Journal of Law and Medicine* 7: 35.

Partners Task Force for Gay and Lesbian Couples. 2000. *What Rights Come with Legal Marriage?* Seattle, WA: Partners Task Force for Gay and Lesbian Couples.

Parvin, P. 2000a. "Kissing on a Delta Plane Lands Couple in Hot Water." *Southern Voice* (31 March 2000): 14.

———. 2000b. "Ruling against Lesbian Mom Appealed to Georgia Supreme Court." *Southern Voice* (27 April 2000): 27.

Patterson, C. J. 1995. "Sexual Orientation and Human Development: An Overview." *Developmental Psychology* 31: 3–11.

Pelton, R. W. 1992. *Loony Sex Laws That You Never Knew You Were Breaking.* New York: Walker Publishing Co.

Pennington, S. B. 1987. "Children of Lesbian Mothers." In *Gay and Lesbian Parents,* edited by F. W. Bozett. New York: Praeger.

"Pentagon Cost of Discharging Gays Put at $500 Million." 1992. *Los Angeles Times* (19 June 1992): A14.

Peplau, L. A. 1993. "Lesbian and Gay Relationships." In *Psychological Perspectives on Lesbian and Gay Male Experiences,* edited by L. D. Garnets and D. C. Kimmel. New York: Columbia University Press.

Perkoff, G. T. 1985. "Artificial Insemination in a Lesbian: A Case Analysis." *Archives of Internal Medicine* 145(3): 527–532.

Pietrzyk, M. E. 1994. "Queer Science." *The New Republic* (3 October 1994): 23.

Plant, R. 1988. *The Pink Triangle.* New York: New Republic Books/Henry Holt.

Rangel, B. 1987. "Brooklyn Youth Acquitted in Slaying of Catholic Priest." *New York Times,* (5 February 1987): B3.

Reed, R., and T. A. Lang. 1987. *Health Behaviors.* New York: West Publishing Company.

Remafedi, G. J. 1987a. "Adolescent Homosexuality: Psychosocial and Medical Implications." *Pediatrics* 79: 331–337.

———. 1987b. "Homosexual Youth: A Challenge to Contemporary Society." *Journal of the American Medical Association* 258: 222–225.

———. 1987c. "Male Homosexuality: The Adolescent's Perspective." *Pediatrics* 79: 326–330.

Remafedi, G. J., and R. Blum. 1986. "Working with Gay and Lesbian Adolescents." *Pediatric Annals* 15: 773–783.

Repetti, R. L., and K. A. Cosmas. 1991. "The Quality of the Social Environment at Work and Job Satisfaction." *Journal of Applied Social Psychology* 21: 840–854.

Report of the CUNY Study Group on Domestic Partnerships, The. 1993. New York: City University of New York.

Richards, D. 1991. "Activism=Arrests." *The Advocate* (9 April 1991): 48–50.

Richter, P. 2000. "Armed Forces Find 'Disturbing' Level of Gay Harassment." *Los Angeles Times* (25 March 2000): A1.

Rig, C. A. 1982. "Homosexuality in Adolescence." *Pediatric Annals* 11: 826–831.

Robson, R. 1997. *Gay Men, Lesbians, and the Law*. New York: Chelsea House Publishers.

Roesler, T., and R. W. Deisher. 1972. "Youthful Male Homosexuality." *Journal of the American Medical Association* 219: 1018–1023.

Rogers, S. M., and C. R. Turner. 1992. "Male-Male Sexual Contact in the U.S.: Findings from Five Sample Surveys, 1970–1990." *Journal of Sex Research* 28(4): 491–519.

Rudofsky, B. 1971. *The Unfashionable Human Body*. New York: Doubleday.

Rushdoony, R. J. 1973. *The Institutes of Biblical Law*. Phillipsburg, NJ: Presbyterian Reformed—A Chelcedon Publication.

Rust, P. C. 1996. "Monogamy and Polyamory: Relationship Issues for Bisexuals." In *Bisexuality: The Psychology and Politics of an Invisible Minority*, edited by B. A. Firestein. Newbury Park, CA: Sage.

Rutledge, L. W. 1989. *The Gay Fireside Companion*. Boston: Alyson.

Saenger, G. 1953. *The Social Psychology of Prejudice*. New York: Harper.

Saghir, M., and E. Robins. 1980. "Clinical Aspects of Female Homosexuality." In *Homosexual Behavior*, edited by J. Marmor. New York: Basic Books.

Sarbin, T. R. (1991). *Homosexuality and Personnel Security*. Monterey, CA: Personnel Security Research and Education Center (PERSEREC).

Scruggs, A. 1996. "Tying Legalities into Tangled Knots." *Cleveland Plain Dealer* (7 October 1996): 1B.

Selland, D. 1998. "Will Maryland Enter the Twenty-First Century in the Right Direction by Rescinding Its Ancient Sodomy Statutes?" *Law and Sexuality* 8: 671–698.

Servicemembers Legal Defense Network (SLDN). 1999. "Soldier Pleads Guilty to Non-Premeditated Murder in Murder of PFC Barry Winchell." Press release on Servicemembers Legal Defense Network website: www.sldn.org/templates/press/index.html?section=2&record=102. Accessed 7 December 1999.

———. 2000a. "New Gay Discharge Figures Up 73 Percent since 'Don't Ask, Don't Tell, Don't Pursue' First Implemented." Press release on Servicemembers Legal Defense Network website: www.sldn.org/templates/press/index.html?section=2&record=98. Accessed 1 February 2000.

———. 2000b. "Antigay Harassment in Military Surges Even after Pentagon Announces 'Zero Tolerance' for Harassment." Press release on Servicemembers Legal Defense Network website: www.sldn.org/templates/press/index.html?section=2&record=21. Accessed 9 March 2000.

———. 2000c. "Military Surveillance of Gay Bars and Nightclubs." Press release on Servicemembers Legal Defense Network website: www.sldn.org/templates/press/index.html?section=2&record=146.

Shavelson, E. S., M. K. Biaggio, H. H. Cross, and R. E. Lehman. 1980. "Lesbian Women's Perceptions of Their Parent-Child Relationships." *Journal of Homosexuality* 5(3): 205–215.

Shein, B. 1986. "Gay-bashing in High Park." *Toronto Life* (April): 65.

Sheppared, A. 1985. "Lesbian Mothers II: Long Night's Journey into Day." *Women's Rights Law Reporter* 8(4): 219–246.

Shettles, L. B., and D. M. Rorvik. 1997. *How to Choose the Sex of Your Baby: The Method Best Supported by Scientific Evidence.* New York: Doubleday.

Shilts, R. 1982. *The Mayor of Castro Street: The Life and Times of Harvey Milk.* New York: St. Martin's Press.

———. 1987. *And the Band Played On: Politics, People, and the AIDS Epidemic.* New York: St. Martin's Press.

Shipp, E. 1981a. "Murder Suspect in Village Found Not Responsible: Defendant in 2 Slayings Held for Mental Tests." *New York Times* (25 July 1981): 27.

———. 1981b. "Defendant Facing Psychiatric Tests: Man Is Ruled Not Responsible in Two Murders in 'Village,' But Future Is Unclear." *New York Times* (26 July 1981): 25.

Simon, D. R. 1996. *Elite Deviance.* Boston: Allyn & Bacon.

Smith, P. 1993. "School Programs Should Not Stress Acceptance of Homosexuality." In *Homosexuality: Opposing Viewpoints,* edited by W. Dudley. San Diego, CA: Greenhaven Press.

Smolowe, J. 1990. "Last Call for Motherhood." *Time,* fall special issue, 76.

Snyder, Patricia Ginger, producer. 1984. *Silent Pioneers: Elderly Gays and Lesbians Tell Their Struggles.* (30 min.). New York: Filmmakers' Library.

Sperm Bank of California. 1997. *Donor Identity-Release Policy.* Berkeley, CA: Reproductive Technologies, Inc.

Stammer, L. B. 2000. "Gay Unions Affirmed by Reform Rabbis." *Los Angeles Times* (30 March 2000): 1.

Steckel, A. 1987. "Psychosocial Development of Children of Lesbian Mothers." In *Gay and Lesbian Parents,* edited by F. W. Bozett. New York: Praeger.

Stewart, C. 1993. "How Effective Is AB2601?" *Edge* (8 September 1993): 12.

———. 1995. "The Efficacy of Sexual Orientation Training in Law Enforcement Agencies." Ph.D. dissertation, University of Southern California, UMI Dissertation Services, 9614075.

———. 1996. "How Effective Is the Department of Labor Standards Enforcement at Protecting Our Rights Under AB2601?" *Edge* (7 August 1996): 30.

———. 1999. *Sexually Stigmatized Communities—Reducing Heterosexism and Homophobia: An Awareness Training Manual.* Thousand Oaks, CA: Sage.

Strage, M. 1980. *The Durable Fig Leaf.* New York: Morrow.

Strasser, M. 1997. *Legally Wed: Same-Sex Marriage and the Constitution.* Ithaca, NY: Cornell University Press.

Strong, C., and J. Schinfeld. 1984. "The Single Woman and Artificial Insemination by Donor." *Journal of Reproductive Medicine* 29(5): 293–299.

"Supreme Court Refuses to Review HIV Benefit Case." 2000. *Lesbian/Gay Law Notes* (May 2000).

"Suspects Get Youth Status." 1984. *New York Times* (17 September 1984): D17.

Tasker, F., and S. Golombok. 1995. "Adults Raised as Children in Lesbian Families." *American Journal of Orthopsychiatry* 65: 203–215.

Thompson, M., ed. 1994. *Long Road to Freedom:* The Advocate *History of the Gay and Lesbian Movement*. New York: St. Martin's Press.

"Three Teenagers Sentenced in Killing of Homosexual." 1984. *New York Times* (6 October 1984): 6.

"Transgender Legal Complications Abound." 2000. *Lesbian/Gay Law Notes* (April).

Tremblay, P. J. 1995. "The Homosexuality Factor in the Youth Suicide Problem." Paper presented at the meeting of the Sixth Annual Conference of the Canadian Association for Suicide Prevention, 11–14 October 1995, Banff, Alberta, Canada.

Udis-Kessler, A. 1996. "Challenging the Stereotypes." In *Bisexual Horizons; Politics, Histories, Lives*, edited by S. Rose, et al. London: Lawrence & Wishart.

Uribe, V. 1992. "Homophobia—What It Is and Who It Hurts." In *Project 10 Handbook*. Los Angeles: Friends of Project 10, Inc.

U.S. Bureau of the Census. 1990. "Marital Status and Living Arrangements: March 1989." In *Current Population Reports, Population Characteristics Series* P-20, No. 445. Washington, DC: Bureau of the Census.

U.S. General Accounting Office. 1997. *Defense of Marriage Act Report*. OGC 97–16: 58. Washington, DC: Government Printing Office.

U.S. House. 1986. Committee on the Judiciary. Subcommittee on Criminal Justice. *Antigay Violence*. 99th Cong., 2d sess. 9 October.

Valdes, F. 1995. "Queers, Sissies, Dykes, and Tomboys: Deconstructing the Conflation of 'Sex,' 'Gender,' and 'Sexual Orientation' in Euro-American Law and Society." *California Law Review* 83(1): 1–378.

Valente, J. 1984a. "Two St. John's Students Given Probation in Assault on Gay." *Washington Post* (15 May 1984): A1.

———. 1984b. "Gay Community Seeks Judge Nunzio's Ouster." *Washington Post* (19 May 1984): B1.

Waldron, M. 1979. "Homosexual Foster Children Sent to Lesbian Homes." *New York Times* (27 November 1979): B2.

Walters, A. S., and M. Curran. 1996. "'Excuse Me, Sir? May I Help You and Your Boyfriend?': Salespersons' Differential Treatment of Homosexual and Straight Customers." *The Journal of Homosexuality* 31(1/2): 135–152.

Walworth, J. 1998. *Transsexual Works: An Employer's Guide*. Westchester, CA: Center for Gender Sanity.

"We've Come a Long Way . . . Maybe." 2000. *Frontiers* 18(22): 12.

Weeks, R. B., A. P. Derdeyn, and M. Langman. 1975. "Two Cases of Children of Homosexuals." *Child Psychiatry and Human Development* 6: 26–32.

Weinberg, M. S., C. J. Williams, and D. W. Pyror. 1994. *Dual Attraction: Understanding Bisexuality*. New York: Oxford University Press.

White, M. 1997. *The 700 Club. The Justice Report*. Video. Laguna Beach, CA: Soulforce.

Williams, W. 1992. *The Spirit and the Flesh: Sexual Diversity in American Indian Culture*. Boston: Beacon.

Wurzel, J. 1986. "The Functions and Forms of Prejudice." In *A World of Difference: Resource Guide for Reduction of Prejudice*. Boston: Anti-Defamation League of B'nai B'rith and Facing History and Ourselves National Foundation, Inc.

Yared, C. 1997. "Where Are the Civil Rights for Gay and Lesbian Teachers?" *American Bar Association Human Rights*, 24(3): 1–6.

Yeoman, B. 1996. *Out*. Available at www.out.com/out-cgi-bin/article?a=9605/hesse.htm.

Young, P. D. 1982. *God's Bullies: Native Reflections on Preachers and Politics*. New York: Holt, Rinehart, and Winston.

Youth Runaways. 1999. Los Angeles: Jeff Griffith Gay and Lesbian Youth Center.

Index

About the Author

Chuck Stewart received his Ph.D. from the University of Southern California School of Education in 1995. He specialized in intercultural education and was funded by the California Commission on Peace Officers Standards and Training (POST) to conduct research into effective means to reduce heterosexism and homophobia through the design and implementation of educational programs. His master's thesis, *Homosexuality and Public Education Law,* led to the Police Advisory Task Force hiring him to write the curriculum and teaching materials for use in sexual orientation training within the Los Angeles Police Department. He wrote the award-winning book *Sexually Stigmatized Communities—Reducing Heterosexism and Homophobia: An Awareness Training Manual* for Sage Publications. He is a twenty-year member and cochair of the Los Angeles Gay and Lesbian Scientists, assistant to the president of the Southern California Lambda Medical Association, and a member of the American Civil Liberties Union Gay and Lesbian Caucus. He teaches ballroom and western dancing for the gay community.